Poking a Dead Fr🐸g

Conversations with Today's
Top Comedy Writers

MIKE SACKS

PENGUIN BOOKS

PENGUIN BOOKS
Published by the Penguin Group
Penguin Group (USA) LLC
375 Hudson Street
New York, New York 10014

USA | Canada | UK | Ireland | Australia | New Zealand | India | South Africa | China
penguin.com
A Penguin Random House Company

First published in Penguin Books 2014

Text from the cartoon "Item #3715 - Cozy Cardigan" by Roz Chast. Used by permission of Roz Chast and Conde Nast Licensing.

Excerpt from "Step Brothers" movie review by Roger Ebert. Used by permission.

Excerpts from "Freaks and Greeks" character bible by Paul Feig.
Used by permission of Feigo, Inc.

Late Night with Conan O'Brien submission packet by Todd Levin.
Used by permission of Todd Levin.

"Temple of Laughter" by Edward Jessen (pages 448 and 449). (www.edwardjessen.co.uk)

Other illustrations by Louise Pomeroy. (www.louisezpomeroy.com)

Photograph by Seth Olenick. (www.setholenick.com)

LIBRARY OF CONGRESS CATALOGING-IN-PUBLICATION DATA
Sacks, Mike.
Poking a dead frog : conversations with today's top comedy writers / Mike Sacks.
pages cm
ISBN 978-0-14-312378-1 (paperback)
1. Stand-up comedy—United States. 2. Comedians—United States—Interviews.
3. Comedians—United States—Anecdotes. I. Title.
PN1969.C65S23 2014
792.702'8092—dc23
2014005646

Printed in the United States of America
1 3 5 7 9 10 8 6 4 2

Set in Sabon
Designed by Spring Hoteling

For K & Little D,
and for my parents, Elaine and Jerry

"Sometimes magic is just someone spending more time on something than anyone else might reasonably expect."

—Teller

"I was not the class clown. . . . I've always maintained that the class clown, the guy [who] when the teacher is out of the room sets the clock back, makes noise, throws water balloons around the room, those kids . . . grow up and they're killed in a motel shoot-out."

—Conan O'Brien

"I wanted to play on the dark side, a little bit under the center of tonality. Not really flat, but just on the underneath side."

—Chet Baker

"And now I'll serve you the beans you so justly deserve."

—Chris Elliott as Marlon Brando,
Late Night with David Letterman

CONTENTS

INTRODUCTION

The late comedy writer Jerry Belson, a veteran of *The Dick Van Dyke Show*, *The Odd Couple*, and *The Drew Carey Show*, among other classic sitcoms, wrote a joke that became one of the most well known, and most retold, in the history of television. It's from a 1973 episode of *The Odd Couple*:

"Never ASSUME. Because when you assume, you make an ASS of U and ME."

The joke is undeniably great. But perhaps the best and most effective joke that Belson ever wrote—and he wrote untold thousands—is the inscription that he wanted engraved on his tombstone:

I DID IT THEIR WAY

In other words: Hollywood's way. The executives' way. The *wrong way*.

Belson's tombstone epitaph never made it beyond the first-draft stage, but regardless, one would think that Belson had done it *his way*. Plenty of credits. Plenty of money. Plenty of respect from those within the industry. And yet, if there's one motif evident in the lives of comedy writers, it's the nagging feeling that one can never have it his or her own way. That a comedy writer must always genuflect to those with the power, with the money—those who deem themselves arbiters of What Is Funny.

Whether through executive negligence or creative bartering on the part of the writers, the most beloved comedies of our time have avoided this trap. When Monty Python created their four-season television series, *Flying Circus*, they did so with minimal help from the BBC. In fact, as one of the Pythons, Terry Jones, explains in this book, BBC executives were disinterested in the result—until they saw the final product. Then they came terribly close to erasing the entirety of Monty Python's first season for the grand purpose of reusing the tapes to record more "serious" entertainment.

The creators of *The Simpsons* made it clear from the show's inception that there would be no executive meddling. James L. Brooks, also interviewed in this book, declared, in essence, *Stay away from our jokes, and we will produce a show for the ages.* Actually, Brooks might have hired a lawyer to say as much in very clear legalese, rather than "in essence." Whatever the case, Brooks saved the show and helped to create a classic.

The creators of the U.K. version of *The Office*, Ricky Gervais and Stephen Merchant, flew so low under the radar that by the time executives became even vaguely aware of what their money had wrought, it was too late. Due to this neglect, the show set an influential precedent for its combination documentary-style format and cringe-inducing humor.

It's clear then: All great comedy has managed to circumnavigate executive meddling. But this is easier said than done.

Since at least the fifth century B.C., when the playwright Aristophanes needed the financial help of a *chorêgos*, or rich benefactor, to help stage his comedies, writers have had to rely on others. The creative have never been fully in control of the marketing and distribution of their creativity. Playwrights have needed sponsors and performance space. Screenwriters have required even wealthier sponsors than the playwrights: Hollywood production studios. Humor writers for print have needed the acceptance, and then distribution, provided by magazines and publishing houses. The keys to the kingdom have been controlled by the less creative.

Until now.

I cannot overstate that there has never been a better time for writers of comedy—or, for that matter, writers of *anything*. A twenty-one-year-old in her room in Oklahoma who writes hilarious jokes on Twitter is potentially just as important (or influential) as any professional comedy writer for *The New Yorker*. A teen making funny videos in his suburban garage can reach just as many people—certainly, just as many of the *right* people—than any director of a movie to be distributed by the large studios.

We are now all on equal ground. If you want to write comedy, you can. There's no one to stop you. And there's no one to tell you what to do. This can be bad. It's far too easy to create sloppy, forgettable work. On the other hand, it's no longer a requirement to work on *The Harvard Lampoon* to eventually earn a professional living writing jokes. That can only be a good thing.

It is also so much easier to communicate with our peers and mentors than ever before. We can access material in a few seconds and reach out to others almost instantly. I have fond memories of growing up in suburban Maryland, biking to the local library to look for inspiration, and staying up late to watch *Letterman* and whatever obscure, random shows that might air in the wee hours. I compiled dozens of files of clippings and took them with me when I went to college and everywhere else I eventually moved. Many of these clips were written by comedy writers; others were in-depth interviews with comedy writers. I pored over the mastheads of my favorite humor publications and the credits for the shows that I thought were the funniest. I occasionally wrote to these writers, seeking advice or attempting to sell jokes.

This book is really an extension of my youthful attempts to contact those in the business whom I admired most. If there is a common trait among those I chose to interview for this book, it's that each of these writers has always done it his or her own way and no one else's. Each came to this business primarily because he or she wanted to create the sort of comedy that they themselves enjoyed the most. For all of them—be they writers of sketches, graphic novels, screenplays, *New Yorker* cartoons, fiction, nonfiction, television, stand-up, the radio—success was a by-product, not the goal.

I am no humor expert; I don't think anyone is. If something

makes you laugh, it's good. But if there is anything about which I am certain, it's that we are now living in a comedic Golden Age.

Never before have there been as many comedy writers in the early stages of their careers producing the type of work that means the most to them and to others. By the time my five-year-old daughter reaches my age, most, if not all, of the young writers in this book will have already become the comedy legends of the next generation. Who are these writers? How did they choose this very odd profession? What do they want to accomplish? How exactly do they do what they do? And, perhaps most important, *why*? One of the reasons I wrote this book was to find out and to share what I learned with others who might find all this of interest, too.

Luckily, there also still exist a good number of elder statespersons of "classic" TV comedies, film, and radio. Soon this ratio will be tipped more toward the young, and a bridge to another time will no longer exist. This is another reason I decided to write this book. How do these older writers want to be remembered? How do they think they changed the industry? Who influenced *them*? I feel lucky to have been able to connect with these older comedy writers, some of whom have not been interviewed in many years or at all.

The writers in this book have played major parts in everything from creating what's been called the first-ever sitcom to coining the term "black humor" to writing for Monty Python, *Cheers*, *The Office* (both the U.K. and U.S. versions), *Saturday Night Live*, *The Daily Show*, *The Onion*, *The Colbert Report*, *Parks and Recreation*, *National Lampoon*, *The New Yorker*, *Seinfeld*, *Mr. Show*, *Bob's Burgers*, *30 Rock*, *Anchorman*, *Juno*, *Ghost World*, *Get a Life*, *Cabin Boy*, *Late Night*, *Late Show with David Letterman*, the *Tonight Show*, and more. A writer or two may have even written the jokes you read this very morning online.

Interspersed throughout this book, between the fifteen full-length interviews, are "Ultraspecific Comedic Knowledge" and "Pure, Hard-Core Advice." The former includes specialized materials and information that might appeal to the comedy geek. "Pure, Hard-Core Advice," as you may have guessed, contains straight advice—no muss, no fuss—from successful comedy writers or those within the industry, such as agents, that might prove helpful to writers just starting out or for those writers wanting to improve their standing in the industry.

If you're not familiar with some (or even most) of these writers, I hope that you will find them as interesting as I do and seek out their work. If you *are* familiar with these writers, I hope you might learn something new about their writing, their careers, their lives—and their humor.

As E. B. White once wrote for *The New Yorker*: "Humor can be dissected, as a frog can, but the thing dies in the process and the innards are discouraging to any but the pure scientific mind. . . . [Humor] won't stand much poking. It has a certain fragility, an evasiveness, which one had best respect." This bit of wisdom is often misquoted or, at least, cut short, with the second half making no appearance. Yes, it's true that the poor frog dies (and as the owner of five dearly departed African clawed water frogs, this strikes particularly close to home). But the crux is that the process can be fascinating to a certain type of person.

Not the type who wants comedy dissected to the point of death, necessarily, but the type interested in understanding the art and business behind comedy; of what it takes, exactly, to make a career out of attempting to induce laughter from complete strangers with only the words or images that you create. It is a fragile art. And as you will read here, it is a tough, yet fascinating life. These are writers who do it their way (and always have), and the rest of us, as well as the world of comedy, are much better off for their efforts.

—MIKE SACKS

Poking
a Dead
Fr🐸g

JAMES DOWNEY

Saturday Night Live has employed hundreds of comedy writers in its four decades on the air, but no writer has been associated with the show longer—or had more of a lasting impact—than James Woodward Downey. If Lorne Michaels is the face of *Saturday Night Live*, Downey is its behind-the-scenes creative force.

Downey first began to consider the possibility of making a living as a writer while at Harvard, where he served as president of the *Harvard Lampoon*. There he caught the attention of writers Michael O'Donoghue and Doug Kenney (both already stars at *The National Lampoon*), who suggested he come work with them in New York. But after graduating in 1974, with a major in Russian studies, he decided instead to accept a fellowship to tour Eastern Europe by way of ship and train. After a few run-ins with the KGB, and after meeting a Hungarian who partly inspired the "Wild and Crazy Guys" sketches he would later co-write with Marilyn Miller and Dan Aykroyd, Downey headed back to the U.S. and saw, for the first time, a new televised comedy show that he had only heard about through friends. "As soon as I saw it, I thought, 'Oh, this is hilarious,'" Downey says. "I would love to be a part of that."

After submitting a ten-page packet to Michaels that included a short piece about his pet peeves—"I guess my biggest pet peeve is when you're just sitting there, waiting for a bus, and a guy runs up with one of those fileting knives and opens up your intestines and takes one end of it and runs down the street screaming, 'Ha ha! Got your entrails!'"—Downey was hired by Lorne "more based on instinct, I have to believe, than on the packet itself." He became one of the first *Harvard Lampoon* writers to break into TV comedy writing, setting a precedent that would change comedy-writing rooms thereafter. "Jim Downey is Patient Zero," said Mike Reiss, a former *Harvard Lampoon*er and long-time *Simpsons* show-runner.

After finding his feet, Downey—the show's youngest writer—began to make a deep impact on *Saturday Night Live*, working closely with, among others, Bill Murray (with whom he shared an office for four years), Dan Aykroyd, John Belushi, Gilda Radner, Jane Curtin, and Laraine Newman. For the last four decades, Downey has worked with and written for every star the show has produced, including Martin Short, Jon Lovitz, Mike Myers, Eddie Murphy, Chris Farley, Norm Macdonald, Phil Hartman, Dana Carvey, Jan Hooks, Rob Schneider, Adam Sandler, Will Ferrell, Bill Hader, Amy Poehler, Julia Louis-Dreyfus, Fred Armisen, Kenan Thompson, and dozens of others. Downey is one consistent on a show that has experienced an untold amount of changes, and has throughout earned a reputation as being a kind, patient mentor to countless young writers (most of whom he personally hired), including Jack Handey, George Meyer, Robert Smigel, and Conan O'Brien. "If anyone taught all of the young writers how to properly write a sketch," Smigel says, "it was Jim Downey."

Called by Michaels the best political humorist alive, Downey has been responsible for most of the political-centered pieces during *Saturday Night Live*'s run (many of which he co-wrote with now Senator Al Franken), starting with Jimmy Carter in the mid-'70s and ending, five administrations later, with Barack Obama. The power of Downey's political comedy extends beyond laughs; more impressively, his work has influenced the actual political landscape. In 2008—during a live, televised debate seen by millions—Hillary Clinton referred to one of Downey's recent sketches to make her point that perhaps the press was going just a bit too easy on her opponent. "I just find it curious," she said, "if anybody saw *Saturday Night Live* . . . maybe we should ask Barack if he's comfortable and needs another pillow?"

In 2013, after working on *SNL* off and on for thirty-three of its thirty-eight seasons—and serving as head writer for *Late Night with David Letterman* in 1982 for two years (where he created the Top Ten List)—Downey retired from the show, and now divides his time between New York City and rural upstate New York, where he hopes to achieve his goal of "harmless eccentric."

Do you have any comedy pet peeves?

What has bothered me most for the last few years is that kind of lazy, political comedy, very safe but always pretending to be brave, that usually gets what my colleague Seth Meyers calls "clapter." Clapter is that earnest applause, with a few "whoops" thrown in, that lets you know the audience agrees with you, but what you just said wasn't funny enough to actually make them laugh.

Bill Maher is a funny guy, but he seems to prefer clapter instead of laughs. A lot of his material runs to the "white people are lame and stupid and racist" trope. It congratulates itself on its edginess, but it's just the ass-kissiest kind of comedy going, reassuring his status-anxious audience that there are some people they're smarter than.

My own politics are sort of all over the place in terms of issues, but as far as the writing goes, the only important thing is that it's funny, and that it's an original comment. That the audience agrees with me isn't necessary and probably isn't even a good thing. It's so easy to coast by, just hitting the same familiar notes you know are popular and have been pretested for effectiveness. The audience will always at least applaud, so you never have to risk silence.

How about pet-peeves specific to *Saturday Night Live*?

Celebrity walk-ons bother me. I remember there was a piece from the final show in 2009—Will Ferrell was hosting—and he's sitting in a restaurant with a few buddies, one was Bill Hader, and they were talking about Will's experience in Vietnam. And Will starts singing the Billy Joel song "Goodnight Saigon." It ends with the lyrics, "And we'd all go down together. And we'd all go down together." What started out as a comedy sketch quickly became a vehicle for name-droppy celebrity walk-ons. And by airtime there were about thirty-five celebrities in that piece. It became a massive wankathon, star-fucking extravaganza. Some of the other writers had predicted the piece wouldn't survive dress, and I would have said the same thing after read-through, but when I learned that Anne Hathaway, Tom Hanks, Paul Rudd, and so on were going to appear, I knew it would be the *least* likely piece to go. "I absolutely flat guarantee you the piece will make air, and if the show starts to spread, that piece will be protected. It is a pure display of star-fucking power."

And sure enough it ran, even though funnier pieces were cut to make room for it, including a great sketch by the same writer. I suppose it's all part of the business, but, to me, that seemed almost like a commercial. But, hey, it pays the bills.

How about appearances by such quasi-celebrities as Monica Lewinsky or Paris Hilton?

I found it especially embarrassing when Paris Hilton hosted the show [in 2005]. What was really humiliating was that, on that very same week, *South Park* was doing that brilliant "Stupid Spoiled Whore-Off" piece that just annihilated her. The contrast was dramatic and not to our advantage.

And then when Monica Lewinsky was on the show in May 1999, that was the week poor Cuba Gooding Jr. was hosting, and apparently he became increasingly annoyed as the shape of the show became more of a cohosting thing: "With Cuba Gooding *and* Monica Lewinsky." And I don't blame the guy at all.

I wrote something for Monica Lewinsky that week that she refused to do. It was hardly a savage piece, just one of those C-Span histories about presidential inaugurations; in this case, the history of the presidential knee pads. How during the Andrew Jackson administration there were knee pads made of hickory and leather, forged by harness makers and so on. And we were working our way through history up to Monica. In the piece, all she had to do was stand there, and Kenny G —played by Jimmy Fallon—was going to serenade Monica with a creepy saxophone solo. I watched her read the piece and she was like, "No, not interested," rather contemptuously, as if it weren't up to her standard. You know, the *Monica Lewinsky* standard.

I thought the piece was funny in and of itself, but I'd also add that it would have helped her, and us, by letting her do some penance, by acknowledging that we booked her for her scandal value.

This, to me, was a real indicator that the show was well past the days when we could book strange types of hosts and music acts like [old-timey guitarist and singer] Leon Redbone or ['70s punk group] Fear, just because we thought it might be interesting. When the show was coming to its last year of the original cast and writers, in 1980, as sort of a graduation present Lorne said that each of us could pick either a musical or a guest host. Just imagine that. I chose Strother Martin, a character actor I'd been obsessed with since *Butch Cassidy and the Sundance Kid* [in which he played a boss at a Bolivian mine]. He was also in Sam Peckinpah westerns, and was the prison warden in [1967's] *Cool Hand Luke*. He was a great, great host.

The notion that we could ever in the modern era book anyone like Strother Martin again is unthinkable. These were just people we liked and wanted to present to the public. The issue of ratings never came up, and the episodes that did get smash ratings at the time were sort of unpredictable.

Over the years, have you noticed any specific traits that a performer must have in order to successfully host the show?

When the hosts come in, they can either be walking premises— certain hosts can just bring certain ideas to audiences, like [NFL quarterback] Tom Brady or Senator John McCain—or they can be just really funny people who are not necessarily great actors but have great comedic minds—Conan O'Brien or Jon Stewart. Or they can be really brilliant actors who aren't necessarily known for being funny but can be wonderful with the right script.

One host, in particular, I just loved was Nicolas Cage, who was there in 1992. He played this kind of passion, this innocence, so beautifully. He was great in everything he did. Jeff Goldblum was like that, too. He was a brilliant comic performer—perhaps not the funniest guy to hang out with—but he approached it as an actor. "What's my motivation? How do I do this?" And then he goes out and he's perfect. Justin Timberlake is another favorite. He started off as mainly a cool presence, but as he's matured, he's become a very funny actor and performer. And he brings that straight line with him, the lady killer.

But of course some of them turn out to be better live performers than others. As a host, you do have to surrender control to us [the writers], which is why we always feel a sense of responsibility for anyone willing to put himself in such a vulnerable position. We have a thing about not bad-mouthing them, although some people have occasionally broken that rule here and there. It's like Alcoholics Anonymous. What goes on in private, when you're here, stays here.

With that said, there have been some terrible hosts over the years, including an infamously bad 1991 show with actor Steven Seagal at the helm.

Yes, that was a case where it was all we could do not to talk about what a douchebag he was.

What was his specific problem? Did he refuse to do what was necessary to put on a good show?

Well, I guess now it can be told. He was just so fucking stupid. Rob Schneider had the funniest idea for a monologue. It was Seagal coming out and doing the "You know, I've obviously made my career with action pictures, like *Hard to Kill* and *Out for Justice* and so on." Applause, applause. "I don't want to apologize for them, I think they were good. But the fact is I've moved past that. To me, it's all about the music now." Then he was going to pick up a guitar and perform a very moving version of [the 1974 hit song by Carl Douglas] "Kung Fu Fighting." Not a rockin' one, but playing it like it was "Amazing Grace" or something. Real slowly: "Everybody was . . . kung fu fighting. Those cats . . . those cats were fast . . . as fast as lightning." And I thought it was a really hilarious idea. So of course, Seagal steps out on stage and decides to go with his "instincts," which were to play it loud and badass, like a Hollywood actor with his own band. It's like when you go to a barbecue joint and realize, "Oh fuck, we came on blues night? Damn!" And you can't have a conversation because the fifty-five-year-old guy is really rocking out.

You worked at *SNL* longer than any other writer in the show's history. And yet as respected as you are, you were actually fired by NBC for a season, beginning in 1998.

Well, that was all due to [then NBC executive] Don Ohlmeyer. Norm Macdonald, the anchor for Weekend Update, and I were writing a lot of jokes about O.J. Simpson, and we had been doing so for more than three years. Don, being good friends with O.J., had just had enough.

Your O.J. jokes were not light taps on the head. These were jokes that would often end with: "Because O.J. murdered two people."

Yeah, we weren't holding back. [Laughs] That's the thing I kind of liked about Don, actually: His friendship with O.J. was so *old school*. It was so un-showbizzy. He ended up firing me, as well as Norm, but I can't honestly say that a part of me doesn't respect Don for his loyalty. Most people in show business would sell out anyone in their lives, for any reason at all, including for practice. Don was the opposite. He threw a party for the jurors after the 1995 acquittal. And he stuck with O.J. through it all.

I don't know that Norm enjoyed the experience of the firing quite as much as I did, but to me it was exciting. It was certainly the best press *I* ever received. We got tremendous support from people I really admire, some of whom are friends and some I didn't really know that well, but who stepped up and called me. It was a fun time.

You had been on the show for twenty years. Being fired must have stung a little.

To tell you the truth, Norm and I had done Update for three and a half seasons. I felt like we had made our point. What I did like about the way we approached Update was that it was akin to what the punk movement was for music: just real stripped down. We did whatever we wanted, and there was nothing there that we considered to be a form of cheating. We weren't cuddly, we weren't adorable, we weren't warm. We weren't going to do easy, political jokes that played for clapter and let the audience know we were all on the same side. We were going to be mean and, to an extent, anarchists.

Shouldn't there be *some* connection with the audience? Can you be a *complete* anarchist when it comes to humor?

Yeah, well, that's Norm Macdonald. He does things for the experience of doing it, and he doesn't fear silence at all. Take his performance at the 2008 Bob Saget roast where he did jokes that could have come out of a 1920s toastmaster's manual: "[Comedian] Greg Giraldo is here. He has the grace of a swan, the wisdom of an owl, and the eye of an eagle. Ladies and gentlemen, *this man is for the birds*! [Actress] Susie Essman is famous for being a vegetarian. Hey! She may be a vegetarian, *but she's still full of bologna in my book*!"

One summer, when *SNL* was on hiatus, Norm and I read a story about a newspaper published by and for the homeless. We were improvising around that idea, doing the tough newspaper editor handing out assignments to his homeless reporters: "Edwards! I want a thousand words on going to the bathroom in your pants! You! Davis! How about a human-interest feature on urine-stained mattresses! Bernstein! Can you give me a long 'think piece' on people whose brains are being monitored by the CIA?!"

I had forgotten all about this conversation, but the first *SNL* episode back that fall, Norm says to me, "Hey, Downey. Remember that homeless idea we had? About the newspaper by and for the homeless? Well, I was out in LA, you know? And I was doing this benefit for the homeless . . . "

And I'm thinking, Oh no . . .

And he says, "Yeah, I did that bit for the audience . . . at this benefit, you know? And they *hated it*!"

He's just the most courageous performer. Norm would sometimes hang on an Update joke because he wanted to make it clear to the audience that yes, the joke was over, but we still thought it was funny. He didn't make the panic move of quickly jumping to the next joke so he didn't have to hear the silence. He wanted to give people a chance.

I'm not sure how big a fan Lorne was of our Update. I think it was probably too mean for his sensibility, and he didn't like the deadpan aspect of it. But he supported us as long as he could, bless his heart. And I stand by it. I'm proud of what we did there. Nearly all of those Update segments have been edited out of repeats, by the way.

Over the years, critics have had a strange relationship with *SNL*. They take very personally what they perceive as the show's low points, almost as if a good friend has let them down.

I remember there was the most cretinous review of the show in the fall of '84. I will never forget this. It was a new cast with Chris Guest and Marty Short, and there was a review in *People* disparaging the show. Now my idea of the lowest rung in hell is to be surrounded and condescended to by idiots. In fact, I tried to write a sketch one time about that. It was Galileo getting teased by other astronomers at the [seventeenth-century] Papal Court. He'd be surrounded by these other scientists, who'd be like: "Oh, geez, Galileo! I'm getting sick to my stomach. It must be all this *spinning* from the earth *rotating on its axis*!!! Awww, I'm just ribbin' ya!" Galileo would be getting this constantly and he'd be losing his mind.

Anyway, in the *People* review, the critic was talking about the [October 1984] "Synchronized Swimming" bit with Chris Guest, Harry Shearer, and Marty Short. It was about two guys training for the Olympics as male synchronized swimmers. And Chris did this brilliant turn as a not-very-funny, inarticulate gay choreographer: "I've been directing regional theater . . . and if I ever do that again, I'm just going to kill myself with a Veg-O-Matic." So the *People* review says, "How bad is the new *SNL*? They do *Veg-O-Matic jokes*." Which, of course, misses the entire point of the reference. The lame Veg-O-Matic reference was a *character* joke, you fucking moron.

It seems that the sensibility of many TV critics rarely matches those found in professional humor writers. There seems to be a disconnect.

Well, I think most of them have terrible senses of humor. Tom Feran, a guy I knew in college, was the critic for the *Cleveland Plain Dealer* and had a great sense of humor. He always championed smart, funny stuff and always tried to get it noticed. He wasn't mean, but he wasn't the kind of easy mark for fake "genius" that gets pushed on you all the time. Most critics, though, have no sense of humor. And all of the mean ones have crates filled with humor pieces rejected by *The New Yorker.*

There also sometimes seems to be a disconnect between the censors for *SNL* and the writers. Over the years, have there been many instances in which you've written sketches that you've loved but were ultimately not allowed to air?

I can think of two: One was a commercial parody written by me, Jack Handey, Al Franken, Robert Smigel, and probably some others. It was one of the few times all of us have worked on the same piece, one that was gang-written. It was for a car called the DWI, the only car built expressly for driving drunk. We wanted to get James Earl Jones to do the voice-over: "It. Is. A. Drunk. Driving. *Machine.*" One of the jokes was that the car keys would be gigantic. I don't remember the rest. But I do remember the network saying "Absolutely not!" And I honestly did not understand. There was nothing dirty in this piece. This was not making light of drunk driving. It was making fun of people who drive drunk. It was holding them up to ridicule; it was fighting the good fight as far as that goes. But their attitude was, Nope, we don't want any letters along the lines of "I wish I could laugh, but, you see, I lost my fifteen-year-old daughter to a drunk driver." So it's that defensive thing.

The other piece [in 1990] was called "Pussywhipped." Jan Hooks was playing the host of a talk show and there were a few male guests, one of whom was Tom Hanks, and they had to keep excusing themselves to go call their girlfriends. The piece did run, but the censors absolutely would not let us use the title "Pussywhipped." And I kept saying, "C'mon, it doesn't mean vagina. It means female-dominated." But that's where the NBC standards lady says, "Well, *as a woman* . . ." Which was her way of reminding me that her sense of humor had been removed at birth.

And so I lost that one, and we called it "P-Whipped" or something. I always hate it when you have to do a lame euphemism that no normal person would ever use.

Overall, though, I never really chafed under the restrictions, even when sometimes they got really crazy. One of the points I pride myself on is that I avoid anything I feel is a cheap laugh based on shock or just being dirty. You can always get a laugh, but you don't want it to come at the price of your dignity.

You wrote a sketch for an October 1990 *SNL* episode that's often listed as an all-time favorite from fans: a very fit Patrick Swayze and a very unfit Chris Farley compete with each other for the last spot on the Chippendales male exotic dance team. But as much as fans love it, there have been some comedy writers who have taken offense to the sketch, thinking that it was demeaning to Farley's true character.

Well, I don't think they understood what I thought was funny about it, and what the audience liked about it. I think they read it as just making fun of the fat guy dancing. But, to me, what was crucial was that Farley wasn't the least bit embarrassed. To me, it was all about the reactions from the judges. The whole point was that not only did they make Chris audition in the first place, but then the judges took the time to patiently explain, at great length, why they were going to choose Swayze over him.

Does it upset you when other comedy writers are critical of your pieces?

No, not really. We disagree sometimes. I know there was another piece I wrote with Jack Handey that a few writers hated; it was the one [that aired in October 1989] about Dracula, played by James Woods. It was the one piece we ever did on the show that dealt, however indirectly, with AIDS. Dracula would engage his female victims in conversation, subtly sounding them out about their sexual histories before he sucked their blood. If I remember the specific objection, it was the kind of instance when writers don't like an idea because they can imagine a hack version of that idea. I suppose you can conjure up a vision of a bad comic out there doing "Hey, how about Dracula! What with AIDS, he's probably asking to get a blood test! Am I right?!" But that's not what this piece was. You can turn *any* idea into a hack version of itself, but sometimes comedy writers just go crazy with overthinking these things.

Sometimes the audience just wants to laugh.

They do, that's right. But sometimes writers overlook this. Not performers, though. If the audience is laughing, they're happy.

Do writers and performers on *SNL* tend to write different styles of sketches?

I think so. Writers tend to write ordinary people in weird situations. Performers tend to write weird people in ordinary situations. That's a broad generalization, but it's fairly true.

With a performer-written sketch, often the criticism that will come from a writer is that the situation is something the audience has seen a million times. And it often bothers the pure writer that audiences don't seem to mind. As writers, we get so frustrated: "Why don't those people—that is, the audience—object?" Writers are much more interested, and maybe even obsessed, with originality. We sometimes treat comedy as a science, where advances are made, and we must always move forward, never backward. So that once something has been done, it should perhaps be built upon, but never, ever repeated. For performers, the fact that something has been done before is, I think, neither here nor there. For writers, it's a real problem, and sometimes we can tie ourselves up in knots worrying, "Is this too similar to that other thing?"

As for me, I wish originality were prized more highly by audiences than it is, but I have to say it doesn't seem to be that important to them. I think we need to be ahead of our audiences, but not so much that we lose them. Figuring out the right balance is everything.

I suppose it can always be taken too far in the other extreme: the repetition of characters to the point of overkill.

Writers tend to be very resistant to repeating characters. We always feel that it's somehow unethical, that it's cheating. "I did that piece already. What? I'm going to do the *second version* of the same piece?" Generally speaking, you do the best jokes the first time around. Now, it's true that over the course of the following three months, you'll think of jokes that if you'd thought of them at the time you would have put in the first version—but there's usually only one or two of those. From a writer's standpoint, not enough of a reason to do it again.

I haven't written a lot of those recurring pieces in my career. Most of what I do is topical one-off things. I have written tons of presidential addresses, but they never involved the same comedy premise—at least, I hope some of them didn't.

One idea I did write a few times was The Chris Farley Show. That was basically putting Chris Farley, the real Chris Farley, on stage in a structured way. I did it the first time when Jeff Daniels was guest host [in 1991], and Lorne kept asking for another one. But it seemed to me such a one-off thing. Lorne finally said, "Well, if you won't do it, I'll ask someone else." And I said, "No, I want to at least control it." So we did it two more times, once with Martin Scorsese and again with Paul McCartney, in 1993.

I must say, none of this seems to bother performers at all. They'll tend to go and go and go with essentially the same sketch until someone makes them stop. We've all seen repeat pieces on the show that are basically the same sketch spray painted a different color, but with the same dynamic, same jokes.

As a writer, I would love to say it's all about the writing. But like the way good pitching beats good hitting, good performing can lift a mediocre premise, and bad performing can sink the best-written piece.

Lorne Michaels has called you the best political humorist alive. In 2000, you coined the George W. Bush-ism "strategery," which many people mistakenly came to believe was actually uttered by the president

himself. But there's been some criticism over the years that you lean more right than left. I think it goes without saying, of course, that this criticism tends to come from those on the left.

In the political sketches I write, I think I just go where the comedy takes me. I honestly never want a political agenda to be the leading edge of the piece. I want the piece to be funny, but only because it's based on an observation that I think is fair to make and that no one else is making. I don't think anyone could ever accuse me of going for clapter. And what's sometimes even better than the laughter is making audiences laugh when they don't particularly want to, or when they're not sure that they should.

Can you give me a specific example?

Well, in 2007, I did a couple of debate pieces with Hillary Clinton and Obama that were generally perceived as being pro-Hillary. Our audience, meanwhile, was probably 95 percent pro-Obama.

One fellow *SNL* writer, who shall go unnamed, criticized you for that particular sketch. He thought that you were promoting Hillary over Obama.

To me, what was funny about that situation was that, for years, Hillary had been very much the official candidate of the media, even right up to the announcement of her candidacy. She was like the wife who put them through dental school, and suddenly they dumped her for the hot, young hygienist, Obama, the trophy wife. And the change in the media was so quick and so extreme. To me, what was funny was Hillary thinking, "What the *fuck*? Two months ago everyone loved me!" It was like the media was doing to Obama what Monica Lewinsky had done to Bill Clinton. And now Hillary was in the same spot all over again. When I write these sketches, I want them to be fresh in comedy terms but also something that resonates: "That's true, that's true." As opposed to something I know damn well reflects the viewpoint of 90 percent of the audience but what would feel to me like cheating or ass kissing: "Well, about time someone took on Big Oil!"

I like to think that unless you're making an observation, and that observation is true—and I hope fresh—it's not worth writing a piece. I'm not saying that I always have a particularly original observation to make, which is why if I had my druthers, I'd write fewer political pieces. For me, this is more about the characters in politics than politics itself. It's about the human aspect of these people we don't usually get to see; the way a person would react in these situations if they were in any field but politics.

Can you give me some examples of sketches, political or otherwise, you've written over the years that you thought would kill with an audience but ended up bombing?

There was one [1985] piece I wrote with Jack [Handey] that absolutely destroyed at the table and then just played to exquisite silence from the audience. It was called "The Life of Vlad the Impaler." And it was [fifteenth-century ruler] Vlad the Impaler's wife, Madonna, gently trying to explain to Vlad why he was so unpopular with his subjects. This came as a terrible shock to him, and he was really stunned and hurt. He couldn't understand why. And her theory was, "I really think it's the impalings." "What?!" "Yeah, they really hate them." "Are you *sure*?" "You know, Vlad, they try to tell you. You don't listen."

God, it bombed. Absolute silence. We figured, Well, maybe they don't know the story of Vlad the Impaler. [Laughs] Maybe they don't know what *impaling* means. Anyway, Larry David called to say how much he liked the piece, which was enough for me.

Here's another one: It was when Bob Newhart hosted in May 1980 and he loved the piece, which was also enough for me. The sketch began with one of those Civil War scenes you've seen a million times. I saw it as recently as *Black Hawk Down*. Officers are walking through the wounded tent, and there's a boy soldier dying. "You're going to be okay, son. You'll be back with your regiment in no time." "You don't have to lie to me, Major. I'm gut shot. I know I'm a goner. But I want to ask you one thing. Will you write my mother and tell her that I did my duty, that I was a good soldier?"

Everyone's tearing up. The music is somber, and the officer, played by Newhart, says, "I'll do that, son. Don't you worry." And then the kid dies and you dissolve to a series of Civil War–era photographs and music, with the graphic "Three Weeks Later." When we come back, we're in Newhart's tent, which he shares with Bill Murray, a fellow officer. And Murray asks, "Hey, did you ever write that kid's mother?" And Newhart sheepishly says, "Not yet, but I'm going to." "Geez, it's been like a month!" "I'll get to it, I'll get to it!" And the rest of the piece was more dissolves to "Three Weeks Later," "Six Weeks Later," and so on, and Newhart still hadn't written the letter. By now, Bob is suffering from writer's block. "See the problem is, I've waited so long that now I can't just write 'Your son was a great soldier. He died a hero.' It's got to be *better* than that." He was trying to come up with good ideas. It was like someone putting off a term paper.

I think the opening of the sketch with someone dying, particularly a young person, chilled the audience from the start.

One thing I've noticed over the years is that when *SNL* airs sketches with graphics—particularly graphics that express the passage of time, such as "Three Weeks Later," "One Day Later," whatever it may be—these sketches tend to confuse the audience. At least, the audience in the studio.

It does take the audience out of the sketch. The only way the studio audience for the Civil War piece could know about the passage of time would be to see the graphics on the monitors. But there was nothing about that piece that suggested to the audience they had to watch the monitors and not the stage. There were no special effects, so most watched the live action.

Do you think the home audience responded differently to that sketch?

I think the home audience would have liked that piece a lot more. But I still think the biggest factor was that the audience felt, Ooooh, a sixteen-year-old kid died.

Is it true that you discovered the legendary and reclusive comedy writer John Swartzwelder, who later wrote more episodes of *The Simpsons*— fifty-nine—than anyone else? He's the Thomas Pynchon of the comedy world. I think there are only a few known photographs of him.

I was head writer for *Letterman* at the time [1983], and we would read unsolicited joke submissions. [Producer] Merrill Markoe showed me this small postcard and it was from Swartzwelder. It had just a single joke on it. It went something like: "Mike Flynn's much-publicized attempt to break every record in the *Guinness Book of Records* got off to a rocky start this week when his recording of 'White Christmas' sold only five copies."

I just loved the shape of that joke. I became obsessed with it. John had signed the card but had left no address. Nothing, just his name and a Chicago postmark. So I began a desperate attempt to track him down. He wasn't in the Chicago directory, and this was way before the Internet. So I went to the New York Public Library and looked up big-city phone books for Swartzwelders, figuring that there couldn't be that many. I found his mother's number in Seattle. She said, "Yes, that's my son, John. He's at an ad agency in Chicago."

I got in touch with John and set up a meeting with him and Letterman, and it was one of the most spectacularly awful interviews in history.

What happened?

Swartzwelder shows up just as we finished taping for the day. Chris Elliott says to me, "Hey, this guy is here to see you." I went to say hi to John—I had never seen him before—and he's a really imposing figure, about six foot eight, standing there in a navy peacoat, like Randy Quaid in *The Last Detail*. At the time he looked like a combination mountain man/biker/Edmund Kemper [1960s and '70s necrophiliac serial killer]. He had a droopy mustache and long, greasy hair, and he was just a real presence. He was carrying a little 1930s-style hip flask. And he asks, "Is there a kitchen here?" "Yeah, down the hall. I gotta run and do something, but I'll be right back." I took longer than I thought, and when I come back Swartzwelder is gone. Chris tells me, "I think he's in with Dave." "Oh, no, no, no, no, no. No, I needed to talk to him first!" Dave is a wonderful guy, but he's a very private person, and it's important that people be warned not to come on too strong when meeting him.

So I ask Chris, "How long has he been in there?" "I don't know, about five minutes." I run back to Dave's office and Swartzwelder is sitting there, making himself completely at home. I want to say he had his feet up on Dave's desk, but I'm not sure. I *am* sure, however, that he was both smoking and drinking, a move not recommended in the Dress for Success guidebooks. Meanwhile, Dave is sitting there stiffly, like an orderly at a mental institution trapped alone with a patient. Swartzwelder is holding forth, as I recall, about his views on television, which amounted to everything on television was shit—including, I think, much of what we had done on our show. Dave looks over at me and his eyes tell me "no way."

He wasn't hired at *Letterman*, but we did bring him to *SNL* for a year [in 1985], and then he went on to do legendary work at *The Simpsons*. I'm sure that he preferred the freedom of writing for animation over writing for live action. He's a brilliant guy, although I haven't seen him in twenty years.

Have you ever felt constrained within the parameters of the sketch form? Have you ever had the desire to write for the big screen or, perhaps, long-form television?

No, not really. I kept retooling myself and changing the kinds of things I did. I wrote *SNL* sketches and then I did *Letterman* for a few years, which is a totally different thing, and then I returned to *SNL* and was writing new types of pieces. Then Update was something different all together. More recently, I was just writing political material and it was a change because I had the freedom to do whatever I wanted. Within that, I also had the chance to write filmed pieces or live performance or whatever.

I really am conscious of the fact that I have been very fortunate. There are certain moments when I felt that better decisions could have been made on the show, but in the big picture I feel I have been treated very well, a couple of firings aside. Because *SNL* is a variety show and because it's ninety minutes long, there is always plenty of room to maneuver. I never got bored with doing the same thing or getting stuck in a rut. I could always go back and retool. Like certain bands do when they just emerge with a totally new kind of sound.

Your attitude seems to be a rarity. It seems that most TV comedy writers constantly yearn to write for the movies. It's almost as if they have a chip on their shoulder, that television is too small.

Actually, I'm glad you said that because I honestly feel that TV is a better form for being funny, generally speaking, than movies. I have never really seen what it is that movies give you that makes things funnier. I think that the smallness and the immediacy of TV—where you can do something on Saturday based on an event that happened on Wednesday, and where the important elements aren't overwhelmed by the scale and production—is great. There are limitations that TV has compared with movies—especially live TV—but I don't think they're the important ones in the scheme of things.

If you look at movies many *SNL* performers have participated in over the years, you can't help but wonder why there's any appeal at all. Is it purely the money?

I guess it's just that for their whole lives some people think you do TV in order to *get to* movies, and that therefore *any* movie is better than *every* television show.

I think it's fair to say—as a general matter—that most of the people who have been in the cast of *SNL* did their best work *on SNL*. Or they do good movies, but it isn't any better than what they did on the show. For example, I think Will Ferrell is brilliant, and I love him in his movies, but I don't think he is any funnier than he was on the show. Same with Kristen Wiig in *Bridesmaids*, or Eddie Murphy. And, of course, some people have done much worse than they did on the show.

I think you're always going to see more odd, original comedy on TV than you will in a movie. I love the *Hangover* films, but weird, eccentrically funny stuff is usually going to appear on TV or online. *Tim and Eric. Portlandia. Reno 911!* [Stephen Merchant's HBO series] *Hello Ladies.* Brilliant.

When have you laughed the hardest over the years at *SNL*?

Um, let's see. . . . Damon Wayan's audition in the fall of 1985. He was doing two kids on a playground. "Your mother is so fat you have to grease her up to get her through the front door." And the other kid's responses keep getting more and more deadly serious: "Yeah, well, your sister had a baby when she was only eleven!" . . . Ben Stiller pitching me a sketch idea in the spring of 1989. I was laughing so hard I fell on the floor. He was improvising a character, a college kid on spring break in Florida—his name was Jordo—being interviewed on MTV, asking his parents for money. . . . Phil Hartman at a table read doing Mace, his psychotic ex-con character with a hair-trigger temper. I couldn't breathe I was laughing so hard.

All of those examples took place *off* the air.

Funny, I never thought of that. There's something about being right there, seeing it fresh before makeup and wardrobe. And seeing it for the first time. After that it's only the audience that gets to see it that way.

As for moments on the show, I'd say Dan Aykroyd doing Julia Child. Bill Murray doing Nick Rails, the entertainer on the auto train to Orlando, Florida. Eddie Murphy doing James Brown's Celebrity Hot Tub Party. Fred Armisen's character, Nicholas Fehn, the political comedian with no material. Maya Rudolph doing the national anthem at the World Series with every conceivable grace note and gimmick. And Will Ferrell doing his "Get off the shed!" guy.

How about beyond *Saturday Night Live*?

Probably *Team America*, the British *Office*, or *The Simpsons*. Sarah Silverman. The stand-up of Chris Rock. Any number of Monty Python or Phil Hendrie bits. S. Clay Wilson, a seventies comic artist known for disgusting but hilarious sex and violence. And any phone conversation with Jack Handey or Andy Breckman, who's written for *SNL* and *Letterman* and created *Monk*.

You just mentioned Phil Hendrie. Can you talk a bit about who he is?

Phil Hendrie had a syndicated radio show [based in Los Angeles] which, in its golden age, from 2000 to 2006, was to me the most consistently brilliant and original comedy of the last generation.

Hendrie did about forty different voice characters so beautifully performed that he could interview himself in character on radio with half the listening audience unaware that only one person was talking. The fake "guests" would be involved in outrageous situations which would get angry listeners phoning in to complain, and a brilliant three-way conversation would ensue with Phil playing the voice of reason and refereeing the fights between the callers and himself in character. The performance, the writing, and the improvised elements together made some of the best comedy I have ever heard.

Bill Murray is a fan. *The Simpsons* writers are huge fans—I'm told they would stop their rewrite sessions to listen to the show. Eric Clapton is a gigantic fan. Phil Hendrie is my comedy hero.

What advice would you give to young writers hoping to make a career out of writing sketch comedy for television?

Comedy is a hard thing to teach, and the work aspect of it is not fair in many ways. I mean, you can spend hours and hours and focus and hard work and pain, and a piece will still not be good. There's no equation where the result is in proportion to the effort. But it has to start with a funny take on something, one that's special, that you've never seen before. I've known funny people who don't write particularly well. The non-comedy parts of the writing may not be all that fresh or interesting, the grammar and vocabulary may be shaky, but all that can be handled later. That can be handled later. It's just mechanics. What you must have is a funny sensibility. You also need confidence to communicate what it is you do that's different from what everyone else is doing.

And then it's a matter of exercising the muscles, hanging out with like-minded people, being out in the world and having experiences. It's not that you have to stand to the side and observe, but everyone notices things as they go through life and everyone has experiences. All of these will matter at some point in some way.

I'd also say to writers that when you're starting out it probably helps to work with other people. Choose a group where you can make a contribution while they get to know you, as opposed to doing it all by yourself and just walking in with the finished product. That's the entrepreneur's way. "I'll own it, it'll be a hundred percent me." But because of that it may have flaws that limit its acceptance. As an approach, it's probably better to be collaborative. Also, it's good for your confidence, and for others' confidence in you, because they begin to think, Oh this guy's good.

It can all be nerve-racking. There are few things in white-collar life where you're more vulnerable than when you drop a ten-page script on a table and it's read cold by a room full of people and the piece eats it. It's terrifying to go through, especially when people are trying to be nice. And you always get that one guy, that one wiseass, who says, "Ooooh! That one *rolled foul*!" That kind of thing. I don't want to say it toughens you up, but I respect anyone who goes through it.

Which is why I think it's important—and I'm going to sound like an industrial psychologist here—but I think it's vital for a show to create a zone where writers can try different ideas out without the fear of being made fun of or even giving a shit. And that's why, when I used to read writing submissions, I would ask a writer to give me three pieces, and make one of them something that only *he* thought was funny. The other two could be something everybody liked. Just make one piece something that you've been unable to convince anyone else is funny but that *you* believe in. I want writers eventually to produce work that no one has seen before and that is definitely only them.

A good writing staff is one where you can look around the room and say, "*This* guy does this thing better than anyone else" and "*She* does that thing better than anyone else." It's not necessary that everyone scores the same amount of points on every outing. But at the end of the year everybody on the show has had some success, something that could not have happened without them—whether they wrote it all by themselves or just contributed. I don't mind taking chances, and I'm less worried about a bad piece than about missing a great one.

Writing comedy is like the high jump, where you get three tries at each height and the misses aren't held against you, or shouldn't be. So you're judged by the best you're capable of. You have to figure out how to clear that height each and every time.

Most of the time. [Laughs]

ULTRASPECIFIC COMEDIC KNOWLEDGE

TERRY JONES

Writing for Monty Python

Can you remember the first joke you wrote?

The first joke I can remember coming up with by myself—not necessarily writing, but creating—was when I was about four or five. My family and I were sitting around a table. My granny asked all of us, "Does anybody want more custard?" I raised my hand, but instead of giving her my plate, I handed over my table mat. She poured the custard all over the mat. Everybody turned to me and said, "You silly boy! What did you do that for?!" It taught me at a very young age that comedy is dangerous business. If you try to make people laugh and they don't, they can become very, very angry. People do not become angry if you're writing a tragedy and you don't do a good job. But people get extremely angry when you create comedy that isn't funny—or, at the least, with the comedy *they* don't find funny.

Did you always know you wanted to write?

Yes, since about the age of seven. I was always writing poetry, which tended to be terribly gloomy. I think my family got worried at some point. I was a compulsive writer. I've got essays I wrote when I was very young; my granny kept them. I used to write poems and huge, long essays for that age. Just writing, all the time. There was a wonderful teacher at school, Mr. Martin, who would read out my essays to the class. I loved that. That gave me a great base. It gave me confidence. But Mr. Martin left, and it was then that I began to hear different things from teachers. I would be told, "You can't make a living as a writer. The best you can hope for is to become a teacher."

Do you think there's a connection between poetry and comedy writing?

I think there is a great connection, actually. The [nineteenth-century poet] Robert Browning, in essence, said that you can take three separate ideas, and from those three, you produce not a fourth idea, but a star. I've always found that lovely. It's a somewhat similar theory with comedy. But the difference is that with comedy you take different ideas and put them together and you produce not a star, but a *laugh*. There's a magical element to it.

Can you give me an example from Python where vastly different ideas were combined to produce a laugh?

Mike [Palin] wrote a [1970] TV sketch called "The Spanish Inquisition." I think that's a very good example of taking separate ideas—twentieth-century locations and Spanish Inquisition priests—and producing a star. How did Mike go from England in 1911 to then having three torturers from the fifteenth century burst into the sitting room and announce, "Nobody expects the Spanish Inquisition"? Where did he make that connection? And how did he make it work? In the end, you get a laugh. But when you reverse-engineer it, it's quite hard to follow how he came up with the original spark, the original idea. And yet it *still* works.

Now that I think about it, there's another similarity between poetry and comedy: distillation. Both have to be distilled. For both poetry and comedy, the words, the concepts have to be boiled down, and the essence is what you want to say.

It was tremendously difficult to keep up that level of quality with Python. We made it a point to end sketches when they might have just been beginning on other shows. Writing was very serious business; we took it very seriously. But it did take a lot out of us.

Michael Palin has said that the six members of Monty Python worked together to produce a harmony that they couldn't have produced individually. This reminded me of something I once read about the 1960s vocal group the Mamas & the Papas. Individually, they had four distinct voices, but when they sang together they produced a fifth harmony—almost another distinctive voice—which they nicknamed "Harpy."

That's a good image, actually. I think that's true. The six of us produced a harmony that was somebody else. We'd write together, and we were almost writing for this seventh voice. There was always that image of another voice that was there. It was the Python voice, really. And it couldn't quite be duplicated with any other combination—or alone. With Python, we had a lot of different minds at work, and we worked very well together.

I rewatched some of the early Python TV episodes from 1970, and I noticed that the crowd was very quiet for the first few episodes and only seemed to grow more and more animated as the series went on.

For the very first show, the audience consisted of a lot of old-age pensioners who actually thought they were coming to see a real circus. They were a bit puzzled. By the end of the second and third series, two years later, we actually had to take a lot of clapping and laughter *out* of the shows. We had to speed up the shows. I think people got used to it by the end of the first season. There was a great doubt whether the BBC would actually commission another series [season]. We were lucky they did, actually. They hated the show—until they were told it was funny and it was good.

That wouldn't happen today—executives not being happy with a show, but leaving it completely alone and providing the show time to find its feet.

With Python, the writers were completely in charge, and this was very unique. We were the only people writing for us, so we had a certain strength. We knew what we could perform. We knew what we couldn't.

With the BBC, we didn't start off with any problems, but we soon faced some difficulty with the censors. We wrote a sketch [for the third series] called "The All-England Summarize Proust Competition." It was about a beauty pageant where contestants, instead of impressing judges with singing or flute playing, would attempt to summarize the works and philosophy of Proust. And this was one of the first instances, if not the very first time, that the word "masturbation" was ever used on television. Graham [Chapman] was playing a contestant. The host of the pageant, played by me, asked Graham what his hobbies were, and he said, "Well, strangling animals, golf, and masturbation."

The BBC edited out "masturbation." Keep in mind, the BBC was okay with strangling cats. But masturbation was definitely out. [Laughs] If you watch the edited sketch, there's a lag time after Graham says "golf." His lips move but you can't hear him say "masturbation." And then there's a huge laugh from the live audience. But this is puzzling to the home viewers. It sounds like the studio audience is laughing at "strangling animals." It becomes even stranger.

Would Python overwrite? For instance, I've heard that the original script for *The Holy Grail* was much longer, and that only about 10 percent of the first draft appears in the movie.

Yes, we'd usually write a lot of material, or at least pitch material, and then cut down. The first draft of *Holy Grail* was much longer. The first half took place in the present day. Arthur and the rest of the knights found that the Holy Grail was being sold at Harrods [department store, in London]. You could find *anything* there. But we ultimately decided to have the entire film only take place in the Middle Ages.

For *Life of Brian*, we had a few scenes that were cut. One of the original ideas was for it to be the story of the thirteenth apostle who missed the last supper because his wife had invited friends over to eat back at their house. That was changed. We spent a lot of time on re-writes. Not so much for *Meaning of Life*, but certainly for the first two films.

We were talking earlier about how comedy is often created by bringing disparate ideas together. You wrote a scene for *The Meaning of Life* that might just be one of the strangest scenes in the history of film—at least for a comedy. I'm thinking of the Mr. Creosote scene, played by you (in what I would assume, and truly hope, was heavy makeup). A gigantic man, dining in a very fancy restaurant, vomits until he explodes.

[Laughs] Well, for that one, I just sat down and wrote a sketch in the worst possible taste. In fact, at the top of the paper it read: "Sketch in the Worst Possible Taste." The first time I ever read that in front of the rest of Python, we had just eaten lunch. No one liked it. That was *not* the time to do it. It was decisively rejected. But then a month later John [Cleese] rang me up and said, "I'm going to change my mind about this." I think he spotted that the waiter could be very funny. It was John who came up with the "wafer thin" line and to offer the mint to Mr. Creosote just before he explodes. That's the only sketch I ever co-wrote with John.

The Mr. Creosote scene took four days to shoot. On the fifth day, a wedding took place in the ballroom where we shot it. That wasn't a set! The fake vomit was Russian salad dressing, and some other food ingredients. By the fifth day you can imagine the smell. And the poor people getting married had to come into that stench. Not a good way to start off the married life.

Fellow Python Eric Idle has called *The Meaning of Life* a "kind of a punk film." Do you agree with that?

I think so. I think that might be accurate. But it was really no different from how we always wrote. We weren't concerned with making anyone but ourselves laugh. And that's clear in the Mr.

Creosote sketch. I mean, we certainly weren't pandering with that sketch.

Nor with the "Fishy, Fishy" sketch, also in *The Meaning of Life*. The sketch consists of you, dressed in a tuxedo, with drawn whiskers on your chin, waving large double-jointed arms. Meanwhile, Graham Chapman is dressed as a drag queen. And there's another character wearing an elephant head. All are looking directly at the camera, asking the audience for help in finding a "fishy."

I was surprised with that one. I pitched it and was shocked after it was voted in. I was totally surprised by that vote. Each of us had different styles of comedy. Mike and I would write, I suppose, zany sketches. John would write bits more having to do with character and human nature. This sketch was silly, with no greater purpose. So it was sort of extreme, and we didn't always agree on extremes. But when we did fight, it was always over the material. It was never personal. Or mostly never personal.

What's amazing about *Monty Python's Flying Circus* is just how close those original TV shows came to being erased by the BBC.

That's true. The BBC came very close to erasing all of the original Python tapes, at least from the first season. What happened was that we got word from our editor that the BBC was about to wipe all the tapes to use for more "serious" entertainment—ballet and opera and the like. So we smuggled out the tapes and recorded them onto a Philips VCR home system. For a long time, these were the only copies of Python's first season to exist anywhere. If these were lost, they were lost for good.

This happened quite often with BBC comedy shows from the sixties. It happened with Spike Milligan's show from the late 1960s, *Q5*. All those shows are gone—or mostly gone. It happened with Alan Bennett's [1966] show, *On the Margin*. It happened with a British TV comedy series from the late sixties, *Broaden Your Mind*, a show I worked on before *Python's Flying Circus*. All these tapes are gone. They were taped over in order to record sporting events.

Comedy shows from the fifties, sixties, and seventies were often erased in order to save money. It happened in the U.S. with the first eight years of *The Tonight Show Starring Johnny Carson*, as well as with shows featuring the comedian Ernie Kovacs. And it happened, as you were just saying, in the U.K. with many BBC comedies. But how much, exactly, was the BBC saving when they would reuse these tapes?

I don't know. I would guess around one hundred pounds per tape reel.

So to save roughly $150—in today's money, at least—the BBC was willing to erase original comedy that could never again be duplicated?

If they'd been wiped, I don't think we'd be talking now, actually. Python wouldn't have been discovered in America. And we might not have made as many series for TV. And we may not have created any movies. It goes to show how tenuous history is. It can go in any direction.

Which direction would you recommend young comedy writers head?

If you want to create comedy, try to make people laugh. If you can make people laugh, head in that direction. If nobody laughs . . . well, that's not good news. [Laughs] Head in the opposite direction.

PURE, HARD-CORE ADVICE

DIABLO CODY
....

Screenwriter/Director, *Juno, Young Adult,*
Time and a Half, Sweet Valley High

I couldn't have grown up less connected to Hollywood. I lived in a very conservative Polish-Catholic community in the south suburbs of Chicago. I went to Mass and received communion six mornings a week. The idea of a "professional writer" was a fantasy. My parents told me that I couldn't write for a living, that it was just a hobby some people had outside of their real jobs. I love my folks, but they're the two most practical, risk-averse people I've ever met. As a result, I truly appreciate Hollywood. It's full of grandiose, insane dreamers with entitlement complexes. Some people find that obnoxious, but to me, it's fun. I never knew characters like that growing up. I never knew anyone who said, "I deserve to be famous." In Hollywood, that's every other person you meet! God bless these douchebags.

I'm really lazy, and I'm not proud of that. I'm usually just thinking about what I'm going to have for dinner. People say, "There's no way you're lazy; you have such a steady output of work." But writing isn't work for me. I enjoy it. If it felt like work, I wouldn't get past page two. That's why I have difficulty relating to a lot of comedy writers. They might seem rebellious on the surface, but a lot of them went to Ivy League schools and are ambitious people-pleasers at their core. I've always been straight-up lazy and defiant. I wouldn't last a week at Harvard, or at *SNL* for that matter. It would be like, "What can I write that Lorne will really hate?"

When I first decided to try screenwriting, I was seeking inspiration from small, offbeat films. I think this is a good way to start. I knew if I read the script for say, *Armageddon*, it wasn't going to connect. I was a nerdy, chubby chick on the fringes, so of course [the 2001 comedy film] *Ghost World* appealed to me. As I started experimenting with my own voice, I found myself interested in suburban misfits like Enid Coleslaw [from *Ghost World*] and like those characters in *Napoleon Dynamite* and Lester Burnham [the Kevin Spacey character] from *American Beauty*. They didn't have to save the planet to be interesting. Their stories were accessible to me. And *Ghost World* was funny, but also melancholy in a way that resonated with me. I think that tone has informed a lot of the stuff I've tried to write.

Always be working on your own material. *Write specs* [noncommissioned, unsolicited screenplays]! Though I've been hired to write studio projects, everything I've ever gotten produced has been an original spec script that I just wanted to write on my own. I wasn't being paid for them. Other people's ideas are never as important as yours. I wrote *Young Adult* while I was supposed to be working on a shitty studio movie, and I'm so glad I prioritized my own idea. Make everything as personal and specific as you can. Sometimes people bitch about, for example, certain screenwriters who make their writing too specific to their own lives, not realizing that that's why it works! The specificity is what makes it brilliant.

We're lucky enough to live in an era where you can write, produce, publish, and distribute your own writing through the magic of the Internet, so there's no excuse not to be creating. Just keep writing. If you really love it, you'll keep doing it even if you're not successful. If you don't love it, you don't belong here.

MIKE SCHUR

If you want to understand the creative nuts and bolts of Michael Schur—a writer for such NBC comedy institutions as *Saturday Night Live*, *The Office*, and *Parks and Recreation*—you should probably read novelist David Foster Wallace's 1996 novel, *Infinite Jest*. At least the first thousand or so pages of it.

Schur didn't just enjoy *Infinite Jest*. It's in his bloodstream. While a student at Harvard University, he wrote his undergraduate thesis on the novel and somehow persuaded Wallace to travel to Cambridge, Massachusetts, to receive an award from the *Harvard Lampoon*. (More on that later.) In 2011, Schur directed a video for the Decemberists' "Calamity Song," which featured teens playing the fictional game Eschaton, a reference to *Infinite Jest*. And an episode from *Parks and Recreation* written by Schur—"Partridge," which aired April 4, 2013—was brimming with *Infinite Jest* references. Schur also owns the *Infinite Jest* film rights. So you can rest assured that if there's ever a movie adaptation of the least filmable book ever written, Schur will be at least somehow involved.

Schur has a popularity that extends beyond those who read the closing credits of sitcoms and enjoy excessive footnotes. Most people would recognize him first as Mose Schrute, the quiet, bearded cousin of Dwight on NBC's *The Office*. Mose co-owns a beet farm with Dwight, thinks it's fun to throw manure, loves *Jurassic Park* (he has a pair of *Jurassic Park* pajamas to prove it), and has suffered from recurring nightmares ever since "the storm." Mose is Schur's creation—he named the character after Mose Gingerich, one of the stars of the 2004 reality series *Amish in the City*—and one that, for better or worse, has become his most visible mainstream identity.

But there's another, entirely different audience for Schur. Mindy Kaling, a writer and actress who collaborated with Schur for many years on *The Office*, knows a very different man than most of the world has seen. "The greatest gift you can give Mike Schur is a Swedish dictionary," she said. "Because he just loves nonsense words, which [is] like a toddler sensibility for a guy who is an Emmy-nominated writer and one of the most well-read, serious guys." Schur enjoys broad comedy, Kaling said; as proof, she pointed to one of her favorite Schur-penned *Office* episodes—"Dunder Mifflin Infinity," October 4, 2007—in which Michael Scott, played by Steve Carell, blindly follows his GPS and maneuvers his rental car straight into Lake Scranton.

Schur was born in Ann Arbor, Michigan, in 1975, and raised in West Hartford, Connecticut. While at Harvard University, he became a member of the *Harvard Lampoon*, which may or may not have prepared him for a future in comedy writing. (As he said once in an interview, writing for the *Lampoon* didn't prepare him "for anything, really . . . [except] perhaps if I had a career as a guy who lounged around drunk in poorly maintained Flemish castles.") Almost immediately upon graduating in 1997, he was hired to write for *Saturday Night Live*, where he worked for seven seasons (1997–2004), three as producer for Weekend Update during Tina Fey and Jimmy Fallon's reign on the segment. Schur found his way to *The Office*, and co-created *Parks and Recreation*, a mockumentary-style, single-camera sitcom about the parks department of Pawnee, a fictional town in Indiana, starring former *Saturday Night Live* colleague Amy Poehler.

In 2013, he co-created Fox's *Brooklyn Nine-Nine*, starring Andy Samberg and Chelsea Peretti.

As a television writer—someone who works behind the scenes—is there a frustration that your name may not be attached to a specific idea or joke? That if you were to write for *The New Yorker* or publish books, you'd receive a byline and full credit?

Not really. TV writing is collaborative—if I want solo credit for everything I write, I'd write a novel. Actually, that sounds really hard. Forget the novel.

But credit can be a very prickly issue for some writers—most TV scripts are constantly rewritten and punched up. It gets very hard to track who did what and whose joke was which and when and where and how. When I got my first half-hour writing job, at *The Office* [in 2005], there were times when I felt slighted because something I had contributed didn't get "properly" attributed. And since I equated "proper attribution" with succeeding at my job, it would upset me. But then I realized that Greg [Daniels, the showrunner] couldn't have cared less about who pitched what. He saw the process of writing and rewriting as a collective effort, and as long as everyone was working hard and the collective effort was producing good scripts, the specifics didn't matter. It was a very enlightened point of view, I thought.

TV comedy writing is a team sport. That's just the deal. In most cases, I could not begin to tell you who wrote what in a given script. And I have very often had the benefit of other great writers' contributions in scripts that bore my name, so it would be crazy for me to complain about not getting credit on other writers' scripts.

Writing for sitcoms, and especially being the showrunner, or head writer, is a notoriously brutal and exhausting job. What exactly does it take to maintain a level of excellence over the course of an eight-month season—twenty-two episodes? How intense is the schedule?

It just takes tons and tons of hard work. In network TV, from the moment you start shooting, you're basically behind. Something David Mamet once said sums it up perfectly: "Doing a movie or a play is like running a marathon. Doing a television show is like running until you die."

How is this particular day at *Parks and Rec* shaping up?

I just got back from the sound mix for Episode 515 of *Parks* ["Bailout"], which is now complete. We're shooting the season five finale, featuring a giant parade in Pasadena, and it's supposed to rain tomorrow, and if it does we're completely screwed. Tomorrow morning, I have a network-notes call at 9:15 to discuss the first cut of episode 517 ["Partridge"], which I have to lock by Thursday. One new episode of the show has to be edited, noted, and locked every week for the next six weeks. Tomorrow afternoon I have a show-and-tell for the sets, costumes, and shooting style of the pilot I'm doing for Fox [*Brooklyn Nine-Nine*], which has a network table read Monday. By the end of the day today, my partner on the pilot and I have to finish the draft of the script to send to the studio and network to get their notes so we can turn it around by Friday. This happens to be a very busy week, because of the pilot, but this is not atypical for network TV. It's a Looney Tunes schedule.

Who's the audience for television these days? Do you write for the home audience or the audience later seeing it on Hulu and downloading short scenes?

We just went through a very specific situation on *Parks*, wherein, due to a scheduling quirk, we had to air two episodes back-to-back. The first was scheduled to be the biggest episode we'd ever done—the wedding of Leslie Knope and Ben Wyatt, years in the making, very emotional, and obviously a benchmark episode for the show. The second one—scheduled originally to air a week later—was a regular episode about Leslie attending a luncheon with members of the local media. So, obviously, this was upsetting. There was going to be this huge, massive, life-changing event in the lives of the two main characters, and then, literally, one second later: "Today, I'm attending a luncheon . . ."

We had a lot of discussions about what to do—shuffle the order somehow? Extend the wedding to an hour? But ultimately we let it be. And our reasoning was that this will matter exactly once—on the night it airs this way. The number of people watching TV on their own schedule, through Hulu or iTunes or whichever platform they prefer, is rising exponentially. And it's never going back the other way.

I'd think that this would put more pressure on you as a writer. You aren't merely writing jokes to be seen once and then forgotten. You're writing for multiple viewings, to last years.

Audience expectations are sky-high, and they get bored very easily because they've seen it all. Add to that the multitude of choices the consumer has—if you slip up even once, people have dozens of other shows dangling in front of them. And they can watch them *on their phones*. When I was a kid, I watched every single episode of *Empty Nest*, a show about a sixty-year-old doctor living in Florida. I was a twelve-year-old kid in suburban Connecticut. Why did I watch it? It was on. Today, if you're a twelve-year-old in suburban Connecticut, or a forty-eight-year-old lesbian taxidermist in Tennessee, or an eighty-one-year-old diabetic glass-blower in Yakima, Washington, there are somewhere between one and three hundred better choices for you than *Empty Nest*—shows that someone somewhere made with you and your friends in mind.

Beyond *Empty Nest*, what were your major comedic influences?

I was a crazy, voracious reader of comedy. I read Woody Allen's books, *Without Feathers*, *Getting Even*, and *Side Effects*, when I was around twelve, and it was like I was seeing in color for the first time. Reading *Without Feathers* is probably the most important "holy crap" moment of my life. I read all these books over and over. I then tried to write Woody Allen comedy pieces, but they were just terrible. I recently found this giant document that I had been keeping that I thought was my great masterwork—it was basically a Woody Allen book rip-off I worked on all through middle school and high school. And it's just so horrifying.

I have never laughed harder than when I saw [1973's] *Sleeper* for the first time. I get my love of goofiness directly from Woody Allen and Monty Python. But in some way the most important movie to me is *Midnight Run* [a comedy released in 1988, co-starring Robert De Niro and Charles Grodin and written by George Gallo]. Maybe the tightest screenplay ever written—not one wasted word—and a dozen indelible characters with strong personalities, each with specific goals and realistic motivations. You can learn everything you need to know about building strong characters by watching *Midnight Run*.

It sounds like you took comedy seriously from a young age.

Every year for Christmas or my birthday, I would receive books of comedy pieces. I remember someone telling me that Mark Twain was really funny, and I started reading Mark Twain short stories. If you're an NFL quarterback, you watch a lot of games on film, and if you're a comedy writer you have to watch a lot of game film—you have to watch comedy, read comedy, write about comedy. You have to treat it as seriously as if you're a law student studying for the bar exam.

When I was a kid, I constantly wrote. I kept notebooks and journals where I jotted down ideas for movies and sketches or whatever. I wrote submissions to shows I wasn't even planning to submit to. I would write sample scripts of TV shows that I liked, just to practice. I wrote a *Cheers* script around 1998, long after the show had been off the air. I didn't really know whether something was good until I had written it down and I could look at it. I would see if I could write in the style of shows that I liked. That's not a job-getting tool, that's a way to practice your craft. When it comes to writing, there's no real secret except to keep doing it. In my experience, the only way to get better at writing is to write.

Do you have any influences that one might consider nontraditional for a comedy writer?

The Mayor of Casterbridge [1886] by Thomas Hardy. Hardy's novels are insane, many of them, because they have a theme of random chance and unpredictability—sort of the nineteenth-century equivalent of the chaos theory seen in *Jurassic Park*. Someone will be delivering an important message, and then, out of nowhere, a bull will escape from a pen, gore a guy to death, and the message will never get delivered. That book in particular struck me when I read it because it's about a man who made one awful, miserable, terrible mistake [auctioning off his wife and daughter] when he was young, drunk, and stupid, and he spends the rest of his life trying to make up for it. What a lovely, simple character detail—and a funny one when you then have a brilliant actor such as Adam Scott inhabit a similar character, and a team of excellent comedy writers writing jokes about it, like we do on *Parks*.[1]

Another influence is David Foster Wallace. I owe a great debt to Wallace—*Infinite Jest* is very funny, but, more important, Wallace spends a tremendous amount of time in that book, and in his others, dealing with the theme of sincerity and honesty. It's something that is very tricky for comedy writers, because sincerity is the opposite of "cool" or "hip" or "ironic," all of which comedy writers wield like swords to fend off feeling gooey or mushy. Nothing terrifies comedy writers more than heartfelt emotion. Wallace ended that for me. His entire body of work was an attempt to reconcile jokes, postmodern games, and "coolness," which he admittedly loved and reveled in, with what he saw as the most basic job of writing: to make the readers *feel* something. To make them feel like they are not alone in the world. That is very moving to me and certainly changed the way I write.

I wholeheartedly agree with one point Wallace made, which was, and I'm paraphrasing: "If the world is terrible and awful and screwed-up, there isn't much point to writing something about how the world

---

1 In a backstory on *Parks*, the character of Ben Wyatt becomes the mayor of Partridge, Minnesota, at age eighteen, but is quickly impeached after bankrupting the town by building a disastrous winter sports complex called Ice Town.

is terrible and awful and screwed up." What made more sense to him—and, subsequently, to me—was to write about how people attempt to navigate this awful screwed-up world and to then find a way to be happy within it, and to make things better.

Did you ever meet Wallace?

I met him in 1996, when I was writing for the *Harvard Lampoon*. *Infinite Jest* came out in February, and after I read it I decided unilaterally that he would be receiving our "Novelist of the Millennium Award," which was a thing I had just made up, so that I could give it to him, just so that I could meet him.

We invited him to the *Lampoon* building through his agent, and one day, as I sat in my dorm working on my senior thesis—which was about *Infinite Jest*—he called me to see what the hell this award was all about. It was very surreal. He was notoriously press-shy and wanted to make sure it wasn't a dog-and-pony show, but I assured him I had just made the whole thing up, and it was only an invitation to come and hang out in a cool old building.

The point of all this is: He wanted to come, ultimately, because he'd been a fan of the *Lampoon* while he was at Amherst. He knew a lot about it, like that John Updike and [novelist] William Gaddis and others had once been members, and that there was a *Lampoon-SNL-Simpsons* connection, which meant something to him. It turned out to be an easy sell.

There are passages of *Infinite Jest* that I think are monstrously funny. He's funny and his writing is complicatedly funny. That might seem reductive, but I think it's true. He was funny in a way that most people who are funny are not.

What was your thesis on *Infinite Jest* about?

I wrote about Thomas Pynchon's [1963 debut novel] *V.* and *Infinite Jest*, positing that they served as bookends for a type of postmodern fiction that dealt with irony and identity cohesion. I got really into it and worked very, very hard, and I think if I read it today I would have absolutely no idea what it meant, or indeed whether it held water at all or was completely full of shit. I strongly suspect that it was full of shit.

Wallace had a complicated relationship with television. He was raised on it and said it was his "artistic snorkel to the universe." But he also felt that television changed our perception of reality. Did you ever talk to him about TV, sitcoms, and comedy?

A little. We corresponded for a while after we met, and I kept him up-to-date on my budding career in TV. He was very interested in that. I invited him to come to a live *SNL* show, because it was a TV touchstone for him, but it never came to be. I think a Wallace essay about *SNL* would've been amazing.

And it wasn't just TV—obviously TV loomed large for him, and he wrote about it frequently, but I think he had a complicated relationship with all of pop culture. He told me a great story about when he was teaching at Illinois State and he was given an audio tape of a band that he fell in love with, and he came into his graduate seminar and said, "I might be crazy, but I think this band is great and you all need to hear this right now." He then played for his students *Nevermind* by Nirvana. It was about seven years after the album had been released.

You wrote for *SNL* for six years, and you've mentioned in the past that the show was a big influence for you. But were there any other TV shows that influenced you?

Late Night with David Letterman. I would tape Letterman every night, watch it in the morning before school, and then steal all his jokes and stories and tell them to my friends. It was the perfect crime, because I knew that no one else my age could stay up that late.

Mary Tyler Moore was huge for me, and when I stayed home sick from school I would watch *The Dick Van Dyke Show.* The character of Laura Petrie was my first ever TV crush. I remember my young brain being surprised that something shot in black and white could be so funny. Later, I loved Mary's relationship with Lou Grant—the relationship between Leslie and Ron Swanson on *Parks* definitely has shades of that platonic friendship.

I also remember loving individual characters within shows. I think Alex P. Keaton from *Family Ties* is one of the greatest sitcom inventions in history, but I also loved Michael Gross, who played the father. I became fascinated by actors who had great timing, and Gross's timing was impeccable. Same with Kelsey Grammer, Woody Harrelson, Ted Danson, Shelley Long—pretty much everyone on *Cheers* gets an A+ for pure comedic timing.

Cheers avoided a lot of current, topical jokes. In many ways, this allowed the show to age better than other sitcoms. Was this a philosophy you tried to adopt with *Parks and Rec*?

Well, we had more rules on *The Office*. Producer Greg [Daniels] really didn't want that show to seem pegged to any particular era, so he always resisted showing dates on office memos, or mentioning a specific Beyoncé song that came out that month, or saying "the 2006 company picnic," or whatever. The idea was, with a show called *The Office*, we were trying to be maximally relatable to all persons who had ever been in an office, not just people who were in offices from 2005 to 2013. We took that idea to *Parks and Rec*, but loosened it up fairly quickly. It became increasingly clear that many of our stories were going to mimic specific things in the political and social Zeitgeist, and some stories were direct parallels to—or commentary on—national political stories of the time. Plus, Aziz Ansari [who plays *Parks and Rec* staff official Tom Haverford] improvised so many great jokes about hip-hop and the *Fast & Furious* movies that it seemed silly to throw them away.

Cheers is a classic sitcom known to have taken awhile to catch on with an audience. *Parks and Rec* also took a little while to catch on with viewers.

In my opinion, really good pilots don't often later make great shows. Great pilots are like movies—they have big exciting concepts or hooks that grab people and draw them in, and cut through the white noise of the two hundred new shows that crop up every year. But the problem is, those hooks and concepts elbow out room that should be given to the characters—explaining who they are, what they want in life, and so on—and TV comedies only work long-term if the characters are three-dimensional and great. That's why *Cheers* is the best TV comedy ever—it's just great characters sitting in a bar talking to each other. And in that *Cheers* pilot [that aired September 30, 1982], you learn everything you need to know about the characters.

But that *Cheers* pilot tested terribly—there was nothing for the audience to grab on to, and at the end they probably felt like they hadn't been treated to a big, entertaining half hour. It takes awhile to learn about the characters and enjoy their funny traits. In the *Cheers* pilot, for example, Cliff is basically an extra. It wasn't until a few episodes later that they moved him to the other end of the bar and sat him next to Norm, forming the most famous 275-episode tableau in TV history.

It frustrates me sometimes, because shows get picked up based on their pilots, which is directly analogous to judging a book by its first ten pages. And then critics weigh in on pilots when they air, which contributes in some way to shows' being successful or not successful in the long term. In the perfect world, no one would discuss a new TV show until it had aired eight episodes, and the creative team had already worked out all the kinks. Sadly, the world—and you might not know this—is imperfect.

You've been quoted in interviews as saying that, as the showrunner for *Parks and Rec*, you care more about story than individual jokes. Why is that?

This is just personal preference, but I find the world so tumultuous and hardscrabble and generally terrifying that I will never tire of stories about people caring for each other, and doing nice things for each other, and in a very basic way trying to make each other feel less alone on Earth. All stories need conflict, but conflict can come from anywhere.

It seems counterintuitive, but when you have well-drawn, three-dimensional characters, and a dozen funny writers in a room thinking about them, chances are that one of the writers can always pitch a good joke at any given point in a script. But those jokes are pointless and empty if the story doesn't hold together. Good stories beat good jokes every day of the week and twice on Sundays.

It's also very obviously the case that jokes are fleeting, but good characters and emotional stories are forever. TV is about presenting an inviting world in which audiences want to invest their time, regularly, over many years. Jokes help because, you know, they make people happy. But what makes people *love* a show, and get attached to it, is great characters having great adventures.

I just like that kind of show better—where the characters are generally positive and the comedy comes from goofiness and satire instead of cattiness and negativity. It's explicitly the theme of *Parks and Rec*—that people need each other to be happy, that communities are important, that nobody achieves anything alone. A show with that theme needs its characters to support each other. So ours do, generally speaking.

Can you remember an instance when a joke was cut because it sacrificed character or overall story?

It happens every single episode. Usually because the joke in question is slightly "off-story," meaning that it doesn't line up with the character's specific attitude in that given scene, and it slipped through the writing-vetting process all through the script stage because it made everyone laugh. Our cast includes some of the world's greatest improvisers, and we always carve out time for them to goof around. Quite often they will add amazing material to the script. But sometimes, we have to chop off that amazing material, because what they improvised unintentionally changes their characters' story or attitude, so its inclusion would just muddy the waters.

This seems like the exact opposite of the philosophy behind an *SNL* sketch. Or is it? Can a joke in a sketch sacrifice a character and still work?

Character isn't important in sketches, where everything is two-dimensional by design. You can't really "sell out" a character in three minutes. It's a much, much bigger deal when you're talking about a show for which you want to do more than one hundred episodes.

What do you look for in character growth? What do you want to achieve at the end of each season?

Someone said that the best ending for a story is at once inevitable and surprising. That it was the only way it could've happened, and yet the audience didn't see it coming. I'd like every episode and every season to end that way. It's a reason I loved the ending of *The Sopranos*, which, as I've been told by many people, who are usually shouting at me, is not a universal feeling. The entirety of that show, and that character, led to that ambiguous cut to black. To me, it made absolutely total complete sense to end the show that way. Even the debate about what had happened—which I don't imagine [the show's creator] David Chase anticipated, in its extant form—felt inevitable, because it was a coda to the way we'd all been debating the show for years.

Great endings come from giving a character big hurdles, great successes, tough failures—testing a character's resolve and defining that character by word and action—and then putting the character into a situation where he or she stands precariously at a fork in a road. I say this as if it's all super easy.

But here's the real problem in all of this. And I've been thinking about this a lot recently: Television used to be a *quantity* business. They created around thirty *I Love Lucy*s a year, and Milton Berle just walked onstage in a dress every week and everyone fell over laughing because their minds were so completely blown by what was happening. The production values were entirely secondary. "Did you see the flimsy set shake back and forth when Ricky slammed the door?" "Who cares? *I'm watching this show inside my house!*"

Stories were new, characters were fresh, stereotypes not yet created. Everything was new and juicy and fifty million people were watching.

Television is not about quantity anymore; it's very much about *quality*—and specificity. It's a giant beautiful smorgasbord of fiction, nonfiction, comedy, and drama—about every conceivable subject—

delivered to the consumer at low cost and with nearly maximal convenience. It is also dissected, analyzed, and reported on with alarming speed by professional and amateur critics alike, who have at their disposal an online database of every single thing that has ever happened in the history of screen-based entertainment for comparison. Maximal speed, maximal scrutiny, maximal convenience, and maximal skepticism in the viewing audience that it's going to be worth their time investment.

We make twenty-two episodes of our show a year. Some shows make twenty-four episodes. On *The Office* we once made thirty, I think, including six or so hour-long shows. So at a time when it's never been harder to do something new and interesting, we still have to churn out episode after episode at breakneck speed.

The entire network TV system is creaking under the weight of this brave new world. I'd actually argue that this is good, in many ways, for the creative process. Obstacles are good, generally, for writers, and the increased scrutiny for television is the natural result of its massive leaps forward in quality; it's being treated, as it should be, like an art form worthy of criticism and discussion.

And please do not think I am in any way complaining about my job. There is quite literally not another one I would rather have. I write largely exactly what I want to, spend my days giggling like a goon, work with my friends, and get paid well—a scenario which makes me, by a wide margin, the luckiest son of a bitch in America, if not the world. I only intend to delineate the unique dilemmas currently faced by network TV writers: Make it great, but make it very fast and make a whole lot of it, and also make it appeal to a wide swath of the American public who have a billion other tailored-to-them choices.

What do you look for in a writing staff? Who do you want in your writers' room?

Staffs should ideally be like the X-Men—lots of different weird mutants with specific voices and talents. If everyone on your staff is an improv performer from Chicago, or a sci-fi nerd from an Ivy

League school, or a stand-up, you'll only get the specific kind of joke that that group provides. There's no specific ratio. Just variety is all. Ideally, we have ten or twelve different weirdos with bizarre life stories and unique experiences we can mine for stories and jokes.

Writers' rooms can be ugly, no question, but the *Parks and Rec* writers' room rivals Disney World as the happiest place on Earth. We have our bad days, and our grumpy days, but overall it's a very supportive, goofy, and joyous place to work. We're very lucky.

Do you think the atmosphere of the writers' room can affect the tone of a show?

Absolutely. There are basically two kinds of comedy writers— laughers and nonlaughers. Nonlaughers bum me out at a very deep level. It's almost as if they think that laughing at other people's jokes is a sign of weakness or something. I've never understood it. If your staff is filled with a bunch of nonlaughers, the show can take on a bloodless, cold tone.

In the past, you've spoken about the "click" that takes place in a writers' room when a joke hits. You call it the "sweet spot." Can you remember any instances of this "click" happening on either *Office* or *Parks*?

It happens constantly. [*Parks* writer] Dan Goor wrote a line for Ron Swanson where someone asks him if he is scared to eat in a bowling alley restaurant, and he says, "When I eat, it is the food that is scared." That click was so loud it rattled the furniture. I wrote a joke for Dwight Schrute [on *The Office*] where Jim offers him a shamrock keychain, saying it's good luck, and Dwight says, "'A real man makes his own luck.' Billy Zane. *Titanic*." That was a "click" for me. It just seemed so Dwighty that he would identify with that character in that movie. Those moments are few and far between, and they're surrounded by millions of crappy jokes and clumsy stuff that you throw away, but when you hit one it's the best feeling. Seth Meyers described the Weekend Update equivalent—writing a joke that you know is going to kill—as swinging the bat and being so sure you've hit a home run that you don't even watch the flight of the ball. You just put your head down and trot around the bases. The millions of crappy jokes you write make that rare feeling that much better.

What do you look for with submitted spec scripts from potential writers? What are some dos and don'ts?

I would say that the most valuable and unteachable asset in a comedy writer is a unique voice. That is my top priority in hiring people—does this person sound like everyone else, or is there something about how he or she puts words and sentences and ideas together that sticks out? So many writers on *The Office* and *Parks and Rec* have owned irreplaceable voices, and so many actors as well. It's something I'm incredibly proud of on this show—the uniqueness of the voices we present. It makes jokes more interesting, characters more interesting, stories more interesting.

When we hired the writer Emily Kapnek for *Parks*, I was given one of her scripts—it was an original—and I knew almost instantly that I wanted to hire her. I was sold with one particular joke midway through. It made me laugh out loud, which happens rarely when you're reading hundreds of scripts at a time.[2]

Do you see any common mistakes, across the board, with young comedy writers?

Complacency is a classic mistake. Some people get to a certain point and go, "Okay, I've figured it out!" Writing isn't a thing you figure out—ever. My favorite things I've ever written, I hate. That might sound like a weird thing to say. But anything I've ever written that I felt was really great, I inevitably will look at two years later

---

2   Emily Kapnek: "Mike read a TV pilot of mine called *Wiener Park*, which actually wound up getting shot [in 2005, but was never aired]. The joke that Mike liked wasn't really a joke but more of a funny moment: The dad character offers to show his house guest a home video of his son playing clarinet in a school talent show. The guest agrees to watch the video, but it's very uneventful. In fact, nothing appears to be happening, but the dad turns to the guest and proudly points out: 'He's wetting the reed.'"

and think, Oh, God, this is so amateurish and terrible. But that's a good thing. If you ever feel like you've solved anything in writing, you're just setting yourself up for a huge fall—and you're wrong. Because it's not math or science; it's a weird, nebulous, hard-to-define thing. One person's favorite show in history is another person's least favorite show in history—or worse, it's a show they're indifferent to. And to stay vibrant and successful, you can't ever feel like you know what you're doing. Your attitude has to constantly be, "Who is this rank amateur, and how can I teach him how to write?"

The tricky thing about TV is that there's a lot of money involved. It's very easy to get to a certain point in your career, whether it's your first staff job or whether you become a producer on a show, and then go, "I can breathe easy now." No writer should ever breathe easy. You should constantly figure out how to write better stories and better jokes, more three-dimensional characters, how to change what isn't working. If you don't, you're gonna lose your touch. It's not like riding a bike; you can't just put your pen down for a year, pick it back up, and be right where you were.

Writing is an art that has a weird aspect to it.

Weird in what way?

Part of its success depends on how the audience reacts to it. You can get philosophical about it and say that a perfectly written script just exists in space and time as a beautiful testament to the power of the human soul or something, but the practical reality is that you have to film it and put it on TV, actors have to act in it, and the audience gets to weigh in at some point. If you ever feel complacent with yourself, then you're basically saying you don't need the other part of the equation. And if you're a TV or movie writer, you definitely do. Not just for your career, but to have people who weigh in on whether or not you successfully communicated what you wanted to communicate.

It's a strange business. It's really where the rubber meets the road—the rubber being art and the road being commerce.

TODD LEVIN

Writer, *Conan*

....

Writing a Submission Packet for Late-Night TV

What follows is the writing packet I submitted for *Late Night with Conan O'Brien*. (I submitted this sample in 2008, was hired in early 2009, then followed the show to Los Angeles to write for *The Tonight Show with Conan O'Brien*. I now write for *Conan*, on TBS, and by the time this book is published, I will most likely be writing for *O'Brien Nights* on eBay.tv.)

Accompanying each entry, in italics, are my thoughts on each specific idea: what I think I did right, what I think I did wrong, what I'd now do differently. I've also assessed each idea with a handy, though purely speculative, "Prognosis for Ever Making It to Air." I'm making these calls based on my perceived merits of the piece, weighed with my experience in seeing what types of pieces and jokes tend to make it out of the writers' room, through rehearsal, and to air.

Todd Levin's Submission Packet for
Late Night with Conan O'Brien

....

"Riff," the Late Night Bully

Riff was Conan's school bully all through high school. Although he hasn't seen Riff in years, now that Conan is a very big success he's decided to bring Riff on the show and finally settle his score. However, when Riff comes onstage it becomes immediately clear that something horrible has happened to him, which has temporarily rendered him physically vulnerable. (In one appearance, Riff is in an electric wheelchair and can only speak through an electronic voice synthesizer.)

Because of Riff's delicate condition, Conan always feels too awful to make fun of him, even as Riff taunts him. Eventually, Riff pushes Conan to his breaking point and he finally halfheartedly insults Riff, leaving everyone aghast. When Conan tries to apologize, Riff claims there is only one way he'll accept an apology, and that way usually involves Conan humiliating himself in front of the entire show to Riff's delight as Riff exits the auditorium shouting, "Smell ya later, Boner O'Cryin'!"

....

Current Thoughts:

In my mind, this was a classic Late Night *bit—a loud-mouthed character interrupting Conan, making him uncomfortable somehow, and then humiliating him before making his exit. That said, this premise has two immediately obvious red flags. Riff is a consciously "character-y" name. Putting your character in a crazy outfit or assigning him an implausibly cartoonish name like "Pudge O'Shaughnessy" or "Benedict Cumberbatch" are loud announcements that the audience is about to experience a wacky comedy sketch. As I've spent more time doing this, I've discovered it's often better to let your character play it real, unencumbered by a silly comedy name, so it's a little more unexpected when he inevitably says or does very foolish things.*

This idea also has two really dangerous built-in expectations of the audience: They must sympathize with an asshole character and then turn against the show's host—the reason they're watching the show in the first place. Good luck!

Prognosis for Ever Making It to Air: *Highly Unlikely*

Bootleg Round-Up

In New York, you can find someone selling bootleg DVDs, CDs, and even computer software on every corner. They're dirt-cheap, but you have to be careful, because sometimes the quality can be sort of dubious. Conan shows off some of the bootlegs he's purchased off the street in this consumer awareness segment:

DVDs—you never know what you're going to get, so you have to read the packaging very clearly.

- *Sicko* (In small print: "the Michael Moore sex tape")
- *The Fantastic Four* (The four pictured on the box are Mr. Fantastic, the Invisible Girl, the Human Torch, and an older-looking Asian man dressed up as Dracula)
- *Law & Order: Special Victims Eunuch—Season Three* (CONAN: "I thought it was a translation problem until I watched the DVD"—plays a clip from it, and it's just a regular episode of SVU but all the male characters' voices are incredibly high-pitched)
- *Ratatouille* (Conan plays a clip from it, and it's just cheap news footage of real, live rats running around in a KFC)
- *Girls Gone Wild, Vol. 4* (Conan plays a clip from it, and it's footage of college-aged girls who have been raised by animals. In one scene, a feral girl with matted hair sucks from the teat of a wolf.)

Current Thoughts:

Kind of a mixed bag here comedically, but I actually think the premise is sound. Plus, it's one of those types of segments that are essential to a nightly late night show—an easy-to-produce and easy-to-repeat "desk piece." (Named so because they're typically bits the host can present right from his desk. Conan's Celebrity Surveys and Fallon's Thank You Notes are good examples of this kind of joke delivery system.) The simplicity of this format is deceivingly hard to crack. It must be generic enough to accommodate all kinds of jokes, familiar enough to require very little setup, and fresh enough that it hasn't already been attempted in more than a half century of late night comedy. Most desk pieces on late night shows typically fulfill one or two of those requirements; all three is pretty rare. In the history of late night talk shows, I don't think there's been a better desk piece than Late Night *with Conan O'Brien's Actual Items. Familiar but totally unexpected, highly visual, and it came with an endless supply of inspiration.*

On paper, desk piece pitches are often not inherently funny— Celebrity Surveys is basically "Conan asks three celebrities to answer a single question, and the third celebrity's answer is very crazy!" That's why it's good to include several beats as proof of concept.

FYI: I was tempted to remove the Michael Moore joke because I still can't believe I sent in something so awful, but I felt it was more important for others to learn from my mistakes. Hero? You decide.

Prognosis for Ever Making It to Air: *Pretty Good*

Late Night Recession Survival Tips

There's no denying that this current economic crisis has really gotten all of us down. That's why Conan has put together some great tips to help viewers save money and fight the recession blues.

Don't have enough money to take your kids to Six Flags this year? Why not turn your own home into a first-rate theme park? Video montage includes:

- Kids step into a clothes dryer with an amusement park sign attached to it that says "The Tumbler."
- A young boy stands in front of a microwave set to cook for thirty minutes. An amusement park sign reads "The Sterilizer."
- Two kids enter through a door marked "House of Horrors," to discover an old man sitting on the bed, completely naked, clipping his toenails.

Turn even the most depressing meal into a feast fit for a king with Dinner Jackets, zippered pouches designed to look like high-end foods. (We see a mom ladling a thick, gruel-like substance into a Dinner Jacket styled to look like a T-bone steak.)

Bam Bam Banker: Who says you can't have fun while the economy craters around you? Next time you're stuck in a dull meeting, why not play "Bam Bam Banker," a recession-era twist on the popular road game, Punchbuggy. [We see a group of businessmen in a conference room, all staring out the window. They are each yelling the names of various colors—"Come on blue!" "Let's go red!!" etc.—until, suddenly, a body dressed in a white shirt and blue tie plunges past the window. One of the businessmen shouts, "Bam Bam Banker Blue!" and punches each of his co-workers in the arm, etc.]

....

Current Thoughts:

At Conan, this kind of piece is called a "thrasher." It's a term I still don't fully understand, although I know it when it applies. A thrasher is a long piece built around a basic theme, and incorporating many types of comedy executions—video, live walkthroughs, curtain reveals, short sketches, etc. This one has a bit of variety in it. The theme park idea would probably work best as a taped piece, while "Bam Bam Banker" could probably be done live in the studio, with a small set.

I didn't even remember this piece from my packet, but I think it's aged better than some of the other ideas. Also, I realize now I've stolen from myself, because later, when I was (briefly) writing for The Tonight Show with Conan O'Brien, *I produced a piece about Disneyland suffering from cutbacks and included the joke about an industrial clothes dryer standing in for a theme park ride.*

Prognosis for Ever Making It to Air: *Extremely Likely*

Desk Piece—DVD Commentaries

Late Night previews some of its favorite special-edition DVD commentary tracks.

- *The Bourne Ultimatum,* Special "Commuter Buying Newspaper" Actor's Commentary: One of the film's extras from the scene that takes place in a crowded London train station gets his own commentary track, in which he spends all of his time prepping the audience for the split-second moment in which his character gets bumped into by Jason Bourne.
- *The Constant Gardener,* Gardener Audio Commentary: During an especially harrowing scene in *The Constant Gardener,* two professional gardeners point out and discuss various gardening techniques evident in the film.
- *Incredible Hulk,* Hulk Audio Commentary: An enraged, barely verbal Hulk provides a running commentary on the action, growling statements like "Hulk found Liv Tyler joy to work with" and "Hulk really admire mise-en-scene here. Think Zak Penn truly visionary director."
- Two Guys on the *Into the Wild* Audio Commentary Who Are Pretty Confident They Would Have Fared Better Than Chris McCandless: Sort of self-explanatory, two skeptical jerks constantly point out obvious mistakes Chris McCandless makes in his attempts to live in the wild.

Current Thoughts:

Another desk piece that would have been easy to produce—pre-existing footage from film with a new audio track. I would bet this idea, or some variation on it, has been pitched dozens of times before and since, on many different talk shows. I wouldn't even be surprised if someone has attempted it. Here, I hope the specificity of the jokes saved a pretty generic concept. If not, I hope the show's head writer accidentally skipped past this one while reading my packet.

Prognosis for Ever Making It to Air: *Decent, Though It Could Be Dismissed Outright Purely on Suspicions That Another Late Night Show Must Have Already Done This Idea*

Characters: Candidates for the "New Characters" Parade

THE JIHADIST WITH BEAUTIFUL LEGS

A man walks out in a cleric's robe and threatens to blow up the entire show. When he tears open his robe to show the bomb strapped to his chest, we can see he's also wearing daisy dukes and high heels, and has smooth, beautiful legs. Stripper music plays as he laments, "It is my gift and my curse!"

Current Thoughts:

Character walk-throughs were a big part of Late Night *and I included these once I felt like I'd already fulfilled my submission packet requirements with other ideas. I would imagine that most writers would have a difficult time submitting a packet for* Late Night *without including a few ridiculous and pointless characters.*

This specific character is kind of a lame idea, really, but I think it could be salvaged with a very good performance. (Even now, if I've written a semi-decent script, I know it will be improved significantly by casting Brian Stack, one of the show's longtime writers and maybe the single best sketch performer I've ever seen.) When I see a lot of sketch comedy, I am surprised by how much its creators will underestimate the importance of casting. (One of my comedy pet peeves—this is meant to be a platform for my grievances, right?—is seeing a twentysomething sketch actor with an uneven coat of silver spray in his hair attempting to play the father of another twentysomething sketch actor when there are thousands of great older actors who would be game and could very naturally play the comedy straight.)

Prognosis for Ever Making It to Air: *Questionable*

EDDIE AMPLIFIER, THE HUMAN SOUND EFFECTS MACHINE WHO JUST WANTS TO TALK ABOUT A RECENT PERSONAL TRAGEDY

Instead of entertaining the audience with his arsenal of vocal sound effects, Eddie grimly recounts some recent bad news, adding realistic vocal sound effects in the most inappropriate and sad places.

Current Thoughts:

I would have loved to do this, even if it had the potential to be a huge bummer on the show. Sadly, though, well after getting hired, I learned that the stand-up comedian Jerry Minor has performed a similar bit onstage. Points off for lack of originality.

Prognosis for Ever Making It to Air: *Cut in Writers' Room*

WHIZMORE, THE CHEEZ WHIZ WHIZZING WIZARD

A man dressed in a full wizard costume, including long white beard, stands onstage and "pees" Cheez Whiz out of his robe and onto a cracker, and then eats the cracker. That's pretty much it.

....

Current Thoughts:

I will fist-fight any one of you in defense of this pitch. I still think it would be a delightful thing to see on television. And yes, that comment at the end—"that's pretty much it"—was actually in my submission.

Prognosis for Ever Making It to Air: *Snowball's Chance in Hell, Though It Has the Novelty of "Worst Thing We've Ever Done on the Show" Potential*

....

Summary:

Your reward for trudging through my submission packet is some advice I hope you will find as simple as it is practical. That is, please try to remember that demonstrating a clear understanding of a show's particular comedic voice might get your packet read past its first idea, but it's not necessarily enough to get you into that malodorous den of zero-moral-boundaries thinking known as the writers' room. For that, never underestimate the importance of carefully weaving your own voice into your submission well enough that it cannot easily be separated from your ideas. That's the balance that I think is important to strike: supplying something familiar that no one ever saw coming.

PURE, HARD-CORE ADVICE

ANDRÉS DU BOUCHET

Comedian; Writer, *Conan, The Tonight Show with Conan O'Brien, Late Night with Conan O'Brien, Best Week Ever*

Recently, I was trying to think of some sound advice for aspiring comedians and comedy writers, and the thing I kept coming back to was how different the comedy landscape is now to when I was starting. There are two big differences: 1) There are way, way, way, way more people now pursuing stand-up, comedy writing, and acting as a career, and 2) There are many more tools and institutions in place to facilitate the pursuit of comedy as a career. Between the ability to take classes at UCB, to network on Facebook and Twitter, to post your own videos on YouTube and Funny or Die, and the endless avalanche of blogs and Tumblrs, aspiring comics can instantly begin creating comedy, finding an audience, and receiving feedback on their material. But, like I said, these tools have increased the number of aspiring comedians exponentially. Currently, it seems that comedy is no longer the exclusive territory of the emotionally confused person drawn to it as a means of finding themselves and working through their anger and fear—that would have been me. Now it's become legitimized as a career that you can pursue after college. You can basically take Comedy Grad School if you go to the Upright Citizens Brigade or any one of the other improv programs.

That being said, my advice to aspiring comedians and comedy writers would be to start with one very basic question: Is this really what I want to do? Because it is for a ton of other people. And since there's so much white noise of constant, relentless comedy content pouring out of all these aspiring comics and writers, you're going to need a very unique comedy voice to stand out, and you're going to need to work very hard for a very long time to separate yourself from the pack.

Actually, perhaps an even better question to ask yourself would be: Do I *need* to be doing this? Most of the comedians I know, myself included, felt there wasn't a choice in the matter. It wasn't, "Oh, neat, this will be a fun career to pursue." It was, "I need to figure out who the fuck I am by making people laugh." So once you've worked through all those questions and feelings, my advice becomes simple: Write and perform comedy constantly and relentlessly for years and years until you're awesome at it, all the while making tons of great friends in the comedy world. Eventually, one of those friends will get their foot in the door of "showbiz," and opportunities will begin to open for you.

If you *can* do anything else with your life and still be happy, do it, for crying out loud.

HENRY BEARD

"'Do you like what you doth see...?' said the voluptuous elf-maiden as she provocatively parted the folds of her robe to reveal the rounded, shadowy glories within. Frito's throat was dry, though his head reeled with desire and ale."

So began the opening paragraph of *Bored of the Rings*, a 1969 full-length book parody of the J. R. R. Tolkien fantasy novels. The book is remarkable for a few reasons: Unlike most parody books, it's remained in publication for more than forty-five years. Also, as one of the first parodies of a modern, popular bestseller, it's inspired several generations of pop culture parodists, including future writers for *Saturday Night Live*, *The Onion*, and Funny or Die. But perhaps most significant, *Bored* was the first major work from two young writers named Henry Beard and Doug Kenney, recent graduates of Harvard University who were just a year from co-creating one of the most influential—if not *the* most influential—comedy magazines of the twentieth century: the *National Lampoon*.

Born on June 7, 1945, Beard grew up from the age of nine at the Westbury Hotel on Manhattan's Upper East Side. He first discovered his writing talents at the *Harvard Lampoon*, but comedy writing was just a recreation for Beard, not a serious career aspiration. After graduating from Harvard in 1967, he planned to attend the university's law school, but after applying in a "halfhearted way," he was rejected. In an equally fortuitous spurning, he and fellow Harvard scribe Doug Kenney were booted out of Harvard's ROTC program, in Beard's case for failing to attend a military ball. "We all went up to the ROTC offices to try to get a hearing," Beard says, "but the colonel in charge refused to see me." Instead, he ran into a sergeant, who recommended that he join the local Army Reserve. He did, and it saved him from a stint in Vietnam.

In 1970, Beard—along with Kenney and Rob Hoffman, with a generous loan from Matty Simmons, one of the publishers of *Weight Watchers* magazine—founded the *National Lampoon*. Within a few years, the *Lampoon* had more than one million readers. Nobody was safe from its take-no-prisoners, slash-and-burn satire, from Richard Nixon to John Lennon. Even the Kennedy assassination was open for ridicule. "My insurance company?" Kennedy asks in a full-page *Lampoon* ad parody, as Oswald points a rifle out a sixth-floor window behind him. "New England Life, of course. Why?"

Beard served as the *Lampoon*'s executive editor from 1970 to '72, and then editor-in-chief from 1973 to '75, where he watched over a motley crew of brilliant satirists including Christopher Cerf, Michael O'Donoghue, Sean Kelly, Chris Miller, P. J. O'Rourke, Bruce McCall, Michel Choquette, and Gerry Sussman. Beard has often been described as the magazine's "calm center," especially during moments of crisis or tension, which were constant occurrences. In an article published by the *Columbia Daily Spectator* in 1972, Beard recounted how the *National Lampoon* received numerous death threats, including nine sticks of dynamite sent from Utah. One letter from American soldiers in Vietnam read: "We would all like to hang you by the Toes and Beat you with a big stick until you couldn't walk."

Far from just an editor—and one of the very best editors of humor in the publishing world—Beard was also an accomplished writer, penning many of the *Lampoon*'s most popular recurring sections, such as News on the March, and larger features, like 1974's "Law of the Jungle," an incredibly dense document, written in legalese, that delved into the complicated rules of the animal kingdom. A short excerpt: "The crows are still paying royalties to the heirs of an obscure, long extinct reptile, for their [copyrighted] use of their 'caw-caw' cry. Interestingly, the heirs are a subspecies of flounder, who are, of course, mute. Animal law is full of such fascinating arrangements." The twelve-thousand-word piece, according to Beard, was written "in less than a day." In comparison, this entire interview—including introduction—runs less than half that length.

Unlike his *Lampoon* peers, Beard never made the transition from print into other comedy genres. He had no involvement with any Broadway musicals or radio shows or TV shows or the wildly successful *Lampoon* movies like *Animal House*. Instead, he quietly retired from the magazine in 1975 and went into near seclusion. Beard, in the years since, has been described as "enigmatic," "reclusive," and "odd." He is not known for giving interviews, having turned down every opportunity to participate in the numerous biographies written about the *Lampoon*.

Over the past three decades, Beard has written, or co-written, thirty-five books, including *Latin for All Occasions* (1990), *French for Cats: All the French Your Cat Will Ever Need* (1991), *The Official Politically Correct Dictionary and Handbook* (with Christopher Cerf, 1992), *O.J.'s Legal Pad: What Is Really Going On in O.J. Simpson's Mind?* (1995), and *Encyclopedia Paranoiaca* (with Christopher Cerf, 2012).

In doing research for this interview, I read that your father was born in 1881. I find that incredible. The distance between 1881 to the 1970s-era of *National Lampoon* feels like it could never, in any possible way, be bridged. Such two vastly different worlds.

It's true. And it *is* incredible. Even more incredible is that my great-grandfather was born in 1834. Try connecting the pre–Civil War era with America in the 1970s. Just a huge gap. But, yes, my father was born in the nineteenth century. Believe it or not, he had a friend who was on the *Titanic*.

Did his friend survive?

Lawrence Beesley was his name, and he survived. He was in second class, a few decks below the top deck. Like my father, he was a Christian Scientist, and clearly he did not smoke or drink. He was reading in his bunk when he felt a bump. He walked to the top deck, where he saw a few people milling about. No one seemed in a great panic. That's really what fascinated me. Everyone was calm. There was very little noise.[1] He returned to his room to read and then heard from above a shout, "All passengers on deck with lifeboats on." Beesley went up to the lifeboat deck, and everyone was saying that the men should be on the left side, the port side, and they'll be picked up there. And Beesley, being no fool, said to himself, "Hmmm, I think my chances are better here on the starboard side." He wasn't pushing women aside—I believe this to be true.

He stayed and saw a rescue boat being lowered. The guy operating the boat yelled, "Hey, you. We got room in here. Do you want to jump in?" So Beesley jumped off the rail and into the lifeboat, which floated away. It was one of the first to escape. Beesley later said that everyone in the boat thought they'd have to later slink back in shame when the *Titanic* didn't sink. And they'd all look like a bunch of cowards. Well, that was a problem they did not have to confront. Beesley later wrote a book about his experiences [*The Loss of the SS Titanic: Its Story and Its Lessons by One of the Survivors*].

Did you ever meet Lawrence Beesley?

No, he was long gone. I spoke to my father a little bit about it and he told me the story of what Lawrence had told him. Lawrence also

---

1   From *The Loss of the SS Titanic: Its Story and Its Lessons by One of the Survivors*, by Lawrence Beesley, Houghton Mifflin Harcourt, June 1912: "To illustrate further how little danger was apprehended—when it was discovered on the first-class deck that the forward lower deck was covered with small ice, snowballing matches were arranged for the following morning, and some passengers even went down to the deck and brought back small pieces of ice which were handed round."

told my father that when the *Titanic* went down, he saw the boat tip over. He said it broke—not quite in half—and he heard the boilers come loose in their mooring and go out the side of the ship, like a huge locomotive going under. He saw the funnels go down. And this description of the splitting of the ship turned out to be accurate when [in September 1985] they found the pieces on the ocean floor. It had broken exactly where he had said it had broken.

Did you, too, grow up under the Christian Science faith?

No. My father was a Christian Scientist, but he had come from a long line of Protestant Irish who ended up in the South, in Birmingham, Alabama. When they came over from Ireland, Alabama was a pretty prosperous place. My father was born there, and then lived for awhile in Louisville.

You weren't raised in the South. How did your family eventually end up north?

My father's mother, my grandmother, was very smart. She was also a very difficult woman who lived to be one hundred. She was evacuated out of Atlanta ahead of Sherman's army when she was a child, and I think she ultimately came to realize that, at least for the time being, the South had no future. So she packed up the family and moved north. My father eventually ended up in New York City, where I spent a few years, before I was sent off to boarding school at the age of ten, in 1955, first to the Rectory School and then to Taft, both in Connecticut.

Do you think that attending boarding school molded you into the comedy writer you later became?

Oh, completely. I don't recommend it. But if you want to get a perfect education as a writer, and if you want to have eight years of Latin before you go to college, well then, this is the place to go. Basically all we were taught was how to read and write the English language. We had to write a thousand-word essay every week. At Taft, in the English class, they had an exam called the 2-8-2. You had a little blue book, and the teacher would write a phrase from a Shakespeare play on the board. You had two minutes to think, eight minutes to compose, two minutes to correct, and then you put your pencils down: 2-8-2.

That is how you train writers.

Often writers have all the time in the world.

Absolutely, and we don't do shit. Then again, in boarding school, with no girls, there wasn't a hell of a lot to do besides write that thousand-word, stupid-themed essay each week.

I'd assume that Latin later came in handy when you wrote *Latin for All Occasions*. The book, published in 1990, helpfully provided readers with the Latin translation of hundreds of phrases, including "You have shit for brains." That would be *Stercus pro cerebro habes*.

That's right, as well as the Latin phrases for "You are a total asshole" [*Podex perfectus es*] and "Screw you and the horse you rode in on" [*Futue te ipsum et caballum in quo vectus est*]. So, for that alone, maybe all those years of boarding school were worth it.

Were you allowed a television at boarding school in the late 1950s and early 1960s?

No, we weren't even allowed a radio. I can't ever remember hearing or watching much comedy at all, although later, I clearly remember Ernie Kovacs. More than anyone, Kovacs had a huge impact on me. Completely unexpected and original. There was no one else like him.

His shows were so primitive. Very low-cost sets. Everything was shot on kinescope, which is just filming off a TV screen. But the comedy was amazing. He had a skit called "The Nairobi Trio," which was three performers dressed as gorillas with derby hats and overcoats, pretending to play music. Beyond bizarre, but it worked. Where did that idea come from? The guy was a space alien. Every once in a while, you run into these space aliens. There's no other explanation.

A space alien in the sense that he was disconnected from the rest of us?

Yes. But he was also connected—I suppose a space alien who fit in on Earth—and that's the only way to produce resonant humor. If you're too connected, it becomes tedious. If you're too disconnected, it doesn't work. You have to be separate but still secured. Genius, absolute genius.

One of the things I love about your career is that it's strictly geared to print, which almost seems like a lost art. Most comedy writers now only seem interested in print if it somehow leads to a TV or movie career.

My generation came along when there was a huge changeover. I graduated from Harvard in 1967. When people graduated from the *Harvard Lampoon*, they went to law school, they became architects, a few of them went on to medical school, or they went to work on Wall Street. If you were a writer—and there weren't many—you mostly wrote for print, not Hollywood. Most clung, of course, to *The New Yorker*, *Playboy*, and books. Within ten years of my graduation, however, all the writers headed west, to write comedy for television shows.

Do you ever wonder if future generations will have either the interest or the talent to concentrate solely on humor for print?

Print is a totally different beast. It requires, without patting myself on the back too hard, some discipline. Television comedy is very tight, very carefully written and rewritten and rewritten and rewritten and rewritten. But it's not quite the same. And you know you've got the backup; you've got funny people to make faces when a line doesn't work. It's different. I suppose some writers will still keep writing humor for print, but it doesn't seem quite as natural as when I was coming along.

And to be fair to comedy writers just starting out, there really isn't much money in it.

No, there isn't. There never really was, but there's a whole lot less now. It's just not a viable thing. It really isn't. *The New Yorker*, to its credit, is still viable, but often they'll just publish an unfunny piece by somebody you've heard of instead of a very funny piece by someone you've never heard of.

It's just so difficult to write humor for print. I tried to figure this out recently. When I was at the *National Lampoon*, I think I wrote a million words. God help me, most of them were supposed to be funny. I can't imagine anyone doing that again. I can't imagine *myself* doing it again. Send the guys in the white jackets and nets. Looking back, you just can't believe it.

You once said that it was Doug Kenney, the co-writer of *Animal House* and *Caddyshack*, who—more than any other *National Lampoon* writer— was able to get things done in Hollywood. Why was that?

The real beginning for *National Lampoon* in Hollywood was Doug Kenney. Doug was a naturally funny writer of print. In retrospect, and I didn't realize it at the time, he was also a gifted writer of movie comedy. Doug just had a great, natural comic instinct, which could be applied to anything. When he got the opportunity to do *Animal House* [in the mid-seventies], it was clear that that was what he was really meant to do.

It was mostly because Doug had a fundamentally cinematic sort of sensibility and he was quite relentless in his pursuit of projects he cared about. It takes a profound sort of focus and determination to get anything done in the movie world, and he had both. He was also a very, very good collaborator with everyone he worked with.

Over the years, there's been much discussion about Kenney's death in Hawaii in 1980 at the age of thirty-three. According to some, he jumped off a cliff. According to others, he slipped or was pushed off a cliff. What do you think happened?

I don't know. Honestly, I just don't know. I think it's possible that he killed himself. The whole thing is so murky. Doug had his ups and downs; there's no question about it. I guess it comes with the territory. Years before, Doug had gone to visit friends in the Caribbean, and he was caught with marijuana in his luggage. It wasn't very serious. He knew people who had good political connections, and he got off. But he would never travel with drugs again. So I think he was out in Hawaii and he may have tried to score some drugs. This might have been a drug deal gone bad, and he might have been killed. But I honestly don't know.

There are stories about Doug being unhappy with the way *Caddyshack* turned out. Do you think he was unhappy with the movie or unhappy with his life?

I think a little of both. When *Caddyshack* was released [in 1980], he was kind of depressed. He said, "Oh, well. It wasn't another *Animal House*." And I said to him, "Man, give it time." It was one of the funniest movies I think I'd ever seen. But he was comparing it to the great success that *Animal House* achieved, and that wasn't fair.

You collaborated with Doug on *Bored of the Rings*. Can you tell me how that came about?

I convinced Doug, who had not read *Lord of the Rings*, and who had correctly thought it was kind of a stupid thing, that we should write a parody of it. We were able to sell the idea to Ballantine, the publisher that originally put out the paperback edition of *The Lord of the Rings*. And again being careful, we sent a letter to J. R. R. Tolkien saying, "We're thinking of parodying your books. What do you think?" And he sent back this sweet, very quirky letter that said, in essence, "Well, I don't really know why you'd want to bother, but if you're silly enough to want to do it then that's okay with me. Go ahead."

After we managed to get a small advance from a publisher, Doug speed-read *Lord of the Rings* in one day and ended up writing probably three-quarters of the parody. I remember sitting across from him at a sort of double desk in a Harvard library, each of us with a portable typewriter, and I sat there fussing over a paragraph, and he was writing *pages* as fast as he could type. It was unbelievable. He wrote thirty-five or forty words per minute. And it was hysterical. I mean, it was just unbelievable. That was Doug—that was pure Doug.

When we turned it in, the head of Ballantine, Ian Ballantine [who published *The Lord of the Rings*], basically picked up the manuscript with a pair of fireplace tongs. It was noxious to him. He wasn't thrilled about it. Meanwhile, over the years, that book [published in 1969 by Signet] has helped support the *Harvard Lampoon*. Simon & Schuster published yet another edition in the fall of 2012.

The *National Lampoon*'s style of print humor was very dense, and not wedded to one cookie-cutter premise. There were many different types of genres that were parodied, from comic books to game instructions to yearbooks to magazines. It must have been an exhausting publication to put out month after month.

Absolutely, and going back to Doug, he had a great gift for the visual. He was the one who more than anyone said, "Listen, the material in the magazine can't just be words on a page. We should do absolutely strict and accurate parodies." Doug completely and instinctively knew that this was a great opportunity to do funny work. It was just in his blood. Once we all caught on to how it was being done, it became very clear that this was the direction to take.

In the very early issues of *National Lampoon*, the art direction appeared looser. It wasn't necessarily very accurate to what it was parodying.

It was clumsy in the beginning. Until [art director] Michael Gross came in around the sixth or seventh issue, it was not working. To his great credit, Michael called up our publisher, even before he was hired, and he said, "You know, this is a funny magazine, but it looks like crap. I'm an art director. Hire me. I'll fix it." And we did, and he did. He saved us, really. Total accuracy for what was being parodied. It was easy to confuse the real with our version.

This very talented comedian named Ed Bluestone came to the office in 1972 with the line, "If you don't buy this magazine, we'll kill this dog." The next day Michael found a dog who would turn its eyes away from a pistol, with a little prodding. The photo was shot for the January 1973 issue. I saw this picture and simply couldn't believe it. And it was, like, with a wave of his left hand. Magic. So that's the type of thing that made all the success possible.

How often was the magazine sued for depicting *too accurate* a parody?

We were continually sued. In one [1973] issue we published a Miracle Monopoly Cheating Kit. We printed out $1,000 and $5,000 pieces of Monopoly money to be slipped among the game's $5 and $10 pieces of Monopoly money. The only reason we didn't get sued is because *Lampoon* writer Christopher Cerf had gone to college with the son of one of the Parker Brothers, who called off the dogs. People were always suing us. Oftentimes, we had to settle out of court and just tell them, "We're sorry. We won't do that again."

Do you think the magazine could work as well today as it did in its prime? So much of this type of humor depends on the audience's knowledge of what's being parodied, and a lot of the print formats you dealt with aren't as popular as they used to be.

That's absolutely right. It was a moment of shared experience. With the visualization of a lot of print and the introduction of television after World War II—and this was for my generation—you had this attic stuffed with shared experience and memories. Everybody had read *The Saturday Evening Post*, everybody had read the stupid comic books, and we connected. It was just an entire world of visual references, and we ran through them at the speed of light. The amount of material we consumed in a few years at *National Lampoon* was shocking. We just used it up.

Most of the humor in *National Lampoon*—and it's now more than forty years old—remains fresh. This even includes material that, in lesser hands, would feel very dated, such as Watergate or the Vietnam War.

It's very lasting. It was very difficult to produce, but I do think most of it has lasted. Some of those parodies I can still look back at and laugh out loud. I reread the *1964 High School Yearbook* parody recently. That was unbelievable; I mean, just great.

A lot of comedy fans feel that the *1964 Yearbook*, published as a book in 1973 and edited by Doug Kenney and P. J. O'Rourke, invented nostalgia. At least a certain type of nostalgia—looking to the past, but with the knowledge of what we know now.

I wouldn't argue with that. Well, I'm not sure we invented nostalgia. We did package it well and gave it momentum. But as a symbol of it, yes. The format of a high school yearbook is the one complete true universal, at least in this country. That's gone. I mean, are we going to now have people sharing their first experience via Twitter? No. So everybody lived through high school. And the high school yearbook was the distillation of this experience.

This is a very specific type of nostalgia. When you have references to high school girls "out sick a lot" and "crying in Home Ec," really a euphemism for being pregnant during a time when such a thing was not accepted, that's a different type of nostalgia than looking back fondly on concerts held in the town square, musicians playing oompah music.

Right, it's completely different. There's a depth to the nostalgia, or a width or a breadth, or whatever geometrical metric you want to use. I think that partly had to do with us growing up in a time, the sixties, when it was unbelievably straightlaced and tight-assed. Things started to loosen up a bit after Kennedy's election, but the first time I ever heard of anybody using drugs was in 1965. It was marijuana. I remember someone saying, "My God, if they ever catch that guy, he's going to federal prison for life!" Can you imagine? Two years later, you couldn't walk through Harvard Square without getting a contact high. It just all fell apart. So the *National Lampoon*'s timing in that sense couldn't have been better. We got a chance to draw on this shared, weird background of the boomers at a time when everything was coming loose. I think the *National Lampoon* was the first printed magazine that published every single four-letter word.

I remember early on the publisher telling us, "I've got some bad news. I got a call from the printing plant. They won't print a particular cartoon." I think the cartoon's punch line was, "Oh well, go fuck yourself," or something like that. Within six months, though, they were printing everything. They just gave up.

This was before even *Playboy* began publishing four-letter words.

Absolutely. To their credit, *Playboy* was more careful, because they were smart. They were printing bad pictures and they didn't want to get involved with bad words. Hugh Hefner wanted a clean-dirty magazine. We were very content to have a dirty-dirty magazine. Hefner was a very smart man. When I was on the *Harvard Lampoon*, we wanted to do a *Playboy* parody. We cold-called Hefner to ask his permission. His secretary said, "Just a minute." Hefner came on the phone practically immediately. Not only did he say he'd love to have it parodied, but he said, "I'll arrange for you to use my printing plant. I will tell them that you're solid citizens. And all you guys have to do is make sure you get signatures from some of your rich graduates on the bill to make sure we don't get stiffed." We printed around 635,000 copies in September 1966, and we sold them in eleven days.

That was really the beginning of me thinking, My God, I don't have to go to law school.

That was the first inclination that there was something big out there?

That was the first really big one. We realized that not only could we do something that was going to be on newsstands all across the country, not just on the East Coast, but we realized that certain production values could be achieved, which was a necessity for accurate parody.

The material from the *Lampoon*, both *Harvard* and *National*, is very much druggy-based. Was there ever any drug use for you?

No. And not because of any sort of moral rectitude. I guess, like Bill Clinton, I didn't inhale, because when a friend offered me a puff on a joint, I took a deep drag and almost choked to death. The perfect negative reinforcement. No one ever offered me anything stronger—they probably figured like that classic Woody Allen gag, I would sneeze in midsnort and blow all the high-priced coke away.

Do you feel that comedy writers can improve their humor—and reach areas they wouldn't have been able to reach otherwise—if they are drunk or stoned?

No.

It must be strange to talk about some of your college classmates who later become such comedic icons. Is it all surreal?

Totally surreal. Everything seems completely accidental. It's that philosophy that if you cross Sixth Avenue at Forty-second Street instead of at Forty-third Street, you'll end up alive instead of being hit by a car. I mean, it was all so completely, unbelievably accidental. I went to Harvard. My father went to Yale in the class of 1913. I went to Harvard to piss off my father. It was youthful rebellion. That was the only reason. If I had gone to Yale, none of this would have happened. No way. I have no idea where I would have ended up. All so trivial.

So much luck really does seem to play into it all, both in terms of achieving success and not achieving success.

You hate to admit it, but it's all luck. It's just really all luck. And that's why it always frustrates me, as a lifelong Democrat, when I hear the Republicans talking about hard work. "It's all hard work." Well, yes, it *is* always hard work, but there are a lot of people who work very hard and are unlucky and they get screwed.

The people who started the *National Lampoon* were very fortunate. We came along at a very particular time. All the restraints were coming loose; it was probably one of the last times when you could start a monthly humor magazine. When we first went out, we were one of the first magazines of its kind to have a seventy-five-cents cover price. That was considered a wild, wild gamble. Who would pay seventy-five cents for such a thing? Well, of course it made it possible for us to exist. For a long time we couldn't get advertising. The advertisers would say, "I'm not going to advertise in that disgusting magazine." But that soon changed. At 295,000 it was disgusting. At 305,000 it was an important audience that needed to be reached on its own terms.

It's notoriously difficult to get advertising for a comedy magazine, as opposed to say, a golf magazine.

If the *National Lampoon* was being started today, we'd have all those ads of two people sitting side by side in bathtubs, with the man trying to get an erection. There are very few advertising categories for a humor magazine. With golf magazines, you can advertise clubs, clothing, golfing books, anything related to golf. For us, cigarettes was a major advertiser, to our eternal shame, but I do not apologize. We never hesitated to take cigarette advertising. My God, we needed it. We would have been dead without it.

You've been leery over the years to talk about your *National Lampoon* days. In fact, I don't think I've ever seen you interviewed for any books about the magazine or its writers—and there have been many.

Well, it's not any sort of hidden agenda. It just gets exhausting. I didn't think most people writing those books were very fair witnesses to what had gone on. It just seemed easier to not get involved with it. Also, it's very hard to tell the story. Part of the problem is that a lot of the story is just damn dull. Other than occasionally receiving a box of dynamite sent to us at the offices, like what happened in 1972, it was just grind, grind, grind. Day in and day out, the deadlines were just brutal.

A couple of years after I left [in 1975], I remember giving an interview to a reporter for *Esquire*, who misquoted me, and some of those misquotes hurt a few people. I swore to myself for a long time thereafter that I would never speak of it again to anybody. I felt I couldn't trust them. But now I've kind of mellowed. It's all sort of become part of history. Sad to say that most of the people who would have been hurt by such things are now dead.

Did you ever have any regrets about leaving the *Lampoon* after only a little more than five years?

No, it probably saved my life. I had a college friend who was a psychiatrist who told me, "If you hadn't gotten out of there we were going to come and get you. You know, there's no way you would have lasted much longer." Selfishly, I don't feel any particular guilt. I had the best of it. By the time we got Nixon out, and things were sort of cruising along, we'd kind of done it. And the really great gifted people began to leave. Even though he could be really difficult, Michael O'Donoghue was an extraordinary talent, but he had gone on to *Saturday Night Live*. I knew we couldn't compete with *SNL*. And Doug had moved on to Hollywood and was not coming back. There were not a lot of other people of that same caliber. And it was becoming a bit more of an uphill fight and a little bit more of a routine. I just got burned out. You can only do something at that level for so long.

Are you content with your writing life now? Publishing a humor book every year or so?

Sure. No one is really ever completely content, but yes. Things worked out much better than I could have ever imagined. I love writing books, although publishing has become more competitive and so difficult. It's hard to come up with these little trivial books and really expect to get them out in the marketplace. But I write books now like I used to write magazine articles. *French for Cats: All the French Your Cat Will Ever Need* [Villard, 1991] would have been the shortest magazine article I ever wrote. And it's a book!

Were you ever conflicted by your choice to become a comedy writer? Did you ever feel that you should have pursued another occupation?

Even though I really sort of stumbled into humor writing as a profession, I can't imagine doing anything else.

National Lampoon **has had its ups (and mostly downs) since you left. Are you at all affected when you see the magazine and its brand struggling from a business and creative standpoint?**

Well, in my heart of hearts I think I always knew it was likely to have a somewhat fleeting golden age. Once *Saturday Night Live* came along, and the new generation of smart, very contemporary situation comedies started coming on the air, there were far more interesting and lucrative outlets for the kind of highly talented writers we were deeply dependent on and never could find enough of. It was always a struggle to come up with a month's worth of often quite highly produced pieces—a typical ninety-six-page issue was about half editorial material and half ads, or nearly fifty blank pages to fill. In a way, I think we had a pretty narrow window of opportunity creatively, culturally, and financially. It really seems in retrospect like we came along at just the right time, and we were just unbelievably lucky.

So, what advice would you have for a young humor writer? Or for someone wanting to improve his or her lot in comedy writing?

The only advice is you just have to do it. I think you just have to start writing early. I think one of the other things is to just go to Hollywood or to go work for *Saturday Night Live*. But the thing with those jobs, while often remunerative, they're also all-consuming. I don't think there are a lot of people who write television comedy, or for movies, who are writing books on the side—unless you get to the point where you've made your bundle and you can just write anything. But, at that point, you don't, do you?

Maybe it was always this way for the comedy writer. S. J. Perelman was always complaining that he never had two nickels to rub together. He never seemed to have enough money. Robert Benchley did well out in Hollywood but it killed him; he was just never happy there. So, I don't know. Things happen, things change. It's not the same as what I went through; it's just different. I'm just grateful that I had a shot.

JAMES L. BROOKS

Screenwriter, Director, Producer, *Terms of Endearment,*
Broadcast News, As Good as It Gets; Creator/Writer,
The Mary Tyler Moore Show, Taxi, The Simpsons

....

Getting the Details Right

The shows you created, such as *Mary Tyler Moore*, *Taxi*, and *The Simpsons*, have influenced an untold number of comedy writers. Who would you count as being an influence on your own writing?

Certainly high on the list would be Paddy Chayefsky, who wrote the screenplays to *Network, Marty, The Hospital,* in addition to historically great television. When you talk about someone unique among American screenwriters, he's way up there. A great writer. And his position was very rare: He exercised final control over his movies. In other words, he hired the director—in one instance, he was even able to *fire* the director—and he was able to control the final cut. He was the controlling force on his films as the writer. Which is as rare as it gets. And he was prominent in both movies and in television.

On the original poster for *Network*, which came out in 1976, the tagline reads: "Prepare Yourself for a Perfectly Outrageous Motion Picture." That outrageousness quickly became commonplace. The movie now almost appears to be a documentary.

Well, I remember when I first saw *Network*—and I'm a Chayefsky lover—but I was cranky when I first saw the movie, because I thought the heroine played by Faye Dunaway was farcical to the point of utterly no connection with reality. And then a heartbeat later, not only was this character not farcical, but she suddenly was all over the place. Chayefsky stone-cold saw the future—and he did that a few times.

That's a tough trick for a writer to pull off, especially when it comes to comedy: to be prescient while also not confusing audiences with anything too new and too unrecognizable.

Well, Chayefsky's [1971] movie *The Hospital* was just as prescient as *Network*. He predicted the current state of today's health-care situation when there wasn't a whisper of it.

Paddy Chayefsky has been criticized for writing dialogue that was considered, by many, to be too "written." That the words out of his characters' mouths were perhaps too preachy and too poetic.

That was the big argument about Chayefsky, because he was making films at a time when films were supposed to not be about words, but just all images. And there were these arguments—endless, really, they just went on and on—that the minute you're aware of the writer's hand, the screenplay could no longer be good. But my point was and still is: If you're aware of glorious writing, so what? I never had a problem with that. Chayefsky's dialogue was also brilliant in its variety. His writing was always big-hearted and full of emotion. He could write dialogue for regular people: Marty, Marty's mother, the characters in [the 1957 movie] *The Bachelor Party*. But he could also write totally convincing dialogue for geniuses: *Network*, *The Hospital*, *Altered States*.

And these days there are any number of writers following in Chayefsky's footsteps in television, which has become the place for the best of our writers to be supported in wherever their talent takes them. I believe great writing should make you aware of it. I think it's a fun thing.

There are stories about Paddy Chayefsky being an incredibly intense, obsessive writer. That he thought of writing, as well as life itself, as almost being a contact sport.

And that's something that I completely understand.

How so?

I see writing as righteous. There are a lot of things in life that we spend time worrying about, agonizing over, being involved with, having it assume distorted proportions. We end up embarrassed by how much priority we give to so many things that, ultimately, we can't control. But that doesn't happen when it comes to writing. Writing dignifies any turmoil it puts you through.

Would you consider yourself to be an obsessive? Many of the characters in your movies seem to suffer from obsessive compulsive disorder. I'm thinking in particular of Jack Nicholson's character in _As Good as It Gets_, as well as Holly Hunter in _Broadcast News_ and Téa Leoni in _Spanglish_.

I can't imagine that any writer doesn't suffer from obsessiveness— a humility that you feel toward your work. Writing is not something you do offhandedly. It should continue to mean as much to you after years of doing it as it did when you first started. I sort of think it's supposed to be ever humbling.

This intensity hasn't seemed to wane over the years. I was listening to the DVD audio commentary for 1987's _Broadcast News_, and you were talking about some of the jokes that you wished you could rewrite, from a distance of more than ten years.

When you write and direct a movie, you are legally insane. It's an absolute distortion of reality—it just is. You're not thinking straight. So when you see the movie again as a rational human being, with some detachment, it becomes a different thing. I saw *Broadcast News* for the first time after many years of not having seen it. I was channel-surfing and then stayed with it. I finally realized what the movie was all about. It's about three people who lost their last chance at real intimacy.

Now, at the time of making the film, I couldn't accept my ending, thinking it should be more definitive. But with the passage of time, I saw that same ending as correctly defining the journey.

You're a writer with a reputation for doing a tremendous amount of research before you even begin the process of starting on a script. For *Broadcast News*, you spent a full year doing research on the news media. How important should research be to a screenwriter, even if the script is going to be a comedy?

It's extremely important—at least for me. I love doing research. The script, the characters, the comedy will always benefit from research. It was one of the best times of my life doing research for *Broadcast News*; just hanging around with journalists was fun. I have this rule: If I hear something being said three times while I'm doing research, then I believe that it's generally true. Well, while in the midst of hundreds of hours of research, I heard it said at least three times that some powerful women in TV journalism would privately cry in the course of their working day. And so I had Holly Hunter's character in *Broadcast News* cry on a schedule to release tension. There are countless similar examples of things that work in your film that never would have been there without research.

Have there been other occasions when your research has helped you either define or create a character that wouldn't have existed otherwise?

Lots. It is always important. When we were researching for [the 1978–1982 sitcom] *Taxi*, we spent twenty-four hours at a New York

City garage called Dover Taxi. We read about the garage in a *New York* magazine article ["Night-Shifting for the Hip Taxi Fleet," by Mark Jacobson, September 1975]. And we came away with a character that we never could have ever have created on our own—the Louie De Palma character [played by Danny DeVito]. I saw a cab driver bribe a dispatcher in order to get one of the cleaner cabs. This was clearly something that went on all the time. But when the dispatcher saw me watching, he did a bit of theater, slapping the cab driver's hand away in an effort to look innocent. And that's how Louie De Palma was born.

You once said that if someone writes a good script, it will eventually be read. That sounds encouraging, but it's also a sentiment that many struggling Hollywood writers might be surprised to hear.

Well, that's the great edge a writer has. Somewhere, somehow, you can get your script read. And if it's good, you will be noticed. If you're an actor, you need other people in order to act; a director needs other people in order to direct. But writers can be alone in a room and do what they do, without any help. It's all in their hands. And sooner or later, someone will give it a read.

Has writing become any easier for you over the years?

You know, I had a nightmare the other night—a *literal* nightmare—that I was talking to someone about writing a screenplay and he told me that he wrote fourteen pages a day. Now, I've written more than fourteen pages in a day for a lot of television shows. But never for a movie screenplay. And when you're working on a movie, there are just so many days when nothing gets written down. That can be tough. Hence, the nightmare.

But I have learned that if you awaken each morning and know the questions you're asking yourself and know exactly the problem you're attacking, then the writing process—even if it's really slow, even if nothing gets on paper—becomes a genuine process. And if you're in a genuine process, there are no mistakes. If nothing gets down that day, it's supposed to be that way. As long as your unconscious is preoccupied with the work, you can get into a kind of zone where what seems to be inactivity is progress. The novelist Jonathan Franzen made a comment that brought me to my knees. He said something like, "You can't call yourself a writer if you can get the Internet on your writing machine." That's brutal. But the fucker is telling a hard truth. So, right away, the bar is that far from your grasp.

Other writers have told me they have the same personality tic that I've experienced over the years. People used to ask, "What do you do for a living?" It took me more than twenty years to answer, "I'm a writer," without my voice breaking and without me feeling self-conscious. To be a writer always felt too big to be true. I grew up in New Jersey, where my ambition was to survive. I don't mean that in a sad or dramatic way; I mean that in an absolute factual way. It's not rhetoric; it's just a real basic fact. I could only picture myself selling things, like working as a shoe salesman. I did not have the ability to dream of being a writer. I did not have any of the self-confidence you need in order to try to become a writer, and I think I only achieved what looked like self-confidence because I did love to write and I could lose myself in the work. Others saw my focus as self-confidence. But it was just me getting away from myself for a little while, writing what I wanted.

And that's all you can hope for: to lose track of time and to get into a zone to produce writing that you're happy with. So I'd recommend that to all young writers. Just write. Lose yourself. And when you look up, maybe you'll be somewhere you always wanted to be.

PURE, HARD-CORE ADVICE

MEGAN AMRAM

Writer, *Parks and Recreation*; Author, *Science . . . for Her!*

Even though comedy writing is inherently goofing around with really funny people for ten to seventeen hours a day, it's also very disciplined. And I am only just starting to figure out how to do it. It's something you need to exercise. Try to write material—try to write *good* material—as often as you can. You also need to consume a lot of comedy so that you can figure out what makes something good.

What's also important is to make sure that you actually *like* writing. I've always wanted to grow up and move to Hollywood—since I was a kid I've always had a vague idea that that's what I wanted to do. But I didn't know until a few years ago that I actually *enjoyed* the art of writing. There are a lot of people my age who are trying to get their foot in the door, who want to be famous, or who want a cool job. But if you don't enjoy the act of actually sitting down and writing for hours a day, it's probably not the correct choice for you.

I started Twitter because one of my friends did it. I thought, Okay, if I tweet one joke a day to myself and my college friends, this will make me better at writing, and I will have some jokes saved for a pilot or whatever I want to do. I didn't know anyone who worked in the industry, but as it happens, there are some people who are really into trolling Twitter for new talent. I think some of the assistants at *Family Guy* saw me first. That could be patient zero of my Twitter spread. Assistants to assistants. Basically, kids right out of college who were helping out the writers and producers. A lot of them have gone on to other jobs now, and I'm still friends with them. So the contagion started that way. They started following and retweeting me, and I was getting some real comedy people as followers. And then [comedian and writer] Rob Delaney became a supporter, and he already had his huge following [more than 930,000]. Once Rob found me, a few months after I started tweeting, that's when it really hit me: "Oh, my God, this guy is using this for a specific purpose that's very exciting and new, and maybe I could get a piece of that pie, too."

I kept tweeting for a few months. I was really working hard at the idea of writing jokes. And then, in maybe one of the greatest things that's happened to me, I had this meeting with writer and comic Jordan Rubin, who had e-mailed me. He told me, "I have a thing that I'm working on. I might want you as a writer." He was head writer for the Oscars. He said, "Do you want to write for *The Academy Awards*?" That was my first job. Just an insane amount of luck, which I am forever grateful for.

Then I was hired on *Parks and Rec*. I had never written for a sitcom like this. I was hired as a staff writer, so I was brought on as a funny person who knew how to write and someone who had potential to be a good TV writer. Mike [Schur], the head of *Parks and Rec*, was a fan of mine from Twitter and from my blog. So it was pretty incredible. I still can't really believe that they hired an Internet weirdo. [Laughs] I think Mike felt, Well, we can always teach her how to write for *this* show.

I started writing with the single goal to make myself a better writer and then, later, to get a job. And I did; I got my dream job. I still love Twitter because it really is a fun way to connect with people, and it feels amazing to have a ton of people [more than 370,000] follow me just by virtue of them thinking I'm funny. That's the most pure, wonderful validation of one's career, basically. But that being said, if I'm at work sitting in a writers' room, I'm definitely not thinking about Twitter. I'm trying to think about my show and trying to do the best job that I can. So I don't tweet an insane amount, and I tweet less than I used to. My number-one responsibility is my job, and my number-two responsibility is my Twitter.

If I had to give any closing piece of advice, it would be to make sure you like what you're doing, to put yourself out there, in terms of your work. Also, just be a human being. Be nice to people and don't be crazy, which sounds very general, but that's appreciated professionally. You can be a nice, energetic, funny person, but still not alienate anyone.

Sampling of Tweets from Megan Amram

I'm giving up spell check for Lant

This is a pretty shitty flash mob. It's in my living room, only my family showed up, and they're just telling me to stop drinking

Such a double standard that when a guy sleeps with a ton of people he's "cool," but when I do I'm "lying"

Face down, ass up, that's the way I want my open casket funeral

They call me the Titanic *because I once went down on a bunch of Irish peasants*

After my ex and I broke up, I was in a really bad place (Florida)

PEG LYNCH

"The big events in one's life occur only now and then, but there are smaller events that are familiar to every family. It's these daily incidents that make up the private lives of Ethel and Albert." So began every episode of *Ethel and Albert*, a hugely popular radio (and then television) series that ran for most of the 1940s and 1950s, on multiple stations both small and national.

Almost half a century before Jerry Seinfeld became famous for his "show about nothing," Margaret Frances "Peg" Lynch was already exploring the comedic possibilities of life's minutiae. *Ethel and Albert* followed the everyday lives of a young married couple, the Arbuckles, living in the fictional small town of Sandy Harbor—no state was ever mentioned. Only the two lead characters were ever heard—at least until 1946, when their baby Suzy was "born"—and they mostly stayed in their house, discussing the most trivial of subjects. In one episode, Ethel challenges Albert's assertion that he could go the entire day by just using his peripheral vision. In another, Albert misses a dinner party because of a six-cent shortage in the company's books, and Ethel asks, rather logically, why Albert couldn't have just paid the six cents out of his own pocket to make it home in time.

Many shows were inspired by Lynch's own experiences, both as a single woman and, later, as a wife. As she told the *Miami News* in 1955, she "once lost a beau because we argued over which side of the street a Chicago department store was on." This simple premise was later the inspiration for an entire episode of *Ethel and Albert*.

"What I loved about her humor was that she dealt in the realm of real domestic life, not the goofier stuff you found on similar shows like *My Favorite Husband* and *Burns and Allen*," says Gerald Nachman, radio historian and writer. Lynch's work "was a very different, more mature kind of comedy writing that didn't depend on jokes but on character and situation, before *situation comedy* was even a term."

After graduating from the University of Minnesota in 1937, with a major in English and acting, Lynch was hired as a copywriter by local radio station KATE in Albert Lea, Minnesota. For a monthly salary of sixty-five dollars she penned scripts for commercials, radio plays, and a weekly farm news program. She soon came up with the Ethel and Albert characters and convinced the station to produce three-minute episodes as fillers between regular programming. As the show grew in popularity, first in Minnesota and then for another station in Maryland, it was expanded to fifteen minutes.

In 1944, Lynch moved to New York City, where she began writing regular episodes of *Ethel and Albert* for the Blue Network, which would later become the American Broadcasting Company (ABC). Not only did the national network hire her to write all the shows—a rare vote of confidence for a relatively unknown writer—they also asked Lynch to play the lead. In the fifties, *Ethel and Albert* moved to TV, first as a ten-minute segment on *The Kate Smith Hour* in 1952, and then in 1953 as its own half-hour program on the NBC network. Over the next several years, it moved between all three major television networks, from NBC (1953–1954) to CBS (summer 1955) to ABC (1955–1956).

Ethel and Albert officially ended its TV run on July 6, 1956. But in 1957, Lynch revisited the Arbuckles for a CBS radio show called *The Couple Next Door*. Lynch reprised her now classic role, but because CBS wanted new character names (and because Peg refused),

Ethel and Albert were never named for this series, and they only referred to each other as "dear." Margaret Hamilton (better known as the Wicked Witch of the West from 1939's *The Wizard of Oz*) was the third adult to join the *Ethel and Albert* cast, as Aunt Eva. The series lasted for three years.

Peg lives with her husband of sixty-five years, Odd Knut Rønning, in Becket, Massachusetts. At the age of ninety-six, she continues to write comedy.

Let's start with where you were born.

I'm originally from a little town called Kasson, near Rochester, Minnesota. It was only a town of about fifteen thousand people, located very close to the Mayo Clinic. I was without a father. My dad died during the [1918] flu pandemic, when I was only two. My mother worked full-time as head orthopedic nurse at the Mayo Clinic. Her boss was Dr. Charlie Mayo, who had cofounded the Mayo Clinic [in 1889].

Dr. Charlie—that's what we called him. He sort of brought me up; he kept an eye on me. My mother once brought me to see him because I wasn't eating. And he made a joke: "Maybe she doesn't like the food." My mother ignored it, and she said, "But look at her! She's mad all the time! Look at her fists! They're always clenched." So Dr. Charlie said, "Margaret"—which is what they called me then—"Margaret, doors are going to open for you when you grow up. Be sure that you walk through them." And that was a good lesson. I'd like to think that I have.

How did you first get involved with radio?

In school, I had a classmate who told me that his father just bought the First National Bank Building in Rochester. Located in the same building was a radio station that had the call letters KROC. I perked right up. "Oh, really?" I asked. This was in 1931; I was fourteen. I had wanted to write ever since I was eight years old. I said,

"Gee, can I work at the station?" And my friend said, "Sure, ask my dad."

I went down to the building, all by myself, and I asked my friend's father, "Can I work at your radio station?" You have to remember that when radio first started, stations were built by the wealthiest merchants in town. These merchants had money, but they didn't know a damn thing about radio. I said, "You gotta get some sponsors." And he said, "Well, what's that? We don't sell things over here at the network."

So I said, "I'll show you. Let's try the shoe store first." I knew the owner was a good friend of his. I walked on over to the store and I said to the owner, "Listen. You're going to sell shoes on the radio. And you're going to need a slogan." I said, "I'll be back tomorrow with a slogan for you." Overnight, I made one up: "Don't spend your life two feet away from happiness." He loved it.

I then went to the fancy grocery store in town—it was called the Vegetable Man. The doctors' wives bought all their groceries there. I told the manager of the grocery that he needed to advertise on the radio. He loved the idea, and he wanted to be a sponsor, too. But we couldn't decide what the slogan should be. He said, "You work at the hospital sometimes with your mother, right? Why don't you introduce celebrities on the air, and we can sponsor the interviews?" I said, "That's a marvelous idea!" The town was small, but we had a thousand new people a day going through the clinic, and there were oftentimes celebrities. It didn't bother me to talk to them. I never experienced that awestruck feeling that I think has sort of ruined the country. Celebrities aren't really celebrities, you know; they're just people. One of the first interviews I got was with [movie actor] Bill Powell. Do you remember [his 1934 film] *The Thin Man*? No, you're too young to remember *The Thin Man*.

Well, Bill Powell was a patient at the Mayo Clinic, and he was adorable. He was so sweet. Beforehand, I talked to Dr. Charlie, and he said, "Don't discuss their ailments. You don't want to get into that. It's their private thing; don't do that. Always be nice and make sure a patient has his dignity. His backside is always waving in the breeze, so make sure he has his dignity."

I disagreed with him. When people are sick, they'll discuss

anything. You see them sitting in the lobby, and you know damn well they don't know each other, yet they're talking about each other's bowel habits. So I told Dr. Charlie that the patients would be willing to talk about *anything*—and I was right. The interviews for the radio were great.

Another person I interviewed—who was the baseball player who retired before his time? Gary Cooper played him in a movie.

Lou Gehrig?!

Yes, I interviewed Lou Gehrig on the morning he received his results [for amyotrophic lateral sclerosis]. I think he already knew what it was, though.

Do you remember what he said to you?

I don't. I do remember him being very sweet and nice. Most of the time the patients would want to talk about where they lived and about their family. They were sentimental, you know.

That's incredible. You perhaps conducted one of the final interviews with Lou Gehrig.

I never even thought about such a thing. I expect I did. But it didn't mean much at the time. I wasn't interested in baseball.

There were others. Have you heard of Knute Rockne [the Notre Dame football coach from 1918 to 1930]? Well, my very first interview was him. He was at the clinic, and he was staying at a hotel in town. I can remember ringing the doorbell at his hotel on the seventh floor. And he came to the door and I was terrified. He looked down at me and he said, "Well, look what we have here! You come right in, honey." And what I remember is not the interview, but the very fact that he lifted me up to him and asked, "What would you like for breakfast, Margaret?" And I said, "Well, sir, I've already had breakfast." And he said, "How about a waffle? Maybe you could eat a waffle?" And I said, "Well, maybe I could." I spent the morning there. I was just numb, but thrilled that he picked up a telephone and ordered breakfast. I'd never heard of such a thing as ordering breakfast. And then the table came up with food on it! I was more impressed with that than with Knute Rockne and football!

Ernest Hemingway was also there, but I never interviewed him. He was there for erectile dysfunction. I'm just joking.

But it was very, very hard, too, because I worked in the hospital to earn some extra money. I was in tears every night that I worked at the clinic. A writer should never be around sick people, because you only end up getting all of their diseases, as you well know. And I told mother, "I simply can't stay here, Mother. I've got to get out." I cried all the time. It was so terrible to hear patients say, "I'm going to visit my daughter in New Mexico" and "I'm going to visit my son," and you knew damn well they were going to be dead before then because you had just seen their tests that read "Inoperable Cancer of the Stomach" or something like that. I just couldn't take it any longer.

Where did you work after your first radio job at KROC?

I landed a job at KATE, in Albert Lea, Minnesota, about sixty miles southwest of Rochester. This was in 1937, just after I graduated from the University of Minnesota with a degree in English and acting. I did everything. I wrote commercials. I worked on a thirty-minute woman's show—it was a daily—and a show about theater that was on once a week for thirty minutes. I'd also write plays and sketches, and I'd give the news, a lot of it about farming. I worked there for a number of years, earning sixty-five dollars a month.

Did you find your university degrees helpful after you graduated?

Literally, I learned nothing at university. *Nothing.* I always taught myself. I was a big reader when I was young. I completed *War and Peace* when I was ten. I can remember a neighbor saying, "Margaret, why are you always going out to the hammock? What do you do there?" Reading was my favorite thing to do. Whenever I could get away with it, I would go out and lie in the hammock with my dog, eating a green apple, and I would read. I *still* read. I would hate to die for a lot of reasons. But mostly because of all the books I haven't yet read.

When did you create *Ethel and Albert*?

I began *Ethel and Albert* in the late thirties. It started as three- or four-minute filler. Actually, the show was first called *He and She*. I thought it was something I'd only be doing that week. The show eventually ran every day, for fifteen minutes. And then the station asked for a second show per day, different from the first. Two new shows a day. But I loved it. I was just bored writing copy for the station. It was a great way to sell products, to have a husband and wife in a domestic setting each week. You know, something happens every day to couples that might not seem funny as it's happening. Later, though, at dinner, it can be hilarious.

The show had a very naturalistic tone to it, in terms of both plot and dialogue. It still sounds very modern.

It's the little things in life that've always interested me. How people in relationships talk to one another. What they say when they really mean something else.

The jokes, too, are much more natural-sounding on *Ethel and Albert* than on the other radio comedies of the time. On *The Abbott and Costello Show*, Costello might say, "You have a cold. How can you keep the germs from spreading?" And Abbott would reply: "I'll make 'em wear a girdle." Whereas on *Ethel and Albert*, the joke would be entirely based on a situation: Albert heads off to work while still wearing his old Boy Scout hat that he had put on as a joke and had forgotten about.

When I started, I didn't write well. I tried too hard to be funny. I was trying too hard to write a Gracie Allen type of character [the not-so-bright comedic foil to George Burns]. But it hit me eventually that I don't have to try to be funny, for God's sakes. Life is funny!

I never considered what I wrote for Ethel and Albert to be jokes.

I didn't write gag lines. All of the humor was based on everyday situations. The comedy came from character traits that we can all recognize and find funny.

For instance, I remember once eating dinner at a well-known restaurant in New York, and the waiter was too busy with the table of twelve next to ours to bother with us. I went home and immediately wrote a script about that. I called the restaurant's manager and said, "If you want to know what level of service your restaurant gives, you can listen to *Ethel and Albert* two weeks from tonight on the radio." So two weeks came and he had to go sit out in his car, because he didn't have a radio in his office—I later learned this from someone who knew him. And he called me up after the show aired, and he said, "I apologize. Come back here and have a free meal." And I thanked him very kindly and said, "I didn't do it for that. I'm too busy to come around, but thank you very much." But that's how I got my ideas. From all over, at any time. Psychologically, it was useful. The show gave me a marvelous sense of freedom.

So, you never felt you wrote "joke" jokes?

No. I think I was certainly capable of doing that. I remember one joke I wrote that went: "How can you put your foot down if you haven't got a leg to stand on?" But what I tended to write were funny situations tied to character.

I wanted it all to sound real. A few things bothered me about radio. I thought the sound effects were not realistic. The only sound effects I liked were the phone ringing, the doorbell, or just clatter. I hated footsteps. Always footsteps. Didn't any of the characters on these radio shows ever walk in rooms with rugs in them? The footsteps weren't realistic, you know? And I'm a very realistic person.

That's how I ended up playing Ethel. We auditioned a lot of actresses, but they weren't natural-sounding. They were too slow. They were too dramatic. They sounded too much like they were on the radio. Why couldn't they just read the way they talked? Why couldn't they talk like normal people in everyday settings?

Can you see the influence that your show had on subsequent radio and TV sitcoms? I've seen *Ethel and Albert* called the very first sitcom.

I've heard from various people over the years that the conversational style in *Ethel and Albert* is similar to a show I've never seen. *Siegfield? Zigfeld? Feigold?* Something like that?

Seinfeld?

Yeah, well, you know. I don't have time to watch all these shows. But I think that show, too, was about the little things that happen in our lives. I realized when I first started that there were a lot of ideas all around me. I didn't have to knock myself out trying to come up with funny situations. They were already there to be discovered.

Yes, but even if a show is based on real life and realistic situations, you still have to write the scripts.

I did, and I had to produce a lot of material over the years. I had to come up with an idea every day. Every single day.

Over the years, how many scripts did you write for *Ethel and Albert*?

More than twenty thousand.

Twenty thousand?! How is that possible?

Well, listen. I wrote for the show for many years, first for radio and then for TV. This was off and on, but mostly daily. And we'd often broadcast two shows a day. They wouldn't ever let me repeat an episode. Can you imagine? But it worked out well. I've always owned the rights to the show and could take it wherever I wanted. And I was also in charge.

Did the show have any writers besides you?

A lot of great writers submitted, but not a single person had a script that would've fit. [Novelist] John Cheever once submitted a script. He was a good writer, but it just didn't fit. People never seemed to believe it was about anything. They all thought I wrote about nothing. No, it was always just me doing the writing. And I've always typed with two fingers, if you can believe it.

I wrote constantly. Every single day, nonstop. One night—and this was when I was living in New York in the fifties—my doorbell rang at three-thirty in the morning. I was up writing. I was *always* up writing. I said, "Who is it?" And I heard a man say, "Don't open the door, please God, don't open the door!" And I asked, "What do you mean don't open the door?" And he said, "Don't open the door! I don't have any clothes on!" And I said, "So you're naked?" And he said, "Yes. And you know me, I'm from downstairs." And I said, "You don't sound like you're from downstairs. What is it you need?" And he said, "Could you get me a coat?" And I answered, "What, am I *crazy*? Opening the door at three-thirty in Gramercy Park? Well, just a minute." And I opened the door a crack and handed a coat to him. I made him walk down to the end of the hall before I opened the door again. He had changed and was walking back to my apartment.

And I recognized him. I had screamed at him six months earlier because he was having a musical jam session in his apartment while I was trying to write. It was so noisy! I couldn't get anything done. So I recognized him, and he began to tell me that he worked for *The New Yorker* as a cartoonist.

He was a *New Yorker* cartoonist? What was his name?

I'm not going to tell you. He later became a big seller in *The New Yorker*, but I'm not going to say things like that. And we sat there in my bay window overlooking Gramercy Park—I lived at 12 Gramercy Park—waiting for the police to arrive with a locksmith. I didn't have a key to the guy's apartment. He told me that he had been taking a shower and had locked himself out of his apartment by mistake. He's sitting there in a raincoat and I'm in a bathrobe, and I said, "Do you like working at *The New Yorker*?" And he said "Yeah, but if I can't get back in the apartment, I can't work on my cartoons for to-morrow."

I said, "Tomorrow, I have to produce a show, and I haven't even written the script yet. So, thirty-seven million people will eventually be turning on their TV sets to watch and hear what I'm saying, and I haven't even got an idea. And here you are, complaining to me because you can't get into your apartment!"

He laughed and said, "Do you know Jim [James] Thurber? He listens to your show when he works, and so do a lot of the other cartoonists." A few months later a group of *New Yorker* cartoonists sent me fan letters. So I've got a scrapbook full of those.

[Playwright and humorist] George S. Kaufman once said a nice thing about me. He saw a TV episode I had written, and he told a mutual friend that he liked it.

What was the episode about?

I had written a script where Albert returned home just as Ethel was getting herself ready for a Halloween party. There was a pumpkin on the front porch that she had scooped out and put a candle in. And Albert thought it'd be funny if he took out the candle and then put the pumpkin on top of his head and pulled a sheet around himself. He ran in—the silly way that people do to be funny—in order to scare Ethel. And he screamed, "Oooooh!" And she said, "For heaven sakes. Go upstairs and get that thing off! The guests are going to be here at eight o'clock." But he couldn't get the pumpkin off. [Laughs] He couldn't get the thing off his head, and Ethel then had to drive him to the hospital to have a doctor try to surgically remove it. It was very realistic.

I heard from a friend that George Kaufman told her, "I saw the funniest damn television show. This writer guy had an idea that comes once in lifetime." He said, "God, he did it so well. I don't know who wrote it." I ended up meeting Kaufman later, and I told him, "I was the one who wrote it. And that writer guy is a writer *dame*."

When you created the television version of *Ethel and Albert* for NBC in 1953, you remained the show's sole writer. Did you find any difference between writing for radio and writing for TV?

Not a bit. Not a bit.

A lot of radio writers had a tough time transitioning from a descriptive medium to an entirely visual medium. Many radio writers would tend to overwrite for television.

When we started our show on radio in 1944, there were about one hundred television sets in all of New York City. Think of it. One hundred. The medium was all radio. But that changed a little by 1950. But it was still so new. I once attended a taping of George Kelly's [1924 play] *The Show-Off*, down in the RCA building, at one of the studios. It was horrible. The lights were so strong. It was incredibly hot. The men had great sweat stains under their armpits. The temperature was 115.

So, when it came time to shoot our show, I knew we had to shoot it in an air-cooled studio, which we did up in Schenectady [New York]. We nearly froze to death, but it worked. It was all so new and everyone was so nervous. The cameraman twisted up in the coils and fell off his feet. Two people in the control room got up to see what was going on and, in their frenzy, they bumped heads, and one knocked the other one out. And then the one who wasn't knocked out came out of the control room and tripped over the cable. It was total shambles.

I have to say, though, that I was fine. I can't talk for other writers, but the reason I didn't have any trouble with the transition from radio to TV is because I always envisioned exactly where we were going and what we were doing. It was an easy transition. It was nothing.

But it frightened a lot of people. A lot of stage actors couldn't make the transition. It terrified them. Performing live in front of millions, as well as a live crowd. It could ruin their timing.

I want to tell you a story about [Academy Award–winning British movie actor] Charles Laughton throwing up.

Please.

In 1952, *Ethel and Albert* was on *The Kate Smith Hour* as a ten-minute segment. There were other performers on the show. Musicians, actors, jugglers. On this night, Charles was going to read Shakespeare on the show. This was the first time he'd ever been on television, and he was nervous as a cat.

A few minutes before the show went live, the producer ran into the backstage area and asked me, "Can you make a two-minute cut in your sketch?" And I said, "No, I'm not cutting anything out. I can't do that. I wouldn't know where to do it."

He said, "Well, we have to cut the Shakespeare thing," which is what Laughton would be performing. "We have to cut it down." The producer just drew a line down the Shakespeare script. He crossed off some sentences and wrote something else. He said, "Make the cut like that." He then walked out of the room and, as he passed Laughton, he said, "Miss Lynch is going to make cuts in your script."

I was putting on my makeup, and I could see, in the dressing room mirror, Laughton standing behind me in the doorway. I said, "Don't worry about it, Mr. Laughton. Miss Lynch is not going to do any such thing." But I noticed he looked strange. I said, "Are you sick? Do you feel ill?" He said, "I feel terrible. I wish I'd never done this damn thing. I usually never accept it, and I hate television. I think I'm going to throw up." And he looked around and saw my bathroom, my tiny bathroom. He quickly headed toward it, and I said, "Oh, don't throw up in the sink, please. All my makeup is there."

He just kneeled down by the john, then he looked up at me and said something like, "My mother always held my head." And I said, "All right," and I got down on one side of him. He wasn't quite as fat then, and I put my arm around his waist and held his forehead, and I said, "Go on now, throw up." And he did. I thought, Here I am, kneeling in front of a toilet with Captain Bligh. He had played that character in [the 1935 version of] *Mutiny on the Bounty.*

Afterward, I grabbed a wet wash cloth and I wiped his face, and said, "Do you feel better? Now straighten your shoulders. You're going on down to the studio and you're going to do the show!" And he kept saying, "Television, I hate it!" I straightened his tie, I brushed his hair back, and I said, "Do you have any clean shirts? Get down there now and put on a clean shirt. This one is all wrinkled."

He did perform and then afterward he said, "I didn't like that. I'm never going to do it again." And I said, "Yes, you will. You were *marvelous.*" Actually, I didn't like it at all—he was fine, but I hated

Shakespeare. And I certainly wasn't going to tell him that he was bad after he had just thrown up!

The great Charles Laughton.

I never saw him again. He sent me three dozen roses the next day. And thanked me.

TV was very time-consuming. I went back to radio after six years of television. I had had it. I only got three and a half hours of sleep a night while doing the TV show. And it was a dirty business.

How so?

Ethel and Albert was sabotaged.

What do you mean?

When the *Ethel and Albert* TV show was on the air, it had replaced another show called *December Bride* for the summer. The sponsor, General Foods, had invested $4 million into that show—a lot more than they spent on *Ethel and Albert*—and they wanted to force my show off the air, even though it was doing well; in fact, better than *December Bride*, and that was the problem.

I started to notice strange things happening. Once, an enormous party of tourists barged into the control room where we were shooting *Ethel and Albert*. We thought it was an accident. They started talking very loudly and bothering the director. Another time when we were shooting the show, all of the actors were in front of the cameras, performing live. The characters were playing a game of bridge. And suddenly a man—not an actor, and someone I'd never seen before— walked through the front door of the set, right through the scene. And all four of us actors looked at him and waited for him to say something—*anything*—but he didn't even look up at us. He just continued walking, maybe nodding his head or something, and then walked off the set. And Alan [Bunce], who played Albert, looked at me with alarm and improvised, "Oh, that's Mariel's friend and he's fixing our faucet, dear. I forgot to tell you. I'm sorry."

Wait. So you think General Foods sabotaged your show in order to get *December Bride*—**a show they happened to have spent more money on—back onto the air?**

Yes. About three years after all of this, I met a man on a train. He looked at me and said, "Peg Lynch?" I said, "Yes?" He said, "I used to work as an ad exec for [New York–based advertising agency] Benton & Bowles and we used to handle General Foods. And I thought I might have a nervous breakdown when I was working there. My wife said either you get out of the business or I'm going to divorce you. And I left. I was sick about what happened to your show." I said, "What do you mean?" And he said, "Don't you know? Word went out through the whole industry that General Foods would do anything they could to sabotage your show—to make it look bad; to make it look unprofessional. And it broke my heart." I said, "Now that you mention this, I do recall a few things, yes."

We should probably make clear that these are *alleged* accusations, right? These were never proven.

You're a babe in arms. I've gone through this thing and I'm ninety-six years old and I've got stories to tell and I know where the bodies are buried.

You're starting to scare me.

What I mean to say is that television is a rough business. But I've been lucky over the years. Very, very lucky. I got to make the show I wanted to make, and I did it on my own terms.

Have you ever thought about working on a current version of *Ethel and Albert*? Perhaps now that the characters would be in their eighties and nineties?

I'd like to, yes. I'd like to write an *Ethel and Albert* now, and what their problems would be and how they would get through them. It would be interesting. Life becomes different when you're in your nineties. People treat you differently. People are always asking, "Are you warm enough?" or "Are you hungry? What can I *do* for you?" No, I'm fine, thanks. I'll do it myself.

It used to be fun. I used to keep in touch with all my fans. I answered all their letters; it was such a bright spot in my life. And now they're all gone. Years ago, my father-in-law was celebrating his ninetieth birthday. For a surprise, I decided to make ninety cupcakes and have candles all over them. I thought it was so cute. It took me and four other people to get all the damn things lit before the first ones started to go out. So I said to my father-in-law, "When you're ninety years old, do you still feel sixteen?" And he said, "Yes, you do." But he looked at me kind of sad and said, "But all your friends are dead."

It's a terrible feeling. My big address book that I have sitting in front of me is scratched through, all of the names are X-ed off. *X, X, X.* All your friends are gone. You won't appreciate this until you're ninety-six.

But I do think anything can be written about it, and done in a funny way. It would be a challenge. Ethel and Albert still getting into fights, still having funny conversations. Maybe this time about doctors and gout.

Wow! Look at the time! I've talked your arm off!

You know, before you called, I was talking with my daughter. She said, "Mother, I wish you had told me these things. You never told me all of these stories." And I said, "Well, I never thought they were important!" I've got a lot more, too.

Like the time when John Kennedy came into the studio while we were shooting an episode of *Ethel and Albert*. Kennedy's sister, Pat Kennedy Lawford, worked as an assistant on the show. So Kennedy told me, "You *have* to have dinner with me tonight." He was only a senator at this point. Can you imagine? "You *have* to have dinner with me."

And how did you respond?

I said, "No, I'm not. I *have* to write a script tonight." He left and then came back later and asked me again. I said, "I really can't. I have to get up at 3:00 a.m. in order to write." He looked at me in shock.

He couldn't believe it; I was turning him down once again. He then walked out. And I went home and I wrote.

Now that's a dedicated writer.

You have to be.

Did Kennedy ever ask you out for a third time, perhaps after he became president? Did he phone you from the emergency red telephone in the Oval Office?

If he did, I didn't answer. But that's another story. [Laughs]

PETER MEHLMAN

Writer, *Seinfeld, It's Like, You Know...* ; Journalist, *GQ, Esquire,*
The Washington Post, The New York Times

....

Writing for *Seinfeld*

You wrote twenty-two episodes of *Seinfeld*. Quite a few lines from these episodes became well-known and found their way into the popular vernacular, including "yada yada yada" and "double-dip." Did you have any idea while you were writing these scripts that a particular line would later hit with the public?

No, I never had an idea. I never knew, really, what would become popular. It always surprised me, actually.

So none of the lines were written to be a catchphrase?

No. Every line was written just to be funny and to further the plot. But, actually, there was one time that I did think that a certain phrase would become popular. And I was completely wrong. In the "Yada Yada" episode [April 24, 1997], I really thought that it was going to be the "antidentite" line that was going to be the big phrase, and it was not. That line went: "If this wasn't my son's wedding day, I'd knock your teeth out, you antidentite bastard." The man who said it was a dentist. And no one remembers that phrase; it's the "yada yada yada" line that everyone remembers.

But it's interesting. When a phrase or word becomes popular on a show, it's like a pop song. Everybody remembers the hook. Nobody really listens to the verses.

In 1993, you wrote a _Seinfeld_ script called "The Implant" that included the "double-dipping" line. Did that story come from a real-life experience?

It did, yes. I was at a party and somebody flipped out because someone else double-dipped a chip. They didn't say "double-dipped." I had to make up the phrase, but that wasn't exactly a tough phrase to make up. To me, "double-dipping" sounded funny and it fit, but I never intended it to stand out. I never consciously thought, Oh, my God, I can actually add to the lexicon.

How about the "shrinkage" line from 1994's "The Hamptons" episode, in which George claims that it's the cold air after swimming that has made his penis appear smaller?

Larry [David, the co-creator] had the idea of George going into a pool and coming out cold, and I said, "Oh, and he gets, like, shrinkage?" And Larry said, "Yeah! And use that word. Use it _a lot_." So I don't know if I thought it would be a big term, but Larry may have.[1]

---

1   George: "Ordinarily I wouldn't mind, but . . ."
Jerry: "But what?"
George: "Well, I just got back from swimming in the pool. And the water was cold . . ."
Jerry: "Ah. You mean . . . shrinkage?"
George: "Yes. _Significant_ shrinkage."
Jerry: "So you feel you were shortchanged."
George: "Yes. I mean, if she thinks that's me, she's under a complete misapprehension. That was not me, Jerry. [Voice breaking] That was not me!"

The brilliance of the writing on *Seinfeld* was, among other factors, how seemingly easy it is to emulate. I'd imagine you were constantly being bombarded with scripts from people thinking that they could effortlessly write for the show.

We would receive thousands and thousands of submissions. Mostly, they were just terrible ideas. We had a boilerplate rejection letter, and once a month one of the writing assistants would come in with about a hundred copies of that letter that I would have to sign, and she'd then send them out. One year, I took stats on the letters, and I found that we had received scripts from forty-six U.S. states.

What four states did *not* participate?

Alaska, Montana, and North Dakota, and then one deep in the South—Mississippi or Arkansas. Most of the ideas were terrible.

Do you remember any?

I remember there were a ton of "Jerry dates woman who turns out to be a transsexual." Most of the ideas were unwitting parodies of the show. The main problem with most of the scripts was that in the first couple of pages it would always have some run of dialogue completely off the subject. The scripts had *pages* of dialogue devoted to digressions. I was always amazed when writers thought you could pretty much go on for pages and pages on completely irrelevant subjects. In reality, our scripts were ridiculously tight. And beyond that, 90 percent of the time we ended up five or six minutes long in the episode, and the scripts would then have to be tightened even further.

Were all of your waking hours dedicated to coming up with ideas for the show?

It became addicting. Every news story, every anecdote I heard at a party, every idea became a potential plot or piece of dialogue for the show. It was all-consuming. I was on vacation once in Arizona, at the

Canyon Ranch Spa. It was Mother's Day weekend, so there were a hundred women with their daughters taking a spa weekend together. I met one of these daughters, and we were hanging out and spending all this time together. Then, on my last day, we were standing on this little bridge over a dry water bed and we started making out. As we were kissing, I remember thinking, It's amazing how every girl's got her own style of kissing—hands *here*, lips *there*, left eye open. . . . And then I thought, Oh, my God, look at this, I'm in the middle of making out and I'm *still* observing! That's when I realized, I've got to figure out a way to back off this a little.

Were your friends and family constantly suggesting ideas for the show?

Constantly. And they never worked. Except in two cases. A friend once told me about his father who worked in the jewelry exchange district in Manhattan, and he would openly say to women, "You know, you're very pretty. You should get a nose job." And my friend would say, "God! You can't just tell people to get a nose job!" And his father would say, "Believe me, they end up thanking me." And that later ended up in the episode called "The Nose Job" [November 20, 1991].

That same friend was once telling me a story—not for the show, but just as a story. He said, "You won't believe what happened to me. I was at Marix Tex Mex restaurant [in LA] and I get the car back from the valet parker, and the car stunk unbelievably bad." Never for a second did he think of that as a *Seinfeld* idea. At first, I didn't either, but then I began thinking that if the smell starts attaching itself to people, then I can get all four characters into that one story—which is what you would dream about as a writer. It later became the "Smelly Car" episode [April 15, 1993].

As a writer for more than twenty episodes of *Seinfeld*, can you still make a good living to this day off residuals, years after the final show aired?

Obviously it depends on your definition of a "pretty good living," but you know, I certainly could survive on it. I could pretty much come out better than even if residuals were my only income.

There are at least two Twitter accounts with jokes about how *Seinfeld* would have changed had the show continued to the present day. From a comedy writer's standpoint, was the complete absence of cell phones and the Internet easier for you? Or do you think the show would be easier to write for now?

If written now, there would be a million instances of one character being able to call another character and saying, "Don't do that!" For instance, in the episode where Elaine is dating a guy with the same name as the famous [1990s] serial killer Joel Rifkin ["The Masseuse," November 18, 1993], Kramer goes to a stadium to pick up football tickets but he doesn't have his ID with him. So the stadium makes an announcement to sixty-five thousand fans: "Will Joel Rifkin please come to will call . . ." This caused the breaking point when the guy wants to change his name—he's tired of everyone in the city confusing him with the serial killer. But if there were cell phones available back then, Kramer could have simply called Elaine and asked, "Can you meet me downstairs?" and that would have been that.

Also, the constant coming in and out of Jerry's apartment would have really changed. It would have changed the logic. It no longer would have been necessary.

We could have still written *Seinfeld*, but it would have just been different. It would have really put a new twist on some great story lines. Like in the Chinese restaurant episode ["The Chinese Restaurant," May 23, 1991]. Instead of all four characters waiting and talking in the lobby of the restaurant, they just would have told the hostess, "Give us a call when there's a table available." Or when Jerry and George were stuck with Elaine's intimidating father [in "The Jacket," February 6, 1991], they could have just said, "Excuse me," and then left to call Elaine: "Where the hell are you?!" When you think about it, convenience doesn't make for good comedy.

Did *Seinfeld* have a writers' room?

No—unless somehow a script was in total crisis. The writers would come up with their own story lines, and then we'd pass them to Jerry and Larry, who would either accept or reject them. If you couldn't come up with story lines, you were let go. But there was no one room in which the writers had to sit and write and pitch out ideas.

You know, having a writers' room is very conducive to getting *nothing* done. You get a lot of people in there and you go off on tangents and people are going to the bathroom and going out and getting coffee. Everybody just wants to get out of that room.

I never would have survived in an atmosphere of shouting out jokes. There's a lot of pressure trying to come up with a better joke than the person sitting two feet away from you. It just doesn't seem like it's the kind of contemplative atmosphere that you usually associate with creativity.

How long would it typically take for you to write a *Seinfeld* script?

Some faster than others. "The Yada Yada" script was unbelievably fast. From the time I pitched it to Jerry to the time it was on air, it was about a month. There were others that took forever.

The most difficult aspect was combining four story lines in order to make a complete episode. There wasn't an episode, really, where all four characters weren't part of the show. That was difficult right throughout, but if I had a story lying around where Jerry was dating a masseuse and all he really wanted was the massage, and I had another story lying around in which Jerry was dating someone who just hated George, that's where I could say, "Wait a minute, the masseuse can hate George," and then we're connected. But it was really tricky.

It would then be up to Jerry and Larry to rewrite the script that I'd turn in to them, and for them to inject their own magic into the scripts. As far as how much they would rewrite, it depended on the episodes. Sometimes it would be A to Z. Sometimes it was lighter.

What were the writing differences between Jerry Seinfeld and Larry David? Would they have a different way of attacking a joke?

There was an episode that took place in the Hamptons, where George has a girlfriend he hasn't slept with yet ["The Hamptons," May 12, 1994]. George goes off to buy tomatoes, and while he's doing so, this woman goes topless in front of Elaine, Kramer, and Jerry. When George returns, he's upset that he was the only one who didn't get to see the breasts. Jerry then wrote a line where George says, "It's like I'm Neil Armstrong. I turn around for a sip of Tang and you just jump out first!"

Jerry's synapses work really well on analogies. He was really big on analogies. It's a great line, but jokey. And Larry just didn't write jokey lines. All his jokes were funny because of the situation. As an example, he once wrote a line for George: "I've never had a meeting where I really wanted the other person to show up." And that was Larry.

You didn't start off as a TV writer. You were a freelancer for various magazines. How did you make the leap from magazine writing to being a writer on *Seinfeld*?

In 1990 or so, I ran into Larry David, whom I had known a bit. He also attended the University of Maryland, but he was about ten years older than I was. He said, "I'm working on a little show with Jerry Seinfeld." He asked if I had a script. I didn't, but I said that I did have a recent funny article I wrote for *The New York Times* called "Star Trekking." It was about me walking around Manhattan, trying to spot famous celebrities. Larry and Jerry liked it, and they gave me an assignment to write an episode, which eventually became "The Apartment." That script idea was changed a bit from the original concept, which was to have Elaine moving farther away from Jerry. Larry Charles [a *Seinfeld* staff writer, and later the director of *Borat*, *Brüno*, and *The Dictator*] suggested it would be funnier to have Elaine moving *closer* to Jerry, into the apartment above his, and he was right. This was also the episode where George wore a wedding ring to a party thinking it would improve his chances of meeting women. It aired in the second season [April 4, 1991].

That is such a rarity. Magazine writers don't usually—if ever—get asked to write for TV.

I know. It *never* happens. And it's what a lot of freelance writers wish for, but it just never, ever happens. The funny thing is, years later, I think on Facebook, somebody sent me this blog that they wrote—this woman in New York—and it was called "In Search of Peter Mehlman." This woman was wondering whether it was just apocryphal that there was this guy who was a freelance writer and then he became a writer on *Seinfeld*. And that was the first time I ever heard that people even aspired to that kind of thing if they were free-lance writers. The difference is that I didn't hope to write for TV. Magazine writing was fine. I actually prefer writing full sentences.

So you're not apocryphal? You're no Bigfoot or Abominable Snowman? You do exist?

I do exist. [Laughs] By a thread.

PAUL F. TOMPKINS

Writer, *Mr. Show with Bob and David,*
Real Time with Bill Maher, Best Week Ever, Bob's Burgers

There can sometimes be a division between different artistic expressions. Writers sometimes look down their noses at people who are actors, and actors do the same with writers. And that's too bad. What you have to remember is that it's always a team effort. That is how great things get done. You can arrive at a movie like *Citizen Kane* just as easily through team effort as you can with the auteur method. Bear in mind, Orson Welles was an actor, as well as a writer. He understood all those disciplines. That's what makes a successful auteur. Somebody who understands those disciplines and has respect for all of them. I think respect for people who do the things you don't do is very important. The writer of the movie is just as important as the director, who's just as important as the makeup artist, who's just as important as the key grip and the lighting guy. And the guy who carries the tiniest cable is just as important as the actor who ultimately stands on the red carpet.

Networking is extremely important. I hate the word *networking* because it feels very crass. To me, networking used to be going to parties and insinuating yourself into conversations. Now, the better definition of networking is that you socialize and find like-minded people and either work with them or have conversations with them about creativity. Networking does not have to be, "How can I get someone to give me a job?" It's, "How do I establish relationships with like-minded people that will eventually lead to work?" It doesn't have to be about, "Hey, you got a show. Are you going to put me in the show?" If you approach everything from a pure creative angle, the work and employment will take care of itself. People don't like others who constantly ask them for work. People find that off-putting. That's not the way to do it. Just be around and engage people in a pure way and you're going to get more work that way.

People like to talk about selling out. I don't think most people understand what that really means. To me, selling out is if you're set for life with money, and yet you still decide to do an M&M's commercial. That's selling out. That's you saying, "I want a bunch of money." But if you are someone who wants to do good work but you're not set for life and you can't pick and choose what you want to do, then you do what you have to do to pay the bills. It's just that simple. I'm forty-three, so I kind of feel like that's just life. That's fucking life. I have a wife. We can't be precious artists who starve anymore. We're too old to starve. I base decisions on, "I need to work. I need to do this." I'm fine with that. Honestly, even with the things I've done that were more for money than art, I had fun and I enjoyed the people I worked with. I'm not ashamed of anything. Do whatever is going to pay the bills for you while you are trying to get your foot in the door. There is no shame in that.

When you're younger, you're very concerned with appearance. You're very concerned with how you look to the outside world. Are you cool? Do people think you're cool? When you get older, you don't give a shit about that anymore. The more you do it, the longer you do this, the more it becomes about the work itself. I love the stuff I'm doing, and I'm excited by the prospect of how my artistry is going to evolve over the years. To me, it's exciting. I see the journey in a way that I did not see when I was starting out.

What it really comes down to is that life is short and these things should be fun. That's why we get into this business and the arts. It's because it's fun; it's like nothing else. The idea is to get paid to participate in this wonderful fun with other fun people.

10.06.1995
2PM, W OHIO STREET, CHICAGO IL

ADAM McKAY, 26
WILL KILL HIMSELF.
THIS IS NOT A JOKE.

ADAM McKAY

Will Ferrell doesn't mince words when describing Adam McKay, his longtime friend and comedy collaborator. "He's kind of a dangerous individual," Ferrell says. "He's extremely funny; there's no doubt about it. But he's dangerous. I wouldn't stay in a room with him, one-on-one, for any longer than I had to. There's a criminal tendency there. We have a great working relationship because I don't ask him much about his past. He just frightens me." Ferrell is joking, obviously. But there was a time, years before McKay found Hollywood success directing and co-writing films such as *Talladega Nights: The Ballad of Ricky Bobby* (2006) and *The Other Guys* (2010), when he might very well have been the most dangerous man in comedy.

In June of 1995, McKay was making history at Chicago's legendary Second City, in a sketch revue called *Piñata Full of Bees*. It would prove to be one of the most seminal and groundbreaking productions in the theater's history. Set apart by its aggressive approach to political and social satire, *Piñata* tackled such seemingly unfunny subjects as wealth corruption, racism, and the massacre of Native Americans. McKay is often given sole credit for masterminding its strong political point of view.

McKay hadn't always aspired to create political satire. The Pennsylvania native grew up idolizing mainstream comics such as Jay Leno and Jerry Seinfeld. While studying English at Temple University, he performed what he calls "family-friendly" stand-up in local bars and restaurants. But less than a year shy of graduation, he dropped out of school and moved to Chicago to study improvisation, and he soon became one of the most popular (and notorious) performers in the city's vibrant comedy scene. With such pioneering groups as The Family and The Upright Citizens Brigade, he became infamous for interactive theatrics and elaborately staged pranks. During one show, he led an entire audience back to his apartment, where they witnessed a brutal (and entirely staged) murder from his bedroom window. During another show, he staged his own suicide.

Performing storefront improv for free soon led to a gig at the Second City, and within a few months of *Piñata*'s premiere, McKay was hired as a writer for *Saturday Night Live*. (He was promoted to head writer after just his first year.) He wasted no time trying to infuse *Saturday Night Live* with a sharper satiric bite, but it wasn't always easy. "We did a commercial parody about a luxury car with an aperture that you could have intercourse with," says Tina Fey, whom McKay hired to the *SNL* writing staff in 1997. "Adam insisted on calling it the Mercury Mistress. Well, it turned out that Lincoln Mercury had just signed on to advertise at NBC, and obviously they didn't want someone fucking their car. The commercial only aired once and it will never air again."

While he was never able to make sweeping changes to *SNL*'s content, McKay eventually found small ways to be subversive. During his fifth year, he began writing and directing short films that were hidden in the show's final minutes. The films—which starred such diverse talent as Steve Buscemi, Willem Dafoe, and Ben Stiller—were typically dark and disturbing. In *The Pervert*, for instance, a group of sexual deviants are disgusted by a fellow pervert's attraction to the Cream of Wheat chef.

In 2001, after six seasons at *SNL*, McKay left to pursue a career in filmmaking. But Hollywood didn't exactly welcome him with open arms. "It's difficult if you've only ever made short comedy films about Doberman attacks and a brutal 'rape' involving [Eagles guitarist] Glenn Frey," McKay admits. "There was at least one studio that was so horrified they asked me never to contact them again." Despite that studio's reluctance, the 2004 release of *Anchorman: The Legend of Ron Burgundy* eventually grossed (for the DreamWorks studio) more than $90 million worldwide and became a cult classic on DVD. It was McKay's feature debut as a director and screenwriter, and his first big-screen project with Will Ferrell.

More movies followed—*Step Brothers* (2008), *The Other Guys* (2010), and *Anchorman: The Legend Continues* (2013). McKay and Ferrell also hit Broadway with the 2009 George W. Bush–skewering one-man show *You're Welcome America*, as well as infiltrating the Internet with Funny or Die, the wildly popular, user-generated video website they launched, in 2007, with their production company, Gary Sanchez Productions. Today, McKay is a mainstream juggernaut, one of the few dependable comedy writer/directors with a loyal following, whose name alone is enough to sell tickets. But has all the success softened the edges of this once subversive comedy writer?

Filmmaker David O. Russell, who coexecutive produced the first *Anchorman*, doesn't think so. "Just spending time with Adam McKay sharpens my rebellious spirit," Russell says. "He's the pure stuff, as far as I'm concerned. We typically go from having a serious political conversation to an insane improvisational digression and back. It cracks me up that anyone would suggest that he's become more traditional. Adam McKay is a cultural gem and he's gonna shine and he's gonna fuck shit up."

Was there a particular comedy movie, or TV show, that influenced you as a child more than others?

It was the [1980] movie *Airplane!* Everything up to that point had been fairly predictable. Story structures had always been sort of the same in movies. With the comedies until then, you would see setup, a beat, and then a joke. Most had this kind of a structure, but *Airplane!* changed that.

There's a specific scene in *Airplane!* that I love. A newspaper spins and it stops with the headline: "Disaster Looms for Airline Passengers." And then it spins and stops with the next headline: "Chicago Prepares for Crash Landing." And then it spins again and stops with the final headline: "Boy Trapped in Refrigerator Eats Own Foot."

That was the first time I ever saw anything like that. That joke was just so out of left field, and yet it still made sense. It was one of the first times I ever saw something where I felt, Oh, my God, you can do whatever you want with this form! Someone's imagination had taken a leap four steps ahead. It was just the utter surprise of it. It was almost wrong or naughty or crazy. It was just so exciting to me. I've talked to other comedy writers who have said the same thing, that they distinctly remember that joke: "Boy trapped in refrigerator eats own foot." I remember my eyes just going wide.

On one level it's pure absurdist comedy. The first couple of beats of the spinning headline are parody, then it becomes a bit of a satire about the media blowing stories out of proportion, and then all of a sudden, it becomes pure absurdism. The premise almost ate itself at that moment—or its own foot.

Your movies tend to contain that very same combination: parody, satire, absurdism.

If you just do parody, it can get pretty boring. You'll just be hitting the old formulas that we've all seen before. We always try to make our movies one-third satire, one-third parody, and one-third original storytelling. We're very conscious of that. We like to use the old tropes to ground the movie in familiarity, and then jump off and go in different directions. At that point—and, really, only at that point—can you then get as sincere as you want. I love getting really sincere off an insane joke or a tail-eating-itself kind of joke, but it has to be grounded first. It's like grounding a live wire. It's the only way good comedy works.

When did you first make the leap from loving comedy to actually devoting your life to it?

I dropped out of Temple University [in 1989] during my senior year. I had a buddy go out to Chicago to perform. He came back and told me about this thing going on out there, long-form improv. I couldn't believe it. At that time, I was only doing stand-up. He said to me, "You go onstage, and whatever you say is what happens. You make up *anything* you want. If you want to be on Mars, you're on Mars. The only rule is that you can't say 'no' to the other performers. You have to say, 'Yes, and . . .' If another performer starts to go off in another direction, you say 'Yes, and . . .' and then you follow."

I was like, "You gotta be kidding me!" My friend also told me about improv teacher Del Close, this old hipster who was the mastermind behind it all. There were other improv groups, led by other teachers, but they didn't really do long form like Del taught. This is what I was waiting to hear. I called up my parents and said, "I'm leaving college." I had a semester and a half to go. And they were so fucking pissed at me. My mom had just remarried a guy who was a doctor, so they had a little bit of money. She said, "Look, if you stay, we'll buy you a car. We'll pay for you to go to law school." And I was like, "No, no. I'm going."

I literally sold my entire comic book collection that I owned growing up. I had the reboot of *Captain America* No. 1. I had *Iron Man* reboot No. 1. I had *Captain Marvel* No. 1. Yeah, I had a bunch of good ones. I had been smart enough to bag all of them. I had some good comics in great condition. I bought a Chrysler New Yorker with shag carpeting, power windows, and an eight-track player—there was already a tape in the player—from an elderly guy who could no longer drive. I then sold my baseball card collection for four hundred dollars, which paid for car insurance. Then my buddy and I put a gag lobster claw over the Chrysler emblem on the front of the car's hood and drove out to Chicago.

When you purchased the car, what tape was already in the eight-track player?

Jethro Tull's Greatest Hits.

Now, why would an elderly man in the 1980s be listening to Jethro Tull?

That's the question that will haunt me for life. My Rosebud question, right there.

When you headed out to Chicago, had you already given up on your stand-up act that you had started in college?

I had given it up. I had been doing stand-up all throughout college, on the weekends, and I just didn't like where my act was headed. It was more original and interesting when I started than what it eventually became. I had to create this bulletproof act that I could perform on the road, lasting about twenty minutes, that could get me through a rough night. In the end, I was doing airplane jokes and girlfriend jokes. I had a couple of original jokes, but I just wasn't that into it.

Hearing about this whole other world and this scene in Chicago sounded so intriguing to me. I was just looking for a change. At that point, I was writing short stories and thought maybe I could be a serious writer. I still had those ambitions. And that's what mostly attracted me to Chicago. It was a great blend of artistic ambitions combined with comedy, with maybe a slight commercial bent. It was a mix of artistic ambitions with straight-up laughs.

It didn't take long to meet, and then work with, Del Close.

How did that come about?

I got into Del's improv class and then started an improv group with a few other players. We had a pretty unique style to our group, so other players were attracted to it. It just kept getting more and more interesting. Del began to pay attention to our group, and he sort of adopted us. We invented all these improv forms, including something called "deconstruction."

With deconstruction we would take long scenes and then just break each of these scenes apart: thematically, narratively, symbolically, psychologically. We'd shatter the scenes and then put the pieces back together in different forms. We could revisit the beginning, jump to the end, reimagine each of the characters—anything, really.

We'd also do other types of improv, like "improvised movies." We'd improvise an entire movie in a three-act show. We'd do something called "The Dream." An audience member would tell us what happened to them that day, and we would show them the dream they were going to have that night. In its rawest form, it was a montage of their day. But when done well, we could bend the images and combine them and make it dreamlike. But it was also showing the audience the process: "Look, here are all the cards. We're not putting any of them up our sleeves. *Here they are.*" And then we'd start working off what was given to us.

Is it true that in the mid-nineties, while you were in the Chicago improv scene, you publicly improvised your own suicide?

Yes, that happened. I had an actor's photo, a horrible eight-by-ten glossy, that I inserted into a poster. And the poster read: "On such-and-such-a-date, Adam McKay, 26, will kill himself. This is not a joke." I put up the poster everywhere, and on the assigned location and date, there was a huge turnout. I went to the roof of a five-story building and yelled down to the crowd. We had a CPR dummy dressed exactly as I was dressed, and we threw it off the roof. Someone else was playing the character of the Grim Reaper, and he collected the dummy and hauled it away. Meanwhile, I ran downstairs and "came to life," and we all ended up back in the theater where we finished the show.

Good luck not getting arrested in New York with that stunt.

It was the type of thing you could only get away with in Chicago. [Laughs] Anywhere else, I'd have immediately been hauled away. But it was also the perfect time. Nowadays with the Internet, people would just go, "Oh, it's performance art" or "It's a flash mob" or whatever. But it wasn't commonplace back then. There weren't as many hidden-camera shows. Nowadays, this stuff is so common, you can't truly surprise people.

There was just this freedom. There was just a freedom to try to get away with whatever you felt you could get away with. Del Close encouraged that.

So Del would actually encourage improv that took place on the streets, in front of unsuspecting people?

Oh, my God, he loved it! You know, when I faked my own suicide, Del was on the street literally screaming, "Jump! Jump!" He had always thought our improv group was pretty good, but once we started doing these kind of stunts—we once even staged a fake street revolution, with audience members hitting the streets with lit torches and fake guns—an extra fondness came in. That's when Del really started knowing our names and caring about what we were doing.

Do you think you ever went too far with these stunts?

I might have done things differently if I could do them over again. There was one time when Scott Adsit [the actor who later played Pete Hornberger on *30 Rock*] and I and the rest of our group were performing in front of an audience. This was when Bill Clinton was president. Scott came out and said, "Ladies and gentlemen, I have some terrible news. President Clinton has just been assassinated." Scott's a really good actor and he played it very real. The whole crowd completely believed it. We then wheeled out a television to watch the most up-to-date news coverage. We turned it on and the audience saw NFL bloopers—we had already inserted a VHS tape. One of us yelled, "Wait, don't change it!" The whole cast came out and hunkered down and just started laughing at these football bloopers. The people in the audience slowly began to file out, dazed. That was the end of our show.

And you know, that's the kind of thing you do when you're twenty-five or twenty-six. Now that I'm a forty-four-year-old, I think, You can't do that. What happens if someone starts sobbing? What happens if. . . . There are too many *what ifs*. But at twenty-six, you're not quite that compassionate. I'll now bump into members of the improv group and say, "Can you believe we did that?" But that was part of the process. We were pushing things as far as they could go. And the only reason I accept it now is that there was real satire there: entertainment and silly pop culture trumping real information. But we probably should have popped it. There probably should have been some reveal at the end. Something to clue the audience in to the fact that what they had just seen was staged.

What did you take away from Del's improv teaching that you later applied to writing and directing?

He had two key tenants: one was to always go to your third thought. Sounds really simple, but when you're onstage, your first thought is knee-jerk. Your second thought is usually okay, but not great. Del would make you stay in a scene until you found your third thought, which was a little above and beyond what most other teachers would suggest. Basically, he wanted your third thought for your character choice, your third thought for your premise or your scene, your third thought for your heightened move.

Also, Del would make you do slow improv, and it was actually torturous. I don't know if you know the book *Thinking, Fast and Slow* [Farrar, Straus and Giroux, 2011]. It relates a lot to comedy, and just the creative process. The author, Daniel Kahneman, is a psychologist who won the [2002] Nobel Prize [in Economics]. His specialty is the psychology of decision making. The book is all about how we think: fast thinking and slow thinking. Fast thinking is what we do every day. It's intuitive; it's quick. Slow thinking is when you stop, shut out everything, really look into the foundations of the decisions you're making, and then make changes. It's extremely painful and uncomfortable. Kahneman performed all of these tests on slow thinking and found that the heart rate goes up; people begin to sweat. Especially in our fast-moving society, people hate it. But it's the key to everything. The people who are more comfortable in slow thinking are more successful, have higher IQs, earn more money. They're the innovators.

It was exactly what Del Close was doing. He was basically forcing us into slow thinking. Because of that, a lot of students were dropping out of Del's classes. There were many people who didn't enjoy working with him. There would be these other improv teachers who would create a sense of, "Everything's cool, everything's free and fun." People would go to those classes, and those people never got any better. The ones who hung with Del, you could see tangible changes. He was not there to make you feel comfortable or put a big smile on your face or stroke your esteem. He wanted you to change the way you were thinking, and he wanted to help you achieve that change.

Another lesson was to always play to the top of your intelligence. If you treat the audience like poets and geniuses, that's what they will become. Del never—*ever*—believed in playing down to the audience, in making cheap jokes. His feeling was, If you're going to make a stupid joke, make it brilliantly stupid. Our group started doing it, and we were like, "Holy shit, this actually works!" Audiences are way smarter than people give them credit for. Now, this doesn't mean that you can't do silly stuff. But when you play a kid, don't play a dumb kid. When you play someone drunk, don't play them overtly drunk. If *you're* drunk, play the character as if he's not acting overtly drunk.

Just very, very honest comedy. Improv is all about taking chances. You're going to fail at first, maybe even fail the first few times. But you don't have to be Oscar Wilde on every take. You can also be Frank Stallone on certain takes.

Let's talk about the films you've made. The characters you and Will have created for your movies—from Ron Burgundy in *Anchorman* to Ricky Bobby in *Talladega Nights* to Brennan Huff in *Step Brothers*—are filled with a tremendous self-confidence and bravado, most of it unearned. It's a type of bravado that seems different from the type seen in comedies from the seventies and eighties, in movies like *Slap Shot*, *Risky Business*, *Stripes*, and *Ghostbusters*, in which the characters actually accomplished something.

Well, I think America has changed so radically from the mid-seventies. I mean, to me, the mid-seventies was a kind of peak in America. It seemed that everything was working well. We withdrew from Vietnam, poverty was at an all-time low, people were properly suspicious of power in the right ways—as opposed to in manipulative ways. Now Americans think their country is number one despite all the numbers that prove to the contrary, and this fascinates me. I just think we let go of the reins in the last twenty, twenty-five years. It's a ridiculous, foolish confidence that America seems to have, for the most part.

Whereas back in the seventies and eighties, you saw this sort of mocking confidence, like in *Stripes*. You saw characters who had their asses kicked by higher, corrupt powers. You saw a lot of cynicism toward power and old establishment. You had *Caddyshack* making fun of country clubs and how ridiculous all that status was. You had *Animal House* mocking old blue-blood college institutions.

Nowadays, I think it's just a totally different game. There are different forces at work. The character of Ricky Bobby and the characters from *Step Brothers* are all idiots, and yet they have total confidence as they rule their domain. They have no skills, none whatsoever, yet they're completely entitled. Will and I are endlessly fascinated by this cockiness; it's all just completely unearned. It's not connected to any reality whatsoever. It's free-floating. They're not getting anywhere. They're stuck and impotent. I find this to be one of the most fascinating things about America right now.

So the characters in *Step Brothers* are cocky and entitled, but, at the same time, they don't have the least amount of power, beyond what takes place in their basement?

Exactly. That's what I mean. Two guys who have no life skills, no actual power, but who walk around completely entitled as if they have *all* the power. And that's so much of the American character right now. I remember once having an argument with a guy who was telling me that America has the best health-care system in the world. I said, "Well, based on what metric? Why are you saying that?" And he said, "Because we do." So I threw numbers out at him: life expectancy, infant mortality, time allowed in the hospital. America is ranked twenty-sixth, twenty-seventh in all those categories. And he said, "Yeah, but that doesn't matter because America's special, so we don't apply to those numbers." And I asked, "But how can you say we're number one?" And he said, "Are you saying I'm stupid?" That kind of conversation just says everything to me. "We're number one, and I don't care what anyone else says, or what reality says. We're number one!" And that's America in the last thirty years, really.

Does that tie into the Refusal-to-Grow-Up syndrome that a lot of your characters suffer from? Their insistence on remaining stunted? To continue to perform bong hits in their parents' house long past the age of thirty?

Totally. You never leave the bubble of your assumptions. You never think, Oh, shit, it's a much bigger world than I thought. Oh, I'm wrong! And, Wow, that's a whole new perspective! You just stay in the bubble of your own creation—or advertising's creation, or the media's creation. You just never leave it, and the more you're in it, the more you become invested in defending it, and the more cocky you become about it all, and the more you roll your eyes over anything that's to the contrary. That to me is the spiritual force that is behind the American decline. That's exactly what's been happening in the last thirty years. When you stop looking at reality, and you just start walking around like you're the best, you don't evolve. You're stuck in amber. You don't find roads for improvement. It's death, basically.

But it seems that one of the major reasons why your characters are so beloved is *because* they're stuck and are still doing bong hits in their parents' basements. Are the audience members picking up on the satire, many of whom might still be watching and doing bong hits in their parents' basements?

It's an interesting question. Maybe there is an artful way to be more overt while also keeping the comedy alive. I don't know. It's a tricky next step. Rather than just presenting the problem and laughing at it, we could somehow share how to go about fixing it. I don't know.

I think if you create the characters who confront the CEOs, you're writing [the 2007 George Clooney film] *Michael Clayton*. There's something a little old-fashioned about that, a character going after the big corporations. It feels like those movies from the seventies, like [1974's] *The Parallax View* and [1975's] *Three Days of the Condor* and [1976's] *All the President's Men*. It no longer feels realistic. It's not where America is right now. To me, it's more . . . I don't know. Everyone attacks this from a different angle. To Will and me, it becomes very, very funny when characters deny that the ship's sinking, even as the water's rising past their knees. Other people can write about characters confronting CEOs. We did do that a little bit in *The Other Guys*. That was in there. That was the first time we ever did anything like that. We did have the characters go into the belly of the corporate world in a way. But what we found was that our comedy swamped the story line a little bit. We thought it was really obvious, but when people saw that movie, they didn't really pick up on what we were doing.

What do you think they missed?

I remember people were blindsided by what we were saying. I was like, "Did you *see* the movie? The villain is from The Center for American Capitalism. The whole movie is about how chasing small-time drug crimes is meaningless. The real crimes, like the Bernie Madoff situation, are always taking place *behind* the scenes." That was the whole premise for the movie. And I was amazed when no one picked up on it. To me it was glaring.

Will Ferrell's character in *The Other Guys* is interesting. As opposed to the rest of the characters in the film, he did, in fact, have the guts to take on those in power. He was a bit strange, a bit of a nerd, and yet he was in no way meek.

When I was a freshman in college, my mom and her husband got this dog, a pure-breed Border collie. He was really inbred, so specific, so smart—but he was a little crazy. He would chase little movements around on the lawn, digging bizarre little holes. His hearing was incredible. He'd hear things that no other dogs, or people, could hear. The Ferrell character in *The Other Guys* is like that. He almost had an Asperger's quality to him. I remember learning about this financial analyst [Harry Markopolos] who uncovered, years before anyone else—way back in 2000—the Bernie Madoff crimes. He knew what Madoff was doing was a Ponzi scheme. He went to the SEC and even *The Wall Street Journal*. Neither did a thing. Meanwhile, Madoff was making comments about this guy, really dismissive comments: "This guy is a joke. Everyone on Wall Street laughs at that guy." Well, guess what? The guy was right, and he had the guts to stand before everyone and say as much.

When you put that type of heroism on the right rail, it's unstoppable. When it's on the wrong rail, it doesn't make sense. I thought, at the time, maybe we should start listening to these guys who aren't the best dressed in the room, who aren't the most charismatic. Maybe we should start focusing on the right answers as opposed to those people who have the best haircuts. And that's how Will's character in *The Other Guys* came about.

The actor John C. Reilly, who was in *Talladega Nights* and *Step Brothers*, has said in interviews that the most subversive people he knows in Hollywood are solely focused on creating comedy. Do you agree with that?

I do. To me one of the most heroic acts of the last fifteen years was Stephen Colbert doing his character right in front of George W. Bush at the 2006 White House Correspondents' Dinner. I mean, it was really amazing. I think in ten years you're going to see a movie about that. That was incredible. At a time when our press just had their tails between their legs, this guy stood up and called out the inanity and insanity, the criminality of what was going on. It was amazing.

There are so many great, bold comedies. Look at the [2006, Mike Judge–directed] movie *Idiocracy*. It's about a future where everyone is an idiot. If we were living in slightly hipper times that would have been our *Dr. Strangelove*. Brilliant movie. Just a buck knife down the middle of the tree. Mike Judge went after specific targets, like Starbucks. But it was kind of overlooked, which happens. In the future, according to the movie, Starbucks will be giving out hand jobs. So brave. Maybe audiences just didn't get the satire, but it is brilliant.

Do you think comedy is more effective for change than drama?

I think what's great about comedy is that it's like pornography and horror. In the sense that if you're not feeling the tingle that's promised by the genre you know it's bullshit. There's no greater truth detector than comedy. You can tell when someone is full of shit immediately. Also, comedy tends to travel. If someone laughs at something, they'll laugh at it in South Carolina and they'll laugh about it on the Upper East Side of New York. So I think what's great about horror and comedy is that both travel. If someone's funny, anyone can see it. I've found that just as many Republicans love *Anchorman* as left wingers. In fact, maybe even slightly more.

I remember [former United States Army] General McChrystal saying *Talladega Nights* was his favorite movie. It's bizarre. Huge right wingers just love that movie even though the film was inspired by George W. Bush. It just travels really well. That's what's exciting about it, actually. In these crazy times when the truth is sort of hazed out, a movie like that always tends to work really well.

There was a study from a few years ago where it was discovered that Stephen Colbert has a lot of Republican viewers who don't quite understand that he's joking. It's amazing. I've heard people say, "I kind of like him." I'll ask, "You do know he's completely making fun of such and such, right?" And they're like, "Oh, no. He's just a cheeky kind of guy, but he's basically a Republican." I'd think, Oh, my God, I know Stephen. He's not! He's most definitely not a Republican!

In some ways, this happens with our movies, too, which is okay by me. Our movies are fun, hopefully. They're fun, bright movies, so there's a lot to enjoy on different levels.

Since you began making comedy films more than a decade ago, it seems that the genre has only exploded in popularity.

I saw a guy the other day at a wedding, and I told him my theory on why we've seen this explosion in comedies in the past fifteen years. Number one, America is tacking hard to the right. That sort of extremism always kind of kicks up the need to create comedy. But the second thing is Avid.

What's Avid?

It's a digital movie-editing program that directors use, and it's incredibly helpful. I think Avid is hugely responsible for this boom in comedy. In the past, one would have to shoot the film and edit it, which was a big deal. Now, filmmakers can record the laughs from a test audience at a screening, and we can then cut to the rhythm of those laughs, the rhythm of the audience. We synchronize the laughs with the film. We can really get our timing down to a hundredth of a second. You can decide where you want your story to kick in, where you want a little bit of mood, where you want a hard laugh line. All of this can really be calibrated to these test screenings that we do. It doesn't mean that it becomes mathematical. It still ultimately means that you have to make creative choices, but you can just really get a lot out of it. Sort of like surgery with a laser compared with a regular scalpel.

We're able to download a movie onto the computer and literally do all our edits in minutes. The precision is incredible. You play back the audio of the test screening and get everything timed just right. Like, "*This* laugh is losing this next line; let's split the difference *here*." You're able to achieve this rolling energy. You can try experimental edits, and do multiple test screenings, and it's all because you can move so fast with this program. Comedy is the one genre that I think has just really benefited from this more than any other.

This process sounds a lot more useful for comedy writers and directors than reading the suggestion cards from audience members left at test screenings.

Test cards are almost useless to me. I can never get any use out of focus groups or test cards. What works best for me is sitting with an audience, which is the greatest thing. There's nothing better than feeling the energy in the room. That's the best, but the audio we use with Avid is incredibly helpful. I think Jay Roach [the director of *Austin Powers*, *Meet the Parents*, *The Campaign*] was the one who started doing it, although the Marx Brothers, eighty years ago, used to take their scripts out on the road to perform them live. They'd then rewrite the scripts based on the audiences' reactions. We wanted to do this with the script for *Anchorman 2*, but for whatever reason never got around to it.

What's the worst audience note you ever received for any of your movies?

There's no greater comedy killer than receiving a note that says a character's not likable enough. The second you see someone write that, you know they don't know a thing about comedy. The entire game is to make your character as awful and irresponsible as possible, while still keeping a toe in the pool of his still being a human being. I mean, that's the game. That's the game you're playing. The more despicable your guy can get away with behaving while still remaining on the side of the audience, the funnier it'll be. *Seinfeld* is the greatest example of that ever.

According to showbiz legend, an audience member left the following note during the previews for 1988's *Rain Man*: "I was hoping the little guy would snap out of it."

Come on! Oh, that's great! That's fantastic. Kind of typical, unfortunately, although I actually do find some negative notes very encouraging. Or negative reviews. There were some bad reviews I received where I thought, Good. This means the movie's doing what it's supposed to be doing. Roger Ebert said that *Step Brothers* was symbolic of the end of Western culture.[1] I thought, That's *exactly* the response he should be having. For me, that's just a sound. It's like when a boxer gets punched, they make a certain kind of noise that clues the other boxer as to how much damage is being done. So reading that from Roger Ebert felt like we had accomplished what we had set out to do.

---

1   "When did comedies get so mean? *Step Brothers* has a premise that might have produced a good time at the movies, but when I left, I felt a little unclear. . . . Sometimes I think I am living in a nightmare. All about me, standards are collapsing, manners are evaporating, people show no respect for themselves. I am not a moralistic nut. I'm proud of the X-rated movie I once wrote [1970's *Beyond the Valley of the Dolls*]. I like vulgarity if it's funny or serves a purpose. But what is going on here?"—Roger Ebert, *Chicago Sun Times,* July 24, 2008.

For three seasons, you were the head writer at _Saturday Night Live,_ a show that's sometimes been criticized for still adhering to a writing schedule more conducive to the coked-out seventies than today. Do you feel that _SNL's_ schedule—including all-night writing sessions on Tuesday nights—is helpful or harmful to the comedy-writing process?

I always found it pretty great, actually. Monday you would get your ideas together. On Tuesday, you'd really start in earnest at around one o'clock in the afternoon. You'd then write for fourteen hours straight. Often, you'd end up writing even longer, until nine or ten in the morning. Some of the best material came out of staying up all night when you were half asleep.

But, yeah, the time we spent at _Saturday Night Live_ was a very different time from the seventies, with all of that craziness. We would go out and drink, but it was all pretty laid-back. You'd be bopping around to different people's offices. You'd dig in with one group of writers, you'd finish writing the sketch, you'd go visit another group of writers. And I remember just writing crazy amounts. That sense of a deadline is so helpful. It forces pages out of you. So some of the highest volume of writing I've ever done in my life was for that show.

Do you remember any specific sketches or jokes that were created solely because you had been up all night?

What usually came from staying up all night were "ten to one" sketches. Meaning, the last sketch of the show that aired at ten to one in the morning. I remember it was once five in the morning, and Ferrell and I found out that Robert Duvall was going to make a guest appearance. We tried to figure out something to write for him. I said, "I'd like for you to give him a sponge bath," and Ferrell said, "Well, I'd like to sing to him." And I said, "Well, I'd like for you to give him a sponge bath while you sing 'Lay Lady Lay.'" And that was it. We wrote a sketch where Will was a weird hospital orderly who ended up giving Robert Duvall a sponge bath while singing Bob Dylan's "Lay Lady Lay." Four days later it was on the air.

Is the last half hour at *SNL* viewed with contempt by the writers? Or is it seen as an opportunity to air more interesting material?

I think for a lot of the writers it's the best. That was the place you wanted to be because you had a chance to get away with a crazy sketch. At the same time, some of these stranger sketches would play well enough that it would then go higher in the show. Which was great, because it just meant more people saw it. But no, no writer ever looked down on the last half hour. The only time you ever saw someone upset would be a cast member who might have written a sketch that was supposed to contain a big, fat hit character and it didn't quite play. Lorne would sometimes drop something like that to the very end of the show.

What percentage of *SNL* sketches, on average, would kill at read-throughs with staff members on Wednesday afternoons but never make it to the air on Saturday nights?

Maybe 40 percent to 50 percent. I remember I once wrote a sketch with Ferrell playing a doctor telling a patient that they were going to die. While the doctor was talking to the patient, he was also eating a giant tuna sub. Real messy. The tuna was dripping onto his clothes, dropping to the floor. It just killed in the read-though. But then in the big studio, the audience didn't get into it at all. It was just dead silence the entire time. Actually, that was a pretty common experience.

Were there certain types of sketches that would hit with audiences more than others?

There were many factors at play. A lot of it had to do with the sketch that came before yours. If you were sort of trying to do something small and funny, and the sketch before yours was the Cheerleaders [starring Will Ferrell and Cheri Oteri], you'd just get swamped. The audience was looking in one direction with cheerleaders and then suddenly your little sketch would come along and it would just get swallowed whole. That big studio floor could make subtle ideas feel very small, and they could get lost. There were a lot of factors at play.

And, quite often, a sketch would kill in dress rehearsal and would *still* get cut. I wouldn't understand why.

Even as the head writer you didn't understand why?

Even as the head writer I wouldn't understand why. Will and I once wrote a sequel to our Neil Diamond storyteller sketch. Will played Neil Diamond as if he were on the show *VH1 Storytellers*. Before each song, "Neil" would explain the songs' origins. "Cracklin' Rosie" was about a hit-and-run. "Cherry, Cherry" was about the time Neil killed a drifter. These were really fun, poppy songs, but they each had these horrific backstories. The first of these Neil Diamond sketches went over really well, so we wrote a sequel with Helen Hunt playing Christina Aguilera singing along with Neil Diamond. It got a ton of laughs the whole way through, and then it got cut. I was really baffled by it. But you know, there's never going to be consistency, really. After you're at *SNL* for a couple years, you learn not to look for consistency. You kind of take it as it is and move on and try to remember to be super grateful that you're working in New York City on a show where you get to write this crazy stuff. My last two years were definitely the most fun I had on that show, because I wasn't as obsessed with "Why didn't that sketch get in?" Your first couple years, you think everything should be perfect. Once you let that go, it's a really fun show to work on.

You came of age pre-Internet, when a site like Funny or Die wasn't even remotely possible. Do you think your writing and comedy style would have been different if you had grown up connected?

Truthfully, I think it would have been bad for me. I think there's a chance that I would never have left my hometown. The reason I left Philadelphia to begin with was that there was no sketch, no improv, and that's what I really wanted to do. If the Internet had been around, I would have found four or five people who also wanted to do it, and we would've just started shooting videos. Back then you had to head to Chicago. I'm curious if that's changed in Chicago. It was like a migration when we were there. There were people from everywhere. In the Upright Citizens Brigade, we had Matt Besser from Arkansas, Ian Roberts from New Jersey, Rachel Dratch from Massachusetts. People were from everywhere.

On the other hand, the truth is that if you've got a group of funny friends and you make videos, these videos will be found. Funny or Die has workers that only look for funny videos. The studios, and the networks, they're all looking for good comedy. It can easily be found now. So that can only be a good thing.

How would you like your movies to be remembered?

As a kid, I just loved watching the Marx Brothers and the Three Stooges and seeing that kind of wild, anarchic craziness. I remember thinking, Oh, my God, someone else gets that feeling! I found that really hopeful. When you're a kid, you just want to throw bottles against a wall. I would love it if my movies played like that. I would love it if in twenty-five, thirty years there are kids watching these movies on Saturday afternoons, and they can't believe what they're seeing. That, to me, would be the best—if these movies had that same kind of anarchic, crazy, head-over-feet kind of quality to them. I think the role of comedy is to break down all those barriers we put around ourselves.

Any last words of advice for those writers who are just starting their careers?

I would say that there are a lot of books out there about how to make it, how to audition, and a lot of these books talk about making connections and networking. It's all about *who* you know. That's actually the biggest mistake a lot of people make. It's really about jumping in and doing it, and just starting to write, starting to make sketches and movies, and just putting them up on the Internet no matter who or where you are. You just have to start doing it—even if you're not getting paid.

How much of success is just sticking with something? It seems that every comedy writer I know has at least one very funny friend who potentially could have made it as a comedy writer if they had only decided to take—or just stay on—that particular route.

I think most of life is just about the choices you make. I don't think there are these special, glowing skills people have. If you or I, at age six, decided that we were going to become swimmers, I'm not saying we'd go to the Olympics, but we would have become pretty damn good swimmers. There's no question that I had friends growing up who were funny as shit. I had a friend who made me laugh harder than anyone. I had another buddy who could have easily been a comedy writer. This guy and I created a fake newsletter in high school that we sent out to fellow students. We created a fake organization; I think it was called Children of the Constitution. It was like an underground newsletter making fun of all of the ass-kissers in our school. He ended up becoming an actuary. Another very funny friend now sells rare books.

All these guys could have made a career out of writing comedy. Part of success is just starting something, working toward a goal, and then living long enough to achieve it.

I suppose that ego also plays a part. Some sense of self-regard that says, I can do this just as well as anyone, so why shouldn't I give it a try?

For me, it wasn't a great burst of "I'm funny!" It was a very slow easing into it.

You usually struggle in the dark for years and years. The trick is that if you love it enough you'll keep going. For people who don't truly like it, those are the people who usually fade away. Those are usually the ones who say, "I wanna be famous. I want everyone to look at me." That type of person weeds itself out at a certain point.

Is that a common sentiment you hear from wannabe comedy writers? "I want to be famous"?

It's the most common mistake out here in Hollywood. The biggest mistake is that people go into comedy solely for the money. It's just a dead end—always. People will ask me, "How much do you get paid?" Or, even more annoying, I'll hear, "It's all about who you know." That kind of approach. I hear it thousands of times. But it's not true. There are corporations out here that *want* to make money. If you're good, they will find you. You could be in North Dakota putting videos on YouTube. If you're funny, believe me, Funny or Die will find you. It's not about who you know at all. That only happens once things begin to percolate, and that happens naturally.

There are two kinds of people in comedy: those who just really love doing it, which is how my group sort of started. We just loved doing it. We weren't making any money. We would have kept on doing it as long as we could have gotten away with it. I'd still be doing it in Chicago. I'd be teaching improv; I'd be making twenty-four thousand dollars a year. It was never about any kind of money or fame or success. We just loved doing it. And then there's the type of person who gets into comedy thinking, I'm going to make it. I'm going to break big! And that is not the attitude to have. There are some people who can have that attitude and still make it, of course, but most won't.

I heard [the basketball player] Kobe Bryant talking the other day about NBA players who love the game versus those players who love the lifestyle the game brings to them. And Kobe felt that that was what separated the great players from the okay players. Athletes who really love to play are the ones who do well, and the athletes who kind of like it, but really want to be successful, well, that's a much harder road to go down. So you just have to make sure you really love it. I think that holds true for most professions, including writing humor.

More than anything, though, I've found through the years that a lot of people try and set rules when it comes to comedy. The second you start believing that, you are fucked. They say, "*This* is the way it is." But these are just general guidelines. The whole basis of comedy is surprise and shock. It has to be. So take all of the rules I just gave you and ignore them. Create comedy that breaks all of the rules. In the end, that's the most exciting stuff. So, yeah, my last words of advice would be, "Fuck me."

A List by BILL HADER

··

Two Hundred Essential Movies
Every Comedy Writer Should See

Here's a list of movies that I find funny and that I think every comedy writer should see. Some of these movies will be obvious (*Airplane!*), others curious (*Eyes Wide Shut*), but it's a personal list, so I don't know what to tell you. I've learned a lot from watching movies over the years—when it comes to both writing and acting—and I've found that these films, in particular, were the most influential. I tried to keep the list to movies that can easily be found on Netflix and the like. Enjoy!

9 to 5 (1980)
1941 (1979)
Abbott and Costello Meet Frankenstein (1948)
Ace in the Hole (1951)
The Adventures of Baron Munchausen (1988)
After Hours (1985)

Airplane! (1980)
Amarcord (1973)
American Graffiti (1973)
An American in Paris (1951)
Animal Crackers (1930)
Annie Hall (1977)
The Apartment (1960)
Army of Darkness (1992)
Arsenic and Old Lace (1944)
Back to the Future (1985)
The Bad News Bears (1976)
Bananas (1971)
The Band Wagon (1953)
The Bank Dick (1940)
Barton Fink (1991)
Beetlejuice (1988)
Being There (1979)
Best in Show (2000)
Better Off Dead (1985)
Big Deal on Madonna Street (1958)
The Big Lebowski (1998)
The Birdcage (1996)
Blazing Saddles (1974)
The Blues Brothers (1980)
Boogie Nights (1997)
Born Yesterday (1950)
Bottle Rocket (1996)
Boudu Saved from Drowning (1932)
Brazil (1985)
Broadway Danny Rose (1984)
Bullets Over Broadway (1994)
The 'Burbs (1989)
Cabin in the Sky (1943)
Caddyshack (1980)
Catch-22 (1970)
The Circus (1928)
City Lights (1931)

A Clockwork Orange (1971)
Closely Watched Trains (1966)
The Cocoanuts (1929)
Coming to America (1988)
The Court Jester (1956)
Crimes and Misdemeanors (1989)
Dames (1934)
A Day at the Races (1937)
Dazed and Confused (1993)
Design for Living (1933)
Dirty Rotten Scoundrels (1988)
Down by Law (1986)
Dr. Strangelove (1964)
Drag Me to Hell (2009)
Duck Soup (1933)
Ed Wood (1994)
Election (1999)
The Evil Dead (1981)
Evil Dead 2 (1987)
Eyes Wide Shut (1999)
Fargo (1996)
Ferris Bueller's Day Off (1986)
The Fireman's Ball (1967)
A Fish Called Wanda (1988)
The Foot Fist Way (2006)
The Fortune (1975)
Four Lions (2010)
Gates of Heaven (1978)
The General (1926)
Get Shorty (1995)
Ghostbusters (1984)
The Gold Rush (1925)
Good Morning (1959
The Goonies (1985)
The Graduate (1967)
Grand Illusion (1937)
The Great Race (1965)

The Groove Tube (1974)
Groundhog Day (1993)
Hail the Conquering Hero (1944)
Heaven Can Wait (1943)
His Girl Friday (1940)
Horse Feathers (1932)
The Hudsucker Proxy (1994)
I Vitelloni (1953)
I Wanna Hold Your Hand (1978)
I'm Gonna Git You Sucka (1988)
The Incredibles (2004)
It Happened One Night (1934)
It's a Gift (1934)
It's Always Fair Weather (1955)
The Jerk (1979)
Jules and Jim (1962)
The Kentucky Fried Movie (1977)
The King of Comedy (1983)
Kung Fu Hustle (2004)
L'Atalante (1934)
The Ladykillers (1955)
The Last Detail (1973)
The Lavender Hill Mob (1951)
Let It Ride (1989)
The Life Aquatic with Steve Zissou (2004)
The Life and Death of Colonel Blimp (1943)
Little Murders (1971)
Lolita (1962)
The Long Goodbye (1973)
Lost in America (1985)
Love and Death (1975)
Loves of a Blonde (1965)
M*A*S*H (1970)
The Man in the White Suit (1951)
The Man with Two Brains (1983)
A Matter of Life and Death (1946)
The Merry Widow (1934)

Midnight Run (1988)
The Miracle of Morgan's Creek (1944)
Modern Romance (1981)
Mon Oncle (1958)
Monkey Business (1931)
Monsters, Inc. (2001)
Monty Python and the Holy Grail (1975)
Monty Python's Life of Brian (1979)
Mr. Hulot's Holiday (1953)
Mr. Mom (1983)
Mystery Train (1989)
The Naked Gun (1988)
Nashville (1975)
National Lampoon's Animal House (1978)
Never Give a Sucker an Even Break (1941)
A Night at the Opera (1935)
Noises Off (1992)
One, Two, Three (1961)
Orgazmo (1997)
Our Hospitality (1923)
Out of Sight (1998)
The Palm Beach Story (1942)
Parenthood (1989)
Pee-wee's Big Adventure (1985)
Play Time (1967)
The Player (1992)
The Princess Bride (1987)
The Producers (1968)
Punch-Drunk Love (2002)
Radio Days (1987)
Raising Arizona (1987)
Real Life (1979)
The Royal Tenenbaums (2001)
Ruggles of Red Gap (1935)
Rushmore (1998)
Safe Men (1998)
Salesman (1968)

Schizopolis (1996)
A Serious Man (2009)
Shaolin Soccer (2001)
Shaun of the Dead (2004)
Sherlock Jr. (1924)
Shoot the Piano Player (1960)
The Shop Around the Corner (1940)
Short Cuts (1993)
Singin' in the Rain (1952)
Sixteen Candles (1984)
Songs from the Second Floor (2000)
South Park: Bigger, Longer & Uncut (1999)
The Squid and the Whale (2005)
Stranger Than Paradise (1984)
Stripes (1981)
Sullivan's Travels (1941)
Take the Money and Run (1969)
Talladega Nights (2006)
Team America (2004)
This Is Spinal Tap (1984)
Three Amigos! (1986)
Time Bandits (1981)
To Be or Not to Be (1942)
Toy Story (1995)
Toy Story 2 (1999)
Toy Story 3 (2010)
Trading Places (1983)
Trouble in Paradise (1932)
Twentieth Century (1934)
Unfaithfully Yours (1948)
Up (2009)
Used Cars (1980)
Vernon, Florida (1981)
Waiting for Guffman (1997)
A Wedding (1978)
Wet Hot American Summer (2001)
What's Up, Doc? (1972)

What's Up Tiger Lily? (1966)
The White Sheik (1952)
Withnail and I (1987)
You Can't Cheat an Honest Man (1939)
You Can't Take It with You (1938)
You the Living (2007)
Young Frankenstein (1974)
Zelig (1983)
Zero for Conduct (1933)

PURE, HARD-CORE ADVICE

SCOTT JACOBSON
....

Writer, *The Daily Show*, *Bob's Burgers*

There's a hierarchy of television comedy writing jobs, and like most hierarchies (the ones you'll find within troops of orangutans, say, or pods of *HuffPo* commenters) it's brutal and a little ridiculous. You see it reinforced in the attitudes of your fellow comedy writers: Work for a smart, boundary-pushing late-night show? Good for you, kid. Think of it as a fun stepping stone. Work on a featherweight multi-cam sitcom starring five hot people pretending to be romantically inept? Congratulations! You have arrived.

There are plenty of exceptions. A job writing for, say, *Saturday Night Live* is more glamorous and carries more cachet than your average sitcom job. And status aside, any working comedy writer is just grateful to be employed.

But comedy writers on late-night shows often aspire to be sitcom writers, for the simple reason that the sitcom world offers more room for professional growth and the potential for bigger royalty checks. Some of the smartest, most charismatic and talented writers I've known have been late-night comedy lifers. They'd like to get hired on a sitcom that insults their intelligence and stuffs them firmly behind the camera (on some late-night shows writers get the chance to perform on-air), but it's a difficult leap to make. Sitcom writers guard their territory with the jealousy of people who know there aren't enough jobs to go around. And there really aren't enough jobs to go around.

Which is easier, writing for a late-night show or a sitcom? If you had asked me right after I started my sitcom job after five years at a late-night show, I would have said sitcoms are easier. The average workday at a late-night show is fast-paced and stressful. You are, after all, turning around material for a program that airs that night. Days at a sitcom can sometimes be just as demanding. But other days—often the ones spent breaking stories—can feel downright leisurely. To an outside observer they look a bit like closing time at an opium den. Writers lounge on couches, staring at a bulletin board with index cards tacked to it and tossing out half-baked ideas. One or two people fall asleep. Snacks are available.

But appearances in this case are deceiving. When I made the jump from late-night to scripted I was what you'd call inexperienced at writing sitcoms—or, if you were being less charitable, awful at it. I was cocky because I had assumed that years of watching half-hour comedies would make writing for one an intuitive exercise. I'd given a bit of thought to writing interesting characters but hadn't troubled myself with the intricacies of story structure beyond getting high once and talking to a friend about Joseph Campbell.

What I now realize is that those slow-paced story days, as numbing as they can be, are really when all the mental heavy lifting happens. Joke-writing days are fast-paced, but they're a much more mechanical exercise. On a good day, jokes are easy. You can churn 'em out. A satisfying story that serves the characters while building the world of the show and hitting all the network-mandated precommercial emotional crescendos—that's something that takes painstaking work.

So . . . which is the better gig for the comedy writer, sitcoms or late-night? My cop-out answer is that both are challenging and desirable in their own way. And while one tends to pay more than the other, both pay roughly a zillion times more than substitute teaching, which is what I was doing before I got my first comedy job. So let's just say the system works and leave it at that.

BRUCE JAY FRIEDMAN

During his five-decade (and counting) writing career, Bruce Friedman has published eight novels, four story collections, numerous plays, and such screenplays as *Stir Crazy* (1980) and *Splash* (1984), for which he was nominated for Best Original Screenplay.

Though he never became a household name, Friedman has many famous admirers and friends. *The Godfather* author Mario Puzo once described Friedman's stories as being "like a *Twilight Zone* with Charlie Chaplin." Neil Simon adapted Friedman's short story "A Change of Plan" (originally published in *Esquire* magazine) into a 1972 movie blockbuster, *The Heartbreak Kid*, directed by Elaine May and starring Charles Grodin and May's daughter, Jeannie Berlin. Steve Martin, who turned Friedman's semiautobiographical book *The Lonely Guy's Book of Life* (1978) into a feature film in 1984, provided a back-cover blurb for Friedman's story collection, *Even the Rhinos Were Nymphos* (2000), that perfectly, if sarcastically, summarizes the sentiments of so many of his contemporaries and would-be imitators: "I am not jealous."

In 1962, while working full-time as an editor of various men's magazines, Friedman published his first novel, *Stern*, which is widely considered to be his masterpiece. The book, which Friedman wrote in a mere six months, when he was in his early thirties, tells the story of a man who leaves the city for the suburbs, only to discover his new home is far from the tranquil residential development of his imagination. He's attacked by neighborhood dogs. He develops an ulcer. His family is harassed by an anti-Semite, who, during one altercation, pushes Stern's wife to the ground. The reader never learns Stern's first name.

Born in the Bronx in 1930, Friedman's initial ambition was to become a doctor—at first. Switching gears, he ultimately decided to earn a bachelor's degree in journalism from the University of Missouri. But his true literary education came while serving as a first lieutenant in the United States Air Force, from 1951 to 1953. According to Friedman, his commanding officer suggested he read three novels: Thomas Wolfe's *Of Time and the River*, James Jones's *From Here to Eternity*, and J. D. Salinger's *The Catcher in the Rye*. After consuming these novels in a single weekend, Friedman realized that he wanted to attempt to write fiction for a living.

Along with Kurt Vonnegut, Friedman is often credited as being one of the pioneers of "dark comedy." In 2011, Dwight Garner, a book critic for *The New York Times*, wrote that Friedman's *The Lonely Guy's Book of Life* "makes low-level depression and ineptitude seem stylish and ironic, almost a supreme way of being in the world." From plays like *Steambath* (1970), in which it's revealed that a Puerto Rican steam-room attendant is God, to short stories such as 1963's "When You're Excused, You're Excused," in which the main character tries to convince his wife to let him skip Yom Kippur to work out at the gym, Friedman's take on humanity is bleak, but always amusingly realistic.

In his foreword to *Black Humor*, an anthology he edited in 1965, Friedman argued that the thirteen writers presented in the collection weren't just "brooding and sulking sorts" determined to find levity in the world's misery. Rather, they were "discover[ing] new land" by "sailing into darker waters somewhere out beyond satire." Not surprisingly, the very same sentiment could be used to describe Bruce Jay Friedman.

I've read that you don't like to be known as a humorist.

I don't, especially. James Thurber, Robert Benchley, S. J. Perelman—they are the great humorists. They set out to make you laugh. That's never my intention, although it's often the result. As a writer, I couldn't possibly be more serious. Sometimes the work is expressed comedically. The hope is that it's unforced and doesn't seem worked on, which, of course, it is.

So you agree with Joseph Heller that humor isn't the goal, per se, but the means to the goal?

I'm not comfortable with the idea of "using" humor to achieve a purpose. I can't imagine Evelyn Waugh, while writing [the 1928 satiric novel] *Decline and Fall*, saying, "I think I'll use a little humor *here*." But there's a theory that a writer can't make a claim to greatness unless there's a streak of comedy in his work. There may be some truth to that.

I'm not much good at jokes, can't remember them. However, once upon a time, I volunteered to be the master of ceremonies at a sorority event at the University of Missouri, which I attended in the late forties and early fifties. The mic went dead after about six jokes, all of which were borrowed from a Borscht Belt comedian. One was, "I don't have to be doing this for a living, folks. I could be selling bagels to midgets for toilet seats." The room was filled with gorgeous women who began to talk among themselves and to cross and uncross their legs.

I became rattled and shouted out, "Will you please quiet down? Don't you see I'm trying to be *funny* here?" I then fainted. Someone named Roth helped revive me. "What did you have to faint for?" he asked. "You were terrific."

In 1965, you put together *Black Humor*, a collection of short stories featuring such writers as Thomas Pynchon, Terry Southern, John Barth, and Vladimir Nabokov. In the foreword, you coined and popularized the term "black humor." You've since said that you feel somewhat stuck with that term.

I do. I hear it all the time, and it makes me wince. Essentially, it was a chance for me to pick up some money—not that much, actually—and to read some writers whose work was new to me.

In retrospect, a more accurate term would have been *tense comedy*—there's much to laugh at on the surface, but with streaks of agony running beneath. I had no idea the term *black humor* would catch fire to the extent that it did—and last this many years. The academics, starving for a new category, wolfed it down.

What similarities did you notice among these "black humorist" writers' works?

Each one had a different signature, but the tone generally was much darker than what was found in most popular fiction at the time. There was a thin line between reality and the fantastical. Their works featured ill-fated heroes. It also confronted—perhaps not consciously—social issues that hadn't been touched on. Pressed to the wall, I'll use a term that's sickeningly in vogue today: It was *edgy*.

Why do you think the term "black humor" became so popular, so quickly?

It's catchy, and that's appealing to publishers, critics, academics. Some of it may have had to do with the political and social climate of the mid-sixties. The drugs, the Pill, the music, the war—comedy had to find some new terrain with which to deal with all of this. I imagine each generation feels the same.

After the book was published in 1965, my publisher threw a huge "Black Humor" party—I still have the invitation—and the whole world showed up. I recall Mike Nichols and Elaine May having a high old time. The "black humor" label started to get reprinted and quoted after that party, and it never stopped. Ridiculous.

When did you begin writing your first novel, *Stern*?

In 1960; it took about six months. I had been trying to write another book for three or four years, but it never came together. Certain notions aren't born to be novels. I figured that out—at great expense.

I wrote *Stern* on the subway and train to and from work. I wrote it in a heat, like I was being chased down an alley.

Stern seems like a break from the type of books that came before it. It seems more ethnic; more psychoanalytic. The main character is an anxiety-ridden Jewish nebbish who feels taken advantage of by his Gentile suburban neighbor. The book was very influential for a lot of writers, including Joseph Heller, Nora Ephron, Philip Roth, and, later, John Kennedy Toole, the author of *A Confederacy of Dunces*, who called it his favorite modern novel. When you were working on it, did you feel as if you were working on something new?

I was simply trying to write a good book—and an honest one—after struggling with a book that kept falling apart. I was living in the suburbs and feeling isolated, cut off from the city. I constructed a small and painful event, and I wrote a novel around it—a man's wife falls to the ground, without any underwear, and is seen by an anti-Semitic neighbor. I hoped the book would be published and that afterward I wouldn't be run out of the country. I'm quite serious. I thought I'd hide in Paris until it all blew over. Such ego. It's not as if I had a dozen book ideas to choose from. *Stern* was the one I had—the story felt compelling—and that's the one I wrote.

This main character was not your typical macho, male literary hero; he was fearful about many things, including sex.

I certainly had that side at the time. All writing is autobiographical, in my view, including scientific papers.

Stern was a book that was in direct contrast to the short stories I had written up to that time. I'm told that it was a departure from much of the era's fiction. *The New Yorker* literary critic Stanley Edgar Hyman called it "the first true Freudian novel." It only sold six thousand copies. The editor, Robert Gottlieb, who edited *Catch-22*, which was published just before *Stern*, told me that they were the "right copies." I remember wondering what it would have been like if it sold a hundred thousand *wrong* copies.

The only book that had a distant echo was Richard Yates's

Revolutionary Road. And, of course, John Cheever's stories, which touched on suburban alienation in New England.

Do you think that *Stern* influenced *Revolutionary Road,* which was written around the same time?

I doubt it, but I do know that Yates was aware of it. I knew Yates when I was working as an editor in the fifties and sixties, at the Magazine Management Co., which published men's adventure magazines. He just showed up without explanation for a few weeks, this man with a handsome and ruined, disheveled look, and attached himself to our little group—and then he disappeared. From time to time he'd call me from the Midwest to ask if I could get him a job. It annoyed me that he thought of me as a publisher or producer. Never once did he acknowledge that I was a writer. But I later learned that *Stern* was one of the few novels that he taught in his writing classes.

Yates had a difficult life. He was a major alcoholic, and he always struggled for money. In other words, your basic serious novelist.

It's a shame that Yates's life was so difficult. He was a brilliant writer, and a very funny one.

I agree. He was a gifted man—his writing was pitch-perfect—but he probably had a demon or two more than the rest of us. He'd complain that if *Catch-22* hadn't been such a big hit, *Revolutionary Road* would have been a bestseller.

There was an incident in which a few writers and editors, including myself, went out for a drink in the early seventies, and Yates joined us. He drank so much that he collapsed and fell forward, hitting his head on the table. My secretary at the time, who hadn't paid much attention to him, pulled him to his feet, and off they went together. I never saw either of them again. They ended up living together.

Tell me about your experience editing adventure magazines in the 1950s and 1960s for the Magazine Management Co. What were some of the publications under the company's umbrella?

There were more than a hundred, in every category—movies, adventure, confession, paperback books, Stan Lee's comic books. Stan worked there for years and years. The office was located on Madison Avenue in Midtown Manhattan. I was responsible for about five magazines. One was called *Focus*. It was a smaller version of *People*, before that magazine was even published.

I also worked as editor of *Swank*. Every now and then the publisher, Martin Goodman, would appear at my office door and say, "I am throwing you another magazine." Some others that were "thrown" at me included *Male, Men, Man's World*, and *True Action*.

Swank was not the pornographic magazine we know today, I assume?

Entirely different, and I don't say that with pride. Mr. Goodman—his own brother called him "Mr. Goodman"—told me to publish a "takeoff" on *Esquire*. This was difficult. I had a staff of one, the magazine was published on cheap paper, and it contained dozens of ads for automotive equipment and trusses, which are medical devices for hernia patients.

When I was there, it wasn't even soft-core porn; it was flabby porn. There was no nudity, God forbid, but there were some pictures of women wearing bathing suits—not even bikinis—and winking. There were also stories from the trunk—*deep* in the trunk—from literary luminaries such as [novelist and playwright] William Saroyan and Graham Greene and Erskine Caldwell [author of the novel *Tobacco Road*]. When sales lagged, Mr. Goodman instructed me to "throw 'em a few 'hot' words." *Nympho* was one that was considered to be arousing. *Dark triangle* would be put into play when the magazine was in desperate straits. We once used it in an article called "The Rock-Around Dolls of New Orleans."

In doing research for this interview, I read issues of these magazines and found many of the articles to be incredibly funny and entertaining.

We tried to keep to a high standard, within the limits of our pathetic budget. Some awfully good writers passed through the company. The adventure magazines had huge circulations and were mostly geared to blue-collar types, war veterans, young men—up to one million readers, with no paid subscribers. But their popularity faded when World War II vets grew older and more explicit magazines became readily available. The only reader I've ever actually met in person is my brother-in-law.

Were these types of magazines called *armpit slicks*?

Only by the competition. They were also called *jockstrap magazines*.

Believe it or not, there was a lot of status involved. *True* magazine considered itself the Oxford University Press of the group and sniffed at us. We, in turn, sniffed at magazines we felt were shoddier than ours. There was a lot of sniffing going on.

We published a variety of story types. People being nibbled to death by animals was one type: "I Battled a Giant Otter." There was no explanation as to why these stories fascinated readers for many years.

"Scratch the surface" stories were also a favorite. These were tales about a sleepy little town where citizens innocently go about their business—girls eating ice cream, boys delivering newspapers—but "scratch the surface" of one of these towns and you'd find a sin pit, a cauldron of vice and general naughtiness.

The revenge theme was popular, as well—a soldier treated poorly in a prison camp, who would set out to track down his abuser when the war ended. And stories about G.I.s stranded on Pacific islands were a hit among veterans—especially if the islands were populated by nymphos. "G.I. King of Nympho Island" was one title, I recall.

Sounds convincing.

Mr. Goodman always asked the same question when we showed him a story: "Is it true?" My answer was, "Sort of." He'd take a puff of a thin cigar and walk off, apparently satisfied. He was a decent but frightening man.

Walter Kaylin, a favorite contributor, did a hugely popular story about a G.I. who is stranded on an island and becomes its ruler. The

G.I. is carried about on the shoulders of a little man who has washed ashore with him. There wasn't a nympho on the island, but it worked.

Who, by and large, wrote for these magazines?

Gifted, half-broken people—and I was one of them—who didn't qualify for jobs at Time-Life or at the Hearst Company. I don't think of them as being hired, so much as having just ended up there. In terms of ability, I would match them against anyone who worked in publishing at the time. We just didn't look like the cover models for *GQ*.

Walter Wager was a contributor, and he went on to write more than twenty-five suspense novels, including, under a pseudonym, the *I Spy* series. He had a prosthetic hand that he would unscrew and toss on my desk when he delivered a new story. Ernest Tidyman worked for the company; he wrote the *Shaft* books and the first two movies. Also, the screenplay for *The French Connection*.

In the early sixties, I was editing *Swank* when Leicester Hemingway—pronounced "Lester"—came barreling into my office. He was Ernest's brother, and he looked more like Ernest than Ernest himself. He called Ernest "Ernesto." He was bluff and cheerful and handsome in the Clark Gable mold. He had gotten off a fishing boat that very day and wanted me to publish one of his stories. How could I say no? This was as close as I'd ever get to the master.

He left. I read the story. The first line was "Hi, ho, me hearties." It was totally out of sync with what we were doing, and it was unreadable. I remember it being called "Avast." So, I was in the position of having to turn down Ernest Hemingway's brother.

A few years later, I went to a party given by George Plimpton, and I met Mary Hemingway, the last of Ernest's four wives. I told her that I'd had the nicest meeting with Leicester. "What a wonderful man he is."

"That *swine!*" she said. "How dare you mention his name in my presence!"

Apparently, this highly decent man was considered the black sheep of the family—at least by Mary. And that's really saying something.

How many stories did you have to purchase for all of your magazines in a typical month?

Fifty or sixty.

Per month?

Yes. I was an incredibly fast reader—a human scanner. My train commute to work took more than two hours each way, a total of close to five hours. I got a lot of work done on that train—much more than I do now with a whole day free and clear. I wrote most of *Stern* on that train.

My best move at this job was to hire Mario Puzo, later the author of *The Godfather*. The candidates for the writing job got winnowed down to Puzo and Arthur Kretchmer, who later became the decades-long editorial director of *Playboy*. I knew how good Kretchmer was, but I needed someone who could write tons of stories from Day One, so I hired Puzo in 1960 at the princely salary of $150 a week. But there was an opportunity to dash off as many freelance stories as he wanted, thereby boosting his income considerably. He referred to this experience as his first "straight" job. When I called him at home to deliver the news, he kept saying in disbelief, "You mean it? You *really* mean it?"

Was Puzo capable of writing humor?

He was concerned about it. Now and then, at the height of his fame and prominence and commercial success, he would look off wistfully and ask, "How come Hollywood never calls me for comedy?"

There is some grisly humor in *The Godfather*. As for setting out consciously to write a funny book—I'm not sure. At the magazines, one of the perks as editor was that I got to choose the cartoons. There was an old cartoon agent, a real old Broadway type who stuttered. He would come stuttering into the office carrying a batch of cartoons, each of which had been rejected eight times already.

Mario insisted he could have done a better job of choosing the cartoons, but I never allowed him to try. It was the only disagreement we ever had.

What sort of stories would Puzo write for you?

You name it—war, women, desert islands, a few mini-*Godfather*s. At one point we ran out of World War II battles; how many times can you storm Anzio, Italy? So we had to make up a few battles. Puzo wrote one story, about a mythical battle, that drew piles of mail telling him he had misidentified a tank tread—but no one questioned the fictional battle itself.

There has never been a more natural storyteller. I suppose it was mildly sadistic of me, but I would show him an illustration for a thirty-thousand-word story that had to be written that night. He'd get a little green around the gills, but he'd show up the next morning with the story in hand—a little choppy, but essentially wonderful. He wrote, literally, millions of words for the magazines. I became a hero to him when I faced down the publisher and got him $750 for a story—a hitherto unheard-of figure.

Do you think this experience later helped when he wrote *The Godfather*?

He claimed that it did. If you look at his first novel, *The Dark Arena* [1955], you'll see that the ability is there, but there is little in the way of forward motion. He said more than once that he began to learn about the elements of storytelling and narrative at our company.

I can't resist telling you this: In 1963, Mario approached me and somewhat sheepishly said he was moonlighting on a novel, and he wanted to try out the title. He said, "I want to call it *The Godfather*. What do you think?"

I told him that it didn't do much for me. "Sounds domestic. Who cares? If I were you, I'd take another shot at it."

A look of steel came across his face. He walked off without saying a word. He was usually mild-mannered, but the look was terrifying. Years later, he always denied being "connected," but anyone who saw that look would have to wonder. The thing is, I was right about the title. It would have been a poor choice for any book other than *The Godfather*.

In the mid-sixties, after the sale of the book, I heard him on the phone to his publisher, asking for more money. They said, "Mario, we just gave you two hundred thousand dollars." He said, "Two hundred grand doesn't last forever."

Wonderful man—perhaps not the most intelligent person I've known, but surely the wisest. On one occasion, he saved my life.

How so?

I became friendly with the mobster "Crazy" Joe Gallo when he was released from prison in 1971. The actor Jerry Orbach, who starred [in 1967] in one of my plays, *Scuba Duba*, was also a pal of Joey's.

Joey had a lot of writer friends—he had read a lot in prison. He loved [Jean-Paul] Sartre but hated [Albert] Camus, whom he called a "pussy." When Joey was released, there were about fifty contracts out on his life. He was trying to soften his image by hanging around artistic types. His "family" would hold weekly Sunday-night parties at the Orbachs' town house in Chelsea. I attended a few of these soirees, and I noticed that every twenty minutes or so Joey would go over to the window, pull back the drapes a bit, and peer outside.

I told Mario that I was attending these parties, and that I wanted to bring my wife and sons along. The food was great—Cuban cigars, everything quite lavish. The actor Ben Gazzara [*Husbands*] usually showed up, as did Neil Simon, and a great many luminaries. Mario considered what I told him and said, "What you are doing is *not* intelligent." And that was it. I was invited to join Joey and a group at Umbertos Clam House the very night [April 7, 1972] he was gunned down. Mario played a part in my saying I had a previous engagement.

Let's talk about the characters you create: They are often very likable, even when they shouldn't be. One character, Harry Towns, who's been featured in numerous short stories and in two novels since the early 1970s, is a failed screenwriter and father. He's a drug addict who snorts coke the very day his mother dies. He sleeps with hookers. He takes his

son to Las Vegas and basically forgets about him; he's much more concerned about his own body lice. And yet, in the end, Harry Town remains very funny and likable.

The late Bill Styron [author of *Lie Down in Darkness* and *Sophie's Choice*] paid me a compliment that I treasure. He said, "All of your work has great humanity." Maybe he said that to all of his contemporaries, but he seemed to mean it. I tried to make the character of Harry—for all of his flaws—screamingly and hurtfully honest, and that may have provided some of whatever appeal he has. I'm a little smarter than Harry; he's a bit more reckless than I am.

I have about a dozen voices that I can write—my *Candide* voice, the Noël Coward voice—but I keep coming back to Harry.

One Harry Towns story, "Just Back from the Coast," ends with Harry watching the NASA moon landing in his ex-wife's house, with her overseas and his child off at summer camp. He's alone. Your characters, including Harry, tend to be very lonely, but your life seems like it was anything but.

I'm not sure what other lives are like—but one of my favorite words is *adventure*. With that said, for a Jewish guy an adventure can be a visit to a strange delicatessen. I have plenty of friends, acquaintances, family, but much of the time I enjoy my own company. Most of writing is thinking, and you can't do much of it in a crowd. Whenever I used to duck out on a dinner with "the guys," Mario would defend me by saying, "Bruce is a loner."

Can the following be verified? That in the 1970s, you were the one-armed push-up champ at Elaine's, the Upper East Side New York restaurant that was a gathering place for writers?

Yes.

How many did you do?

Who knows? I was probably too loaded to count.

Were you surrounded by a crowd of famous authors, cheering you on? Was Woody Allen anxious to compete?

Not really. But we would have various athletic contests, generally beginning at four in the morning. There were sprints down Second Avenue, for example. It got more macho as the evening progressed.

I remember [the film director and screenwriter] James Toback trying to perform some push-ups and running out of steam. The restaurant's owner, Elaine Kaufman, said, "Put a broad under him."

Is it true that, in the late sixties, you got into a fistfight with Norman Mailer?

Yes, at a party he was holding at his town house in Brooklyn Heights. Mailer was looking for a fight. Instead of getting mad, I patted him on his head and said, "Now, now, Norman. Let's behave." We made our way to the street, and a crowd formed. We circled each other and we tussled a bit. Eventually he dropped to the ground. I helped him up and he embraced me—but he then bit me on the shoulder. I saw the bite marks once I got home. I rushed to the hospital for a tetanus shot. I was afraid I was going to begin to froth at the mouth.

Let's talk about Hollywood.

Must we?

For someone who has a good amount of experience as a screenwriter— you've worked on numerous screenplays over the years, including *Stir Crazy* and *Splash*—you seem to have a healthy attitude toward the film industry.

I don't know of anyone who ever had more fun out there than I did. The work was not especially appealing, but I did have a great time. In fact, I would get offended when I was interrupted on the tennis court and asked to do some work. I thought Hollywood was supposed to be about room service and pretty girls, orange juice and champagne. When I was gently asked to write a few scenes, I was annoyed.

I did my work in Hollywood with professionalism and never took any money I hadn't earned. But I could never tap into the same source I did when I wrote my books and stories—or plays, for that matter. Perhaps if I'd had some hunger to make movies at an earlier time, I could have learned the camera, studied the machinery of moviemaking, and it would have been different. But for me, the gods at the time were Hemingway and Fitzgerald and Faulkner; there were girls in the Village who wouldn't sleep with you if you had anything to do with movies: "You'd actually *sell* your book to the movies?" This was spoken with horror.

Shortly after I arrived in Hollywood, Joe Levine, the producer of *The Graduate*, summoned me to his office. He was a fan of my play *Scuba Duba*. He said, "You will never again have to worry about money." When I left the office, I felt great. *I'd never have to worry again about money!* But he was wrong. Never a day passed that I didn't worry about money. Later, I met Joe at the Beverly Hills Hotel and I reminded him of his prediction. He waved it off and said, "Oh, well, you have so much of it anyway." Not the rapier-like response I'd hoped for.

Screenwriting is the only writing form in which the work is being shot down, so to speak, as you're writing. It's always going to be, "Fine, now call in the next hack." If someone were to submit the shooting script of [1950's] *All About Eve*—updated, of course—it would only be considered a first draft. And a parade of writers would be called in to improve it. Hollywood doesn't want a singular, unique voice. If F. Scott Fitzgerald, over the course of his career, could only earn one-third of a screenplay credit [on 1938's *Three Comrades*] then what does that tell you?

Or Joseph Heller in Hollywood.

Right. He was there for years, but only had partial credits on two movies [1964's *Sex and the Single Girl*, 1970's *Dirty Dingus Magee*], and on a few episodes of the [early 1960s] TV show *McHale's Navy*.

There's an old-fashioned phrase—*pride of authorship*—that I never felt on the West Coast. I'm sure Woody Allen feels it, and maybe only a few others. Still, for a time, I was delighted as a screenwriter to be a well-paid busboy. And, oh, those good times!

Anything you care to tell me about?

I played tennis on a court alongside the actor Anthony Quinn. Back then, I was actually told that I resembled him. He kept glancing over at me. We both had shaky backhands.

I collided with Steve McQueen in the lobby of the Beverly Hills Hotel. A hair dryer fell out of my suitcase. Needless to say, it was embarrassing to have McQueen know that I used one.

And I spent one summer as a "sidekick" of Warren Beatty's. My main function was to console his army of rejected girlfriends.

How did you even come to know Warren Beatty?

He loved *Stern*, and he was convinced he could play the central role in the film. I had to explain, patiently, that it was a bit of a reach. He was no schlub.

We would go to the clubs in LA, including a place called the Candy Store. I never saw anyone who could bowl over women the way he could. He was a sweet, charming man—gorgeous, of course— and he made you feel that you were the only one in the world that he cared about. I don't mean to be a tease, but there were a few episodes I'd be uncomfortable mentioning—especially now that he's a family man with all those kids. Maybe if we have a drink sometime.

Hollywood is something. The name-dropping that goes on there is incredible. I had a friend who was an actor, and he called me one day. I could tell he had a cough. When I asked if he was okay, he told me that he had caught Pierce Brosnan's cold. Another time, while I was on a movie set, a guy offered me a cigar and bragged that he had gotten it from someone who was close to Cher.

Were you happy with the first version of *The Heartbreak Kid*, which was released in 1972? It was based on your 1966 story for *Esquire* "A Change of Plan."

I thought the first version was wonderful. I'm permitted to say that because I didn't write the screenplay—Neil Simon did. It actually sounded like something I might have written. Simon said that in writing it, he pretended he was me—although we'd never met.

What did you think of the 2007 remake, starring Ben Stiller?

I thought the first part—the revelation about the wife—was hysterically funny. The rest, for me, fell off a cliff. There are five screenwriters listed in the credits, including the Farrelly brothers. And Lord knows how many *uncredited* screenwriters. The budget was north of $60 million. You would have thought that a simple phone call to the fellow who invented the wheel would have been useful. Maybe I knew something. Maybe Neil Simon did. I would have helped out pro bono. But it would never have occurred to someone to make that phone call. I'm not upset about this. Just curious . . . amused.

I read a story about you that I assume cannot be true: that actress Natalie Wood once worked as your secretary.

No, that's true. It was either my first or second trip to Hollywood. I was working on the movie version for the Broadway play *The Owl and the Pussycat,* and I needed a secretary. Or, at the very least, it was *assumed* I needed one.

The producer Ray Stark [*The Sunshine Boys, Smokey and the Bandit*] said, "I'll find you a good one. Don't worry." I went over to his beach house and there, sitting by the pool, was Natalie Wood. Stark said, "Here is your new secretary."

As a joke?

I said, "That's very amusing, Ray. But this is Natalie Wood, from *Splendor in the Grass, West Side Story, Rebel Without a Cause.* Every boy's fantasy."

She looked up and said, "No, I *really* am your secretary."

She was between marriages to Robert Wagner and seemed dispirited. I don't think she was being offered major roles, and a shrink might have suggested that she try something different. This is self-serving, but I'd seen her at a party the night before and we had maybe exchanged glances. Who knows, maybe she liked me. What's the lyric—*I can dream, can't I?* In any case, she was my secretary for about a week.

Each morning, I'd pick her up in Malibu and drive her back to the Beverly Hills Hotel, all the while thinking, I'm sitting here with Natalie *fucking* Wood—and she's my secretary. It was difficult staying on the highway.

Can you imagine a Hollywood actress doing that these days?

Unlikely.

What Hollywood project were you working on at the time?

I went out to California to work on *The Lenny Bruce Story*. Lenny had died a few years earlier. The executives wanted a writer who was crazy and strange, but also wore a suit. They wanted someone who would be presentable at a meeting—I was that guy. But I never worked on the project.

Why not?

I had never seen Lenny Bruce, but I knew of his legend. I really wasn't interested in that type of work, actually. I just didn't know enough about him to be a fan or to not be a fan.

I once heard of a woman at one of Bruce's performances who stood up in the middle of the act and started screaming, "Dirty mouth! Dirty mouth!" I wanted that to be the title of the film—*Dirty Mouth!*, but I didn't realize back then that I, as a screenwriter, was nothing more than a busboy. It was just a different world than what I was familiar with. The most important thing back then was to be a novelist. Now it's the opposite.

You left the Lenny Bruce project?

I did, yes. But only after a truck pulled up to where I was staying, with men hauling boxes and files and every scrap of paper related to Lenny Bruce's life—every letter, every deposition, every piece of correspondence. I remember that I hurt my leg carrying some of these boxes up to the attic.

I just got smothered with it all, and I ended up not doing it.

I don't think I've ever discussed this before, but I found aspects of his life troubling. It made me uncomfortable. There were some similarities of his life that brushed up against mine. I was having domestic problems of my own, and the whole story made me uncomfortable.

Plus, I didn't want to be the one to fuck up the Lenny Bruce story. I knew about his legend, even though I never saw him perform, and I knew how important he was to many people.

There was one piece in particular of Bruce's that I thought was absolutely brilliant. It runs a little over twenty minutes, and it's called "The Palladium." I think it's one of the best twenty minutes of comedy ever.

My friend Jacques Levy, who directed the stage production of *Oh! Calcutta!* and then later Bob Dylan's *Rolling Thunder Revue*, once said that all contemporary comedy springs from that half hour.

In what sense?

Bruce uses a few different voices throughout the piece, which I've often found myself slipping into while writing. It's this "What are you nuts? What are you crazy?" type of attitude; it was a very modern sensibility when he performed it in the mid-sixties.

It's about a minor Vegas comedian named Frank Dell who wants to perform in "classy rooms." He just bought a new house with a pool and patio.[1] His manager gets him into the Palladium in London. He

---

1   In the routine, Bruce describes the character's new house in Sherman Oaks, California, as the following: "The pool isn't in yet, but the patio's dry." The Rolling Stones' Keith Richards, thirteen years later, used a slightly different version when writing the lyrics to 1981's "Little T&A": "The pool's in, but the patio ain't dry."

starts off with his bad shtick: "Well, good evening, ladies and gentle-men! You know, I just got back from a place in Nevada called Lost Wages. A funny thing about working Lost Wages . . ." He bombs so badly that he starts to say anything to get a response: "Screw Ireland! Screw the Irish! The IRA really bum-rapped ya." He still bombs and causes a near riot.

What did you make of the Bob Fosse–directed movie *Lenny* when it was finally released in 1974, starring Dustin Hoffman in the title role?

I thought Hoffman was miscast. The movie just barely scratched the surface of that man's life. The film didn't work at all for me.

You're credited with writing the screenplay to 1980's *Stir Crazy*, starring Gene Wilder and Richard Pryor. Were you happy with the finished product?

I liked that movie very much; I just liked the way it worked out. I could recognize my voice every once in awhile watching that movie.

The idea wasn't mine—it was a producer's named Hannah Weinstein, who told me about this phenomenon in Texas where prisoners staged a rodeo. That's all I was given. I wrote the screenplay, and Hannah was able to cast Richard Pryor and Gene Wilder.

There was one instance where I wasn't happy. At the last minute, another writer was brought in to punch up the script or to add some dialogue. I visited the set during the scene where Gene mounts a mechanical bull. He pats the bull and says, "Nice horsey" a couple of times.

Well, I don't write "Nice horsey." I mean, it's simply something that I would never write for a character. Bed wetters say "nice horsey," but not my characters. I didn't know the rules and I was a little offended, so I started to walk off the set. So Richard—someone I had never met before—came running over and said, "Gee, I never met a writer like you. Take the money; don't take any shit." He said, "I've got fifty in cash. I think I'll get out of here, too."

He then said, "You ever get high?"

I said, "Once, in the spring of '63." I was just teasing, but I was in good form. I said, "Jews rarely tend to become junkies. For one thing, they have to have eight hours of sleep. They have to read *The New York Times* in the morning. They need fresh orange juice. So, no, I've never gotten high."

We walked into his trailer and, the second we did, I knew I wasn't going to be comfortable. Everything was foreign to me: pipes and wickers and just crazy things. It was all new to me. If we lit a match, we were finished.

My one regret with *Stir Crazy* is that I didn't do more with Richard's character. I should have fleshed his character out more, and I didn't. I feel bad about that. What's interesting is that Richard treated every word you wrote as if it were scripture. Gene was looser. For Gene, the dialogue was just a starting point.

You knew satirical writer Terry Southern quite well, didn't you?

We were good friends, particularly in his late years.

Do you think Terry's contribution was important to *Dr. Strangelove*? Terry co-wrote the script with Stanley Kubrick and Peter George, but Kubrick later claimed that Terry's role wasn't as significant as many people thought.

I would trust Terry's account in this area. He was always collaborating and getting into awful squabbles about credits. He was a generous man and easily taken advantage of—picked apart, really—by the wolves.

How does a writer like Terry Southern age—where you always have to produce work that has the capacity to astonish?

Some keep it up. Some fade. Others simply push on. Churchill once said, "If you're going through hell, keep going." Terry had an especially tough time throughout the last decades. Had the culture changed? Was he out of sync? There is always that worry.

It's a shame. He had the most unique voice of any writer I knew.

He was a brave man in print, but vulnerable in life—no doubt a familiar story.

I once leased an apartment in New York that had an S&M room. Terry saw the black walls, the mirrored ceiling, the whips and chains stored in the closet. A room that had his name on it. He said, "Grand Guy Bruce, would you mind terribly if I crashed in here for a bit?" I said fine. It was three in the morning.

I then realized that painters were coming at around seven in the morning to ready the room for my young son Drew, who was moving in for awhile. They were going to repaint the all-black walls.

One of the painters said, "We can't work. There's a man sleeping in that room." I said, "Don't worry about it. Just paint around him." Terry fell asleep in this Marquis de Sade room, and woke up hours later with photos of Mickey Mantle on the walls. He didn't say a word, just shook it off and went on his way.

You leased an apartment with an S&M room?

It was a lovely place, had a great terrace, lots of space. It just happened to have a guest room with all that bondage equipment.

What was Terry doing in the room before he fell asleep?

He'd had a big night. Let's put it that way.

Do you think Terry wasn't respected in the latter part of his career because he wasn't producing "quality lit"?

Terry is the one who invented that phrase. He was an easygoing man, contented, amused by life. I don't think he ever felt bitter or resentful with the way things turned out in his career. I know he had grave financial difficulties toward the end of his life—but he wasn't a complainer.

He was respected throughout his life by the people who counted, so to speak. And there are all these new readers coming along. His books and films exist, ready to be enjoyed.

You've written eight novels and more than one hundred short stories. After all these years, is writing still difficult for you?

Actually, I've written more than two hundred short stories—half of them are languishing in an archive.

But God yes, writing is still difficult and always will be. I'm suspicious of writers who go whistling cheerfully to the computer.

Are there any writers' tricks you've learned over the years that have made the process a bit easier?

I'm hesitant to begin a short story unless I know the last line, or a close approximation of it. I'm always apprehensive when I begin work each day. After a lifetime of this, I still can't get it clear that the actual process of writing tends to erase the fear.

I'm not the first to point out how essential it is to, on occasion, discard a favorite passage in the interest of pushing on with a good story. Isaac Bashevis Singer said that the wastebasket is a writer's best friend. He also said that a writer can produce ten fine novels, but it doesn't mean that the next one will be any good. It mystifies me that after a lifetime of writing it would still be like this. I should be able to solve any problem—but it doesn't work that way. Each story or book presents a new challenge. That's probably a good thing, though. It keeps me on my toes.

Do you still write every day?

Yes—or at the very least, I worry about it.

I do some teaching, and I put the emphasis on focus, as well as the importance of making every sentence count. [Novelist] Francine Prose once quoted a friend as saying this requires "putting every word on trial for its life." I believe this. You can read the entire works of a major writer and never find a bad—or unnecessary—sentence.

Do you have any specific instructions for those students who want to write stories with humor?

I'd suggest you stay away from irony or satire; there's very little money in it. You're likely to wind up with reviews—like some of mine—that say, "I didn't know whether to laugh or cry." There's no such question in Dickens. Most readers would prefer to know exactly where they stand, where the author stands, and how to respond. Ergo, no irony permitted.

I'd advise students not to try to be funny. Nothing is more depressing than someone caught making such an effort. If a story or sketch is intrinsically funny, if it deserves to be funny, it will make people laugh. Truth—bitter and unadorned truth—is a good guideline.

Asking yourself "What if . . . ?" is a good starting point for a story. What if I befriended a pimp and he asked a straightlaced character to watch over his stable of women while he was in prison? That later became a story I wrote for *Esquire* called "Detroit Abe."

As for television writers, in comedy or drama, there's a simple rule: Include the line "We have to talk," even if your characters have done nothing but for half an hour. Producers love that line. Writers are brought in and paid a fortune for their ability—and willingness—to write that line.

Finally, I also like the writer Grace Paley's piece of advice: "Keep a low overhead."

BRUCE VILANCH

Writer, the Emmys, the Academy Awards,
the Tonys, the Grammys

···

Writing Jokes for Awards Shows

What's the joke-writing preparation for a televised awards show, such as the Oscars? How much time and effort are we talking about?

A tremendous amount. People have no idea. Billy Crystal came up with the idea of creating a huge playbook, almost like a football team would use for a big game. The script itself is three hundred pages. It's a big hefty tome, and it's kept offstage, generally offstage left. The host will leaf through it during commercial breaks. It's mostly based on what *might* happen during the broadcast. "Suppose *this* happens. What if *that* happens?" You know, just in case. So, you end up creating a lot of material: "Oh, if that happens, we're covered." You study who's nominated to win all the awards, the movies these people are associated with, everything that's necessary to come up with jokes. A ton of research.

How many of these jokes, on average, end up being used during the performance?

Out of the hundreds that we write—really, hundreds—if one or two are used, it's a big deal. We'll start the actual writing process about two months before the ceremony—usually in December for a February or March broadcast.

Is the notebook divided into subjects? Into categories?

There's an entire rundown of the show, and we write potential jokes into the script at the point where they would occur. But we always give ourselves room for on-the-spot improvisation. There are some things we could just never predict.

At the 1992 Oscars, nobody expected Jack Palance, a seventy-three-year-old man, to start performing one-armed push-ups when he won the Academy Award [for Best Actor in a Supporting Role for *City Slickers*]. But we knew something was going to happen. Billy had worked with Jack in *City Slickers* and knew what Jack was capable of.

But, no, we didn't know exactly what he would try to do. And that's the great thing about the Oscars. Something will happen that's unwritten, and it's always way funnier than anything we could have dreamt up. And it's then up to us to work off those situations.

People tend to forget what exactly Jack Palance said before dropping to the ground to perform push-ups.

Right. The first thing that Jack said when he got up to the podium was, "Billy Crystal. I crap bigger than him." Talk about your visuals. And then there was kind of a shocked reaction, and that's what made Jack drop to the floor to do something that would allow the audience to forget that he had just said "crap" in front of most of the universe.

Once Jack did those push-ups, we, the writers, were standing backstage, thinking, Okay, no holds barred. He made this joke about Billy, so now Billy can do anything about him. The floodgates opened.

We wrote a couple of jokes about Jack's prowess, and then Billy came back and said, "Look, do more. Write more." So we did.

It must be frustrating to come up with so many jokes each year, only to have only about 2 percent used. Have there been any jokes you wished had been used but weren't?

There've been a few. We had one joke [in 2003] that involved Steve Martin coming out after the monologue, and he was going to say, "I have good news and bad news. The bad news is that my fly was open throughout the monologue. The good news is the camera puts on ten pounds." But Steve wouldn't say the joke; he said it was a "cock joke." He just didn't feel comfortable doing a cock joke on the Academy Awards. I said, "But it's not a cock joke! It's a *camera* joke." Everybody loved the joke. Even the network censor thought it was hilarious. We could have gotten away with it because it didn't cross any kind of line, but the fact that the network censor thought it was hysterical meant we had done something right.

It might very well have become a classic if he did say it.

I know, but Steve felt it was just a little too anatomically correct. You can see the visual a bit too easily. I can understand why he would come to that conclusion. The host has to decide, "Do I want to take the audience to that place?"

The Academy Awards is a strange show to work on as a comedy writer. You're writing jokes for over one billion people, of all ages, countries, backgrounds. How do you determine what is and what is not appropriate without sapping out all the humor?

You have to be careful not to cross that weird line. There are celebrities you just can't make jokes about, whether because it's cruel or because they'll be in the audience, or just because it's too embarrassing a situation. Keep in mind that whatever a host says is going to live with them for the rest of their career. The choice you have to make is,

Do I, as a comedian, want to be remembered for this joke or not? You can't unring that bell.

Can you tell me about the backstage writing process during an Oscars broadcast? How do the writers work? Together or separately? Writing down jokes? Pitching them out loud?

It's frantic. It's chaos. It makes the fall of Saigon look tame. It's all happening so, so quickly. My favorite example is from 2003, when Steve was hosting. Now, this goes back to something happening just before the commercial break that you can work off of. Michael Moore had won for Best Documentary Feature for *Bowling for Columbine*, and he made a speech against the second Gulf war. Some in the audience booed, but we also noticed that some of the stagehands started booing him, too. When we returned from commercial break, Steve came out and said, "It's so sweet backstage, you should have seen it. The Teamsters are helping Michael Moore into the trunk of his limo." That was a joke that we came up with in the wings.

Who are you writing for? The live audience in the auditorium? Or the audience at home?

You're playing to the auditorium because they're the ones who are giving the immediate reaction that the home audience will hear. You're always playing to both of them, really, but I think what you want most is a reaction from the live audience, clearly.

The problem is that the vibe in the room changes as the night progresses. As the night gets longer, there are more and more audience members who have not won an award. Their high hopes have disappeared. For every winner, there are at least four or five who won't win. It gets chilly. The audience is not really paying attention. At this point, you're getting down to the big awards; it's been a long day. The audience really would like to get out of there and start drinking—those who aren't already potted, that is. So, by the end, the audience is not really paying close attention. Also, there are a hefty amount of seat fillers, because people have children, have to relieve the babysitter, they get bored, they just leave. Say, for an example, there are ten supporting actor nominees, and those categories are given early. Those ten faces will be gone, generally, by the middle to the end of the show. And they'll be replaced by secretaries from Paramount who might not be too keen to laugh.

But if you're in the audience, you can always sense a degree of excitement. In particular, when Letterman hosted the 1994 Oscars, the live audience was enjoying it; they were having a good time. But his performance did receive terrible reviews.

I really enjoyed watching that show. I think a lot of people did—that is, until Letterman convinced us otherwise.

But that's his persona, you know. That's what you get when you hire him. I liked his performance, too, but I do think the mistake he made was to try and duplicate routines from his late-night show to the Oscars. Nobody had tuned in to see that. I always think it's better to take a fresh approach. That's what the audience really loves. And Letterman also would comment on whenever a joke wouldn't hit, which is something Johnny Carson would do on *The Tonight Show*. But that doesn't work at the Oscars, either.

Were you responsible for some of the jokes that bombed the night Letterman hosted, such as the Uma/Oprah joke? The joke was that *Uma* and *Oprah* sound similar. And the follow-up joke was that *Keanu* sounds similar to both *Uma* and *Oprah*.

No. The Uma/Oprah joke was written by Rob Burnett [executive producer, *Late Show with David Letterman*], who lethally takes credit for it. Just lethal. I told Rob not to do it. I thought it was a bad idea to have David Letterman from New York TV making fun of these huge stars from Hollywood.

Hosts are vital to the show's tone. It's a very specific role that the host plays. You have to bring your personality, but you have to do it in a clever way, so it doesn't feel like a retread of what you do at your other job. I think that's what happened with Letterman. The comedy didn't translate well.

It takes a very specific type of performer to do well at the Oscars. Ellen DeGeneres [in 2007] had a different approach, and I don't think it worked. She was very daytime. There wasn't a sense of occasion. She was scared, I think, and wasn't willing to go the extra mile. James Franco [in 2010] didn't work out well at all. He was really out of his comfort zone. He's not a live stage performer.

It's better if the hosts are comedians. They have to have a bit of an attitude. It's easier for us writers to find words that suit a comedian's attitude. Actors tend to act. It's tough for them to play themselves, to have a persona. You'll never see Johnny Depp performing *An Evening with Johnny Depp.*

What's it like to write for celebrities presenting awards, many of whom are not used to performing comedy before a live audience?

It's tough. It's constantly a negotiation of some sort. Each of these celebrities has a flotilla of assistants who are advising them of what to say and not to say. A lot show up with their own writers, depending on who they are. And it's hard for me to bitch about that. That kind of goes with the territory. So that doesn't surprise me. What does surprise me is when you get people who don't do this kind of performing for a living and they go into a major panic and every single word has to be edited by everybody. By their hairdressers, their yoga instructor, their publicist, their pet psychiatrist. Everybody's got an opinion. And all of those people who are supposedly helping are really enemies of comedy, because they don't want anybody to get into trouble. You can't be funny by saying, "I'm not going to get anybody into trouble." You know, that's the risk you run. Read Freud on jokes and tell me that you're not ever going to get anybody into trouble.

PURE, HARD-CORE ADVICE

KAY CANNON

Writer/Producer, *30 Rock*; Producer, *New Girl*;
Writer, *Pitch Perfect*

The biggest thing that I learned as a writer at *30 Rock* was the importance of self-awareness. You are sharing fourteen hours a day with the same people, and having the same conversation all day long. You need to learn what role you play every single day in that configuration. I think a lot of writers end up not finding success, per se, because they don't have that self-awareness to know where they fit in on any given day. For example, I know now that some days I have to be at the head of the table, I have to run the room, I need to be the leader. And then some days I tell myself, "Oh, this is a day where I have to sit back. This person is taking it. My job today is to be a good listener and support and add whatever I can." I've seen so many people crash and burn from not understanding that, and feeling as if their role is something else. The truth is, in a writers' room—and specifically in comedy, because you do so much together and it's such a group process—if you're not fun to hang out with, and you don't have that self-awareness, you're not going to do as well.

When I was a staff writer on *30 Rock*, one of the most valuable things I learned was to just listen and learn from the people who've done it for a long time and are a thousand times better at this job than you are. If they're stumped on some story problem or a joke, and you feel you have a good idea, that's when you should talk. But just don't talk for the sake of talking. Again, understand where you fit in with the group. And that changes every year, because you get promoted, and the dynamics change and people leave and new people arrive. In the comedy world, at least in comedy writers' rooms, it just feels like your personality is a big deal, almost a little bit more than what you put on the page.

When rewriting or taking notes, trust your gut if you really feel strongly about something. But understand that it's a fine line between "Are you being thoughtful" and "Are you being lazy?" I find that sometimes I'll receive notes from the network or the studio, and I'll be like [emits moan of dread]. And I stop and think, Am I being lazy because it requires a lot of work to make that change? Or am I being thoughtful and just trusting my gut that I know better than they do? You have to really mull it over.

If you want to write for television, I strongly suggest that you watch a lot of television. Like, a *lot*. If you want to write movies, I strongly suggest watching a ton of movies. When someone says they're a TV writer and they don't own a TV, I just want to roll my eyes until they get stuck that way. [Laughs] If you're going into an interview for a very particular show, you've got to know everything about it. I'm always shocked when someone admits that they've only seen a few episodes of a show they now work on. You just think, How did you not watch every episode before coming here?

I was writing [the 2012 movie] *Pitch Perfect* from season three to season six of *30 Rock*. It was pretty tough doing both. So I would write every weekend. And then I would write on the subway ride to work, and then I would write over my lunch hour. I was just constantly writing. And again, it goes back to you just really having to be passionate about what it is that you're writing. I actually have such a love-hate relationship with writing. I kind of hate it. [Laughs] But you have to tell yourself, "I get to do this." More importantly, "I just *have* to do this." There's nothing worse than having it in the back of your mind, that it's something you need to do and you're not getting to. Maybe you've felt that way. You've thought, I'm so tired, I've worked all day writing. How am I opening up this computer and starting this other project? But if you really want it, you'll do it.

I do a thing where when I'm writing I put my television on Bravo, and I pause it on whatever show. Then I write until it unpauses itself, about forty-five minutes in, and then I get to watch for however long it's been paused. When it catches up, I go back to writing and pause again until it undoes itself again. That's my Saturday fun. [Laughs] Aren't I a blast?

CAROL KOLB

Carol Kolb isn't a household name, except among comedy nerds and obsessive fans of *The Onion*, "America's Finest News Source," the most consistently brilliant news parody of the last twenty years. But for comedy aficionados, Kolb is an almost mythical entity. "We're still not convinced that Carol Kolb . . . is a real person," a writer at *Gawker*, the popular New York–based gossip blog, once admitted.

Kolb was born and raised in Spencer, Wisconsin—two-and-a-half hours north of Madison. She enrolled at the University of Wisconsin to study English and Latin, and found her way to *The Onion* only by chance, when Todd Hanson, one of the original *Onion* writers, visited her apartment to see the Madison Museum of Bathroom Tissue. The collection of more than three thousand rolls of toilet paper, taken from such tourist attractions as Mount Rushmore and the Alamo, was just a quirky hobby Kolb had invented for no other reason than to amuse herself. But the museum attracted national attention. She was featured in *Time* magazine in 1997, and later that same year, she was asked to join *The Onion*'s writing staff.

She became indispensable. Kolb quickly went from managing editor to editor in chief, and in 2001 moved, along with the rest of *The Onion*, to New York City. When *The Onion* tried their hand at TV in 2007, launching the *Onion News Network*, a web video series and (eventually) TV show, Kolb was brought on as head writer, helping *The Onion* win its first Peabody Award in 2009 (for creating satirical news that was "not infrequently hard to distinguish from the real thing"). After the *Onion News Network* was canceled in 2012, Kolb moved to Los Angeles with her husband, comedian Tony Camin, and started writing for TV shows such as *Kroll Show* and *Community*.

Was your childhood enjoyable? Were you happy as a child?

I wasn't. I came from a really small town in Wisconsin, population 1,754. I had fifty people in my graduating class. Everyone was really stupid, including the teachers. Half of them were clearly hired just because they could also coach the sports teams. Most of the boys in my class would be gone for a week during deer-hunting season. I was always extremely shy. I got good grades but I never talked, and I had a "crying problem." All the elementary school report cards my mom kept say "cries too easily" and "can't stop crying," all the way up through fifth grade. One report card reads "Crys easily." With a *y*.

What was your home life like growing up?

I did have fun, but basically my childhood was pretty sad and pathetic. My parents fought—and still do. It's now approaching fifty years. My dad worked at the Land O' Lakes cheese factory, the only building in town over three stories, at a series of soul-sapping jobs in departments like "Slice" and "Loaf." He didn't really spend time with us, ever. He got one vacation a year and he'd spend it on a two-week fishing trip to Canada with his friends. I never thought to complain. I saw the other kids at school whose families couldn't pull it together to get them a Halloween costume, or who, when we were older, talked about how their dad got drunk and tried to stab them. So it never really occurred to me to be critical of my dad just for not coming to my Christmas pageants.

My mom didn't work after having kids and she always felt guilty about this—but also I think she was just afraid to get out there. She started losing her hearing when I was still young and that was part of the reason. Also, we only had one car and my dad took it to work—things like that got in her way. Not that she has ever been diagnosed, but she definitely has some anxiety disorder. At *The Onion*, I wrote an article called "Area Mom Freaking Out For No Reason Again" [July 22, 1999], as well as several other articles based solely on her. But she also has this dark sense of humor and would say very funny things in a straight, matter-of-fact way.

For instance, after my dad had a heart attack, he would still always be yelling about something, and my mother would mutter under her breath, "How was your heart attack?"

Ultimately, I credit her for my sense of humor.

How did your parents feel about your writing career?

In 2000, when I quit my day job as nurse's aide at a horrible county psychiatric home to work full-time at *The Onion*, my mom wasn't sure that it was a good idea—even though it meant I would no longer have to clean up human shit and get punched in the face. When I moved to New York, she was like, "Oh, no! You have to move to New York?!" I'm not even complaining that my parents aren't supportive. They are proud of me—they get excited when I am on TV. But my mom is an obsessive worrier and she would rather I have a stable job like my sister who teaches Family and Consumer Sciences Education—the modern equivalent of Home Ec—at a junior high school. And my dad isn't going to read or watch something just because I wrote it. I sound bitter, but I'm not at all. My parents are great and cute. They just live in their own world centered in Spencer, Wisconsin.

I'm pretty sure none of the other writers in this book have ever worked in a county psychiatric home. What was that experience like?

There were different floors for different types of issues. There was an Alzheimer's unit. There was one guy, a former police chief, who got Alzheimer's very young. He was probably only sixty or so and in great shape. It took five of us women to put him in pajamas because he didn't know what was going on and his natural response was to fight. He would pull these tricky arm bends and foot sweeps on us. Giving him a shower was crazy. His wife would come to visit and just cry. That was sad.

The upper floors were where the real crazies were, younger people with schizophrenia and so on. These people would sometimes manage to get out for a bit, but then would be back in again after swallowing a handful of safety pins or whatever. There was one guy, thirty-five or so, who believed he was a leprechaun. He'd speak in an Irish accent and offer to grant wishes and stand on his head. I loved that he was so classically crazy—if I had read something with that character, it would have seemed like lazy writing. And then there were just a lot of really loud, demanding crazy people who didn't like to bathe and would get violent very quickly if they wanted a soda and there wasn't any left.

The bottom floor was for elderly people with dementia. The former drunks were always the worst—they tended to get mean when they lost their minds. There were some people who'd been there long enough so that they didn't walk or talk anymore. The worst thing was that we had to spoon-feed these people puréed food. I mean, at a certain point it's time to die—if they were at home they would just stop eating. But the state rules were such that we had to give these poor people three meals and a snack a day—so they lived on and on. Some of them refused to open their mouths. You had to coax them to open their mouths so you could put the mush in. Others naturally opened up their mouths like little birdies. Then there were those who had feeding tubes.

People, make a living will!

How do you think working at the psychiatric institute affected your comedic sensibility?

Well, I think working at a place like that makes you develop a thick skin. You deal with a lot of sad situations and annoying conditions. So

I think you learn to not be emotionally affected by things as much. In that way, I think working there made me more able to make fun of "taboo" subjects. People would get so mad about *Onion* articles that involved certain subjects, whether it was disabled vets or dying babies or whatever. I just wasn't so emotionally attached to the subject. It's not that I don't think certain circumstances or topics were sad or wrong, but to me there's more than one emotional response beyond sadness or outrage. I can distance myself enough to see what's funny about other subjects, too.

From what you were saying earlier, high school sounds like it was far from ideal. Was your college experience in the mid-nineties, at the University of Wisconsin in Madison, in any way an improvement?

Madison was—is—a great city. It's a very liberal city. It has that classic free weekly paper, *Isthmus*, filled with stories about lesbians and medical marijuana and public radio. The college is huge, which I loved. Freshman year you could take classes in giant lecture halls and not have to interact with another human all day long.

These days, when I mention I went to the University of Wisconsin, people always mention the Badgers. Football was a huge deal at our college, apparently. I never went to a single game, a single tailgating party, or even watched a game on TV. It was this whole world I never interacted with the entire time I was going to school there. I guess on game days the entire neighborhood around the stadium becomes a sea of red and white, totally taken over by football fans. But I never went to that part of campus. It was all sports bars and jocks and business students living over there.

How did you come into the *Onion* world?

Madison is small enough that eventually I met people who worked at *The Onion*. I was putting these silly weird flyers up around town on the kiosks, and Joe Garden, one of the writers, called to say he liked them. Joe had been working at a liquor store on State Street, the main pedestrian street in downtown Madison. He had plastered the windows with funny hand-painted signs. One was a diagram of the brain with arrows pointing to "The Frontal Lobe," "The Backal Lobe," and "The Michelob." The *Onion* editor at the time, Dan Vebber [later a writer for *Space Ghost Coast to Coast, Futurama, Daria*], recruited him based on that. Joe ended up working at *The Onion* for close to twenty years.

So, my neighbor across the hallway went to a couple *Onion* writer meetings—he didn't really work out, but after a meeting he brought another one of the staff writers, Todd Hanson, over to a party I was having at my apartment. My apartment was set up like a fake museum. I called it the Madison Museum of Bathroom Tissue, and it was a curated collection of toilet paper stolen from around the country, presented in a very formal, very pretentious way, with an audio tour and lots of brochures.

I eventually wrote an *Onion* headline list and it went over well, and I was invited to come to meetings. I fit in right away.

How exactly did the Madison Museum of Bathroom Tissue start?

It started randomly. When I was a freshman, my friend and I would go to bars in neighboring small towns because they didn't card. We ended up getting a roll of toilet paper from each of these places and then keeping them as a "souvenir." The collection really took off when me and two of my other friends started going on road trips all over and stealing toilet paper from Graceland and MoMA [New York's Museum of Modern Art]—and labeling where it came from with a black magic marker. We collected thousands of rolls and got other people to collect toilet paper when they went abroad. We also got people to mail us rolls from weird locations. The joke, I guess, was that all the toilet paper looked the same. It was just something fun to do. When the rolls had taken over the front room of our apartment, we opened it up to the public as the Madison Museum of Bathroom Tissue. I started making T-shirts and brochures and calendars and getting it in guide books. In no way did I think of it as an "art project," but I guess it sort of was. It was also a way to mess with people.

The Onion is now a professional company with a large revenue and staff. But what was The Onion like when you first started contributing in 1996?

The Onion was so much smaller then. All the writers had day jobs. There were staff jobs for those who sold ads or did graphic design or whatever, but there was only one full-time staff position for a writer and another for the head editor. Maybe there was an assistant editor, too. All the writers just worked freelance for nothing—they got paid around forty dollars to come to meetings. The office was a crappy little place with stained carpeting and beanbag chairs. But it was really fun. It was like a club. Everyone was really invested in it. We acted like a group of friends. At that point we were still cementing the voice of the paper.

The first headline *The Onion* ever ran was in August 1988, and it was "Mendota Monster Mauls Madison." The piece was about Lake Mendota, which is on campus. Another early piece was headlined: "Thompson Changes Title from 'Governor' to 'Sexecutioner,'" which was about then Wisconsin Governor Tommy Thompson. You know, references that only locals would care about. Everything was just sillier in the beginning, and more random: "Pen Stolen from Dorm Study Area," "Everybody's Eatin' Bread," "Angry Lumberjack Demands Hearty Breakfast."

At one point, before I worked at *The Onion*, they did a fake issue of the *Badger Herald*, which was the frattier of the two daily campus newspapers. The *Herald* was just riddled with errors and had all these bad single-panel cartoons. One was a drawing of a hammer and a clock, and captioned "Hammer Time." So, you know, at that time, *The Onion* was still expending energy on something only a small handful of UW students could even understand.

I was a "new" writer. I sort of came in at the right time—just when the writers started to get paid for their work. Right after I started, in 1996, *The Onion* went on the Internet, which of course was huge for increasing readership, and then we got a book deal. Everything was a big deal—when *Mr. Show* used a copy of *The Onion* as a prop in a sketch ["No Slackers," November 1996], that was the most exciting thing ever. When our first book, *Our Dumb Century*, went to number one on *The New York Times* bestsellers list in 1999, it was so thrilling.

For those first six or seven years, *The Onion* was very much an underground hit.

The Onion had always been sort of an underground secret. It was distributed on the streets in Madison and in a few other cities where they set up a local office to sell local ads—Denver, Milwaukee. But also people could order a subscription and they would be mailed the Madison edition. And those subscriptions became sort of an underground hit. People all over the country would get subscriptions and have them sitting around their apartments or office, and it would be a cool thing that not everyone knew about. Subscribers included comedy writers on the coasts. Older people in comedy still talk about how they know the names of all the dumb pizza and sub sandwich shops in Madison—Rocky Rococo and Big Mike's Super Subs—because of the ads in the early editions of *The Onion*.

When *The Onion*'s popularity started to quickly spread, did you feel that things were going to change for you and the rest of the *Onion* staff?

It felt like what we were doing was important. Some of this feeling came from us being in the Midwest. We had something to prove. There was a really strong group dynamic. We were like a band. There was no system like there is now. We barely had an office. We didn't have assistants. Or interns. Or a proofreader. It's now huge, which is great. But it was smaller then.

A central part of the *Onion* sensibility, always, was that we were underdogs. All those early *Onion* stories about pot smokers and dishwashers and nerds and fat guys eating at buffets, or sad housewives buying Swiffer products, tapped into that. We made jokes about political figures and celebrities because we were not them, and then we made jokes about sad sacks because we *were* them. I don't think anyone in the writer's room back then had had a normal, fun childhood.

Do you feel that the paper's humor changed once it went national?

Things got a bit more clever and less silly. I think "Secondhand Smoke Linked to Secondhand Coolness" is an example of that. The humor started to be more about buzzwords in the media and more about using journalism jargon. I'm also thinking of "Clinton Takes Leave of Office to Stand in Line for *Star Wars: Episode I*" and "Lewinsky Subpoenaed to Re-Blow Clinton on Senate Floor." But then I think as it moved into the George W. Bush years, things started to get a little more pointed and satirical: "Bush: 'Our Long National Nightmare of Peace and Prosperity Is Finally Over'" and "Bush on North Korea: 'We Must Invade Iraq.'"

Most of *The Onion*'s staff, not including the A.V. Club, moved to New York just before 9/11. *The Onion* was the first comedy outlet—including TV shows, stand-up comedians, anything or anyone—to tackle the horror of that day. Can you talk about what it was like working on that 9/11 issue?

Oh, man. The *Onion* writing staff had just moved to New York in January of 2001—and then in September, that happened. We were basically just settling in and getting our sea legs. It happened on a Tuesday. All the writers spent the rest of the week freaking out like everyone else. The following Monday, six days after it happened, we went in for a meeting to figure out what we were going to do for the next issue. We decided we'd do a new issue, instead of putting out a reprint issue.

Anything that we could have republished from the years-long catalog of stories just seemed stupid and inconsequential. It almost seemed more offensive to run some old story about Doritos or something. We didn't initially plan to do an all-9/11 issue, but after working on it, it just turned into that. I mean, why wouldn't it? It was all any of the writers were thinking about. We were in New York, smelling the smoke and seeing the crushingly sad photocopied "missing" posters. It was actually really great to be working and focused on something instead of just wandering around in a daze or sitting around watching the news.

We normally never cared at all if we offended anyone. If we felt we were making a point we would stand behind, we didn't care if some people didn't "get it" or didn't agree with us. In this case, though, we all really did care what people thought; we didn't want anyone to think we were being disrespectful or making light of the situation. I just wanted to make things an infinitesimal degree better by giving people a break from all the horror.

In writing that issue, there were a lot of jokes that got thrown out because they were shocking in the wrong way. I think we did a good job of weeding those out. All the staff writers wanted to do the issue except for one. It was contributing writer Joe Garden—and I can understand where he was coming from. He just thought it was wrong and thought it would be the end of *The Onion*. The only bad thing about working on that issue was having to travel into Manhattan every day—it was scary and depressing, a war zone. But also, it was good to be around friends at a time like that, pitching jokes to each other.

We finished the paper and sent it off to the printers. There was a two-day wait before it hit the streets and the Internet. During that time, I was so nervous, second-guessing if we did the right thing, worried how people would react. Then the issue went online and a trickle of e-mails started coming in, and then a flood. And they were 95 percent positive. On a normal week, 50 percent of the e-mails were people complaining—so this was really good. All these people were writing long, long e-mails to say "thank you" and to say how much the issue meant to them and how they cried while reading it. I was so relieved and so happy and proud.

People have said that this particular *Onion* issue was special not because it came out so fast but because we actually made jokes *about* 9/11. Other comedy outlets came back with no jokes at all or unrelated jokes.

We also wanted to avoid any headline like "Thing Everyone Knew Was Going to Happen, Finally Happens." Or a headline like "We Told You So, America!" Even though *The Onion* has a long history of chastising the government, we didn't want to touch on that for this particular issue. Then again, we didn't want to do a bunch of "Rah Rah U.S.A.!" flag-waving headlines, either.

You wrote a now-famous headline for the 9/11 issue that seemed to perfectly sum up the nation's mood: "Not Knowing What Else to Do, Woman Bakes American-Flag Cake." That particular headline was mentioned in newspapers across the world. It was mentioned again and reprinted on the tenth anniversary of 9/11. Were you at all surprised by the positive reaction to it?

I'm glad people liked it. Some of the stories in that issue were kind of cocky and opinionated—if your God tells you to kill people, maybe he's not such a good God. So I'm glad some of the stories were about the sheer sadness and confusion we were feeling. We didn't feel like we totally understood what was happening.

Over the years, have you been the go-to person for any specific type of *Onion* story?

I wrote a lot of stories about the sad mundanity of life. Fat guys, blue-collar workers, starving Africans, emotionally needy women. You know, the stories that really don't have a lot of jokes.

I wrote one [April 1998] with the headline "My Goal Is to Someday Be a Realtor," which doesn't even have a joke. It's just ridiculing this woman for having small dreams instead of just giving up and being totally hopeless.

And yet this Realtor does seem to be content. I was reading through some of your articles again and I saw that a common theme is cheerfulness in the face of adversity.

Or in what would be my idea of hell. Yeah, I guess so. I do like to write about characters who probably should be depressed but who, for whatever reason, find their situation okay, or even a little exciting. I wouldn't be so cheerful. I guess an example of that would be "It's Not a Crack House, It's a Crack Home" [December 3, 1996].

You've also written quite a few stories featuring female characters—usually young and naïve—who might not grasp how bad their lives are about to become.

There's something particularly detestable about people who are stupid and completely wrong but still have attitude. It's funny to hear these characters spout off when you know what's in store for them. I wrote columns by a recurring op-ed character named Amber Richardson, with headlines like "I Hope My Baby Doesn't Come Out All Fucked-Up and Shit" and "My Baby Don't Want No Medicine." She was a teen mom who was always railing against her "bitch social worker." This sixteen-year-old single mother is probably at a high point in her life, complaining about her poor social worker and ragging on her friends.

I earned a teaching degree in college. I did my student teaching at a high school in Madison for pregnant teens. It was pretty sad. A couple of the girls were smoking specifically because they had heard it would make the baby smaller—they thought it would make the labor less painful if the baby was small. One girl "stole" another girl's baby name, Rae Rae, after giving birth first. There was a lot of material that you never would have ever thought up if you were trying to write for a teen mom. You just had to hear it.

Do you see a difference now between your sensibility and the sensibility of the current, younger writers for _The Onion_?

I think writers for _The Onion_ are still mostly weirdos. And _The Onion_'s use of freelance writers contributes to that, too. There are people who can live in Michigan and submit jokes every week out of their parents' basement.

I think there is a new thing that I've noticed where more younger people have begun to see comedy as a viable career and approach it that way. It's not that they're not funny and talented; they are, but they also go about it with a goal in mind. They know they have to work up their résumé and get their foot in the door at various places. This is so foreign to the way I started and how the older comedy writers I know started. They were doing comedy because they felt like they didn't fit into the jobs they were supposed to pursue. So they did this other thing as an outlet. And then when they started to make money, it was almost surprising.

In 2013, you were hired as a writer on the TV show *Community*. What's the difference between writing for *Community* and for *The Onion*?

Writing for *Community* is, of course, very different than writing for *The Onion*. The show is [comedy writer and producer] Dan Harmon's show—he created and runs it. When you're writing for it, you're writing for him. At *The Onion*, our goal was to maintain the consistency of the "*Onion* voice." Because it was this collective thing, and there was no single creator, we could argue endlessly about what was in the *Onion* voice and what wasn't. The whole process was very democratic—in both good and bad ways.

The *Onion* voice at its best is rather cold and stiff and clinical, which I suppose is why the hive-mind system works so well. *Community*, on the other hand, is a very warm show, and that's because of Dan Harmon and his love for his characters. People who don't watch it sometimes have the misconception that *Community* is all genre parody and pop culture references—I myself made that mistake before I actually saw it. But the genius of *Community* is that even within those genre-joke episodes it never sells out its characters or abandons the emotionality of the story.

Dan Harmon, who began his career as an improv performer in Milwaukee and then began writing for TV in 1999, is notorious for breaking down the plots and storylines in a very analytical way.

Dan has a method for breaking stories, a modified version of the hero's journey. The character leaves his zone of comfort, has a road of trials, and returns home having changed. It's physically represented with a circle divided into four parts. We use these circles each time we're working on a specific story. We spend all day drawing them on the dry-erase boards, marking them up, erasing them, drawing new ones. I literally see these circles in my sleep. Last night, I was dreaming about a vacation I'm about to take, and in my dream I was using Dan Harmon's circle to figure out what I should do on the trip. This system is a great way to make sure that your stories aren't too plotty and linear. It helps you wrestle endless options into an emotionally meaningful story. I will definitely use it whenever I write something from now on. I'm learning a lot from Dan.[1]

As someone who's achieved her dream of becoming a successful professional comedy writer, do you now consider yourself a happy person?

For me, writing comedy is about being unhappy. It's about being unhappy with the way things are, and wanting to write something that is critical of those things, but in a way that isn't so self-serious. Or it's about being on the outside of something a bit, feeling left out, and needing to create your own fun. Or wanting to create something that excludes other people—the people who don't get it—in order to circle the wagons a bit around people who *are* like you. I think if you are happy and fit in, you have little reason to develop a sense of humor. There are always exceptions, but swimsuit models and Wall Street dudes aren't funny. They have no reason to question the world. It's working for them. *Life is sweet, bro!*

I'm not actually an unhappy person. I'm not one of those angry or depressed comedy writers. I just think I am distrustful of the world and of accepting things at face value, and I guess that's a result of my childhood.

---

1   Megan Ganz, writer for *Community*: "The best thing I ever learned about script writing has come from working on *Community*. The creator, Dan Harmon, had us write these things called 'spit drafts,' which is basically an outline for your script. It's the shape of that script. You write out the script scene by scene with dummy dialogue that you'll later replace with actual jokes. For instance, the character of Jeff walks into the room, and Jeff says, 'Here's the point where I say that we should all go get a sandwich.' And then the character of Annie will say, 'I don't want to do that.' And then another character will say, 'I have a joke here.' You can have them do whatever you want, but you just have to get through the scene and have all of what needs to happen in that scene baldly stated.

"If you can't get through a script that way, then chances are your story doesn't work. If you're stuck and you feel like you have writer's block, this is a really helpful method because it distinguishes between, 'Okay, do you have story problems or are you having a hard time writing the dialogue?' Also, when you write really quickly, you end up writing really good jokes anyway; it's almost as if you trick your brain into thinking that it doesn't matter."

I think things have to be better for kids these days simply because of the Internet. I'm just talking about weird, shy kids wearing the wrong jeans, not kids who are molested by their gym teachers or have degenerative bone disorders or who are getting shot at. They're just fucked. But these days, slightly different kids can find other people with their interests. It must help them feel like they're not total freaks.

Then again, maybe it's a bad thing. I think young writers feel more entitled to be published now than ever before: "I can publish on my blog. Why won't *The New Yorker* publish me?"

At the very least, I think comedy can help misfits cope. It's not for everyone, so it becomes a place for someone to fit in, either as a consumer or as a maker of comedy. Any area of interest can help someone achieve that sense of community, whether it's astronomy or a particular style of comedy. But comedy is better because it makes you laugh and it physically works those underdeveloped nerd stomach muscles.

What advice would you have for those high school or college students wanting to develop those underdeveloped nerd muscles?

As far as specific advice for those wanting to get into comedy writing, do a bunch of stuff for free. Even if you live in some godforsaken hellhole. There are so many blogs out there and humor websites, as well as people who act or produce and need scripts. Writing for free will make you write a lot, which is the only way to become a better writer. Everyone knows that reading a book about how to write comedy is a big joke. You just have to do it.

College kids used to show me their versions of *The Onion*—often called something like *The Scallion* or *The Bunion*—and they'd want me to be impressed. But it was hard; I was already doing *The Onion*. What could I say? I mean, now *The Onion* is a format, but years ago, *The Onion* was created and developed by a bunch of college kids. The *Bunion* staff would be better off doing something new. So take a two-prong approach—learn how to write for other people but also, in a separate project, find an original voice.

Another thing: If you want to write comedy, I think that you shouldn't watch too much comedy. I think you start to rely too much on other people to tell you what's funny and ridiculous. You become needy for comment. Or else you start to feel that everything has already been done and you inadvertently close yourself off to having an honest and funny reaction to things. This might be bullshit because I do know a lot of comedy writers who are big fans of comedy and who watch a ton of it. But I also know a lot of comedy writers who tell funny stories as opposed to retelling jokes. It just gets annoying when there are five public figures everyone is making jokes about, and the jokes start to take on the same cadence.

So keep writing for free and then almost free, and then after a while, if you are good, you will rise to the top. Good writers are actually in demand. If you are not good, well, you will hopefully start to enjoy your day job as a web designer at an Internet company that sells moderately priced, fashion-forward men's pants. It's a win-win.

WILL TRACY

Editor in Chief, *The Onion*

....

Choosing Headlines at *The Onion*

Each week, the staff of *The Onion* reads an average of fifteen hundred headlines that arrive on Monday morning from both regular contributors and freelancers. Now, that's a lot of goddamn jokes. It's really more jokes than the human brain is able to reasonably and intelligently process within the span of five days. Only a handful of jokes are truly funny and exceptional enough to break through the benumbed haze of our writers' room and see the light of day. The rest, meanwhile, are immediately thrown onto the corpse pile and, like my high school years, never spoken of again.

I have chosen nine rejected jokes from a recent Monday headline list and specified the reason why each joke, ultimately, was not picked. The individual reasons why these jokes were not picked tend to come up over and over again. We are constantly repeating the same death sentences about how a joke is "too this" or "too that." This is how you develop consistency as a joke writer, but this is also how—slowly but surely—you begin to lose your mind.

I have also included five jokes and why they *were* picked.

REJECTED HEADLINE: Next Quentin Tarantino Movie to Offer Slick, Stylish Take on Rwandan Genocide

I could see how this would be written out, and we could probably come up with some funny casting choices and an amusing description of the film's story, as well as a realistic-looking poster. But it just feels like the obvious joke to make about Tarantino at this point. Even though it might be a popular story for us to do, it would be popular because it's telling people, essentially, a joke they've already heard before.

REJECTED HEADLINE: Nation's Environmental Experts Quietly Moving Families Inland

Here's something that happens to us, depressingly, quite often . . . we've already done this joke. "Nation's Economists Quietly Evacuating Their Families" [August 12, 2012]. Hence, we killed this immediately. We have over twenty years' worth of these headlines, so the chances of doing a joke we haven't done before grows a little slimmer with each passing day.

REJECTED HEADLINE: Non-Time Traveler Warns Humanity of Dystopian Present

Here is a similar, yet different problem for us: Someone else has already done this joke. It was on *McSweeney's* ["It's Difficult Convincing Time Travelers That the Present Day Is Not a Dystopia," by David Henne, January 3, 2011]. We generally kill any joke that is similar to another comedy outlet's joke. The most common joke-killer, by far, is *The Simpsons*, because they've already made every joke ever. *Mr. Show* comes up, too, and, occasionally, *The Colbert Report*.

REJECTED HEADLINE: Study: Majority of Americans Covered in Layer of Crumbs

This is a halfway-decent joke, and not one we've made before, exactly, but it's part of a genre of jokes that we've just made too many of recently. Sometimes we hit a certain genre too often and need to take a break. We've opted to take a break from writing about overeating Americans for a bit, although, I'm sure, not for *too* long.

REJECTED HEADLINE: Parents Who Spend Every Waking Moment in Anguish Proud Son Is Serving His Country

This appears to be an interesting juxtaposition and comment, but ultimately, it's not enough of an escalation of reality. It just reads as too real. Also, feeling anguish over your son serving in the armed forces overseas is not necessarily a mutually exclusive feeling from being proud that your son is serving his country. I'm sure many military parents openly hold both opinions at the same time, and feel no conflict in doing so. It feels like a toothless piece of satire.

REJECTED HEADLINE: Instagram Photo Very Unique, Sources Agree

This would be a popular story, but, like the Tarantino joke, it's the joke that everyone is making. We look pretty stupid when we make the same basic joke that everyone else is making, because we have a reputation for doing the opposite. *The Onion* has a long history of snidely pointing out how everyone is making the same point. We're jerks in that sense.

REJECTED HEADLINE: Area Man Stocking Up on Computers for Impending Cyber-War

Something about this still amuses me—I like the idea of someone physically stockpiling computers like they're rifles or something. But it's just too odd, and the logic doesn't actually hold. It's the kind of joke we talk about for a few minutes in the room until the question of "How would you actually write this?" is posed, and then we drop it and move on.

REJECTED HEADLINE: Chuck E. Cheese's Costume Only Halfway Off Before Screaming at Eight-Year-Old Daughter

I'm not a fan of this joke. It's just too easy, and too constructed. You can see the thought process of the writer, thinking, I'm going to take an upsetting situation (a man yelling at his daughter) and then juxtapose it with an easy, go-to example of something silly and harmless (the Chuck E. Cheese's costume). But it has no basis in reality. It's a situation that exists only in Comedy Writer Land.

REJECTED HEADLINE: Only Way to Prevent Gorilla Attacks Is Bigger Gorillas Everywhere, Says NRA Head

This one was not technically a reject, per se, as it led to a reworded headline using the same concept. The gun control joke was, I felt, too convoluted and too jokey. It seemed to parallel the real-life headlines I was seeing. The writers' and editors' room batted around a few rewordings and came up with "Gorilla Sales Skyrocket after Latest Gorilla Attack" [January 10, 2013], which just reads cleaner and sharper. A lot of headlines are submitted to a similar brand of torture.

And now for five jokes and why they *were* chosen as headlines:

Ten-Year-Old Wishes Unemployed Father Couldn't Make It to Just One of His Little League Games

It's a switch I haven't seen before. There is something really elegant and satisfying about a headline that looks almost exactly like its real-world antecedent, the only difference being the addition or subtraction of a few key letters here and there, and suddenly the meaning becomes *completely* different. And yet, there is still a logic in place that completely holds. We all know the cliché of the busy, careerist father who can't make it to his son's Little League game, but anyone who has ever played Little League is just as familiar with the somewhat pathetic, embarrassing father who is way, *way* too into the game because he may not have much else in his life at that point. To me, that's a perfectly clean switch.

Film Character Moves into Beautiful Brooklyn Brownstone after Getting Dream Publishing Job

This is sort of a mini-genre within *The Onion*, wherein we report on a movie or television reality in our dry editorial voice as though it were *actual* reality. The subtext generally being that the reality presented in movies and television is just utter, lying horseshit. Most of our writers are thoroughly—perhaps unhealthily—pop culture literate, so it is generally fairly easy for us to get into this world, inhabit it, and, in so doing, expose exactly what is manipulative and false about these narratives we are fed over and over again. Also, there is always a slight warmth to these pieces, because I think a lot of our writers have an inherent nerdish fondness for bad, junky movies.

Report: Chinese Third Graders Falling Behind U.S. High School Students in Science, Math

I was unsure about this one at first because, while it's a cleverly worded joke, I wasn't sure the story itself would have legs. I also worried the joke might be more "clever" than funny. Ultimately, though, I think it's good for an issue of *The Onion*, or a week's worth of content, to have a certain ratio of smart to silly, and this is just a solid satirical joke. It is all couched in this very official "report" language, as though this were an alarming, surprising trend. It looks *just* like a news headline, which helps, and it calls up so much unspoken subtext for the reader to think about: the state of the U.S. education system, the rise of China, the economic realities that await both countries. And yet you don't have to come out and say any of that; it's all perfectly implied by the perspective of the joke.

Torrent of Soap Issues from Wildly Unexpected Part of Dispenser

This is another entry in the cherished *Onion* subgenre of Small Made Big, in which we take the must prosaic, insignificant, ordinary event that could ever occur and report on it as though it were huge, breaking, front-page news. "Rubber Band Needed" is another entry in this genre. I like this one in particular because the language in the headline is so heightened, so dramatic. And I immediately smile when I see a headline like this—something so incredibly minor—and then see that there are fucking eight hundred words of text beneath it. Overkill like that makes me laugh.

Robert Mapplethorpe Children's Museum Celebrates Grand Opening

Sometimes just the thought of what the finished Photoshopped graphic will look like is enough to sell me.

PURE, HARD-CORE ADVICE

GABE DELAHAYE

....

Writer, *This American Life, Funny or Die, McSweeney's,
Gawker, Huffington Post,* ESPN, CNN;
Founding Editor, *Videogum*

When it comes to advice about humor writing, or really any type of writing, two things seem to stick out. The first is that you should really be looking for better advice. Humor writing? Give me a break! How about advice that might actually lead to the earning of actual money? Or even advice on which specific advice classes to take? That might prove more fruitful. The second thing that sticks out is something I was once told, which I am paraphrasing here: "You aren't good at writing, but if you can get over that, then one day maybe you will be okay at writing." I think that's really solid advice. If you're reading this right now, you might not be a great writer—in fact, you probably aren't. No offense! But if you accept that, then maybe you can start working your way toward the holy grail of writing: not being a terrible writer. But this takes time! You know who starts out great? High school football captains. And you know what they do

204 | Poking a Dead Frog

now? They sell insulated hot tub liners to pay for their alimony. So relax.

When it comes to writing advice, there really is no such thing. No one who's successful knows exactly how their path has led to their success. Every journey is different. It doesn't matter how Erma Bombeck did it because your path is your own and no one else's.

With that said, these ideas have worked for me:

#1. Write what you think is funny. This does not mean anyone else will agree, but if you write what you *hope* others will think is funny, you have already alienated at least some readers.

#2. If you aren't willing to do something for free at first, no one is going to pay for it later. It is called "paying your dues" for a reason. Truth be told, you might never get paid, but how is that different from no one paying for it now? Besides, if this is about money for you, you are very confused about where all the money is hidden.

#3. It is almost never worth arguing with someone on the Internet about anything—*ever*. Unless they think 9/11 was an inside job, in which case it might be funny.

#4. If you are lucky enough to get an audience for your comedy, be nice to that audience. You are lucky to have them.

#5. You don't *have* to be a writer or a comedian. Quitting is allowed. I'm not saying you should quit—I'm just saying that it's an option that a lot of writing and comedy advice books don't provide, even though they should. Writing is boring and solitary and lonely and awful. Comedy is even worse. You're not living in ancient Sparta, Greece. Stop fighting. You can do whatever you want in life. Make a baby with an insulated hot tub lining salesman. He's still got it! Or go back to choosing which advice classes might be most useful.

#6. Make friends with smart, funny, highly motivated, encouraging, wonderful people who are more talented than you. This is obviously easier said than done, so you should stop reading this immediately and go get started on that.

Good luck.

GLEN CHARLES

During an interview with *NPR: Morning Edition* in 2012, famed TV director James Burrows (*The Mary Tyler Moore Show*, *The Bob Newhart Show*, *Wings*, *Frasier*, and many others) shared what he called "one of the biggest laughs [he] ever heard." The laugh in question came during an episode in the second season of *Taxi*, which aired in 1979, when Reverend Jim (played by Christopher Lloyd) attempts to cheat on his driver's license written exam.

"What does a yellow light mean?" Jim whispers to his friends from the Sunshine Cab Company who are standing nearby. Bobby (played by Jeff Conaway) whispers back, "Slow down." Jim considers this, and then responds, "What . . . does . . . a . . . yellow . . . light . . . mean?" The joke is repeated again and again—each time more slowly—until, according to Burrows, the "laugh goes on for forty-five seconds," one of the longest in the history of television.

The script was written by two brothers, Glen and Les Charles. It was one of seventeen teleplays they wrote for *Taxi* and the beginning of a fruitful creative relationship with Burrows.

The brothers were raised just outside Las Vegas by Mormon parents in the 1940s. Both graduated from the University of Redlands with a degree in liberal arts, with Glen pursuing a career as an advertising copywriter and Les working as a substitute high school teacher. But one night in the early 1970s, while watching CBS on Saturday night—which, at the time had a legendary lineup, including *All in the Family* and *The Bob Newhart Show*—both brothers were inspired to try co-writing a spec script for *The Mary Tyler Moore Show*. They submitted the script to MTM Enterprises, the show's production company, but never received a response.

Undeterred, they kept writing, finishing dozens of spec scripts. They were so confident in their abilities that they quit their respective day jobs, devoting themselves exclusively to writing. Les and his wife were living out of a Volkswagen bus when he and Glen finally sold a script, an episode of *M*A*S*H*, which they'd titled "The Late Captain Pierce" (it aired in October 1975). But then came more rejection.

Two years later, almost penniless, they finally heard back from MTM, who not only bought their original *Mary Tyler Moore* script ("Mary and the Sexagenarian," which aired in February 1977) but also hired them as staff writers, where they contributed scripts to *Doc*, *The Bob Newhart Show*, and the *Mary Tyler Moore* spin-off *Phyllis*. This experience led to their friendship with director and producer James L. Brooks, who hired them as writers and coproducers on a new show called *Taxi*. And *Taxi* led to a friendship with James Burrows, a director on the show, who eventually lured them away to launch their own production company, Charles-Burrows-Charles, which resulted in the long-running series that Amy Poehler, in an October 2012 *GQ* oral history, called "the best TV show that's ever been": *Cheers*.

Though ratings for the first season of *Cheers* were poor, both NBC chairman Grant Tinker and the network's president, Brandon Tartikoff, were fans, and the show received critical praise and plenty of awards, earning 4 of its 117 Emmy nominations (it would eventually win a total of 28). Eventually, the world discovered it, and *Cheers* went on to run for eleven seasons, from 1982 to 1993. Nearly everybody in the cast—Ted Danson, Shelley Long, and Kelsey Grammer—became stars. For the final episode, which aired in May 1993, more than 42 million viewers tuned in, including thousands who watched on giant screens set up outside Boston's Bull & Finch bar, the inspiration for the *Cheers* setting. It was a public event, the likes of which will probably never be seen for a final TV show again.

But the real stars of *Cheers* were the scripts. It could be argued that the script Glen and Les wrote for the premiere episode of *Cheers*—"Give Me a Ring Sometime," which aired in September 1982—was one of the best, if not *the* greatest, premiere script ever penned for a sitcom. Megan Ganz, now a writer for *Community*, says, "What's amazing about that pilot is how much exposition Glen and Les were able to do with the characters just sitting down and talking with each other. Nothing actually happens. They were able to do a great amount in a very small space and with very little." When it came time for Megan Ganz to write her first script for *Community* in 2011, she says, "When I was writing that episode, I just kept thinking, Be like the *Cheers* script and it'll be great."

You grew up in the 1950s in Henderson, Nevada, just on the outskirts of Las Vegas. Did your father work in the gaming industry?

Les and I had a yin-yang childhood. Our mother, a very kind and sweet-tempered lady, was an elementary school teacher, a devout Mormon, and determined to get us all into heaven. Our father, a Mormon but an errant one, worked as a dealer in several Vegas casinos, the gambling dens in the City of Sin. Many are gone from memory. Actually, most of them are gone, period. They all deserve it—they never gave the man Christmas off.

By most measures, my father was not a good father. He certainly wasn't abusive either physically or emotionally. Mostly he wasn't there. Neither Les nor I can remember him ever playing a game of catch with us. He did take me fishing once. He kept telling me to be quiet. "Don't talk to me. Or the fish." I finally told him, "You're the one doing all the talking." Male bonding is an elusive thing.

I do remember Les and I watching comedy on television with our father. He had a great sense of humor and a great laugh. I don't remember him ever telling a formal joke. He'd give wry offhand commentary on things. A cheery, "Come and see us again when you can't stay so long," was his idea of good-bye. He'd dismiss envy with, "I wish I had that car and he had a pimple on his ass." I'm making him sound angry, but he was not. He was essentially a sweet man with no driving ambitions. He did dabble with a stamp collection. For a time he had a drinking problem.

Your father didn't abide by the Mormon teachings of not consuming alcohol?

He was definitely a Jack Mormon, meaning that except for funerals he rarely saw the inside of a church. He was not religious. On his days off, he would go with a group of buddies and spend most of the day and night imbibing, and then come home, often just to clean up, change clothes, and then be on his merry way again. He changed jobs quite often. Not always his choice.

Not unlike the Norm character on *Cheers*.

Norm was a composite whose essential ingredient was George Wendt [the actor who played Norm], but yes, there was a lot of Dad in there. He would have loved to have found a bar like Cheers, and, for all we know, maybe he did. We of course never joined him on his convivial travels. He was an amiable guy who enjoyed being in his comfort zone with his own people. Of course my mother was mortified by my father's drinking; she was so afraid that he would be arrested, that he would be involved in some kind of accident, and that all of us, the whole family, would have to change our identities, leave the area, and never show our faces again. And, in fact, one night my father was in a bar, and at closing time he got into his car and immediately backed into a Highway Patrol squad car. Occupied, by the way. Needless to say, he didn't get off with a warning. He spent the night in jail. The good news is that he never drank again. And he later started going to church on a regular basis, although neither his heart nor soul was really in it. But his body in a suit and tie on a pew next to my mother was just fine with her. The problem for us, her sons, was that she could now go to work on us.

Did you ever have an opportunity to meet some of the characters your father hung out with at the bar?

A few. My mother was less than thrilled when Dad brought them home, so he rarely did. These were people who lived on the periphery of casino life and who would scatter when they heard a siren. Some of them I liked. I found them far more interesting than anybody I met in church.

The 1950s Las Vegas that you're talking about was a city vastly different from today's family-friendly tourist attraction.

Everything was adults only. I had a friend who was in the business of making fake IDs. When I got my first driver's license at sixteen, I enlisted his help and suddenly became a very young twenty-one-year-old. I immediately gained access to casinos and shows and the world of [singer] Louis Prima and [comedian] Shecky Greene and, of course, Don Rickles. My first nightclub experience was a young Don Rickles in the lounge at the Sahara. It was so great. It was bright, it was loud, and here was this comedian mercilessly taking shots at everything that moved. This was something me and my buddies did with each other. The first night I saw Rickles, he did a running bit, exchanging double-talk Japanese with his Asian bass player, and they went back and forth bowing politely and jabbering. And Rickles finally said, "I shot your brother out of a tree!" And I thought, Geez, can you say that? During the course of the evening he insulted pretty much everybody's race, color, creed, and wife's looks. I realized then that comedy could be dangerous. So could falsifying your ID, by the way. We were let off with a warning.

Who were your favorite comedians on television at the time?

Jackie Gleason and Sid Caesar were two early favorites when we got our first television set. I watched their series fairly religiously. As

I got older, I also was a fan of comedians who would appear on variety shows like Ed Sullivan. People like Nichols and May, Richard Pryor, Shelley Berman, and Bob Newhart. Newhart was a big favorite not just for his guest appearances but for his comedy albums. I wore out the grooves on the [1960 album] *The Button-Down Mind of Bob Newhart.*

Jack Benny was another big favorite. There's never been another comedian like him. Jack Benny never told jokes. He was the joke. He let himself be the butt of other people's sniping at his cheapness, his vanity, lousy violin playing, and lying about his age long past credibility. It's been said that he made everyone around him funny, and he did. But you always laughed more at his response to these indignities than to the funny people in his stock company. The wait for him to respond to a thief telling him, "Your money or your life," gets funnier the longer it goes. It's supposedly one of the longest laughs in radio history. Underneath it all, I think I like Jack Benny because his persona was of a man who persisted in his vanity and illusions, no matter how often everyone he met would contradict him. Also, he established this comic persona in radio and translated it, intact, seamlessly to television.

Radio was a huge influence on me. Maybe not for Les, who's younger, but I think it's a great training ground for comedy writers. For all screenwriters, actually.

How so?

The great thing about radio is that the listener is an active participant. You're given a soundtrack and the pictures are up to you. Some people said *Cheers* could have been a radio show. We didn't consider that a criticism.

Were you aware, as a child, that there were writers for these radio comedy shows that you enjoyed?

No, not in any real sense. When the credits were announced, they would say "Written by" and "Produced by." That had no meaning for me. When television later came along, I was amazed by the number of people it took to write comedy. A seemingly simple show like *The Honeymooners*, for example, had more writers than characters.

It would have been difficult for me to have fashioned a writing career without radio. It was a tremendous educational tool. It was very informative, but entertaining at the same time. It was all about the dialogue.

I've always loved listening to great dialogue and it seems we're now becoming an entertainment culture where dialogue is not as revered as it once was. With a lot of films now, there will be a line, another line, and then a cut. You look at some of the films from the thirties and forties, and there were long scenes where it's just two people talking. I don't think we have the attention span to stay with something like that right now. We need continual visual stimulation to keep interested.

Do you think that today's pop culture contains an overabundance of stimuli?

I have heard that 3D television can overstimulate the brain. But anyway, who cares really? That monster is out of the cage. I like all the eyeball dazzling as much as anyone. I am getting tired of big special effects and CGI movies about Armageddon and something from the bowels of the earth. But for all the babbling I do about radio and films of the thirties and forties, I'm happy to be around today. Most of the good stuff from that time is available anyway.

How far back does this dream to write go?

My first career ambition was to be a ventriloquist. I liked [the radio comedy team] Edgar Bergen and Charlie McCarthy a lot. So I went and bought a book on ventriloquism. I told my parents that I wanted a dummy for Christmas. Some parents would have been shocked that their ten- or eleven-year-old boy wanted a doll, but mine didn't have any trouble with it. They couldn't afford therapy for me or themselves anyway. So I got my little friend, studied a bit, and performed at family reunions and school talent shows in the area. This lasted for two or three years.

Do you remember any specific jokes?

I had an uncle who'd lost his hair and I'd joke about how he wasn't bald, he just had an "exceptionally wide part." I would mostly just lift material from other ventriloquists.

Were you a fan of any movie comedians?

I was a big fan of the comedians who dealt with misfortune. Those who weren't successful, happy people, but those who somehow triumphed. Even if they didn't, they thought they did. W. C. Fields, a big influence. I was a huge Chaplin fan, but I was a much bigger Buster Keaton fan. Chaplin was obviously brilliant, but he could be a bit mawkish at times, whereas Keaton was all about funny.

Talking to me about influences is difficult, because I've had friends who have influenced my comedy. I have some very, very funny friends. When I was in the army in basic training, maybe the worst experience of my life, there was a guy in there who truly, truly was one of the funniest people I've ever met. I have no idea whatever happened to him, it's been a long time, but if he was able to put something on paper he could have certainly worked in the business. Often that's the difference between those who make it and those who go on to do other things. Just putting something on paper. Over and over and over.

When you later attended college, did you major in creative writing?

I never took a college writing course. I was a literature major. It was only after I graduated in 1965 that I took a course in comedy writing offered by UCLA extension. I had always been interested in comedy. It was taught by a person I'd never heard of who claimed to have written a lot of things I also never heard of. In the end, it was not very productive.

What did this teacher claim he had written?

I think he'd done punch-up for some sitcoms. The only thing I remember him telling us that had any kind of relevance was that the best jokes are the briefest. One of the other students in this class was Garry Shandling. Garry had just arrived to Hollywood. I'm not sure he'd even remember it but we once chatted about how useless this class was.

Many who teach humor writing have never actually made a living at humor writing. The majority tend to be more fans of comedy.

It would be difficult to teach. We're all perpetual students in this. You're always learning something, no matter how long you've been at it. When you're producing a television show and you're talking out a story with a writer, that is—in a way—a professor-student relationship. I've been on both sides of that equation, and it's as much a learning process for the ones running the meeting.

Are you still learning?

You're always learning when it comes to comedy. It's the nature of the game. There just simply aren't any hard-and-fast rules. The margin of error with the writing of a joke can be very, very small.

Many times over my career I had a joke that I was absolutely sure about. It would work all week at the reading and at the rehearsal. But by the time it got in front of an audience, it was lukewarm.

That's one of the things that fascinates me about humor writing. If you work as, say, a plumber or an electrician for forty years, I'd imagine your work tends to become less mysterious over time. Pipe A goes into Pipe B. *This* wire needs to be attached to *that* wire. With comedy, however, it seems that no matter how long you've worked in the field, it remains just as murky as it might have felt in the beginning.

It remains difficult. You never really know. But I think you develop a thermometer of sorts. I think you do become more sophisticated about what's going to work and what isn't. But because comedy is so subjective, what would put me on the floor will have you standing stone-faced. And it could change day to day.

Here's why this business makes you crazy. It was early on in Kirstie Alley's stay on *Cheers*. The beat was essentially Sam comes into her office to talk about something. She gives him a bad time, and he turns to leave and says something to the effect of, "You know, I bet when you smile, you light up a room. You should smile a lot more. It would really help." She pretends to be coy and shy. Eventually she does end up smiling at him. The joke was Sam then saying, "I'll be darned." Meaning, her smile didn't light up the room. And all week it worked. But when it came time for the shoot, it didn't work in front of the studio audience.

Looking back, do you think that joke needed some tweaking?

We figured it out in editing. During production we thought Sam's "I'll be darned" was the joke. In fact, Kirstie's reaction after the line when her smile turned to smoldering hatred was what we'd been laughing at all week. And, fortunately, it worked on film for the audience at home where it mattered most.

How did you go from taking an unproductive comedy-writing course with Garry Shandling to landing your first TV-writing job?

My brother and I wanted to write comedy. We were both dissatisfied with our lives. He was living in a Volkswagen bus with his wife. I began working as an advertising copywriter at a small firm in Los Angeles.

Les and I decided to try our hand at writing for TV. *Sitcom* wasn't the same pejorative term it had been. There were at least three high-quality comedies on the air; they were all different. There was *All in the Family*. There was *M*A*S*H*. And there was *Mary Tyler Moore*. Les and I were big fans of all three but especially *M*A*S*H* and *Mary Tyler Moore*. We watched some episodes and fired off a spec script to both of them. This served as our audition. We just watched and thought we could do it. Simple as that. *M*A*S*H* responded right away. For the *Mary Tyler Moore* script, MTM Enterprises took eleven months to get back to us, during which time we had pretty much decided to quit. But after a couple of scripts they ended up putting us on staff.

MTM, which produced *The Mary Tyler Moore Show*, was where you wanted to be as a TV comedy writer. There were so many good shows going on. It was really a community. MTM had picnics; they had tennis tournaments. It was just a fun place to be. It was a very bright, happening place.

Writing comedy as a team is always a difficult situation, even in the best of circumstances. But how much more difficult was it for you and your brother? Not only being writing partners, but also siblings?

We basically shared comedy DNA; we'd usually laugh at the same things, find the same people funny.

As showrunners, we kind of split functions. With comedy teams, one writer might be more joke-oriented; another might be more story-oriented. But it's very hard to differentiate. Les is very good at organizing and putting stories in order and sequence. He's more analytical. He was a good goalkeeper. I would say I'm a more active pitcher of stories and jokes. Obviously, there was overlap.

Were there ever fights over jokes?

There were, but if we got to the point where there was still a disagreement after discussion, we'd say, "Let's just throw it out." And over the years, arguments declined in frequency and intensity. No joke is worth the time and effort spent on talking about it. If you're unable to come up with a better joke, that's a bigger problem anyway. Also, we had to find a way to get along so as not to spoil family gatherings.

In 1978, you became the showrunners on *Taxi*. The executive producer of *Taxi* was Jim Brooks, who later went on to direct *Terms of Endearment*, *Broadcast News*, and *As Good as It Gets*. In Hollywood, Brooks is talked about in almost reverential tones, but with also a sort of fear. There are stories that to work for him is a rewarding experience that can also be quite challenging.

He was definitely a perfectionist. He always thought we could do better. I had a friend in comedy who said the worst day of his life was the day he met Jim Brooks—he realized he was never going to be the best. Jim has this fertile, fast, unpredictable comic perspective on things. We learned so much from him. He always had a fix. Even if it didn't work, it usually led somewhere.

Jim and the other producers on *Taxi* [Stan Daniels, David Davis, and Ed. Weinberger] had this formula—and this is just my opinion—but they felt that creating a great show has to involve a lot of angst. There has to be pain. If the show has an easy week, it's suspect.

Don't most shows—especially great shows—involve great angst?

I'm not convinced that you have to have a painful process to get a good result. Certainly, you can't be lackadaisical when you want something and it's not coming. When you're not getting what you want out of a scene, you've got to keep working at it. Believe me, Les and I had plenty of painful moments when we were later in charge, but we never insisted on difficulty being an essential aspect of the process.

One of the things that always struck me about *Taxi* is how melancholy its theme song was. It's a very low-key opening for a sitcom.

I remember liking it a lot when I first heard it. Up to that point, it was only big feel-good openings for sitcoms. But for *Taxi*, the theme song is very subdued, and for a reason. There was a sadness to *Taxi*, I think. There's a sadness to all the characters. Someone once described *Taxi* as being a show about hell. All of the characters were essentially stuck in a very bleak environment, struggling to get out. I can definitely see that.

We were obviously not going for a subdued theme when we created *Cheers*. We spent a tremendous amount of time on it; it went through many different versions. Two writers worked on that song, Gary Portnoy, who had written for Air Supply and Dolly Parton, and a writer named Judy Hart Angelo. The first version was god-awful. So pat, so on the nose, rhyming, *cheers* with *beers*. It ultimately took five attempts. But when we heard the final version, we knew. It's interesting that with all of the writing talent that worked on *Cheers* over the years, the five words that are still the most associated with the show came not from any of us, but from the songwriters: "Where everybody knows your name."

Taxi had a huge cast. Was there ever a problem with a specific actor not being able to sell a joke that you wrote?

When you have a gang comedy as we did on both *Taxi* and *Cheers*, you have your leads, but you have to service everybody. This goes for both actors and their characters. Some actors are surer than others. Some characters are more multidimensional than others. Some you have to protect.

How do you protect a character?

You give them foolproof jokes. You give them jokes that don't necessarily have to be played, that don't depend solely on delivery. The cast was mostly very good on *Taxi*. I'm thinking of two characters at most.

One of the stand-out characters on Taxi was Latka Gravas, a mechanic from an unnamed foreign country, played by comedian Andy Kaufman. A lot has been written about Andy's genius since he died in 1984 at the age of thirty-five, but could you recognize his genius at the time?

Andy was excellent in the role and yet I always felt Latka didn't fit in with the rest of the characters on *Taxi*. The rest were all fairly realistic. Alex Rieger, the Judd Hirsch character, would be a point of contrast. The Latka character would have been better for an animated show. We went a little too broad with Latka. He was from a fictional country. He spoke in a completely invented accent and language.

Whether or not Andy was a genius, I don't know. He was sui generis. I've never met or heard a performer like him. I think there was a sadistic streak in his stand-up. Like reading the entirety of *The Great Gatsby* to an audience. I do feel that the character of Latka was the best thing Andy did, and it's how he will mostly be remembered.

What was Andy like to write for, to work with?

If Andy was unhappy he certainly didn't show us that. He was mostly very cooperative—when he was himself. But Andy had it written into his contract that his lounge-lizard character, Tony Clifton, would be featured on two *Taxi* episodes each season. Clifton was everything Andy wasn't. Loud, obnoxious, rude, misogynistic. So when we wrote these episodes, we'd give the Clifton character a minimal amount of lines. I think he had one or two at most. It had nothing really to do with the story. But Andy couldn't even do that. Kaufman, as Clifton, was just all over the place, intentionally. The director would ask, "Can you say a line this way?" And Tony Clifton would say, "I'm doin' it the way I want. You can go fuck yourself!" [Laughs] That may be the first time I ever laughed at Tony Clifton.

The upshot is that Andy wanted to be fired—or he wanted Tony Clifton to be fired. And he wanted the firing to be done in front of a lot of people on the soundstage. He wanted the security to come in. He wanted to make it a performance. Right after lunch one day, he was asked to leave the set. He exploded, "I'm not leavin'! You gotta deal . . . you gotta deal with *me*!" He went crazy, and the guards came in and escorted him out. He was screaming all the way. I guess in his mind, just great fun.

This particular event has become infamous in the comedy community, but I can also imagine that if you were somehow involved—that if the show you were working on was being held up because of such a performance—it might not have been terribly entertaining.

If this happened today, it'd be all over the Internet. Everything Andy did would be. In a way it's too bad Andy was before his time. He would have reached a lot more people on YouTube than he ever did on *Taxi*. Anyway, I found it surreal. I didn't find it funny. I find it even less funny in retrospect that we allowed the indulgence. In the seventies, everything was a little wilder. It was, "Hey, let's be part of this. We're young. We're hip. Let's let it happen."

We were having a party after the shoot on the *Taxi* stage one evening. Andy invited me and Jimmy Burrows, the director for most episodes, to come up to his dressing room and meet a poet. The poet was a lady—young, slender, and blonde. Andy introduced us as the producer and director and asked us to sit on the sofa. He informed us that the young lady preferred to write and read her poetry in the nude. She declined at first but then started to disrobe. At that point Jimmy, obviously not as big a poetry fan as I was, said we'd best be going. He reminded me that our wives were a matter of feet away at the party and would soon be wondering where we'd gone. Looking back on it, I'm thinking maybe that that's what Andy wanted—our wives to walk in. Not out of any animosity toward us but just as, what . . . performance art? If all this had happened to somebody else I might have loved it.

It got stranger. Tony Clifton was once kicked off the set, and he returned with a gun. There were about two or three days when we said, "Well, we can put up with this." But then we concluded that it wasn't fair to the rest of the cast to allow this type of disruption to go on. We were shooting a television show. We eventually decided this was something we couldn't tolerate. Call us party poopers, if you must.

From *Taxi*, you went on to create *Cheers*. You mentioned earlier that the setting for *Taxi* was quite bleak. With *Cheers*, however, I'd imagine it was extremely important, in a visual sense, to create not only an inviting bar for the fictional customers but also for the home viewers.

That's right. Les, Jimmy, and I had sort of settled on Boston as the setting for the series. I had never visited Boston, so my wife and I went to look around. We were staying at a hotel across from a bar called the Bull & Finch. We started our journey of discovery there on a Friday afternoon. All the regulars were already expounding on the state of the world. I loved it. I looked around and told my wife, "We don't need to go anywhere else. This is it." She said, "You know, you're going to spoil this place for their regulars." I said, "Sure, I guess, if we get really lucky . . ." I hope they've forgiven us over time.

The Bull & Finch eventually became the third-biggest tourist attraction in all of Boston.

The regulars later did complain the bar was ruined. It became a huge industry. I feel bad about that. But, look, we had no idea anything like that was going to happen.

On the bright side, the owner of the Bull & Finch reportedly became a millionaire.

He did well, yes.

After *Cheers* ended in 1993, an entertainment company built facsimiles of the *Cheers* bar in airports and hotels around the country. In each, there were two animatronic characters, Bob and Hank, modeled after Norm and Cliff. One was a delivery driver, the other a businessman. They would crack corny vaudevillian-style jokes.

We were asked permission and we said, "Sure." It was pretty much underway by the time we heard about it. I always found that strange. You entered a bar where no one, including the robots, knew your name.

***Cheers* was very much a character-driven show, less gimmicky and quieter than other sitcoms. Is this why it might have taken longer to hit with audiences?**

It definitely took awhile to find an audience. The first year it aired, 1982, we were ranked seventy-fourth out of seventy-seven shows. I think we would have been canceled, but NBC didn't really have any other shows to replace us. Over the summer, our competition showed repeats. It was then that the vast majority of the TV audience on Thursday night had to either talk to each other or tune in to watch us. When we began the second season, we had already made the top twenty. I'm not sure that would happen now. We wouldn't have been given a second chance.

Another advantage was that we had more time per show. Sitcoms now have almost three minutes less content, around twenty-two minutes—we had about twenty-five minutes. The network now wants more room for advertising. Consequently, everything is condensed, and, especially when you're first starting, you have to overwhelm people with comedy. As a writer, you don't have the time to establish a character before they have to earn their first laugh. With *Cheers*, we had the luxury of more time. If you can get a joke right after a character's introduction, that's fine. If not, let's wait.

Is it true that Bill Cosby was once up for the role of Sam Malone?

In the beginning, the network called us about Bill Cosby playing the lead character. We were Cosby fans but we took a vow, a blood oath, before we started the show, that we would never have a "name" in the title of the show, whether it be an actor or a character. Bill Cosby was a star. We wanted to avoid *Bill Cosby in Cheers*. Because if you ever lose that star, the show is over. So that was the main reason we didn't use Cosby and I'm happy that we didn't. I'm sure he's happy, too. Two or three years later he came along with one of the most successful sitcoms in history.

Did the *Cheers* writing staff have any rules regarding jokes? What to avoid?

We had a rule that if writers were pitching jokes and two writers came up with the same punch line at once, it was gone.

Why?

If two writers arrived at the same joke simultaneously, someone in America would, too. Maybe that wasn't the case, but it was one of our superstitions.

When a show lasts eleven years, such as *Cheers*, how can the writers even remember what jokes have already been used?

Jokes you can remember, particularly if they're yours. There are entire plot lines I've forgotten, but I always remember specific jokes.

If you're on the air a certain amount of time, say five or six years, there's no way you can remember all the shows you've done. For plot points, we had a show historian. All she did, essentially, was sit in the writers' room when we were pitching stories and say, "You did that in season three." By the end of our run, that was happening more and more. If you're on the air a certain amount of time, there's no way you can remember the shows you've done.

Cheers had a large writing staff, didn't it?

It varied. We started with five writers full-time, and then a couple of writers would come in to do punch-up, including Jerry Belson [_The Dick Van Dyke Show, Gomer Pyle–U.S.M.C., The Tracey Ullman Show_] and David Lloyd [_The Mary Tyler Moore Show, Taxi, Wings, Frasier_]. It was small for a week's show, but that's how we wanted it. We always considered it a compliment when we were called a writers' show. To us, the writers were the stars of the show. After we'd been on a few seasons we had established writers actually sending us spec scripts.

Cheers certainly never talked down to its audience. I remember jokes that concerned Dorothy Parker and seventeenth-century poet John Donne. I don't recall similar jokes on _Laverne & Shirley_.

We had a publicist at NBC at that time, and we had lunch with him one day. We were talking about the low ratings for _Cheers_, and he sighed and said, "I'm going to be honest with you. I just don't know how to sell a show that does Arthur Schopenhauer jokes."

A joke about a nineteenth-century German philosopher. Not exactly a "can't miss."

That's what we liked about it. Diane met an old friend of hers from graduate school and they were going on and on about this and that. Arthur Schopenhauer was one of the subjects mentioned. Diane's line at the end of the conversation was, "Well, that's enough 'Schop' talk." To them, it was screamingly funny. It would have been a pretentious, pseudo-intellectual pun that would have confused and annoyed anyone else who had heard it. It was very much a Diane joke. It wouldn't have worked with Norm.

Cheers dealt with some very serious issues: homophobia, alcohol, and sex addictions as well as other topics that were regarded as risqué for a network show at the time—and would perhaps even be considered risqué today.

We dealt with homosexuality in the first season in an episode called "Boys in the Bar" [January 27, 1983]. Sam's former Red Sox teammate writes an autobiography and comes out of the closet. There was discussion among Sam and the rest of the regulars about the fear of *Cheers* turning into a gay bar. The episode really wasn't about homosexuality, more about paranoia. Everyone started to turn on each other. I once had a guy at a seminar ask if that particular show was about McCarthyism. I said "exactly." That's the first time I realized what the show was about.

Is it true that, at one time, there were plans to produce a Cheers episode about the AIDS epidemic?

Yes. One of Sam's girlfriends calls to tell him that she just tested positive for HIV. It was toward the end of the series. AIDS was very much in the news. It was an epidemic. The question for our staff was, "Are we being irresponsible by having a sexually active male the central focus of our series and not dealing with the issue in some way?" The more high-minded among us said, "Of course we should deal with it." The writing session went on for three or four hours just deciding if we wanted to do it. The big question was, "How do we make this funny?"

Toward the end of this long writing session, Bill Steinkellner, who was one of our producers, said, "Well, what's wrong with somebody tuning in to watch their favorite comedy at nine o'clock on a Thursday night and, for thirty minutes, to live in a world where things like AIDS don't exist?" When no one could think of an answer, that's how we decided to look at it.

Cheers dealt with some serious issues that were beyond your control, such as the 1985 death of actor Nicholas Colasanto, who played Coach. Was that difficult to deal with as a comedy writer? Not only the death of a character, but also of the actual actor who played him?

We knew that Nick was very sick quite a long time before he passed away. We had him off the show for half a season because he wasn't feeling well. When he felt better, he came in to pay us a visit and frankly, he didn't look well. Putting him on the show would have been jarring to the audience. He was so emaciated and obviously terminal. So we knew that that day was coming, and we had time to prepare. We just tried to soften it, not to spend a lot of time on it. We wanted to give him a tribute at the end of an episode ["Birth, Death, Love and Rice," September 26, 1985] and move on.

The network, in years past, was always giving us notes about adding youth to the show. So this was our chance. We actually named the replacement character Woody even before we found Woody Harrelson. We created a backstory where Woody had been a pen pal of Coach's, and that worked out well.

It seems that as the show evolved over the years, the humor became broader and more physical, and it became less about dialogue.

It did tend to lean that way. There was one show where Sam and Diane grabbed each other's noses and didn't let go ["I'll Be Seeing You," May 3 and 10, 1984]. I think the first time we tried that joke it was just experimental. It worked, so we moved forward. I think the point we were trying to make was that you reach a stage in a relationship when you can no longer reason with your romantic partner. You go back down the evolutionary scale, physically—grabbing each other's noses. Ted and Shelley made it work.

You and Les co-wrote the final episode of Cheers, "One for the Road," which was broadcast on May 20, 1993. I remember the National Enquirer actually publishing the entire leaked script a week or so before the show aired. The build-up to the show was tremendous.

That was strange. I'm still not sure how they got the script. But we ended up shooting the last scene without an audience, just to keep it secret. It was a very quiet scene, and we didn't want anybody to know how it ended. Nobody except for a few people saw the whole show being shot in its entirety.

You once said that all final episodes are very difficult to write. But I would think that final episodes would be easier to write than pilot episodes, in which you're still imagining who the characters are.

First of all, the whole country gets primed for a final episode. There has to be a spectacular finish. It's almost inevitable it's not going to be like the rest of the series because you're going to have to reach conclusions. I think the best ending ever for a television show was *M*A*S*H*. They had an inevitable conclusion: the end of the war and almost everybody going home.

For the rest of us, we have to manufacture an ending. And one of the problems is that the network always wants to make the last episode longer than it would normally be. In our case, it was ninety minutes, three normal programs in length. Way too long.

The final episode does end on a quiet note. Sam and Norm are alone in the bar, very late at night. After Norm finally leaves, another customer, unseen from the waist up, knocks on the door. Sam says, "Sorry, we're closed" and walks into the back office.

Was there any hidden meaning to that last scene? Some fans felt that it was a metaphor for death.

I'm flattered that some feel that the last scene was a metaphor for death. Every comedy writer aspires to that level of hilarity in their work. Actually, any interpretation other than our saying good-bye and leaving Sam Malone in his bar just as he was back in the very first scene of the series would be coincidental and unintended.

Our agent, Bob Broder, played the customer in the last scene. Bob wanted *Cheers* to go on with a revised cast. When no one went along with this idea, he became quite despondent and was required to go through a metal detector whenever he came on the lot. [Laughs] So his being turned away at the door in the last scene could be an apt metaphor for thwarted greed and ambition.

Is it true that the then president, Bill Clinton, was going to make an appearance on the final episode?

Yes, and we wrote a whole segment for him. This character, the president, would have learned that the bar was going to close, and he was going to stop by for one last drink. One of the customers would give him advice on how to run the country. We actually cleared the script with his people. But Clinton canceled at the last minute. He was meeting with [Soviet Union president, Boris] Yeltsin in Vancouver for a summit.

That lame excuse.

I wasn't happy with the whole scenario. We stopped being *Cheers*, and we started to be a "thing." It started to become, "This has got to be sensational. Let's bring Diane back. Let's bring the president on. What about the Royal Lipizzaner Stallions dancing in the bar?" I would like to have that final episode back. We were serving other masters.

We had an episode of *Cheers* that aired just before the final episode. It was called "The Guy Can't Help It" [May 13, 1993]. It was written by David Angell, Peter Casey, David Lee; all three later went on to write and create *Frasier*. David Angell died on Flight 11 on 9/11. But this penultimate episode should have been our final episode. It was a half hour. Sam goes to a sex addiction group. Everybody at the group stands and tells their story. This very attractive lady gets up and talks about how addicted she was to sex: "Going from man to man, not caring, just wanting him." Everybody's shaking their head. She sits down. Sam has been frowning in sympathy and has been expressing understanding throughout her story, but when she finishes he sits next to her and quietly asks, "Do you like Chinese food?"

I think that should've been the end. He's still the same Sam from the beginning. A lecher throughout television eternity. And that's where we should have left him.

I suppose the pressure not to put a halt to a runaway hit show is huge. There's just so much money involved that the network would do anything to keep it going.

The money involved is incredible. It's difficult to stop. In fact, we received overtures from the network to continue *Cheers* with Woody as the head bartender. Both Les and I said, "That's not *Cheers* anymore." It was time to move on. But I think that if Woody had been agreeable—which he wasn't—the network would have brought in another producing team. It was just too big for the network to ever want to stop.

The final episode of *Cheers* was shown on two giant Jumbotron screens outside the Bull & Finch Pub in Boston. After the show, at 11:30, *The Tonight Show with Jay Leno* broadcast a live feed from the bar, which was filled with the show's cast, as well as celebrities, athletes, actors, politicians. The evening has become infamous for how out of control it became. Were you there that night?

I was. It became a circus. The entire cast was upstairs in the restaurant above the bar. We were in a room by ourselves, and they had set up refreshments and, of course, a television to watch the show. There were bleachers outside for fans. Jay Leno was going to shoot live for *The Tonight Show* after the episode ended. This was his first year. The evening progressed and I could see everybody getting tipsier and tipsier. I thought, Wow, this is going to be strange. Two hours from now these people are going to be live on *The Tonight Show*. They're going to have to make some kind of sense.

Well, they didn't. Jay began the interviews at around 11:30 [on the East Coast], and by then everyone was beyond drunk. It was a disaster. I'm not a teetotaler by any measure, but I didn't want to be a part of that. It was chaos. There were spitballs going back and forth. Woody Harrelson was literally trying to shoot spitballs into Jay Leno's mouth. People were cursing, stumbling. I remember Jay telling someone, "These people are drunk off their asses." The cast was all schnockered. So were the VIP guests. It was madness, and all broadcast live.

In your opinion, how would you say *Cheers* influenced the sitcoms that followed it?

It's interesting. I've heard lately that we had an influence that I wasn't aware of. Tina Fey said some very nice things about us, as did Amy Poehler. Actually, we had our thirtieth anniversary of the broadcast of the first *Cheers* episode recently, and people who had been on staff came up and said they worked on a lot of shows and still regard this as their best experience. It's hard for me to say. I see kind of an influence on *Friends*, *Seinfeld*, and other shows with the gang comedy concept. People who hang around each other outside of a work environment.

Another legacy is that sitcoms now have large plot arcs. I've noticed, too, that sitcoms will now end their seasons with cliff-hangers. We would do that on *Cheers*. We wanted to have people talking about the show over the summer, wondering about it, thinking about it.

What advice would you have for those hoping to get into writing for sitcoms?

The common fault I see is that a lot of writers don't hear the show. Every show has a voice. The better the show, the better the voice. I remember when Les and I got our first job with *M*A*S*H*. At the time, the two of us had been writing and sending out spec scripts. [*M*A*S*H* producer] Larry Gelbart told us we'd written a good script. He said: "You *hear* the show. Most spec scripts don't." There's a quality that's missing, almost apart from the comedy. Maybe it's our radio background rearing its head. With really good comedy writing, you can hear the characters say the lines on paper. It's tough to tell anybody what to do about that.

Easier said than done.

Right. I'd advise anyone interested in screenwriting of any kind to do some acting, maybe take an acting class. It'll help you understand that the words you write on paper are meant to be spoken. You'll *hear* your writing.

Sitcom writing is still writing after all. When I was in college, I met [fantasy and sci-fi writer] Ray Bradbury. I mentioned that I'd like to somehow write for a living, although I didn't know what form that would take. I asked him for recommendations on how to proceed. He immediately said, "Well, first get out of college. You can read everything you need to read on your own, but you can't experience in college what you need to write."

His point—and I later came to agree with it, even though I ended up graduating—is that, yes, it's important to be exposed to great literature. At a certain point, though, you have to get out and see things, go to strange places, meet weird people, maybe fall in love with one of them, get hurt, and even act in a play that will allow you to wear tights in public. I think life experience for too many of us is very limited. So much literature, film, and television is self-referential and insular. It's a world of sequels, remakes, and homages.

Another thing is, you can teach specifics. Things like story construction, joke structure, and character delineation can be picked up from watching and reading good things. But, overall, this is not a science, and I've never worked with any comedy writer—and I've worked with great ones—who hasn't been wrong on occasion. I mean, *really* wrong.

The last piece of advice I'd give to any writer would be to avoid envy of your peers and joy at their misfortune. Keep your overheated ego and ambition well-concealed around those less powerful than yourself, and don't carry a grudge in this business, no matter how great the slight. Actually, wait, I'm wrong. All these things can be great sources of inspiration. Set them free. Let them run wild.

JOEL BEGLEITER

Agent, UTA

....

Finding an Agent for a TV-Writing Job

How does a young writer acquire an agent if he or she wants to write comedy for television?

There are a couple ways to do it. The first is to graduate from one of the writing programs. Warner Brothers, Fox, and CBS productions all have their own internal grooming programs where they take writers who have never been on staff and put them through a six- or eight-month-long program in which they write original material and spec scripts. The writer comes out the other side with a stamp of approval from those studios. Warner Brothers is definitively the most successful of them.

After you graduate, the heads of those programs will call agencies and say, "We've got a live one here. This guy or woman just came through and they're exceptional and you should think about hiring them." There are incentives then in place for these studios to hire the writers who have just gone through their programs. So your odds of getting a job are significantly higher than the odds of almost anybody else at your level around town. That's one way to do it.

The other way is to be referred by a writer who's already signed. These clients will call their agents and say, "I work with this guy, or I know this guy, and he's incredible, and you should check out his material." It's an assurance that this writer is employable. That's basically saying, "If I had my own show and I was in charge, I'd hire this guy." That's the second way.

The third way, the most difficult way, is to blindly submit your material to an agent. This is especially difficult in television. The material would have to be absolutely, spectacularly exceptional to be taken on by one of the major agencies without any kind of other connection to the industry already in place.

Is the process different if one wants to write for a sitcom versus wanting to write for late night?

The process is definitely different. For late night, it mostly comes down to referral. Head writers for each of the late shows have a full staff of joke writers, and those people have friends, and they refer their friends. Late-night shows generally take packets as submissions. Each show will put out a set of guidelines and say, "Okay, we need you to write three Top 10 lists in the style of David Letterman, and twenty monologue jokes, and then three desk pieces." They'll then take those submissions, look through them, and bring the funniest people in for interviews and hire them. I think it's easier to get one of those gigs on pure merit than it is to get a traditional sitcom writing job.

Is an agent even a necessity for late night?

I don't think it hurts. It certainly helps in the sense that you are made aware of when these shows have a writing opportunity opening up. Unless you already have friends working on these shows—someone who can give you a heads up every time they are hiring—it will be much more difficult without an agent. I don't know how you'd have the information to know when and where to send your packet.

Now, does having an agent help push you through the door of these shows? Not particularly, in my opinion. It's more based on your writing material. But it certainly helps to have an agent because we do a good job tracking when new openings pop up.

As far as your clients, what's the percentage of those who write for sitcoms compared with those who write for late night?

Ninety-five percent of the people I represent work for sitcoms, and 5 percent of them work for late night. I think that that percentage would probably be relatively identical across the board at all agencies.

What are some of the common mistakes you see writers making who submit material to you?

Some mistakes are very basic. When I open a script, and within the first five pages of that script there are three typos, that tells me how little effort that writer put into this piece. It's an easy way to discourage somebody from reading it. It's a really basic turnoff, but it happens all the time.

Aside from that, I think the only real mistake is not honing the material, not submitting a script that is your best work; just submitting something that has not been vetted by twenty or thirty other people who will be honest about whether it's good or not. This happens a lot. One of my clients will call me and say, "Hey, you should check this stuff out. He's my friend. I think he's great. Will you read his stuff?" And I read it and it's not very good and I call the client back to say, "Listen, unfortunately, this is going to be a pass. Would you like me to reach out to your friend directly to save you from the pain of having to pass on my behalf?"

The answer is never, "Really? I loved it. It's really surprising that you didn't love it." It's usually, like, "Okay, great. Thanks. Talk to you later." And you can tell that they didn't love it either, and they're sort of embarrassed that they had to send it to you. There definitely have been occasions when I have passed on something and the client has fought for it and said, "I think you're wrong about this." But when you get that other immediate response from the client, you know you were right and they were just doing a favor for a friend.

How important is the cover letter?

The cover letter is largely irrelevant. A letter is mostly for writers who are submitting to someone who is not expecting their material. We all receive SPAM e-mails all day long at the major agencies from writers who have bought e-mail address lists. They are deleted immediately. There's not even the slightest consideration. I don't read the letters. When a client has referred a friend of theirs, the letter is not necessary.

Do you prefer original material or scripts based on existing shows?

Definitely original material. I think there was a period more than ten years ago when everybody needed to have material based on pre-existing shows. And that day has largely gone away. It is impossible to work in television without having a piece of original material.

Why did it change?

I think it changed because the industry became significantly more competitive. Reality television happened. *Survivor* happened. Suddenly all the hours on prime time that had been devoted to scripted television shows disappeared. Those hours got eaten up by reality shows. So there are fewer shows and it became more competitive to get onto those shows. You get to a point where you can only read so many *Parks and Recs*, *30 Rocks*, and *Offices*. So how do you differentiate yourself?

Let's say there's a new show that they're staffing and they're accepting submissions from writers. The number of scripts they're sifting through is probably four hundred, five hundred scripts. There has to be a way to differentiate yourself from the pile. The idea of having an original voice has become something of a premium. Everybody feels like the bar has been raised. So you have to be able to prove that you can write something original and unique.

How much material does a writer need to submit? How many scripts?

You need at least one great sample script. But if you are an aspiring writer, you should always be writing. One of the greatest frustrations I have with my clients is that they get staffed on a television show, and then, three years later, the television show goes down and they don't have a piece of new material. And you just want to say, "What the fuck have you been doing for the last three years?" So to get that first job, you need one great piece of material. It doesn't hurt to have a second piece. There are writers and showrunners who ask to read two things, but one great piece can get it done. But the next time out, you've got to have something new. You can't just send the same great script to all the same people again. They've already read it.

Can you submit other forms of humor writing? Say, funny print pieces?

It depends. It depends on the showrunner who's hiring. If you look at animated shows like *Bob's Burgers* or *Family Guy*, those are shows that have hired writers based upon alternative format comedy. Their interest was not generated by a writer's spec half hour. So, you know, it depends entirely on the showrunner. Writers have been hired from Twitter streams or short films they've made for Channel 101 or books that they've written. This can all pique a showrunner's interest. But ultimately most showrunners want to read something structured and narrative before they make a hire.

How do you, as an agent, differ from a manager?

I differ enormously from a manager. Managers are not able to negotiate employment for their clients. Lawyers are. Agents are. Managers are technically not. This is a line that is crossed all the time, every day. It's not upheld, generally. But I view a manager's job as sort of holding the hand of the client and working on a piece of material over a long period of time before it goes out to the world to be judged. And to help a client with long-term career goals.

I view my job of an agent as securing work. But it's become much more than that. It's not just about staffing people, securing people's jobs. It's also about when writers are selling their development deals. It's my job to help put together the right pieces that can make those deals attractive to a network.

Is it virtually impossible to get hired as a television writer without an agent?

It is not impossible. It does happen now and again, but rarely.

It always tends to be one of those chicken-and-the-egg things. You can't get an agent without having the possibility of getting a job because agents are animals who want people who pay commission. On the other hand, you can't get a job without having an agent. So how do you break through that? The most organic way is to move out to Los Angeles immediately after college. You have to move out to LA. New York just doesn't have that many television writing jobs.

Once you get out to LA, try to get a job as a production assistant on a show, and start to get to know writers. Then work your way up and eventually become a writer's assistant. You have to become a known commodity. That's the real way to do it without going through a program. If you work your way up to writer's assistant, eventually you'll get hired on a show that works. And then you start getting promoted. The minute anybody in Hollywood sniffs that you're getting promoted, you'll start to receive phone calls from UTA, William Morris, ICM, and all the rest of the talent agencies, with all of them saying, "Hey, man, I hear you're great. I'd like to read your stuff." And then you'll get an agent.

PURE, HARD-CORE ADVICE

MARC MARON
....

Host, *WTF with Marc Maron*; Performer, *Late Show with
David Letterman, Late Night with Conan O'Brien, Comedy
Central Presents*; Creator/Writer, *Maron*

For awhile, I hit a wall where in my mind the choices were pretty dire.
I didn't have any idea how I was going to continue to make a living.
There was real fucking fear there. For one reason or another, the timing was right in the medium [podcasting] that I chose in 2009, and
things evolved.

Quite honestly, I try not to have regrets in my life, because it is
what it is. But whatever I went through, there was not a plan. My
process creatively is not an easy one. I'm impulsive, I'm filled with
anxiety, I don't have the ability to compartmentalize, I don't have the
wherewithal or the confidence to plan and follow through when
working toward a goal. Everything has always been very immediate
to me, and that is exhausting. It could really have gone either way. In
talking to other people and looking back at my own career, the
people who were more aware of their talent and how to use it, and
more aware of their limitations and what they were really shooting

for, were able to find their place a little easier. If you start out as a comic, you want to be a big comic. But as you get older, you realize, "Wow, there are only a few of those at any given point in time, and it's a tough life." The possibilities of not getting to that level, where you can really bank some money or build a career, are very high. Depending on what your ego can handle at those crossroads in life, you might say, "I do write great jokes, and I know I want to be involved somehow, so how do I adapt?" The ability to get away from your ego enough to recognize your limitations, and to take action toward becoming a writer or working for a sketch group—that's a big moment. The thing I now know is that the people who were aware and cognizant of the business ultimately found a little more peace of mind—a place to express partially, if not more so, their particular sense of humor.

A lot of the dudes I started with, the ones who didn't fall away or end up club comics for life, very early on went into writing. Whether you get into producing, or directing, or management, relationships are built early on; crews start out generationally. You build those relationships when you're all struggling, and those are the relationships that are going to carry you through a career—if you're lucky enough to have one.

As far as whether you choose this career, I have not found that to be a choice. In my experience, somehow or another, your brain has already told you that this is a reasonable life to live, which is nuts. That comes with the territory. You're going to have those things, no matter how crazy or insecure you are, that continue to propel yourself into this life. Some of that may be rebellion; some of that may be, "Fuck you, Mom and Dad." Some of that may be grandiosity. But whatever it is, you're already in it. And the deeper you get into it, it's very hard to get out of it, even when things aren't going well.

Don't kid yourself: A lot of people fade away. A lot of people become tragic, whether they see it that way or not. I don't know. There's always this weird thing in show business where you never know when success is going to happen. It's not a meritocracy; so much of it is about some weird shit aligning that's usually out of your control, and you catch your break. And a lot of people don't ever catch it.

I've learned from talking to people over the last few years on my podcast [*WTF with Marc Maron*] that people who work hard find something. There's a certain amount of entitlement when you're a young comic living the life, like, "Oh, it'll happen," even if you're getting high every day and sleeping until three. The truth of the matter is that eventually you're going to have to do the work. You're going to have to find your consistency and your groove—somehow.

You just have to do it. There's no schooling; there's no anything. Find a place where you can get onstage and do it. Do you have favorite comics? Watch them. It's very self-explanatory: You stand up there, by yourself, and you try to get laughs. I usually say, "Look, you might bomb, you might do great, but you're not going to always do great. You're not always going to bomb." You have to figure out once you do it whether or not you're infected with the bug that makes you keep wanting to do it. When you get off that stage, no matter what happens—whether they hated you or loved you—you have to get up there again. And if you do get up there . . . well, good luck, and welcome to the life.

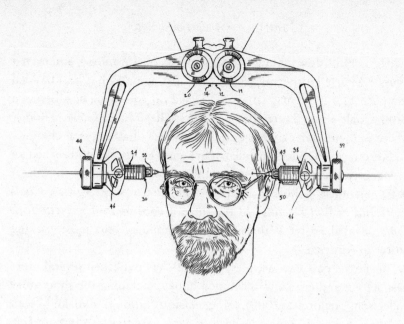

GEORGE SAUNDERS

Comedy isn't always the domain of comedians or traditonal comedy writers. Sometimes a writing professor who works alone in an office, doesn't have a Twitter following or a TV show, and has never told jokes at comedy clubs can have a fundamentally better grasp of how humor works than those who make their living writing and saying things they call "comedy."

Enter, stage left . . . George Saunders, one of the very best writers working today—and also one of the funniest. Born in 1958 in Amarillo, Texas, and raised in the south suburbs of Chicago, Saunders originally sought a career in geophysical engineering. After graduating from the Colorado School of Mines in 1981, he worked as a "seismic prospector" for an oil exploration crew on the Indonesian island of Sumatra (where, according to *The New York Times*, he discovered Kurt Vonnegut's *Slaughterhouse-Five*, having read "virtually nothing" until that time), and then worked later as a technical writer for an environmental engineering company based in Rochester, New York. Saunders has also been employed as a Texas bar band guitarist, a Beverly Hills doorman, a Chicago roofer, an LA mover, and even a slaughterhouse worker in West Texas. (In a somewhat backhanded compliment, online magazine *Salon* used the following headline in a 2000 article about Saunders: "Knuckle-puller Makes Good.") Somewhere in there, during what he calls "a series of attempts at channeling Kerouac," Saunders enrolled at Syracuse University and earned an MA degree in creative writing. And then in 1996, at the age of thirty-seven, Saunders published his first collection of short stories, *Civil-WarLand in Bad Decline*. At the time, according to *The New York Times*, David Foster Wallace declared Saunders "the most exciting writer in America."

Over the past two decades, Saunders has published several more best-selling and critically acclaimed books, including the short story collections *Pastoralia* (2000), *In Persuasion Nation* (2006), and *Tenth of December* (2013); the novellas *The Very Persistent Gappers of Frip* (2000) and *The Brief and Frightening Reign of Phil* (2005); and an essay collection, *The Braindead Megaphone* (2007).

Saunders has received numerous awards, including the coveted MacArthur "Genius" Award, which he was granted in 2006 for "bring[ing] to contemporary American fiction a sense of humor, pathos and literary style all his own."

In the past, you've talked about growing up in South Chicago, and that, as a child, you felt total freedom. But how do you think South Chicago affected you as a writer?

I attended Catholic school. We received a great education from the nuns. They were just merciless in terms of grammar and syntax and spelling, which was incredibly helpful later: They gave us the tools we could later use to build our taste. They forced us to become little language fiends—almost like, say, a great chef might force his kids to become food fiends. That taught us basic discernment. Also, guilt. Guilt and a feeling of never being satisfied with what you've done. And a sense that you are inadequate and a big phony. All useful for a writer. I'm always being edited by my inner nun. So in some ways this is good—it makes for good revision. But it can also be killing—you're never satisfied.

How about as far as humor? Is it tied in any specific way to Chicago?

I think I got the idea that the high-serious and the funny were not separate. The idea that something could be gross and heartfelt at the same time. Some of the funniest things in South Chicago were also the most deeply true—these sort of over-the-line, rude utterances that were right on the money and undeniable. Their truth had rendered them inappropriate; they were not classically shaped, not polite, and they responded to the urgency of the moment.

In Chicago, people often told these odd little Zen parables, ostensibly for laughs, or to mock somebody out, but behind which I always felt were deeper questions looming, like who we are, and what the hell are we doing here, how should we love, what should we value, how are we to understand this veil of tears.

Do any specific anecdotes come to mind?

My whole childhood we lived next door to this family I'll call the Smiths. We didn't know them very well at all. At one point, Mrs. Smith's mother, who was in her nineties, passed away. My dad went to the wake, where this exchange occurred:

Dad: "So sorry for your loss."

Mrs. Smith: "Yes, it's very hard."

Dad: "Well, on the bright side, I suppose you must be grateful that she had such a long and healthy life."

Mrs. Smith (mournful, dead-serious): "Yeah. This is the sickest she's ever been."

My dad came home just *energized* from this. I loved his reaction. My family was such a big influence on me. There was a real respect for language. It was understood as a source of power. Everyone was funny in a different flavor. You could make anything right—diffuse any tension, explain any mistake—with a joke. A joke or a funny voice was a way of saying: All is well. We'll live. We still love you.

Can you talk a bit about your mother and father?

My father was from Chicago and my mother was from Amarillo, Texas. They met at a dance when my father was stationed down in Texas, in the air force. They were nineteen when they married, and had me when they were twenty-one. My dad is one of the most intelligent people I've ever met, but he didn't go to college right out of high school. He got out of the air force and moved back to Chicago and he did a bunch of different things—he was a collection agent for State Farm Insurance and then ended up as a salesman for a coal company. This was when there were still a lot of buildings being heated by coal. For awhile he was selling directly to landlords, and apparently sneaking into basements to do reconnaissance on the type of coal they were getting from other companies. But then he gradually worked his way up, and when I was in grade school he became vice president of the company. Around that time he had a falling-out with his boss and quit. He bought a couple of now defunct fast-food franchise restaurants called Chicken Unlimited, and that's what he did while I was in high school. Well, that's what we *all* did: worked in the restaurant. My mother and sisters worked the counter; I drove the delivery truck; my uncle managed one of the stores.

The main beauty of that job was getting to go in there day after day and see this parade of American characters. For many of those people, our restaurant was the closest thing to family they had: lonely, lonely, lonely. It would have been impossible for me, before that job, to imagine how filled America is with lonely, isolated people.

Many of the characters in your stories, whether they are good or bad, young or old, tend to be quite lonely.

What I remember about all this is that particular gloating teen delight that there were such crazies in the world and that I wasn't one of them. But also the way this got complicated by coming to know them, by seeing them in these sad private moments, in our restaurant, sitting at one of our plastic booths all alone. The other kids and I were actually pretty good and gentle to them when the chance arose. But, of course, among ourselves, it was all posturing and harshness and war stories about what "the wackos" had done that day. Makes me sad to think of it at this thirty-year distance.

Do you remember any customers in particular?

Oh, sure. There was a woman we rather brutally called, but not to her face, "The Wacko." She'd come in around four in the afternoon and chain-smoke and chain-drink Pepsis hour after hour. She used to wear a ratty imitation fur coat and talk to herself. She lived in a complex behind the restaurant. Almost the minute she got home, she'd call for delivery: a pack of cigarettes from the machine we had in the store and a large Pepsi. She'd sometimes order three or four times a night. I was the delivery guy, so I'd go over—I made seventy-five cents a delivery—and she'd be in this furnitureless apartment, shaking and talking to herself. And she wasn't all that old either. She later slit her wrists and jumped in the Chicago River—only to be pulled out by some passing hero.

Then there was a guy whose claim to fame was twofold: He'd try to pick up girls by wearing his old security guard uniform and harassing them at the mall, and it was his "old" security guard costume because he'd gotten fired from his job as a security guard after being caught doing what he described as "allegedly masturbating against the curb of a Fotomat." I didn't even know what that meant, exactly. In his defense, he always claimed innocence. But the charge seemed pretty . . . specific.

And then there was "Gagger"—for some reason he didn't even get an article in his name. He was an old man dying of emphysema, who would come in and sometimes literally cough himself unconscious in a back booth. He had no family and so we were it for him, more or less.

You've talked in the past about how important compassion is when it comes to writing. That writing, in your opinion, is an exercise in compassion. You strike me as someone who is not only a compassionate writer, but also a compassionate person.

Yes, but people think of compassion as, like, kindness. The image comes to mind of some nice New Age guy bending to something with a look on his face like he's about to cry. And I don't think that's it. I think of it more as a quality of openness that comes with being in a state of unusual attentiveness.

Yes, but with other writers, I don't always sense compassion when it comes to humor or satire. I'm not sure if they don't have full control of their toolbox or if they're just not compassionate. Can satire work if the writer isn't a compassionate person?

Sure. I think a harsh truth can be compassionate, in the sense that it speeds us along from falseness to truth. So, if a friend is wearing something ridiculous, you can say, "You look like an idiot," and maybe that will save him. I think we wouldn't want to assume that compassion is always gentle.

I think this quality you're talking about in my work might be more about fairness than compassion. By which I mean one's willingness to stake out a position (*Kevin sucks!*) and have a lot of fun with that, and then run around the table and assert another position (*Although Kevin does care for his sick grandmother*) and then do it again (*But yuck, Kevin masturbates while thinking about whales!*) and another (*And yet Kevin once saved a man's life*).

I sometimes think of this as "on the other hand" thinking—just that constant undercutting of whatever (too) stable a position you find yourself occupying.

You once said that satire is a way of saying, "I love this culture."

It's hard to be sufficiently involved in satirizing something you don't like. That's just sneering. Satire is, I think, a sort of bait-and-switch. You decide to satirize something, so you gaze at it hard enough and long enough to be able to say something true and funny and maybe angry or critical—but you first had to gaze at it for a long time. I mean, gazing is a form of love, right?

Right, but gazing is also a form of fear, too, I'd think. As well as staring at something beautiful, one can also stare at someone, or something, different from the norm, such as a freak at a sideshow.

In either case, it's attention. You are paying attention to the thing, spending your time on it, which is a form of . . . something. Love? Respect? You're honoring the thing with your attention and allowing it to act upon you, to change you. In terms of writing, if you are writing and rewriting a paragraph or section that concerns a person, you are allowing your initial, often simplistic or agenda-satisfying notion of that person to be softened or complicated—you have to, for technical reasons. If you don't, the reader will anticipate where you're going and be pissed or bummed when you go there.

So I think it's the attention that matters. You are paying attention to this fictive creature via paying attention to the words that have caused him to—sort of—exist. It's a kind of double-attention-paying. And the more attention you pay, the more you're going to eliminate the lameness in what you're doing. Even if your idea is to pillory someone, doing this double-attention thing is going to force you to pillory him at a higher level, more honestly.

You seem to be the opposite of many writers who deal in satire, such as Mark Twain, whose work became darker and darker as he aged. For instance, in his uncompleted book *The Mysterious Stranger*, Twain questions whether or not God exists. With your work, however, there seems to be more and more evidence of lightness.

Yes, so far. But Twain was older then and had gone through some really dark shit—he went bankrupt, lost an infant son, outlived two of his daughters and his wife.

But of course some things are just dispositional. I think I've always been a fairly happy person, just in terms of my physiology. Also, I think you have to keep growing aesthetically in whatever way feels essential. You can feel in Twain that when he went toward that darkness he was, in some ways, going against his own early grain. He was facing facts, in a sense, being more honest, striving for his truth. At the moment, I'm trying to resist any kind of knee-jerk darkness that might have to do with some feeling of wanting to remain "edgy," if you see what I mean. At this point, "more light" feels like "more honesty." But, you know, we'll see. One of the perils of any sort of interview is that the thing you are so passionately saying might turn out to be all wet, once you actually start working again.

Another thing I love about Twain is the way his clear-sightedness expresses itself in exact language. Also, to be as funny and loose as he is in *Huck Finn* but also dense enough with his language that it evokes a rich physical world—that is very hard, I think. He hits a lot of different modalities in that book. It's funny, it's smart, it's tragic, some of the language presages Faulkner, but also presages Nathaniel West.

If Mark Twain were around today, do you think he'd have a difficult time finding an agent and getting published? In today's publishing world, humor and comic novels aren't always "marketable."

He'd still be a superstar. I mean that in two ways: I think his work is still great, so great that no one could deny it, so that, if you could erase all cultural memory of *Huck Finn* and then send it out fresh it would still be a sensation. Second, let's say there was never any Twain to begin with and he was then born in 1957 or something—I think he would adjust to and imbibe this contemporary life of ours and do something unimaginable and great.

Who were your comedy influences?

I was a big fan of Steve Martin's. It was absolutely new at the time, the early- to mid-seventies. We'd never seen or heard anything like it. Now I can see that what made his work so radical was that it was so self-aware, so postmodern: He was making comedy about the conventions of making comedy. But then it just felt . . . limitless, and honest. In those days so many comics were completely conventional. You'd see them on *The Tonight Show*, and they felt old-fashioned and sort of dead. I mean, George Carlin was around, and Richard Pryor—both geniuses—but I felt they were kind of outliers. They were radical and angry, whereas Martin presented himself as a sort of mainstream comic who tore the whole thing down from inside, very sweetly. He wasn't really rejecting anything; he was accepting of everything, with the force of his charm and his will. I also picked up from him something that reminded me of the way some of my uncles were funny—that whole comic riff of pretending to be clueless, exaggerating that quality and not flinching. I loved that.

Who else?

I loved Monty Python for the wordplay—this sense that you didn't have to squash your intelligence to be funny. In fact, you could walk right into your intelligence and nerdiness and self-doubt, and *that* could be funny.

I liked the Marx Brothers for the irreverence, the way they tore everything down. That's where humor enters the domain of the philosophical and starts to say: "What seems obvious, isn't; what you think will sustain you, won't; what you trust, will fail you; what you think is permanent, is fading; your mind will go, your body will rot, all that you love will be cast to the wind."

I loved Dr. Seuss. The funny thing was, we never had his books in the house. My mother claims this is because my father confused Dr. Seuss with [pediatrician and child-care author] Dr. Spock, and considered Dr. Spock a communist. My father denies this. And honestly, it doesn't sound like him—the guy who gave me Michael Harrington's [1962 book on poverty] *The Other America* to read when I was in seventh grade, along with Upton Sinclair's [1906 novel on Chicago working-class conditions] *The Jungle*. But who knows? Anyway, we didn't have the Seuss books, but a neighbor did, and I remember whenever we would go over there I would sneak into the kid's room and read all the contraband Seuss.

I loved the simplicity. Very elemental and profound. Also completely weird. You can't trace any predecessor or agenda in those books. Just sui generis. I loved the level of detail—I used to sort of linger on the pages, especially the more panoramic ones.

Somehow I group Seuss with Samuel Beckett and Raymond Carver and Charles Schulz and the Picasso of those famous vanishing bull lithographs: Less is more, if the heart is in the right place.

You once mentioned that you had a stylistic breakthrough by writing Dr. Seussian-type poems. What was the breakthrough? Where and when did it occur?

It happened in a conference room at the engineering company I was working for in the mid-nineties. I was supposed to be taking notes on the call but not much was happening. So I just started writing these goofy little rhyming poems and illustrating them. I liked them enough to bring them home, and later that night my wife read them and . . . liked them. I'd just come out of the experience of having written a seven-hundred-page novel that didn't work and it was mind-blowing to see that she was getting more pleasure and edification out of these ten poems I'd written off the top of my head than from this whole big book.

So that helped me turn the corner on accepting humor into my work. Humor and a whole bunch of other things I'd been denying for some reason: speed, pop culture, irreverence.

Did it take awhile to come to terms with the fact that you were a funny writer? There's a feeling with many writers that if you're not Hemingway-serious you're not as important as you could be. That you're not living up to your full literary potential.

I did have that feeling, yes, in a big way. I spent about seven years trying to keep humor out of my work, but finally had this catastrophic break, where I almost instantaneously rejected my rejection of humor. That was the beginning of my first book. It was sort of powerful: I just realized that I'd been keeping all the good parts of myself out of the fight—all the humor and irreverence and my extensive body of pop culture knowledge and fart jokes, and the rest of it. But I'd also been afraid to embrace, for example, a certain high-speed manic quality I have in person and in my thought patterns. So it was like throwing a switch when I finally got desperate enough.

What I've come to realize is that, for me, the serious and the comic are one and the same. I don't see humor as some sort of shrunken or deficient cousin of "real" writing. Being funny is about as deep and truthful as I can be. When I am really feeling life and being truthful, the resulting prose is comic. The world is comic. It's not always funny but it is always comic. Comic, for me, means that there is always a shortfall between what we think of ourselves and what we are. Life is too hard and complicated for a person to live above it, and the moments when this is underscored are comic. But, of course, they are also deep. Maybe the most clearly we ever see reality is when it boots us in the ass.

You once said that Kurt Vonnegut was more of a purist than Hemingway in his "aversion to bullshit." What did you mean by this, exactly?

Well, it always seemed to me that Hemingway, especially in the later period, would ignore a lot of data, and sort of avert his eyes in order to stay in a certain kind of style we associate with him. His style became a prison of sorts. He had an ethos and a rep and he had all of that fame and I think by the end he was just writing stories that confirmed his view of things. Whereas I always felt Vonnegut was actively investigating. He had less of an agenda and so could present the world as he actually found it. His stuff was weird and weirdly shaped but, based on my experience, it had more of the real America in it.

Or saying it a slightly different way: Vonnegut wanted to investigate how life really is here on Earth. Whereas, especially in the later work, it seems to me that Hemingway had a big investment in turning aside certain realities—maybe in the name of style, maybe because he couldn't see them, famous and enshrined and trapped in his image as he was.

Beyond Dr. Seuss, how well-read were you as a child?

I watched a lot of TV as a kid—I mean, *a lot*. Including hundreds of episodes of *Twilight Zone* and *Night Gallery*, both by Rod Serling. I would never have thought of these as being influential. But they had to be, I guess, just in terms of communicating some early idea of story shape and story expectation. I expect that someone of my generation would have to have had his or her storytelling mode colored—or corrupted?—by the volume of TV we watched and the odd storytelling mode TV occupied in those days.

When I was older, I attended the Colorado School of Mines to study geophysical engineering, so not only was there not much literature studied, there wasn't much time for me to do it on my own either. I did it on the sly, in a spotty way.

Were you unencumbered by coming late to the literary game? In the sense that you didn't feel buried beneath the weight of countless writers and classics?

Well, "unencumbered" is a generous way of putting it. Like saying to a monster that he is "unencumbered" by physical beauty.

When I finally figured out that I wanted to be a writer, I came at it with this combined sense of mission plus inferiority—which can be pretty good. In other words, I kind of conceded early that I wasn't going to be a scholar of literature. I wasn't going to be somebody who'd read and was synthesizing everything ever written. I was too far behind already. But I'd find a writer I loved and read him over and over, and copy him, and then read *his* favorite writers and so on.

I was surprised to learn that there are quite a few writers, like yourself, who also studied engineering: Thomas Pynchon, Kurt Vonnegut, and Norman Mailer, among others.

It might just be that an unconventional background liberates you from knowing the proper way of doing a thing. If you train ten people in a method, and the eleventh comes along untrained, he's going to be off step, and maybe—*maybe*—this will be to his benefit. So when I look at other writers my age, I am struck by how different my life was from theirs when we were in our twenties. Sometimes this feels like an advantage—I read differently and with a different intention and got to do a lot of strange things. But other times it feels like a disadvantage—I lack a solid grounding in, say, the history of the novel, and so lack confidence and am tentative in that area. On the bright side, I do know how to identify many different minerals—or did, anyway.

Sometimes I have to remind myself that, for all my writing life, I'll be coming from behind, and I should be happy to be a sort of mutt running alongside the pack. If I ever make the mistake of thinking I'm one of the alphas, I'll blow the whole thing.

I've heard that, in the early days, nobody in U2 could really play their instruments. But that became sort of central to what they were doing. They played around that fact, essentially. That resonates with me: this idea of deeply musical, deeply feeling people who maybe don't have virtuosic technical skills but who are able to make what they do have work for them.

I actually prefer U2 in the beginning of their career. There were mistakes, but maybe they were better in spite of, or because of, those mistakes. Can this also hold true for writers?

I think so. Maybe not "mistakes," but a certain crudity of expression; this feeling that the writer is bearing so much vital news that he can't slow down and be fastidious about presentation. Or, conversely, that his truth is so powerful that it is malforming the vessel that is carrying it. And for writers, with our infinite powers of revision, we can even go a step further: We can be spontaneous and messy and, liking that effect, revise the text so as to make it seem even more spontaneous and messy—while at the same time actually "clarifying" those qualities.

At the highest level, revision is about anticipating what most writers would do and then asking: Well, is there anything deeper or better or livelier that I could make happen? Not just for the sake of it, but because the new thing might really be richer? Can it somehow contain more "life" by eluding the usual tropes and expectations?

What I find with your writing is that the humor rings in a minor key that resounds in some very dark places. I once read a critic who described this style of comedy as "weighty humor."

I think one trick as a writer is to let all of the people you are come to the table. Or let all of the modalities that reside in you—at least the powerful ones—come to the table. So, in me, there's a maudlin part and a funny part and a dark part and an optimist, a pessimist, a part that loves sci-fi, a part that loves lean language. And this "allowing to the table" can only happen—or happens best—if you loosen up your conceptual expectations in regard to the story. So you might start out thinking that your story is this one thing, but then the trick would be to, at some critical moment, let it become whatever it seems to want to become. Let those other modalities in, come what may. And the criterion there is: Okay, this other modality that's showing up, does it make the story better or worse? More or less interesting or energetic? And again this all happens on a line-to-line level. If it's making the story better, then it stays, and the story has to revise its self-image accordingly. So you might look up from your story and find that something has entered into it that does not at all fit with your initial understanding of it or your original aspirations for it. And when that happens, that's great—it means you've done the important work of befuddling the pedestrian part of yourself.

Your stories have a surreal, dreamlike quality to them. Do you ever dream your story ideas?

I do. I once dreamed that this old girlfriend—someone I had treated kind of shittily at the end of our relationship—came up to me and said: "I just want you to know: I have a baby."

Was it your baby?

No, it was quite clear that it was not mine. This was her way of saying: "I survived, and even thrived, asshole." And in the dream I was like: "That is so great. I am so happy for you." To which she replied: "No. I have a *baby*. And he is just incredibly smart. Watch." And then the baby started talking, reciting all these facts and equations and so on. But then I looked down and noticed a zipper on the back of the baby's head. He was wearing some sort of mask, this smart-making mask. And the dream ended on this realization. So that mixed tonality is even present in the dream, I guess. It's sad, with some sci-fi, but it's also sort of a funny idea.

And then in writing that story—"I Can Speak" [*The New Yorker,*

1999]—what you do is squirm around until you find the right narrative stance. It's a very intuitive thing, when you first stumble on to an idea, of figuring out how to start, what voice to use, and all of that.

This whole story-writing thing is like riding a bike. If the bike is leaning left, you need to lean right. If a story starts to feel maudlin, darken it up. Too earnest? Put in some crude thing. It's essentially your psyche wrestling with your psyche. You have, say, two or three main personality go-to's and they are always wrestling. But this process is not so different from what we do every day, as we try to be charming or functional or liked. "Eek, I've gone too far with Ed. Better say something flattering." Or: "I am sounding strident. Better counteract that with some humility." And of course each of us has his or her own way of doing this, his or her own set of issues that tend to throw the bike off balance, and then ways of rebalancing it along whatever axis is ours.

The most popular types of characters in comedy these days seem to be adults unwilling to grow up. This is common in Hollywood, as well as in literature. The eternal teen. But your characters tend to be real adults who are doing their best to live, struggling mightily. There's no Peter Pan Syndrome at work.

I think I had a little advantage in this, in that I didn't really get started until I already had a regular life—a job, a wife, two kids—so the idea of eternal youth had flown. And it had flown for good reason, by which I mean: I was totally on board with it having flown. I didn't feel reduced or compromised by having a job and family. The whole 1970s idea of "selling out" had been rendered anachronistic and even gross by the extent of my love for my wife and kids. Beatniking was not an option anymore. So then I had to learn that the things that were actually bothering me or challenging me during the day were valid subjects for literature. Mostly, at that time, what was bothering me was 1) not having enough money to provide for my family in the way they deserved, and 2) having a job that required me to spend basically my whole day doing things that I didn't want to do and were simultaneously hard and boring but that were, at that time, the only antidote to (1). So I suppose that's a fundamentally adult conundrum: no place to run, because the trap you're in is made of love. Love plus material paucity.

Your characters tend to be bizarrely optimistic. In your short story "Bounty," one of the characters says, "[My sister] Connie is a prostitute. I'm a thirty-year-old virgin, but all things considered, we could have turned out a lot worse."

That has something to do with American optimism that is really mostly denial energy. Critical thought becomes negative. Negative thought means you're a loser. So don't do it.

Another characteristic I notice about your characters is that even the "bad" ones—the characters who work for big corporations and tend to do evil things—still have a good deal of humanity in them.

I never bought into the whole corporation-as-evil thing after I worked as a geophysical engineer for a company called Radian Corporation, in Rochester, New York. The "big evil corporation" was *us*. All of us. And everyone who was there, including the managers, was there for one reason, and that was to support his or her family, to make a living.

You can see this philosophy in quite a few of your stories. Your 2010 *New Yorker* story "Escape from Spiderhead" is about two prisoners forced to participate in laboratory experiments involving new drugs, one of which is a love potion. And yet, the "bad guys"—in this case the scientists—break the rules by going offsite to buy the prisoners delicious snacks.

Sure. The idea is that even the "bad guys" don't see themselves as such. Have you seen those color photos and videos of the SS guys and gals at Auschwitz cutting up on the weekend, singing and dancing and joking and so on? They thought they were the good guys. Mostly that sort of black-and-white, Cruella de Vil flavor of evil is, I think, a creation of comic books and movies and TV—and one that has, sadly, started to dominate in our epistemology of evil, and is maybe now leeching out into the real world. We'd be better served, I think, to start with the idea that all of our enemies get up in the morning feeling like they're out to serve good. That's a more realistic and effective view of evil, I think, even just in terms of how it actually occurs and also how one might start to defend oneself or work against that evil. If you see the 9/11 guys as pure rabid monsters, there's nothing to do but kill kill kill. But if you can ask: Okay, what was the guy like the day *before* he decided to be a terrorist? What was nascent? What other direction might he have gone? What would the necessary conditions be to get a parallel version of him—or some current version of him—to take that other, more peaceful, path?

In *Persuasion Nation*, there is a terrifying and very effective story called "93990." The story is written in the form of a dry bureaucratic document about a scientific study—or "a ten-day acute toxicity study"—performed on twenty monkeys. The cold, precise language reflects the horrors of what occurs. I bought a used copy of the book, and I found the following Post-it note on the title page of this story. I have no idea who wrote it, but it's obvious that this particular story affected him or her very deeply.

Hopefully he or she meant the story line, not the prose quality. Did they leave a phone number, so I can check?

Was the idea for this particular story dreamed?

No. I worked at a pharmaceutical company in Albany, New York, in the late eighties, just after our first daughter was born. That was based on a true story.

This story was based on a real event?!

I worked summarizing tech reports for the company's FDA submissions. I worked upstairs and the animal labs were downstairs. I have a strong memory of leaving work at five o'clock, liberated, so happy to be going to see my wife and our baby, and taking a shortcut through the lab, and seeing about fifteen beagles in slings—that's right, beagles in slings. They slung them up like that, supposedly, to stabilize their heart rates for the next day's study. Seems like that might have had the opposite effect, if it were me being slung. They also tested rats and rabbits and monkeys.

My job was to summarize all of the animal tests that had been done for a particular proposed drug. This would be maybe five thousand pages. And we had to get the whole thing down, in summary form, to less than a hundred pages to submit to the FDA. So I had to read—or, more honestly, scan—these larger documents and summarize them.

A memo very much like what's in the story one day came across my desk: this miracle monkey who could survive every dosage level. And then they killed it at the end, per the protocol. So I photocopied the summary and took it home and held on to it for a few years. And, as I recall, I was flying home from out west and thought of that, and wrote a quick draft—I can't remember, but I might have had the memo with me. Maybe I'd planned to write it on the trip. It's all kind of hazy. But I was pretty good at that kind of language by then, and also had really internalized the way these studies were done and so forth. So I just turned the volume up a little, to make the movements within the real memo more evident to a reader who hadn't had the benefit of reading the hundreds of nonmoving memos that I'd had.

I wonder if it helps a writer to have worked difficult jobs, such as yourself.

Not necessarily. I mean, look at Flannery O'Connor, Tolstoy, or Proust. It helped me, I think, but it also could have completely messed me up. There was this narrow window of a few years where, if I hadn't gotten something going, it would have been too late, given my fiscal situation—my energy for writing would have been gone and my life would have become too busy to write a first book.

The weird thing about writing is, whatever the question, there's no "one size fits all" answer. Because writing is hard, and subjective. We like to think, you know: "The key must be X!" And the X equals "work weird jobs," or "cut the story down in half," or "show, don't tell," whatever. But it is totally person-centric. Nobody's truth applies to anyone else, at least not completely. So you go into it alone.

But in my case, I do think that the difficult-job period was good. It helped me to get a first read on capitalism and its hardships. It sort of gave me my material. I had a couple early close brushes with real poverty that scared the shit out of me. We had a dog once who almost got hit by a falling icicle when she was a pup and always flinched when she had to go by that side of the house. I am—when it comes to poverty—like that dog.

How easy could it have been for you to have remained in the working world? Not necessarily in a slaughterhouse or as a doorman, but as an engineer in an austere office? Someone who was a little different from the rest of the co-workers, the one not participating in the trust games at the company picnic?

I think it would have been easy enough. There were real pleasures in that life. And people are pretty adaptable. I mean, all kinds of people do it. I think we do what we need to do and our real spiritual and emotional growth occurs around that, no matter what.

The thing that made it easier at the time was that I was far from the only one who felt weird. I'd go so far as to say that most of us felt that way—that we were not supposed to be there, or were too cool for the setting, or that this was a temporary glitch in the greater glory that would be our life. There was definitely an ironic thing in the air. This was especially true of those of us who were below a certain line—basically, those of us who were not in management felt that way.

It was a great chance to get into a more or less "typical" life and just stay there. It was beautiful, actually. And it was a great inoculation against simplistic thinking when it came to "the corporation" or "big business" or "the suburbs" and all of that. I don't like the lazy way of telegraphing those things you sometimes see in fiction or on TV, something that indicates that a concept like "suburb" automatically means: "shallow craphole." That's not interesting, to see things only as simple blocks of meaning.

In previous interviews, you've talked about the presence or absence of magic in writing. How does a young writer create a sense of magic in their work without overthinking it?

Yes, that's the million-dollar question. Or, since we're talking about fiction writing, the five-thousand-dollar question.

I can't speak for anyone else, but my feeling is that you have to first and foremost keep your eye on the fact that your prose has to kick ass. It has to compel and entertain, and your job is to make that happen, per your taste. And my experience has been that this process isn't so much intellectual or cerebral as we sometimes, when younger, think it is. We think of writing as an intellectual act, which of course it is, but it's also an act of entertainment and engagement and arguably has to address those needs before it can do any sort of intellectual work.

So my first job as a writer is to make the prose undeniable. And for me this is mostly a gut-level or "ear" thing. Maybe it's like music—people can talk and think and write endlessly about Miles Davis, but I doubt, in the moment of playing, that Miles Davis was doing much thinking, per se. What he was doing—well, who knows what he was doing. But whatever it was, it was the result of years of prep. Writers also prep themselves with years of reading and thinking and talking and so on. But in the moment of doing, I think we have to admit that something magical and inexpressible and irreducible is going on. And that this moment is what distinguishes an interesting writer from a dull one. And what distinguishes this interesting writer from this other one over here. And what I find exhilarating is that we don't have to worry too much about what exactly that magical thing is—we don't have to reduce it or own it or be able to explain it. We just have to be able to do it. Our job isn't to describe that state, but to learn to get there, and occupy it, using whatever tricks we've learned to get us there.

Does an internal melody come into play when you write? Or a musical rhythm?

Yes. That's just what I mean. There's the "sound" of the sentences, although for me this is internal. I sort of feel it at the back of my throat, which is not separable from meaning, or from the prose's ability to convince. But language is the main tool you have in prose as you are trying to close the deal. Compelling language equals belief. Blah language erodes belief in the fictive reality. At least I think so.

You just mentioned Miles Davis, but Davis was not always a people pleaser; he was known to literally turn his back on audiences. Where's that balance between wanting to create new music—or literature—while, at the same time, not alienating a large portion of your audience who might just want to hear "My Funny Valentine" over and over again?

For me, this hasn't really been an issue. My work first got meaningful when it got entertaining. Maybe because of my background, I'm at my smartest and most intellectually genuine, I think, when I am trying to keep the reader reading.

You have an extremely strong writer's voice, but you've said that it took you seven years to find that voice.

Yes, it took a long time. I think part of getting a voice is accepting the notion that one's natural voice—the voice that's first arrived at—isn't necessarily one's "true" voice. That is: That revision is as important as that first initial riffing impulse.

My early drafts usually don't sound much like "me." They're overly clever and jump around a lot, and have more conversational fill in them—clichés and empty phrases and so on. And they meander in terms of their causality. Things happen for no reason, and lead to nothing, or lead to something, but with weak causation. But in revision they get tighter and funnier and also gentler. And one thing leads to the next in a tighter, more undeniable way—a way that seems to "mean." Which, I guess, makes sense, if we think of revision as just an iterative process of exerting one's taste. Gradually the story comes to feel more like "you" than you could have imagined at the outset, and starts to manifest a sort of superlogic—an internal logic that is more direct and "caused" than mere real-life logic.

The thing is, writing is really just the process of charming someone via prose—compelling them to keep reading. So, as with actual personality, part of the process is learning what it is that you've got to work with: How do I keep that reader reading? What's in my tool bag?

When I was a kid, I had this Hot Wheels set. A car would approach the "gas station," which was just two spinning rubber wheels that would push the car forward to the next "gas station." A story could be thought of as a series of these little gas stations. You want to keep the reader on the track—giving them little pleasure bursts—with the goal of pushing them forward toward the end of the story.

So learning to be a writer could be understood as getting into relation with one's own little gas stations—finding out what sort of micromoments you are capable of creating that will keep the reader moving through the text.

One of the things that interests me about writing humor is this: How does a writer for print, after the one-hundredth reading of a sentence, still recognize that intuitive "pleasure burst"? It's all so internal. It could almost fester, it's so internal. It's not similar to performing a comedy routine where its success is immediately confirmed by applause or laughter.

That's the crux of the whole thing. You become deaf to your own prose after many readings of it. I think that might be the main thing every writer has to learn: How do I refresh my reading mind? And I'd say that this is the one area where I can objectively say I've improved over the years. It takes less time now to clear my mind and read what I've written in a relatively fresh way. I just try to approach the prose as if I'm a first-time reader. I'm trying, in my reading mind, to imitate what I think a first-time reader might feel. Part of this has to do with trying to divest yourself of whatever concepts you've accrued about the story—sort of like wiping fog off a window. Concepts like: *Yes, this part is dull, but that's because it's essential to my critique of provincialism.* Absent those things, what's left? Well, basically, that first-time reader is left: you, if you hadn't already read the thing a gazillion times.

When you're writing, how do you know when an ending feels right? How do you know when to stop?

Well, building off that "first-time reader" idea above: If we imagine that there's this meter in our head, with "Positive" on one end and "Negative" on the other, our job is to keep the meter in the Positive zone. If it drops into the Negative, ask ourselves why it's doing that, and edit accordingly; and better if the answer to "Why?" is an intuitive adjustment of the line rather than some big conceptual overlay.

So to finish a story just means that you can get through the whole thing with the needle up in the Positive—and then, at the very last minute, you are trying to put in something that will make the needle go all the way over. By that time, the theory goes, you will be so deep inside your story that your subconscious will be driving the car, so to speak. But there's no general principle—each story has its own "epistemology of ending." It's maybe like a long car trip with a close friend. You cover so much ground, things get rough, you talk them out, all of that—and then it's time to say good-bye. How do you say good-bye? Well, there's no one answer. Depends on that particular friend and trip but, by then, being so deep inside the trip, you'd know how.

One thing I always do is try to read the story all the way through, remembering that a first-time reader is not reading individual lines but is inside the story. By reading, we enter into this odd mind-state where each sentence is a microadjustment of both our imaginative reality—what's happening in the story—and what we might call our "sonic reality"—the cumulative effects of all those sentences and the internal dynamics and all of that. It's so wonderfully complicated, the act of reading. But I understand it as a very visceral thing, just reading along as if for the first time, and what you're doing is noticing whether you're still charmed. Is the spell still in effect? If not, where did things go wrong?

And when you think of it, it's an incredibly hopeful process—this idea that I, over here, in my place and time and mental state, can actively communicate with someone over there, in some other time, and some other mental state—that I can reach across time and space and circumstance and ring your bell. That argues for a sort of commonality of spirit that I find very thrilling.

ULTRASPECIFIC COMEDIC KNOWLEDGE

BYRD LEAVELL

Literary Agent, Waxman Leavell Literary Agency

....

Finding a Literary Agent for Your Humor Book

Can I just be brutally honest here? Agents never want to admit that they don't do a great job handling the submissions they receive but, well, they don't—or, at least, I don't. I was at a party twelve years ago, which would have put me at all of twenty-two years old, and a book editor I respected tremendously, George Gibson, told me something I never forgot. He said, "Go find your clients. Don't count on them coming to you. You'll always be remembered by the ones you tracked down." And I fundamentally believe that. Don't get me wrong. I do get passed some amazing clients these days. What I don't do, though, is devote very much of my time going through the "my book is called *Death Comes for Everyone*" submissions.

Which is terrible. But, you know, there's never anything good in that submission stack. And I'm just not up to it anymore. Can I say that? I am going to get in trouble for this later. But there really isn't, goddamnit. You know where all the talented people are? They are out there hoeing corn on the Internet. They are putting up great content that people are reading and responding to. And they in turn are learning how to respond to their fans and how to build an audience and how to write what people care about. More than anything, they are learning how to be funny.

No one really gives my client Justin Halpern any credit. In 2009, Justin started a Twitter feed called Shitmydadsays. Shortly after that I signed him and sold the book at auction for a pretty reasonable advance. Then Justin wrote the book and it ended up selling over a million copies in one year. Which is ridiculous. But everyone seemed to focus on how lucky Justin was, and no one seemed to focus at all on the fact that Justin had been out there for years trying to be funny on various sites that were paying him close to nothing. For Justin, that was invaluable. Justin Halpern is now one of the most talented humor writers in the country. Really. He is. Go read one of his books and then come back and say I'm wrong.

So don't even submit to an agent. You are just going to get rejected anyway. Because these days the idea isn't enough. Going to publishers with "I've got a great idea for a humor book" is about as useful as tweeting your breakfast menu. No one cares. Especially not publishers. All they care about is *platform*. They care if you've written something really, really funny and it's gone viral and five thousand people have commented on it. They care that your product is the perfect thing to turn into a book that works in the market. They care how many readers you can make aware of your book when it is finally published. You have to show agents that you can do all of these things, and then, and only then, do you get to show them how good your book is.

One last point. Most humor books are actually not funny. I'd put the percentage somewhere around 97 percent of books as not having a single laugh. So when you do get your book deal, all you have to do is make sure you are a part of that 3 percent and then watch how many copies your book sells.

PURE, HARD-CORE ADVICE

DAVE HILL

Contributor, *The New York Times, GQ, Salon, This American Life*;
Author, *Tasteful Nudes . . . And Other Misguided Attempts
at Personal Growth and Validation,*
The Goddamn Dave Hill Show on WFMU

I think the purpose of writing—and, really, with all comedy—is to fully entertain yourself. I look at my output, whatever it is—be it writing, performance, music, or anything—as more like an excretion, like what a snail leaves behind. It's just what comes out, and the more you can have it be what comes out naturally, the better it ends up being. The more you can remove any stakes or pressure—just write as fast as you can type—it's going to come out better. And then, at the very least, you have the raw material, and you can go back and hone it.

I once got asked to submit a writing packet for a comedy show. My thinking was, I'm not the right fit for this job at all. I'm not even in the running, but my friends are going to read this, and while they're sitting in the office going through this pile, I want to entertain them. So I wrote this packet thinking, There's no way in hell anyone's even thinking of hiring me for this. It's more like I was asked to submit out of politeness or something. [Laughs] Later, they told me, "Your packet was honestly, hands-down the best one we got, and we want to hire you. Nothing was even close." I'm not saying I'd be capable of doing that again in any context, but I think because I wrote only for wanting to crack up my friends, and I was cracking myself up in the process, it worked. It was the first writing packet I ever wrote that I had any fun doing, and that's why I was able to make it good. Normally, you put pressure on yourself. And as soon as you think that you *absolutely* have to do a good job on it, you're in trouble. I tense up when I do that, and then it usually sucks.

When I first started getting into comedy and writing, I thought I needed an agent and a manager. I felt, I have to get my friends to introduce me to people and help me. And my friends would help, which was very nice of them. But I know now that this doesn't matter at first. I mean, it's nice to have an introduction. But you know, I was rejected by everyone. And understandably so. When I was first starting, I called someone who's my current manager, and they weren't even taking my calls. I couldn't even make it past the receptionist. I was crushed by that initial rejection. I thought I'd been rejected by the establishment of comedy. So I was like, "It doesn't matter; I'm on my own. I'm going to do my own thing." And once I did that, once I was truly at the point where I was not trying to get anyone's attention, that's when I got everything I wanted, including a manager. The point is, if you're like, "Oh, I *gotta* do this," that energy and that mental state does not help the situation at all.

Another thing that helped was I was fine with failing and being a complete moron. I think a lot of people in comedy have a slight concern about not being willing to be completely foolish. Not everyone, certainly. But it helped me to not care that much.

With my book, *Tasteful Nudes* [St. Martin's Press, 2012], I knew within three weeks of the proposal going out to publishers whether anyone wanted to publish it. But in that time, I realized probably the real reason that I dragged ass, took several years to put the book proposal together, was because if no one wanted it, it was going to crush me so badly that I would never have written another word. Fortunately, it worked out. And, you know, if no one had wanted the book, I would have been bummed out for a few weeks, but I would have gotten over it. It's going back to not really giving a shit. Do your best to entertain yourself. Or entertaining the fifteen-year-old in you. Or just creating something that you want to see exist.

Find a way to remove that anxiety and pressure. Just do your best, the same way that you would try to do your best with anything, like making spaghetti. Basically, I think life is way more knuckle-headed than people make it out to be. It's making spaghetti, and then it's sitting with someone and having spaghetti. That's basically all life is.

My mom died a couple years ago. I spent so much of my adult life thinking, Oh, man, I've gotta do something to make her proud of me. And it took me right up until the end to realize, Oh, she's been proud of me this whole time. She doesn't give a fuck what I do. She doesn't want me to be a prostitute, really, but otherwise, we're just sitting around watching TV, talking; it doesn't matter. We're just eating Chinese food. I realized the basis of any relationship is way less complicated than it's made out to be.

I'm probably a bit more scattered than I should be. I sort of wish I could rein it in, but when I try to do that, I realize I'm doing the things I want to be doing. Maybe not always on the scale I want to be doing them, but I'm thrilled that I can make a decent living doing what I want to do—just acting like an idiot. It's kind of my job.

TOM SCHARPLING

"In the seventies, Led Zeppelin and the Who spent the hours on the road listening to their prized bootleg Derek and Clive tapes," Rob Sheffield wrote for *Rolling Stone* in 2007, referring to the foul-mouthed, blue-collar characters created by British comedians Dudley Moore and Peter Cook. "These days, Tom Scharpling and Jon Wurster are the traveling rock musician's comedy duo of choice, inspiring a fanatical MP3-trading cult. Like an indie-rock Bob & Ray, they improvise long, absurd dialogues about . . . jerks you know, or maybe the jerk you are."

The cult began with a now-legendary 1997 bit (titled "Rock, Rot & Rule") that Scharpling and Wurster produced and distributed themselves via cassette tapes. The forty-seven-minute phone interview, which first aired live on radio station WFMU near New York City, featured host Scharpling and Ronald Thomas Clontle, a fictional rock critic from Lawrence, Kansas, played with deadpan brilliance by Jon Wurster. Clontle classifies all musical artists into three categories: rock, rot, or rule. Clontle makes maddening statements—"[the eighties British group] Madness invented ska"; Frank Zappa rots because "humor has no place in music"—and it doesn't take long for the phone lines to light up with callers ready to berate him for his ignorance. But the real comedy gold of "Rock, Rot & Rule" is the comedy interplay between Scharpling and Wurster.

Growing up in central New Jersey, Scharpling seemed destined more for a career in music than for one in radio comedy. When he met Wurster in 1992, at a My Bloody Valentine concert at the Ritz in New York City, Scharpling was running a New Jersey indie label and fanzine called *18 Wheeler*. He and Wurster (in real life, the drummer for Superchunk, Bob Mould, and the Mountain Goats) became friends after discovering their shared love for Chris Elliott and his short-lived Fox sitcom *Get a Life*.

Scharpling has gone back and forth between music and comedy writing for his entire career. In the mid-nineties, he was hired by WFMU to host a noncomedic, all-music show. After receiving acclaim from the comedy community for "Rock, Rot & Rule," which Scharpling intended as a one-time bit, his show ultimately evolved into *The Best Show on WFMU*, which made its official debut in October of 2000. (The title of the show, Scharpling has said, was always meant to be self-deprecating. "I was such a footnote up at WFMU that I was making fun of my stature there," he's claimed.) In 2002, while continuing with the show, he joined the writing staff of the television comedy-mystery series *Monk*, where he worked as a story editor and eventually rose to executive producer before the show ended in 2009.

Writing witty dialogue for *Monk* paid his bills, but Scharpling's work on *Best Show on WFMU* was slowly building his reputation as one of the funniest writer/performers in underground comedy. Over the years, not much about the content has changed. Scharpling still plays records and then interviews people, some real and some fictional.

Scharpling and his longtime co-conspirator Wurster have created hundreds of characters, the majority of whom live in the fictional town of Newbridge, New Jersey. There's Roland "The Gorch" Gorchnik, who's absolutely certain that the Fonz (i.e., the Henry Winkler character from *Happy Days*) was based on him. There's "Philly Boy Roy," the former mayor of Newbridge and pencil factory employee who loves everything about Philadelphia, from Tastykakes to the eighties band the Hooters. There's overweight barbershop singer Zachary Brimstead, and two-inch-tall racist Timmy Von Trimble. And there are also guests who don't come from Scharpling and Wurster's imagination—actual comedians who also happen to be *Best Show* fans, like Patton Oswalt, Zach Galifianakis, and Fred Armisen.

Among comics and humor writers (as well as musicians), Scharpling is akin to royalty. Listening to the *Best Show*'s long-form comedy has for years been unofficial homework for Conan O'Brien and his writing staff. When Patton Oswalt guest-edited *Spin* magazine's first "Funny" Issue in 2011, Scharpling and Wurster were given a feature profile. "It's one of those rare things in pop culture," Jake Fogelnest wrote of *Best Show* for *Spin*, "like, say, *The Wire*—that you actually get angry with your friends for not knowing about."

In 2013, a few months after this interview took place, Scharpling—after more than six hundred episodes—left WFMU and took *Best Show* with him. He plans to direct and spend more time writing. Past and "best of" episodes can be found at wfmu.org/playlists/bs.

I've read that you started working at the age of ten. Is this true? If so, it sounds like something out of a Horatio Alger novel.

That's true. When I was around ten, I would run errands for a music store in Summit, New Jersey. It was a store that sold records and other music-related items, like sheet music—just a place I wanted to hang out. I would clean up and run these tasks so I could buy all these records. That was my main goal. I think I made five dollars an hour. Then, when I was twelve, I was a busboy at a New Jersey diner. I worked there for about two years. Eventually, when I was about fifteen, I worked as one of the janitors at my own high school.

Was this something of your choosing? I can't imagine any child wanting a janitorial job, especially at their own school.

Another kid, who was a couple of years older, was working as a janitor, and I liked the guy. We were friends. He said, "So, you do this after school, and you get the keys to the school. You get to push that extra-wide broom down the hall, and you get to spray-clean the floor and you use a mop. Then you get to go into the classrooms. You get the keys to everything."

And what was the appeal of that?

I'd go to the classrooms and look through the grade books to see what my friends were getting.

Did you ever change any of the grades?

No, no. It was not *WarGames*. [Laughs] I wasn't going to hack into the system. I don't know why I did that job, truthfully. It was such a bad decision. It was just horrible. It was clear that it was not helping my social standing by doing that.

I did that for about a year. By this point, I was completely obsessed with music and comedy—equally. Eventually, I was able to afford a color TV for my room. I also bought a Betamax tape machine. I'd rent movies and watch and tape all these comedy shows. I would stay up and watch TV later than most kids. I remember watching that first Letterman late-night show [*Late Night with David Letterman*, February 1, 1982].

Actually, even before that late-night show, I remember watching Letterman's daytime summer show [*The David Letterman Show*, June to October 1980]. It aired in the morning. I remember discovering that show while flipping through the channels. I saw a birthday cake blow up. That was such a ridiculous image. I remember thinking it was funny in a way that really spoke to me. Here was a guy who was younger than most everyone else on television, and he looked different, and he was sarcastic about everything and everyone else. I think I had that streak in me; this was something I could definitely connect with.

Very funny, very strange. Some bits were almost as scary as they were funny. Like the Chris Elliott characters. Almost frightening.

Were you also a fan of horror?

I loved horror as a kid—I'd watch horror movies and read horror comics—but then there came a point when it only repulsed me. When

I realized how rough life actually was, I didn't need to see people getting killed for no reason. I realized that people get killed unfairly all the time anyway. Life is fragile. It was no longer entertainment for me.

But there is a connection between horror and comedy, not to mention other genres. They're all math problems ultimately. When I was writing on *Monk*, I learned pretty quickly that comedy writers were able to write mystery somewhat easily. It was just like writing a joke: the rhythms of the setup, the misdirection, the payoff. That's what mystery ultimately is. The structure is just 1-2-3. There's a long arc, but then there are shorter elements sprinkled throughout. And then there's the big payoff. Just like comedy.

So comedy writers can write mystery, but can mystery writers write comedy?

No, actually. I think you can jump from comedy into other genres, but not necessarily from other genres into comedy. Or at least not so easily or automatically.

Did you have to teach yourself the elements of mystery?

I did. I just wasn't familiar with that genre. I watched all of the Alfred Hitchcock movies and all the episodes of [the 1970s TV mystery series] *Columbo*. I wanted to see how one doles out suspense and how one sets up a ticking clock. I wanted to see what made a scene suspenseful, how to make a whole story suspenseful. If you're open to doing your homework—and really just embracing it—a comedy background is very helpful.

I suppose comedy is like type-O blood. It's the universal donor.

If you know how to build jokes, you can write any other genre, including mystery and horror.

Where do you think the creative drive in your personality came from?

I'm not sure. Nobody can get you there. My parents were doing the best they could, but they had gone directly from high school to working jobs. And that's what I came out of. I was the first person in my family to go to college. My parents just did not know how to deal with some kid who at seven or eight years old was writing crazy things, like comic books or scripts to *Battlestar Galactica*. You know, my parents were working class.

I remember high school as being so frustrating. I hated school, just hated it. But anytime there was a chance to do anything creative, I was all over it. I remember one time we had to break off into groups in history class and write a Civil War–era story. So I broke off into this group, and I remember we ended up creating this story that was so insane. It was so aggressive and hyperviolent. It ended with a fight between a slave and a slaveowner, in front of a cotton-baling press. The slaveowner falls into it and comes out of the machine in the shape of a cube.

We had to read the story to the class, and we were laughing so hard. Everyone else wrote a real story, and we wrote a Bugs Bunny cartoon that ended with someone falling into a cotton-baling press— and coming out as a cube. It was just so out of step with reality. [Laughs] The teacher was horrified. Not that we got in trouble; it was just like, "No. That's not how you do this."

So what did that experience teach you? That you could have fun outside the confines of what teachers and administrators wanted from you?

I didn't even know what it was. I just felt it was this chance to do something. I didn't even know what to do with this feeling, this drive to make something. It was an urge and there was nowhere for it to go. I do not come from a background of performing. Nobody in my family is really creative. There was nobody to say, "Since you are interested in this, you should go do this, or go do that. Or go to this school." There was none of that. I was just dropped in the middle of the ocean, not really sure which way to swim. Or sink.

I was living in New Jersey, thirty miles away from where everything was going down—but it was like another planet. I didn't know how to get from where I was to *there*. It could have been the moon. I was operating as such a second-class citizen, anyway. I felt like I didn't have a place in New York City. I felt like I would always be exposed, that I would hear, "Who in the hell do you think you are?" But at some point, the compulsion and the need to create eventually outweighed any of the insecurities that went with it. I felt that I just had to do *something*. That something was *going* to happen.

So, while still working at the music store, I started writing and publishing a fanzine in the late eighties called *18 Wheeler*. I was about twenty. It was a chance to combine music and comedy. At this time, there were so many awesome music fanzines, and I just wanted to create something similar.

Was there a frustration that you weren't on the inside track? That you weren't writing for the *Harvard Lampoon*? That you weren't meeting contacts in the professional writing world?

I have to say, I'm still haunted by the fact that I did not go to a good school. I went to a community college in Jersey [Middlesex County College]. I worked for ten years in a record store, until I was around twenty-seven or twenty-eight. This haunted me for years. I felt I had fucked up. I just didn't have any kind of guidance. I had to kind of stumble my way through all this. I lost my twenties. I really didn't know any other way to do things. But you have to teach yourself the rules. That's the only way to go through it. And I think I'm happier now because of the fact that I went through it alone. If it means I got to where I am now, then that's where I should be. I'm happy with where I am now. I'm in the right mind-set to be doing this. And there's nothing I can do about the past anyway.

I was alone. Totally alone and isolated. But there were some people who were really important to me. There was one guy in New York named Gerard Cosloy; he was a DJ at WFMU for a while. He was also the owner of a record label called Homestead Records, and he later became one of the owners of Matador Records. He had an amazing track record of putting out these fantastic groups—Sonic Youth, Big Dipper, Dinosaur Jr. He also published a music fanzine called *Conflict*, which had the funniest record reviews ever. Gerard really combined humor and music; he was the gold standard for that. He could be mean with his writing sometimes, but he was always on the right side of things. He was fighting the good fight.

So Gerard was just a huge influence on me doing my own fanzine. This guy was managing to be legitimately funny—as funny as any comedy writer out there—and he also had amazing taste in music. He made a point of pushing the things that people needed to know about to those who might not have known about them otherwise.

I think younger writers might not be aware of how important fanzines were to music or comedy geeks pre-Internet. In many ways, fanzines were the only lifeline.

Yes, absolutely. And they were very accessible, these fanzines. This was the equivalent of the Internet then. You had to piece everything together yourself. You had to reach out to like-minded people, and this was one of the few ways to do that. So from that, I decided to put out my own fanzine.

At some point you either overcome everything and you do your own thing or you don't. You can stay on the one side where you don't ever make things. There are a lot of people who don't create, and that's fine. But there does come a time when you either do it or not. I'm not sure why I did it, truthfully. I'm not sure why anyone does it. But there just comes a time when you have to decide.

Did you ever graduate college?

I did. After I went to community college, I transferred to what later became the College of New Jersey. At the time it was called Trenton State College, but they later changed their name. They didn't want anything to do with the name Trenton. [Laughs] They felt Trenton, New Jersey, wasn't a great selling point. It took a long time for me to graduate. It took me about eight years to get through college.

Did you make any friends?

Not really. I wasn't on campus. I was a commuter. I made one good friend at the community college. Outside of that, I didn't talk to anybody; I just went there. I'd do my time and then get in my car and drive to work. That's what I was doing.

After I graduated, I stayed for a few more years at the music store, and then began to write for basketball magazines. I was a huge fan of basketball. There was a magazine called *SLAM* that was published for kids. It had a hip-hop element to it and celebrated the NBA players. It was not institutionalized the way *Sports Illustrated* was. I wrote to *SLAM* and kept asking them, "*Please* let me write anything for you guys." And they let me. First small pieces, and then eventually a cover story.

Around 1997, they sent me to a reading event in Orlando, Florida. Some players from the Boston Celtics were going to read to kids in the Dr. Seuss section of Universal Studios. I got a plane ticket, flew from Newark to Orlando. At this point, the Celtics were in the ninth overall spot; they had to win that night if they were going to make the playoffs. When I arrived at the Orlando Arena, I heard their coach, Rick Pitino, screaming as loudly as he could. I could easily hear it through the walls. Screaming and screaming. Then these two players walked out—Antoine Walker and Paul Pierce—after having been screamed at for twenty minutes, and they got into a limo with me. They're off to read to the kids. And they're in the worst mood ever.

They start to complain to the NBA rep who was with us: "Why aren't we ever on the cover of anything? You guys promote this guy, you guys promote that guy, you don't ever promote us!" And now they're yelling at her, and I'm just this big dummy sitting there. Sweat is pouring down my face and down onto my little recorder. The NBA rep starts yelling back at them: "You know why you're not on the cover! We . . . we put who *wins* on the cover! *Winners!* That's why!" And then there's quiet and she announces, "So, Tom is going to ask you a few questions about reading." I mumbled something like, "So, ummmm, what kind of books do you like to read?"

I remember one of them said he liked books about money. The other said he preferred books by John Grisham.

I felt like garbage, and I felt as if these two were giving me nothing for this thing. And I wanted to say that being there was beneath me, but that's the part that truly sucks. I felt that I deserved better, but, no, this was *exactly* what I deserved! It was terrible—just awful. But I had zero experience. It was exactly what I deserved.

I'd imagine that this type of experience could have only helped later with your comedy. You didn't directly go from an Ivy League to a writing room in Hollywood, which would have been limiting.

Everything has worked to my benefit, even the things that felt, at the time, like they were working against me. A problem never comes without a gift in its hand. You may not even be aware of it until five years later. Everything I've done in my life has allowed me to have this wealth of real-life experience. And that can only help.

And, actually, I'm grateful that I did not have the Internet back then. All of the missteps I made when I was first starting out would have been made public. For years, I could fail in private. By the time I got my act together, the worldwide distribution method clicked into place. Private failure is not really a luxury these days.

How else do you think real-world experience helped with your comedy?

There's so much comedy that just deals with show business. Jokes about other jokes. References to references. There are so many writers who write movies about other screenwriters. The pitch is something like, "This story is about a screenwriter who has writer's block, so then he goes . . ." Well, you've already lost sight of the real world. Writing about showbiz is such a cheap trick. Everybody wants to see behind the curtain, but there's such a low ceiling for it. It contains no dynamics from real-life experience.

I can't imagine anyone growing up wanting to write a screenplay about a screenplay. People end up there because their worldview has shrunk to include nobody but other screenwriters. I see the same with TV writers, too. They'll know every episode of *The Simpsons*, but what do they know about working shitty jobs? Or, if they do know about shitty jobs, it tends to be the bad jobs that fictional characters have worked, like Fred Flintstone working at the stone quarry, or Apu from *The Simpsons* working at the Kwik-E-Mart.

I don't say all of this from a place where I'm mad at anyone who took that path. I'm just very glad that I have had at least some experience with the real world.

How did you pick radio as your medium of choice?

The appeal of radio to me was simply that I was allowed to do it. Jon [Wurster] and I wanted to do a radio show similar to [the 1970s and '80s TV sketch comedy show] *SCTV*. We wanted to create a large world. We wanted to create characters. Backstories. Plot lines. An entire, very real world. And radio allowed us to do that. We were using the only medium we had at our disposal. We couldn't work in movies or in TV; radio was accessible.

It really worked to our advantage. The most amazing thing about radio is that it allows for long-form comedy. What other medium even comes close? If we were on television, people would stop watching after three minutes. Movies are out of the question.

Radio allows us to really stretch out. We can create bits as long as we want because people will never say, "This is too long." I mean, some people will say that. If you listen to Z-100's Morning Zoo, you'll hear character bits, but they only have ninety seconds to do it. It's joke, setup, joke, setup, joke, setup. But we have the real estate to create something larger, more nuanced. There's no rush on it. We can take the scenic route.

Another positive aspect of radio is that it creates a very personal connection between listeners and performers.

The amount of time you spend with people who listen to the radio is incredible. If you're a Bill Murray fan, you might spend four hours a year with him. If you're a fan of a sitcom, you spend twenty-two half-hours with those characters. But with radio, you're talking about spending hundreds of hours with a person over the course of a year.

Radio is such a passive medium. Listeners are usually doing something else while they listen, like washing the dishes or driving a car or going on a walk. That's a strength, not a weakness. The bond, I think, becomes so much deeper than it would be for other mediums because of that.

It took awhile for an audience to find your show, didn't it?

It did take a while for the show to find an audience, but you can never try to be a version of what everybody else is doing. Even if it seems like the kind of thing that other people might not laugh at, you have to stick with it. Everybody that you admire has come from that same place.

[The comedians] Tim and Eric had a hard time at first, but they stuck with it. Their [Adult Swim] TV show [*Tim and Eric Awesome Show, Great Job!*] wasn't crowd-pleasing—at all. They weren't attempting to win a huge audience. But they stuck with it, they eventually found their audience, and it's what they needed to do. You have to trust what you're doing. There's something running through everybody that others will eventually respond to.

When you started *The Best Show*—which really kicked into gear around 2000—was anyone else even doing long-form radio comedy? Jean Shepherd, Bob & Ray, Firesign Theater—all had been long off the air by then.

I'm the only one that I'm aware of. We're still the only one. The first comedy bit we did was in 1997. I then took a few years off to try and find a writing job. I returned in 2000, and the show became just as much about comedy as it was about music.

Do you remember your first scripted comedy radio bit?

I do. And it was more effective than it might have been, I think, because no listener could have predicted it coming. Jon phoned in to the show as a character and we did a routine that we later called "Rock, Rot & Rule."

In 1997, the tape of "Rock, Rot & Rule" became infamous. It was bootlegged and passed around as cassette tapes, particularly among comedy writers and musicians.

Thankfully, I was taping it. At that point, if you didn't tape a show onto a cassette, you didn't have it. This was before the show was taped and later broadcast on the Internet. So I taped it, edited it down to forty-seven minutes, and handed out cassettes. We got validation from our friends that this was funny. I remember Amy Poehler loved it. There was even a reference on Amy Sedaris's TV show, *Strangers with Candy*, which took place in a high school with blackboards in each classroom. In one episode, someone wrote "Somebody rocks, somebody rules" across one of the blackboards. The funny thing is that when we did that first bit, we were so anonymous. What pedigree did I have? Zero. I was just a guy going to watch live comedy shows every week in the city. And Jon lived in Chapel Hill, North Carolina, and was working as the drummer for the group Superchunk. So zero. Zero pedigree.

What type of pedigree do you really need for comedy, though? And wouldn't that work to your advantage anyway? I mean, no one had any indication that this character you created was a fake.

That did work to our advantage, actually. A lot of people at first thought that [comedian] David Cross was behind it. We also had a lot of people who thought it was a crank phone call. I'd read on sites, "Listen to this guy crank this dumb radio host!" Which, to me, is the greatest compliment ever, because I co-wrote the thing.

It was a great parody of pompous music critics and their ridiculous, wrong-headed theories.

[Laughs] The phones really lit up. I mean, the callers had absolutely no idea that Jon was playing this character—and they were just burning, burning mad. Furious!

Jon told the audience that he felt that David Bowie and Neil Young were "rot" because they had made too many changes to their sound over the years. And yet, he hadn't heard any songs by Neil Young from before 1989. Jon also said that the Beatles fell under the "rock" category and not the "rule" category, because they had so many "bad songs," including "Strawberry Fields Forever." Puff Daddy, on the other hand, "ruled."

I remember first coming up with this idea after reading an article about Texas cattlemen taking Oprah Winfrey to court over a show she did about mad cow disease. They said she had portrayed the meat industry in a negative light, and they tried to sue her, but the case was thrown out. Afterward, Oprah said, "Free speech not only lives, it rocks!" Jon and I were laughing about that, and we thought, What if we apply that to music? We wrote out the script, and I showed it to my wife. She said, "You're going to do this for *how* long on the radio?" But that night when I came home after the show, she said, "Nope. You were right. That was awesome." It ran for about fifty minutes. And that goes back to what I was saying earlier about long-form comedy. What else can run that long, except for a movie?

You've worked with a lot of great comedians and performers, some of the best in the business. How does Jon compare?

Jon is literally the funniest person I've ever met or seen. He's so quick and is able to make everything go down so effortlessly. But I know how much effort is going into it. That impresses me even more because I know how much he's working to just make these calls sound like conversations.

To make it all seem breezy and real and to be able to play the emotions and know when to start to get mad or sad—just to have the perfect gauge—is extremely difficult. He's got so much range, and he's got so much control over that range. He can very smoothly not draw attention to the fact that we're trying to transition from one beat to another; you don't even notice he's doing it. Amazing.

He has no comedic training, right? No acting background?

No, no, he's just a natural talent who has taught himself over the years. He has "it." I can't think of one thing Jon hasn't been great at. He's been at such a high level for so long, whether it's comedy or music. To have two things that you're great at is shocking. Inconceivable.

Over the years, we've performed hundreds of bits. And a ton of characters. And I still receive plenty of calls from people who believe that the characters Jon performs week after week are actual people.

How do these radio scripts take shape?

We spend a lot of time writing these scripts. The scripts are usually 90 percent written, and 10 percent improvised. Jon and I talk by phone or e-mail and come up with some ideas. "Hey, I have an idea about a guy who does this." Or "What about a guy who does that?" We'll start laughing about a situation, and then we flesh out the idea. Most of these are very tightly scripted. It comes down to, "This is how this needs to be said at this point in the call for the joke to pay off or to set up the joke or to make sure that it all comes together." We'll also make notes for what *not* to say. Jon will tell me, "Don't ask me this question because that will tip off a joke too soon."

I was going through some of the characters you've created for your fictional town of Newbridge, New Jersey, and I stopped counting at one hundred. The mythology for this town and its characters is so rich and dense. Newbridge has become almost the comedy equivalent of Middle Earth.

[Laughs] Actually, there are more than two hundred characters. The world is very specific. I can't even keep up with these characters. I have to ask a guy who keeps track of all of this. He's almost like the show's historian. We have characters who are distant relatives of characters we created years ago. We have sons, daughters, parents, grandparents, cousins, nieces, nephews. But I love that. That's creating reality from out of nothing. And once you do that—once this world begins to take shape—the comedy becomes stronger for it.

To me, the things I love the most are these comedy worlds, whether it's Melonville [where *SCTV* took place] or the world that Steve Coogan created for [the BBC situation comedy] *I'm Alan Partridge*, or the Springfield that was created for *The Simpsons*—it's all just so full and wonderful. Characters become more realistic, fully fleshed, instead of just being one-dimensional.

A good example of one of your fully-fleshed characters is Barry Dworkin, who has appeared on the show multiple times over the years. In

one bit that originally aired in 2002, Barry—as played by Jon—calls the show to seek musicians for a band he's starting called The Gas Station Dogs. His requests are incredibly detailed. The keyboardist has to be an "albino who wears vintage late-sixties NASA-approved space suits," and his nickname will have to be "Commander Giggles."

That's a good example of a character who is totally delusional. And narcissistic. Barry is forty-four and his only musical experience is once playing in a Rolling Stones and Who tribute band called Tattoo Who. He's four feet eleven inches tall. He has reddish-gray hair that's balding, and a handlebar mustache. He has a purple birthmark on the top of his head the size of a softball. And his dream is to form a group consisting of only very young and extremely handsome musicians, and to record a song that he's spent nineteen years writing called "Rock 'n' Roll Dreams'll Come Through." The song is pure shit. There are about fifty characters in the lyrics, all with similar-sounding names ["Rodge," "Roddy," "Denny," "Don," "Betty," "Kenny," etc.]. And yet this guy's ego is through the roof. He's looking at everyone else under a microscope but has no quality control for himself. He's just holding everyone else to some insane standard.

It's sad. It's one of those situations when you know someone is doomed to fail, and everybody can see it but them. I'm obsessed with that.

These characters that you create tend to be a bit clueless about their lot in life. A total lack of awareness.

Jon has talked about this before, but a major influence for both of us was a scene from the [1988] documentary *The Decline of Western Civilization Part II: The Metal Years*. It was directed by Penelope Spheeris, who later directed *Wayne's World*. In the middle of the movie Penelope asks a series of horrible LA heavy metal musicians where they'll be in ten years. Every single one says, "I'm gonna make it!" Spheeris asks, "Well, how about if you don't?" And they always answer, "Oh, but we will." None made it. Total delusion.

At the same time, I always admire anyone who even attempts to do something different. To accomplish anything is never easy. The easiest thing in the world is to not make stuff. The easiest thing in the world is to choose to not put your neck out there on the chopping block. That is the safest route you can take.

Even if someone makes something terrible—like the music the Insane Clown Posse makes—at least they're doing something that speaks to them. And they kept going even though people told them it was terrible. And they found their audience, and now they built a community around their work. Look, you couldn't pay me to listen to their music, but I still feel like I have more in common with the Insane Clown Posse than I do with someone who just sits on the sidelines and shits on other people's work and who never puts themselves on the line.

But when meanness comes into the equation . . . when a terrible ego comes into play, then that's something that's always bothered me. Have you ever seen the [2003] documentary *Overnight*? It's about a totally delusional, mediocre egomaniac—a writer and director in Hollywood—named Troy Duffy. I'm fascinated by guys like that. Guys like that are the patron saints of everything we do. Duffy is the type of idiot who thinks he's a genius; there's no doubt in his mind that he's brilliant. And it takes no time for him to start rubbing this fact in everyone's face. When you see someone act like that, it becomes clear that the real geniuses—the ones behind the scenes, the ones who quietly do all the work with little fuss—are not out there mouthing off and making people feel bad about themselves. They just do the work.

On your radio show, you have complete freedom to write whatever you want. I imagine you didn't have that complete freedom when you were working as a writer on *Monk*.

Actually, my writing job on *Monk* was the best position for me to be in. I had one voice among 150 voices on *Monk*. We were all trying to build a TV show and to make that show as good as it could possibly be. I also had something that was completely my own at the same time—my radio show. But I think you have to learn how to play with adults. It's a very valuable experience. You need to go through that experience of working with others. If you don't, it's going to be very hard to suddenly be in charge of your own show down the road.

Look at David Chase, who created *The Sopranos*. He worked for years as a writer on *Rockford Files*. Look at Mitch Hurwitz, who created *Arrested Development*. He worked for years as a writer on *The Golden Girls*. You have to learn how to play nice with others.

So, no, I didn't have complete freedom on *Monk*, but I did learn a lot of valuable lessons.

TV and movies are such collaborative mediums. You have to be ready to not have everything go your way—even if you're in the top position. There were so many times on *Monk* that [writer and producer] Andy Breckman, who created the show and was the showrunner, would face actors who didn't love a certain piece of writing. The actors wanted to change scenes. Now, Andy could have just stomped and screamed and made the actors do it his way, but he didn't. It's a give-and-take. So being a part of that and learning that dynamic is a very important tool that you need in your toolbox.

But when you do achieve the freedom to create what you want, it's important to appreciate what you have. I never take *The Best Show* and the freedom that comes with it for granted.

When you're in a radio studio performing these comedic bits, you're operating in a vacuum of sorts. It's just you, alone with your producer, in a studio. How do you even know when any of the humor is working— or not working?

That comes from just trusting yourself. Basically, I'm talking to myself. You just have to trust that the humor is bearing fruit. It does feel, at times, like I'm on this space walk. There's nothing to grab on to. It feels that if the cable ever breaks, I'll just be lost in space and I will die.

But it's helpful when it comes to writing. If I'm writing something by myself, I don't worry that it's not funny enough, because I have the confidence of working in silence. I don't need everyone to be rolling on the floor because I know—or, at least, I hope—that the end result will be funny. That's very valuable when it comes to writing. It's the opposite of being a stand-up.

I'd think that would be another advantage of long-form radio comedy. Silences are accepted. Not every moment has to be filled with laughs.

That is an advantage. The worst part of stand-up, and the worst part of TV, is that sense of desperation. That *neediness* for a laugh. If people laugh, it works. If they don't, it doesn't work. Silence is death. I don't think I have that same neediness because I'm not moving a hundred miles an hour. If I'm telling a story that I know is going to get funny, I have to just trust that people are going to hang with the straight part of the narrative.

I'm at an advantage. Being onstage in front of an audience creates a different level of expectations. You want to see the audience smile. You can't help that. So that type of comedy is going to have to be front-loaded.

But yours is a solitary existence.

Actually, I wish it would be *more* solitary. I don't find myself writing as much, for the lengths that I would like to write. I wish I could just have all day to work on stuff without trying to hold down the business end of things.

You know, in order to do the DIY punk thing, you have to actually work very, very hard. It's DIY—Do It Yourself. But that takes effort. It takes a lot to do a show like this. I have complete freedom, but I don't get paid a thing. So I have to find other work, and that can take up a lot of time.

It's a bit exhausting. I'm in a strange position. I do a thing that a lot of people love, and I appreciate how much they love it—it's very, very validating. It's the purest version of me that I'm doing. But it does not translate into money. It's very challenging. It's a hustle. For most people, if you do the thing you do the best you'll find a way to get paid for it. Not me.

But at least you've found the thing that you do best. And you have the *opportunity* to do the thing you do best. Most people haven't—and never will.

I could so easily be back working retail in New Jersey. That line is so thin. You look at all these people who never achieved what they wanted to achieve—they're just broken down on the side of the road for one reason or another. They never found the right fit. Or they aged out. It's so easy for something to have never clicked into place. And if that's the case, the rest of it never would have been possible.

Or you have people who are lauded now, but were entirely ignored while they were in their prime. I've gone my whole life idolizing the forgotten people, like Alex Chilton [the lead singer of 1970s rock group Big Star]. Or John Kennedy Toole [the author of the novel *A Confederacy of Dunces*]. Yes, it was a tough life, but at least they got to make the product they wanted! There's nothing more valuable.

There is a great freedom to be allowed to do what you want to do in the way you want to do it. But in order to do that, you need to create a two-track system: on one track, complete freedom but no money. On the other track, money but little freedom. That's just the way it is.[1]

You just said that you could still be easily working in the retail world. Do you really believe that?

Absolutely. I could have easily bought the music store where I worked for years from the owner. When I was leaving, he said to me, "I'm going to sell the place. It's time for me to check out also." I could

---

1 Jon Wurster: "There were years when I constantly worried about whether I'd ever realize my dreams. I applied to become a writer on *The Daily Show*. I wrote a sample packet, but stopped midway through. I wasn't very excited about it. I'm not a super newsy guy. It took me forever to come up with one desk piece. And I realized that I'd probably never be able to ever function in that world. But I think that's a good lesson. You don't have to take the route that others might think you should take. We're so ingrained to think that we have to do things the exact way of the status quo, but 80 percent of the status quo is miserable, you know? Everything came together for me when I stopped caring about it. I was really worried about making a living in music and writing comedy. I was just constantly worried. And then when I stopped worrying about it, that's when all the music gigs came and that's when *The Best Show* started to take off. When I gave up worrying about it all is when it all got better."

have said, "You know, if you're going to sell the place I'm going to buy it from you, and this could be my job." I could now be running that store, and that would have been fine.

Do you ever wonder what that other life would have been like?

Sometimes. But the urge to do other things was just too strong. I think that in some people they're able to tamp down that need—to just be like, "No, I'm going to make the safe play here and go for the steady paycheck." It's kind of like a game show: "Do you want the two hundred dollars or do you want what's behind door number two?" And I went with what was behind door number two.

And you never really know what's back there.

It's a scary thing. But I couldn't have done it any other way. This is my life. This is the life I was supposed to have, for better or worse. I would be so miserable if I had done anything else, because I would have been so untrue to who I really was.

If you truly want to do it, then you're going to have to make the necessary choices in order to do it. You're going to notice a little crack in the wall, with a little light shining through, and you'll head that way. The crack will be the only thing to justify you going for it. And the thing is, other people would look at the situation and be like, "What are you talking about? That's not a sign that you should go for it!" No, but to you it is a sign, because you're *looking* for a sign. You're looking for anything to give you that push.

And then it's up to you. The responsibility is yours. I give everything I have to make this show work. You can't do it if you're not going to do it the right way and if you're not going to be true to it. Because you know what bad comedy is. You know what garbage entertainment is. And the worst thing for me would be to be responsible for more garbage entertainment. It becomes like a mission to do something good in the face of garbage.

Speaking of garbage, when I entered the WFMU studios this morning in Jersey City, New Jersey, to interview you, I noticed an "Employee Tasks" board in the elevator. And I noticed that your task read: "Garbage."

We all have to volunteer here at the station. And garbage is actually not the worst task. I go to the garbage can in the studio, I pull the bag out, I tie it, I throw it off the fire escape into the parking lot and I put a new garbage bag in the can. Then, later, when I go to my car, I'll throw the garbage into the Dumpster. So in the scheme of tasks, it's not too bad. Everybody at the station has a job to do.

You write and produce your own radio show that entertains more than half a million people every week, including a good percentage of top comedy writers, and yet you still have to hit the Dumpster after each show to take out the station's garbage?

[Laughs] I'll do anything for creative freedom.

Radio is such an ephemeral medium. Do you ever wonder how you'll be remembered?

You have to appreciate the journey. You can't control where you're going to end up. You better appreciate the experience; otherwise you'll never be happy. As soon as I'm dead I don't care if no one mentions my name once. I can't get anything from it. It doesn't matter to me. If I drop dead and am completely forgotten, it bears the same impact on me as if I'll be remembered for a hundred years. Regardless, I'm done.

But isn't that the purpose of a creative person's life? For their work to outlive their own mortality so that future generations can enjoy what they struggled so hard to produce?

But that's the kind of thing that people have no control over. You just can't worry about it. It's funny when you hear names of people who were once so enormous in the culture and they now mean almost nothing. Johnny Carson is currently heading toward that point, and he used to be huge. I guess for me it comes down to wondering why it matters to have your work be valued by anyone after you're not here. It's not even that important to me to have it valued by anyone *now*, on some level. If I'm happy with what I'm doing, that's really all that I can control and it's all that matters. It's great when people say nice things about what you do, but that doesn't help you do the work any better, right? And the concept of "future generations" seems like fool's gold. There are authors who sold millions of books during their era but they didn't stand the test of time, and people who didn't sell ten books who are now revered. I can only focus on what I have a say in, and that's what I'm working on today. Everything else is out of my hands, and it really doesn't matter.

If you're trying to make things that will last forever, I can almost guarantee you that you won't. The best things are the things that were made because they were powerful in the moment, and they were immediate, and they resonated with people. But if you're swinging for only immortality, it's just not going to happen.

All you can really hope for is to connect with people and to hopefully put food on the table—and to then get a chance to do it again the next day.

BOB ELLIOTT

Writer, Cohost, *Bob & Ray*

....

Writing for Radio

For more than forty years, you were half of one of the most famous and influential radio comedy teams in history, Bob & Ray. Who were your own comedic influences growing up in the 1920s and 1930s?

Ray [Goulding] and I both grew up with radio. Our whole hopes for the future were that we'd get into radio. That's what we loved the most. That's all we thought about. We both loved comedy, and even though we didn't grow up together, we had the same influences.

One of our favorites was a comedy team named Stoopnagle and Budd. These two were really radio's first satirists. They were very influential. Very clever. They once did a bit where they had a revolving bowl for fish who were too tired to swim around on their own. They broke up in the late thirties. Really far out. Not as broad as other radio teams, even though they had both been in vaudeville. They would invent different items, like an eleven-foot pole for somebody you wouldn't touch with a ten-foot pole. They were my favorite kind of funny. Lots of characters, bad puns. *Purposely* bad puns.

They also played characters that you could visualize. I think that's important.

I guess that's the beauty of radio: You can visualize your own world.

Absolutely. It's a thing that I miss. I do think that some of the mystery has gone out of comedy. Somebody seems to always now describe exactly what the joke is. We would do bits that we could never have gotten away with on television, like describing a world-champion daredevil trying to break the record for the most times walking around a revolving door. You couldn't get away with that on TV. It wouldn't work.

But I guess there was one drawback to radio: Ray and I later did so many characters over and over again that we were afraid to do them in front of people because it would only disappoint. We didn't want to destroy that thing we'd built up.

What fascinates me about comedy on the radio is how hugely popular it was for decades, but how completely forgotten these shows tend to be now. For instance, one of the most popular radio comedies, *Vic and Sade*, had close to eight million weekly listeners in the early 1940s. Eight million!

Vic and Sade was another big influence on our show. It was created by a writer named Paul Rhymer, who ended up writing thousands of scripts. The show had great characters who all lived in a small town. It was just homey kind of stuff. You'd hear real people talk. Real people, but a little odd. And you could visualize every one of them.

Radio was huge. It came right into your home, and only books could do that then. It was magic. When I was seven or eight years old, my parents used to go down to New York from Boston for a week at a time and my father would conduct his insurance business. He knew some guy who could get tickets to live broadcasts. We used to go. I just loved it. My parents had no theatrical background at all, but they backed me up and came along. They were very supportive.

Do you consider what you and Ray did as being different from the type of comedy that was on radio before your show launched?

At the time, a lot of people told us we were different, but it was hard for us to see. I guess one difference was that there was no set "straight man." We were both sort of straight men reacting against the other. We were also the first to use a comic version of a straight interview between two characters. This later became common. Two straight characters talking.

What's interesting, too, is that a lot of your comedy was surreal, almost bordering on crazy. And yet it was performed in a very understated manner. It's a very effective combination. And very modern. In particular, I'm thinking of the sketch about two guys who swim across the country, but only after they purchase a semi truck with a pool on it and swim the length of the truck, back and forth, back and forth, as the truck creeps along the highway.

Mostly, I think we were an amalgam of a lot of the shows that we loved. We never thought of ourselves as being different. Each generation is always influenced by the former. Ray and I never discussed "what humor is." We just did what we felt was funny, and we slowly began to see that people liked it. We started to receive more and more mail. At first it was a small group of listeners, but that group really loved what they heard. They connected with it.

Many current comedians, writers, and actors are huge fans of Bob & Ray, including Paul Rudd, Jack Handey, Bill Hader, and Bob Odenkirk. Also, David Letterman is a huge fan. You once did a bit called "The Bob & Ray Home Surgery Kit." You announced, "Haven't you ever thought, 'Golly, I wish I could take out my own tonsils?'" That's very Letterman-esque.

David was influenced by us, but we were also influenced by many people. You know, one thing that I can see—not only with David, but also with Bob Newhart—is that the humor is character-based, rather than just purely joke-based. We rarely did jokes. It was mostly characterization. I think that type of comedy always lasts longer. We also didn't do jokes about current show business. And I don't think we were ever mean-spirited. We never made fun of these characters.

These characters tended to be very sincere.

[Laughs] Those type of people truly interested us. Ray and I would walk around New York, and we'd look around and find things that would impress us. I remember once walking past a Woolworths in Times Square and seeing somebody playing the character of Mr. Peanut. Out in the sun in a peanut suit, wearing a giant monocle. And a top hat. It struck us as funny. What type of guy would be willing to do that?

You created a lot of characters with horrible jobs.

We once came up with a character who worked at a restaurant and was a shrimp deveiner. It was his job to take that black stuff out of the shrimp. And every day some other guy would come around to collect it. Not a job you'd want, but he was proud of it.

And the porch-swing salesman in New York City. Not an easy gig.

We made fun of a lot of fake products and businesses. It was our take on advertising and how stupid that can be. I remember us talking about a company that only made old-fashioned, homemade paper-clips ["The Great Lakes Paperclip Company"]. And we once did a bit about a store [Friedolf & Sons Shoelace Wash][1] that specialized in cleaning dirty shoelaces. That's all they did. They steam-pressed the shoelaces for the customers.

In the 1950s, Bob & Ray were performing routines that other comedi-ans and performers were afraid to go anywhere near. In particular, you

---

1   "Friedolf & Sons has *never* lost a pair of shoelaces in over forty-seven years of operation."

were taking on Senator McCarthy. This was long before anyone else had the nerve to mock McCarthy and his anticommunist hearings.

Time magazine later singled us out as having been the only ones who did. One of the long-running bits we did was based on the hearings, but it was about a man in a small town who wanted to build a very large home—sixteen stories high—and had to face Commissioner Carstairs [played by Ray] to get approval. Commissioner Carstairs was based on the blustery McCarthy, and he'd go out of his way to destroy any citizen who didn't live up to what he saw as exhibiting small-town values.

We'd watch McCarthy every day on TV and then the next day we'd paraphrase everything he'd done. Ray had McCarthy down like McCarthy wouldn't have known it wasn't him. What upset us about McCarthy was that he had such a reputation for blacklisting guys that never did a thing wrong in their lives. We were angered by this. It was unbelievable. I don't know what you'd call it. He was a steamroller when he was going. Nobody could get a word in, on either side.

I guess you could say we were fearless, but nobody complained. Actually, Ray and I and our families all went down to Havana, Cuba, on vacation years later. We were about the only people on this particular flight from Miami to Havana, and the last guy to get on the plane was Roy Cohn [lawyer to McCarthy]. He gave us a good dirty look and sat down. He threw his overcoat over the back of the chair and pulled out a copy of *Confidential* magazine. Which says a lot. *Confidential* was famous for prying into the private lives of celebrities. An awful man.

Over the years, Bob & Ray hired many comedy writers, some of whom later became famous in their own right.

Neil Simon and his brother, Danny, wrote for us. They were nice guys and they were talented, but they didn't work out. Our show was a very specific sensibility, and it was difficult to get on our exact wavelength. Andy Rooney once wrote for us on some project or other. Another writer named Tom Koch wrote for us for years. He was exactly on our wavelength, and he wrote material for us that we used years before we even met him.

Tom Koch, who contributed frequently to *Mad* magazine from the late 1950s until the mid-nineties, was a fascinating, brilliant writer. And yet, he never seemed to receive the public recognition he deserved. Anyone who has ever read and enjoyed *Mad* magazine would be familiar with his work.

Tom was a news guy who would submit ten to fifteen bits a week to us. He came up with our parody of *Dragnet* [*Squad Car 119*]. He wrote our Lassie parody "Tippy the Wonderdog" and one of our soap opera parodies [*The Gathering Dusk*]. The paperclip bit I was talking about before was written by Tom. We performed that for years. His material never needed any rewriting from us. It was ready to go—nothing needed to be added or taken out. Tom played a big part in a lot of our most successful pieces. He wrote thousands for us.

Tom wrote one of the most famous *Mad* articles of all time, a three-page spread that outlined the incredibly detailed, fantastical rules to a made-up sport called 43-Man Squamish. The 1965 article was so popular that college students around the country formed their own Squamish leagues and played actual games according to Tom's rules.

I think there are groups that play to this day. Tom had a very ironic kind of wit. He was first-rate. He might be the only humor writer to invent an entirely new sport.

Is it true that Kurt Vonnegut wrote for you when he was young?

He wanted to write for us. I think he had a summer place near Boston, where we were based, and he submitted a couple of scripts, but we didn't actually meet him until years later, when Ray and I played characters in a TV special [1972's *Between Time and Timbuktu*] that Kurt had written based on a few of his stories. Then we would see each other often.

In that TV special, you played an ex-astronaut who visited Mars. You described it as looking just like your driveway back in Dallas. You also forgot Neil Armstrong's famous line when he first set foot on the moon. You remembered it as being, quite wrongly: "One step for man, two steps for mankind."

[Laughs] That was really a takeoff on the countless hours of live TV devoted to space exploration. Most of the hours were filled with people just trying to fill the hours. A lot of what we made fun of was the silliness of the media.

Vonnegut once said that as a teenager he attended a taping of your radio show and was surprised that you and Ray both looked so melancholy. That it almost appeared as if it was a burden to create and to be funny hour upon hour, day after day.

Others have described the same thing. That we looked angry. But we weren't. We were just concentrating. And it was a job.

Vonnegut also said that there was a beautiful innocence to your humor. In his foreword to *Write If You Get Work: The Best of Bob & Ray*, a 1975 collection of your scripts, he wrote that your humor seemed to say that "man is not evil. . . . He is simply too hilariously stupid to survive."

I agree with that premise, without ever having thought of it that way. That really was what we were. And I think that you can see that way of thinking in the books and stories that Kurt himself wrote.

How would you and Ray write together?

We worked together in the Graybar Building in New York City [near Grand Central Terminal]. We both had our offices, each with a desk and sofa. Each office was ten-by-twelve feet or so. There was a partition in the middle. Our studio was off to the side. Ray would usually come in to where the typewriter was, which was in my office because I could type. And we'd kick around ideas and come up with a line, and then come up with more ideas and come up with another line, and then keep doing that. We would really sit there, improvising but always taking down the best parts.

Did you and Ray use a broadcast delay on any of your shows?

No, no time delay. That hadn't been invented yet. We were on our own, but we were confident in our characters and in the humor. And, actually, we were the first comedy show to go on the NBC Network without a preapproved script.

You once said you didn't think that you and Ray could work today. That everything moves so quickly now. And yet, I would think that your bits, your sketches—most of which are very short—were tailor-made for the Internet. There's no waste. It's all very tight.

If we ever felt a sketch wasn't working, we moved on to the next one. We also didn't depend on a last line being the clincher to a piece. We hoped that all of our sketches were as funny in the beginning and middle as they were in the end.

That's good for an audience, but we couldn't sell that now. We couldn't get a job today with what we did, I don't think. The vignettes and bits were about three minutes, two and a half. But now the longest they let anybody gab, except on a talk show, is like thirty seconds. But, I don't know. Maybe we could run late at night. And I'm not talking about audiences, really. I'm only talking about executives. They don't think that way.

Really? You don't think that you could now sell your style of humor to today's executives?

I don't, no.

At the very least, you'd now have more freedom with language and subject matter.

I know. But if we were on today, I don't think we would do anything that we wouldn't have done fifty years ago. We did what we wanted to do and we got away with it. And it was fun.

Not a bad life.

Not at all.

PURE, HARD-CORE ADVICE

AMY POEHLER

Actress/Writer, *Parks and Recreation*, *SNL*

Read your stuff out loud. Sometimes the way it reads in your head sounds different when someone says it.

Be open to changing all the material you think is really brilliant. Even the most talented people don't fight every day for every one of their jokes. There's always some better way to do things when you're working with good people. I find the most talented people tend to be the best collaborators.

Being flexible can mean people want to work with you. A lot of people say fight for what you believe in and don't let them change it, but I want to say, fight less, and be open to the fact that other people might have a better idea.

I'm paraphrasing that great quote from [*This American Life* host] Ira Glass—basically the sentiment of, "Keep doing it, even though all your stuff is going to be pretty bad. But don't be discouraged by its imperfections; embrace it if it's half good. Fake it till you make it. Put things up. If they're sloppy, keep trying." I love his thought that nobody carves out this perfect jewel. Everybody struggles and does all these half attempts, and it's really more about time than it is about perfection.

Just put in the time, and don't be too precious about things. Work with your friends. And maybe, eventually, you'll get paid. [Laughs] If you're doing it for the money, then just forget it. When you sit at your computer and think, I'm going to write something really political and interesting, it's like, Okay, good luck with that!

People quit because it's really hard. It's hard to not have a house, hard not to have money, hard not to have insurance, hard not to be married, hard to have your parents ask you every day what you're going to do with your life. It's hard to wait tables while you're doing improv shows. It's hard to get up onstage and bomb. It's hard to lug your props around everywhere. It's hard to submit things that get rejected.

It's not easy! Good people make it look easy, and a lot of people want to do it because they think it looks easy. If you stick around, if you're a good collaborator, if you're open to new ideas and you keep trying, then you'll find there's a lot of different ways you can work as a writer. You can generate original material, or you can be a staff writer, or you can write about the comedy scene—all different things you might find you're good at if you stick around long enough.

ROZ CHAST

During an interview with Roz Chast at the 2006 *New Yorker* Festival, comedian Steve Martin read aloud from one of her cartoons from February 1993. It was a fictional help-wanted classified, touting the opportunity of a lifetime. The job? "To reorganize 760,000 files from top to bottom, fire four people nobody else will, and take care of children aged three and one." In addition, applicants would be expected to have an "up-to-date trucking license" and "knowledge of quantum physics." "There is so much literature involved," Martin remarked about this cartoon, and others. "So much *writing*."

Cartoons are mostly a visual medium; too many words add unnecessary clutter. But Chast, like the early *New Yorker* cartoonists, is a master at finding the perfect balance between the literary and the visual. Her cartoons do not depend on funny pictures, needless explanation, or rambling punch lines to sell the joke. She's a rarity among her creative brood—a cartoonist whose humor can be appreciated *without* the drawings.

Take this *New Yorker* cartoon from October 2002, which

features the following catalog description beneath a simple drawing of a cardigan sweater:

Item #3715—Cozy Cardigan: Snuggle up in this oh-so-cozy cardigan. Once you slip it on, you'll never want to take it off. We've improved the fit and the texture—it's a hug made of wool, a hug that never lets go before you're ready to be let go. Whether you're just sitting at home with your family, who must think you're some kind of automaton and take you for granted day in and day out, who can't be bothered to clean up after themselves, it's a wonder you're not a complete alcoholic, or whether you're going to work at the widget office where all day long, you have the privilege of watching your boss making goo-goo eyes at that thing in the black leather miniskirt that a normal person with her legs would never wear, and finally it's five o'clock and you can go home to your empty apartment overlooking two gas stations and a restaurant that is probably a Mafia money-laundering operation because it has all this expensive but ugly junk in it and about seven waiters per customer because no one ever eats there, and you wonder: Is this all there is?, this is the sweater you'll reach for over and over again. We guarantee it!

As with all great humor writers, Chast has a fascination with the tiny, seemingly insignificant details that are usually and all too easily ignored. Her cartoons—which have appeared in *The New Yorker* since 1978—have featured an array of characters, some of whom bear an uncanny resemblance to her own family members.

But many of Chast's most famous creations are insentient. Chast has devoted entire comics to wallpaper, lamps, boxes, electrical cords. She specializes in finding the "inner voice" of these objects—or, as her mother once referred to it, the "conspiracy of the inanimate." In one late-seventies cartoon, she gave a toaster a bow tie and a vase a string of pearls, and dressed a grandfather clock in a skirt and straw hat. ("You can dress them up," she wrote in the accompanying caption, "but you can't take them out.")

Born and raised in the Flatbush section of Brooklyn in the mid-fifties and sixties, Chast began drawing at age five—her first original comic strip, featuring two anthropomorphic birds, was named *Jacky and Blacky*—but it never crossed her mind that she might make a living in cartoons. However, within only a few months after graduating from the Rhode Island School of Design, where she studied with the future members of Talking Heads, Chast was already publishing her work in *Christopher Street* magazine and *The Village Voice*. A few years later, still in her twenties, she was invited to join the approximately forty cartoonists under contract with *The New Yorker*.

Today, Chast lives with her husband, humor writer Bill Franzen, in Ridgefield, Connecticut, where she continues to write and illustrate her cartoons. Her books include *The Alphabet from A to Y with Bonus Letter Z!*, co-written with Steve Martin; *Theories of Everything*, a career-spanning, four-hundred-page retrospective, featuring an introduction by *New Yorker* editor David Remnick; and *Can't We Talk About Something More Pleasant?*, a memoir about the deaths of her parents.

How much did *The New Yorker* mean to you growing up in Brooklyn in the fifties and sixties?

Not much, truthfully. *The New Yorker* wasn't something that I focused on when I was a little kid, even though my parents subscribed. I read *Highlights for Children*. It wasn't until I was about eight or nine that I discovered the old *New Yorker* cartoonists like Charles Addams.

My parents were both involved with education. My mother was an assistant principal at a Brooklyn elementary school, and my father taught high school. Each summer, we would drive from Brooklyn to Ithaca, New York, to Cornell University, and we'd rent graduate-student housing, because it was cheap. When my parents attended lectures, they'd stick me in the browsing library in the student center. There was one section that contained only cartoon books. I would look through these books and just die.

I especially loved Charles Addams. It was the funniest stuff I had ever seen—just amazing. I still remember the books: *Monster Rally, Addams and Evil, Black Maria, Drawn and Quartered.*

What was it about Addams's cartoons that appealed to a nine-year-old?

For one thing, I "got" them. I couldn't relate to some of the other *New Yorker* cartoons, like the ones in which grown-ups said witty things to each other at a cocktail party. That just didn't make any sense to me; I had no idea what a cocktail party was, really.

But with Addams, I understood the jokes. It was sick humor—very black. They were funny to me. Plus, there were kids in them! A few of his cartoons I've never forgotten. One had an entire family pouring boiling oil onto a group of holiday carolers. In another one, the Uncle Fester character is signaling to the car behind him to pass, even though he knows an oncoming truck is approaching. Or the cartoon where Uncle Fester is grinning as he watches a movie, while everyone else sobs. So many great ones! Kids building guillotines in their rooms. Very transgressive.

Wolcott Gibbs, the *New Yorker* writer, once wrote that Addams's work was a denial of all of the spiritual and physical evolution in the human race. Maybe I related to that.

Even when you were nine?

Oh, when I was a kid I was obsessed with all sorts of weird, creepy, dark things. I was fascinated with medical oddities and bizarre diseases. My mother's sister was a nurse, so we always had [the medical reference book] *The Merck Manual* lying around. I didn't understand much of it, but I did understand the symptoms. Just the faint possibility that I might have leprosy or lockjaw or gangrene . . . tantalizing and terrifying.

I'm still fascinated with that sort of thing. Last night I watched this incredible medical show on television and [laughs] . . . I shouldn't laugh, because it's not funny at all, but the show featured a woman who turned silver.

She turned what?

Her skin turned silver, but I can't remember why.

I suppose it doesn't matter, really.

It doesn't matter—it's true.

Oh, actually, I *do* know why! When she was a kid, a doctor prescribed nasal drops that had silver in it.

And you're not confusing this person with a superhero?

No, she was definitely just a normal woman who turned silver. The condition is called *argyria*.

To me, that's the ideal type of disease show. If I watch a show that features, say, a man with an extra arm growing out of his shoulder, I know that I don't have that condition and I never will. Same with parasitic twins. Horrifying, but not contagious.

Have you ever seen *Dear Dead Days*? It's a book by Charles Addams [Putnam, 1959], and it's a compendium of all of these odd images—weird photos of patients suffering from rare diseases, criminals, revolting or frightening architecture, wheelchairs. I loved that book.

Many writers and cartoonists are fascinated by people who live on the outskirts of society—criminals, the mentally ill, those suffering from deformities.

Those people are more interesting than the everyday humdrum. To quote [photographer] Diane Arbus, "Most people go through life dreading they'll have a traumatic experience. Freaks were born with their trauma. They've already passed their test in life. They're aristocrats."

I suppose it's also helpful for a creative person to look where others might not be looking.

Maybe. If I could, I *would* look where everyone else is looking. But my attention is always drawn elsewhere. When I was in school, trying to listen to the teacher talk about the French and Indian War, I would be distracted by irrelevant things like the ugly shoes she was wearing.

You once drew a *New Yorker* cartoon about that.

I did. It was called "Newly Discovered Learning Disabilities" [December 3, 2001], and one of the entries was "Doodler's Syndrome." The child in the cartoon insisted on drawing and didn't hear a thing the teacher was saying—very similar to my own experience.

You'd be labeled ADD today.

Oh, absolutely! It's still very hard for me to pay strict attention to something that I have to listen to. I once drew a cartoon called "Adult Attention Deficit Disorders" [*The New Yorker*, June 7, 2004]. It included "Financial Information Disorder," "Driving Directions Deafness," and "Technical Manual Fatigue Syndrome." I suffer from all of them—and more.

I'd love to be able to pay attention to a lecture about saving money on my taxes, but I'm always fascinated by the silver person sitting in front of me.

How often does that actually happen?

Not often enough.

Were you a fearful child?

I remember I was afraid of kites, but I have no idea why. Actually, I can sort of guess: I had an uncle who told me that if I were to hold on to a kite long enough I would be lifted into the sky.

Kids believe *anything* you tell them. I did, anyway. I could easily convince myself that something bad was about to happen, or that I was about to come down with a terrible, incurable disease.

My parents were older than all of my friends' parents. They came from a world where people actually did get diphtheria. I remember my mother describing having had diphtheria as a child; she said it was like having "a web across [her] throat." My grandmother supposedly stuck her finger down my mother's throat and pulled out the web. This was very real to me. I heard that diphtheria story many times.

My parents were both forty-two when they had me in 1954. They were a link to another time and place, and that affected me greatly. A lot of my friends had parents who had experienced the excitement and the prosperity of the fifties, whether they were "red-diaper babies" or "Eisenhower babies." My parents didn't seem to know anything of that; I might as well have been raised during the Depression. My parents grew up poor in households that spoke mostly Yiddish. They were from the Old World.

How did your parents feel when you achieved success? Did they understand your cartoons?

Sort of, but they were more excited that I had insurance. [Laughs]

Did your parents allow you to own comic books?

My parents were very serious; they did not like pop culture *at all*. Comics were considered "crap." They did buy me *Classic Comics*, however. Have you ever seen them? They're illustrated versions of *Moby-Dick*, *Robin Hood*, and other works of literature.

They were like pieces of candy that looked great but tasted terrible. The sad part was that an illustrator actually drew them. So much work went into them, and they were really horrible.

I hated *Andy Capp*. A lot of daily strips were so depressing. They have that awful "joke" rhythm. Here's the set-up . . . and now . . . here comes the punch line! Ha, ha, ha! Everyone's laughing at the hilarity that ensued, except you! I could never imagine doing a weekly strip with the same rhythm and the same format week after week after week. You just want to kill yourself. I'm able to work on any subject in any format, and it's freeing.

You were a teenager during a period when comics were beginning to be criticized as being harmful for kids. Were your parents influenced by the 1954 anticomic screed, *Seduction of the Innocent,* by the psychiatrist Dr. Fredric Wertham? The book implied that comic books would quickly lead our nation's children to ruin.

I think it might have been more of a class issue. My parents thought comic books were for stupid people, and if I didn't want to be a stupid person with a stupid job who was going to live a stupid life in a stupid apartment and marry a stupid husband and have stupid children, then I shouldn't be reading comic books.

I did manage to borrow some issues of *Mad* magazine from my cousin. I loved Don Martin and the way he wrote out all those amazing noises his characters made. I loved the way his characters' shoes would bend—you know, the top part of the shoe would sort of bend over at a ninety-degree angle. He just drew *funny.* I've never forgotten one cartoon in particular, for some reason: A man in a bathroom is using a towel-dispensing machine, and a sign says: PUSH DOWN AND PULL UP. This guy takes the whole machine and pushes it down and pulls it up, and rips it off the wall. The joke itself wasn't even that great. It was just the way Don Martin drew the guy's expression. He drew great expressions. He's just hilarious. And so original.

Did your parents allow *Mad* in the house?

No.

Were *Archie* comics allowed in the house?

To my parents, *Archie* was the devil. So, of course, that's what I wanted to read the most. I thought *Archie* comics were fantastic. Even though they already seemed kind of dated when I was reading them in the sixties, Archie and Jughead and Betty and Veronica were very seductive to me.

Seduction of the innocent.

Right. It was sort of a parallel universe with all these people who didn't look like they lived anywhere near Newkirk Avenue in Brooklyn. There were no girls with beehive hairdos, or people who would punch you in the school hallways for no apparent reason.

What did Manhattan represent to you, as someone who grew up right across the East River?

Speaking of parallel universes! It was a different world for me, and it was magical. When I was young, I attended weekend art classes at the Art Students League in Manhattan, and I really liked it. As I got older—after I moved to the city—I loved it even more.

As for my career goals, I never, *ever* thought that I would one day be published in *The New Yorker*. I was hoping that maybe, fingers crossed, I might one day have a strip in *The Village Voice*, because that's where Stan Mack and Jules Feiffer were publishing their cartoons.

Jules Feiffer—just great, funny, insightful social commentary. The writing and drawing were a great combination. To me, it's crucial. It can't be just, *Here's* the writing, *here's* the illustration. The two have to add something to each other and they have to be intertwined in a deep way.

What was the magazine-cartoon market like in the late seventies?

There were very few outlets. When I first began to sell my cartoons in the late seventies, I was mostly dropping them off at *The Village Voice* and *National Lampoon*. I was once assigned to do an illustration for the *Voice* about corporal punishment in schools, and I drew a female teacher standing on a desk, in an S&M leather outfit, cracking a whip. I guess I thought it was funny. Other people didn't think so. The "golden age of cartooning," as the cartoonist Sam Gross used to call it, was finished by this point. It used to be that all of the male cartoonists—and they were pretty much *all* male—would put their work into a portfolio each week. First, they'd go to *The New*

Yorker, because that was the top of the heap. Whatever cartoons weren't bought would be taken to the editors of the next tier, like *The Saturday Evening Post* or *Ladies' Home Journal* or *McCall's.* They would make the rounds and work their way down the list, to the very bottom—maybe eventually even to [the pornographic men's magazine] *Gent.*

That process was already over when I started to pitch my cartoons to magazines in the late seventies. For one thing, there were so few magazines publishing cartoons. It was much more difficult to place them. It was pretty much down to *The New Yorker* and *National Lampoon.* There was *Playboy,* but that wasn't on my list.

Did you always write your own cartoons? Or did you have outside gag writers help you?

No, I always wrote my own. Gag writers were more common in the past. The tradition of the gag writer selling cartoon ideas to an artist had begun to end in the sixties. I didn't even know there was such a thing as gag writers until I became a cartoonist. A lot of famous cartoonists used them, like Peter Arno, George Price . . . even Charles Addams would sometimes buy gags—which really freaked me out.

When I first started, for maybe the first seven or eight years I would receive packets from gag writers. And that was very weird. The envelopes would arrive, and I'd just go, *Arrrghhhhh!*

I knew that these people were going through a list of cartoonists' names, and mine was on there somewhere. The gags were always very traditional and mostly pretty lame: "Two guys standing in a bar talking," and then there'd be a corny punch line you'd read eighty times before. It was obvious they'd never seen a single cartoon of mine.

Who exactly were these gag writers? Were they doing it for fun, or did they actually make a living at it?

I have no idea. I don't think they were young people, because I can't imagine a young person doing such a thing. I always imagined them as middle-aged men living alone in small apartments above stores on main streets in sad, grim towns. Even the envelopes the gags came in were sad—all crumply and yellowed and hand-addressed in a saddish way.

By the time I got to *The New Yorker*, almost everyone wrote their own gags. I think maybe some of the really old-timers were buying gags. When *The New Yorker* just began, for the first twenty years or so, the captions to cartoons weren't usually written by the cartoonist. In the sixties, the balance started to tip in favor of the artist and writer being one and the same.

How old were you when you sold your first cartoon to *The New Yorker*?

I was twenty-three. I went under contract at the end of that first year. I think a lot of it had to do with my being in the right place at the right time. Maybe the magazine wanted to attract younger readers. Lee Lorenz was the art editor at the time. I will always be grateful to him.

Did you feel that *The New Yorker* wanted to include underground cartoonists and their sensibility in the magazine?

No, not underground, exactly. I didn't have that sense at that time at all. I think they just wanted to open it up a little to maybe a "younger sensibility."

The cartooning was becoming less rigid than it used to be, looser. There were no more cannibal jokes. There were fewer cocktail party cartoons. No bums or winos. Or, at the very least, if those were the subjects of the cartoons, then they had to be handled differently by the cartoonist. A lot of subjects weren't considered funny anymore.

Do you think that it helped your chances that you were a female cartoonist? There weren't many at *The New Yorker* at the time.

I'm pretty sure it wasn't only because I was female. I signed my cartoons *R*. They didn't know *what* I was.

I think there was only one other female *New Yorker* cartoonist in the late seventies, although there'd been more in the past, like Mary Petty, Barbara Shermund, and Helen Hokinson. Now there are about five. I didn't think much about the "female" thing. I like to think that everyone I love is an influence in some tiny way. And even with people I hate, I think, That's something I *never* want to do.

Did you find those early *New Yorker* cartoons misogynistic or their humor too male-centric? There has been criticism over the years about James Thurber and his possibly stereotypical portrayal of the harping wife.

Most people drawing cartoons are guys; they draw things from a male perspective. I don't usually get too bent out of shape about that, because it doesn't help me. It just makes me agitated. The subject of what guys find funny, what women find funny, and how sometimes they overlap and sometimes they don't, is a complicated one. I really loved *The Comeback*, a very short-lived comedy with Lisa Kudrow [HBO, 2005]. Whereas a movie like [2012's Seth MacFarlane–directed] *Ted*, and how successful it is—that's a ticket to Depression-land for me. Not that I've seen it. Maybe it's a real side-splitter. I don't care about drawings of harping wives. Some wives harp.

How much were you paid for your first *New Yorker* cartoon?

Two hundred fifty dollars.

How much are you paid today for a *New Yorker* cartoon?

One thousand three hundred fifty dollars.

What was the reaction to your first *New Yorker* cartoon, published in 1978? Even looking at it today, I find it to be very odd and different. It's called "Little Things," and it features bizarre shapes with funny names: "chent," "spak," "kabe," "tiv," and so on. There's no gag—at least in the traditional sense.

I think a lot of readers were pretty perturbed. Some of the older *New Yorker* cartoonists were really bothered by that cartoon, too.

It's strange that Lee chose that one. I had submitted fifty or sixty, and this was the weirdest in the batch. It was so rough and personal, and it was so weird. [Laughs] Later, Lee told me that somebody had asked him whether he owed my family any money.

It was certainly a break from the type of *New Yorker* cartoon that came before.

I knew that my cartoons were quite different, which is why I never really thought they would appear in *The New Yorker*. I never deliberately set out to be different; that's just how I draw. But if I tried to conform to somebody else's idea of what's funny, I'd have no compass at all. I wouldn't even know where to begin.

I don't dislike genre cartoons. In fact, I have done quite a few. I love tombstone gags, end-of-the-world guy gags, pushcart gags. But my favorite cartoonists have been the ones who create specific cartoon *worlds*, not just come up with a good gag line. I like being able to imagine what's in the rooms of the house that I'm not seeing in that particular cartoon. Like what's in those people's refrigerator.

It's hard to draw—at least in detail—worlds that you don't know. I don't know what's in a penthouse refrigerator. Expensive champagne? Maybe some really old capers?

Has *The New Yorker*'s submission process changed for you since you first began?

No, it hasn't changed much at all. I've submitted, let's see: thirty years times forty-six weeks on average a year . . . whatever that is, since I first started, and I still do it basically the same way. Each week I submit between five and ten cartoons. Usually, about six or seven.

And how many, on average, will be accepted each week?

It's really hard to say. I might average one per issue for maybe three or four weeks in a row, but then I might go for three or four weeks and not sell any. And then the next week, for no reason at all, it seems, they'll buy two. I'll feel great, but then I'm back to square one. It's a cycle, but it's frightening because I never know if the cycle will remain stuck on my not selling anything.

Someone once told me about a psychological experiment that was done with rats: If you keep rewarding the rats with a pellet each time they push a lever, they will eventually become bored and stop pushing the lever. And if they receive no pellets at all, they'll get discouraged and stop pushing the lever. But if you provide them with intermittent, random pellets, they just keep pushing that lever. Sometimes I feel like I am that rat.

It's a tough business. You only feel as good as your last sale. Even this many years later, I still get depressed if I haven't made a sale for a couple of weeks. I always feel like that's the end of it, you know—*I really have run out of ideas!*

You would think that by now I would understand that when I get depressed, it's part of the cycle. But it's still hard. The fact is, there are no guarantees. I don't know too many cartoonists who are superconfident people.

Do you hand-deliver these cartoons to *The New Yorker* office?

I used to go every week, but it just took too much time. In the eighties, I'd have a weekly lunch with the rest of *The New Yorker* cartoonists. But when we all moved out of the city, the group disbanded. I feel I can better use my time to stay at home and work. Or procrastinate.

Once a week, I fax a batch of rough sketches to *The New Yorker* offices. I try to draw pretty much what the finished cartoon will look like. You know, if people are standing in a room, I'll sketch the room, but I won't put in all of the fine detail until the cartoon is bought. The initial versions are always rough. If they buy it, I do a *finish*—a finished version of the sketch.

How long does a finish take?

For a very simple drawing, it might take an hour and a half. For a more complicated one, especially those in color, it might take several hours.

What exactly goes on in a *New Yorker* cartoon meeting? To me—and, I think, to many others—*The New Yorker* is like the Kremlin. It's a world of mystery, smoke, and mirrors.

The deadline is late on Tuesday. Every cartoonist either e-mails or brings to the offices a batch of rough sketches, usually about five to ten. I've never been to a *New Yorker* art meeting where the editors talked about cartoons, which takes place on Wednesday. It'd be like peeking in on your parents and accidentally seeing them doing things you know they do, but don't want to think about them doing.

I once read an article that described the process, but I've since repressed it. As much as I would like to imagine the editors saying, "*This* one is really good, but *this* one is even better!," I know the disgusting, painful reality.

Do a lot of these ideas for cartoons gestate for a long time before you sketch them?

Sometimes yes, sometimes no. Often, ideas will crop up when I'm in my studio just doodling and thinking. I remember when I was drawing "The Fantastic Voyage" [*Scientific American*, July 2002]. I had been thinking about the cliché of spaceships and strange submarine-like vehicles that would travel through the body in sci-fi films from the fifties and sixties. I wondered, What if people were in a broken-down bus instead? Or in the family sedan? That's how that cartoon came about.

I once doodled a crazy man holding a sign that read: THE END IS NEAR! I just felt like drawing one of these guys. Who knows why. After looking at the guy for awhile, I realized that he needed a crazy wife. So I drew him a wife, and she was holding up a sign that said: YOU WISH. That one came out of the blue.

What ideas are you currently mulling over?

I'm working on an idea now. I wrote down, "Break Internet." I like the thought of breaking the Internet, as if it were a toy or an appliance. Now that I describe it, it sounds pretty lame. [The cartoon was not bought.]

How extensive is your backlog of unsold cartoons?

Thousands and thousands. It's an ocean of rejection. A lot of them are very dated, and a lot of them are just plain bad, but in that pile I will sometimes find something I want to rework. I have so many rejected drawings that it almost becomes raw material for me. When I'm stuck, I sometimes go into that file, and I'll see if there's an idea hiding that can be fixed.

How much time do you spend on the exact wording of your cartoons?

It really depends. Sometimes a cartoon will be very clear in my head from the minute I conceptualize it. Other times—especially with a multipanel "story" cartoon—it takes longer. I like the editing process. I think—I *hope*—that this is something I've gotten better at as I've gotten older. I probably could have done more self-editing when I was younger.

Specifically, what sort of self-editing?

Eliminating things I don't need; paying attention to the rhythm of a joke. I don't want to make anyone read more than absolutely necessary.

I wonder how many readers even notice how finely structured the wording is in certain cartoons—such as with your work, or Garry Trudeau's *Doonesbury*, or Gary Larson's *The Far Side*. There's never an extra comma or beat.

Bad rhythm is something you see frequently with amateur cartoonists. With that said, there are times when I can feel the rhythm of a cartoon more clearly than at other times. I work on deadline, and I have to do this whether I'm in the mood to work or not. But why I'm in the mood sometimes and not at other times is still a mystery.

Do you have tricks you've taught yourself that have made the process less difficult?

Getting away from work and coming back to it fresh really helps. Also, Truman Capote once said that if you have to leave a manuscript or a chapter, don't finish up the last little bit, because then, when you come back, you'll have to restart from nothing. I've often used this approach. If I'm going downstairs for lunch, I leave something I'm excited to come back to—so I won't be starting from zero miles per hour. But it doesn't always work.

Do you consider yourself as much a writer as a cartoonist?

I don't consider myself as much of a writer as a "real" writer—those writers who write without drawings. And I don't consider myself as much of an artist as a "real" artist—somebody who paints without using any words. But cartooning is a hybrid, and cartoonists are hybrids. We feel incomplete doing just one or the other. When I have to write and I can't use pictures, it's very frustrating. You work in the medium best suited to what you have to say, and, for me, that's cartooning.

So where do you see the art of cartooning in the future? Do you think it'll remain a viable profession?

I don't know how viable it is *now*. It's a very tough profession. I really don't know whether cartooning for magazines will stick around. There's a lot written about teenagers and print media and how irrelevant the nonelectronic media might soon become. I really don't know what's going to happen. But I do know that if someone wants to become a cartoonist they're going to find an outlet.

I'd like to learn more about animation programs. If there was a computer program that wasn't too difficult to learn, I might just give it a shot. Hopefully you can always learn something new. Key word: *hopefully*.

Any advice for cartoonists starting out with their careers?

I'm really grateful for the life-drawing classes I took at art school. Not that anyone looking at my characters would believe it, but I think life-drawing is really important. A cartoonist has to know how a body sits or stands on a page. It's like learning a language.

You can't teach a cartoonist how to have a style. They can improve their own style, but it's impossible to provide a style to someone who doesn't have one. And that has to be learned on your own.

Do you have any regrets? It seems that no matter how successful anyone is, they always have at least one major regret.

I feel that on my deathbed, which is something I hope to eventually have, I'll probably look back and wish that I didn't always look on the dark side of everything. But how can you not? You could die at any time, for any reason. You're walking under an air conditioner, and *kaboom*! My parents actually knew someone who was killed by a falling flower pot. But we have to kind of go along and put one foot in front of the other and pretend that we don't know that everything could take a serious turn for the worse in the next second.

It's all in the pretending.

Yes, it's all in the pretending. Any of us could walk outside right now and Mr. Anvil could suddenly meet Mr. Top of Head. But we pretend otherwise.

Actually, that'd make for a nice cartoon.

And if I'm safely off to the side while it happens to you, and if there's a deadline looming, I would absolutely love to draw it. [Laughs]

HENRY ALFORD

Contributor, *Spy, Vanity Fair, The New York Times, The New Yorker;* Author, *Would It Kill You to Stop Doing That: A Modern Guide to Manners*

··

How to Be Funny as a Journalist

You've been a writer now for over thirty years. Your specialty is humorous first-person journalistic accounts. But how would you define yourself? As a journalist? Or as a humorist?

I usually say both. The writing that I seem to be known for—the first-person, fish-out-of-water, investigative, humor-type pieces—are a hybrid. I usually say, "George Plimpton, but with more leotards."

Do such definitions matter in the industry? How important are labels for magazine and book editors looking to assign articles or seeking to purchase book manuscripts?

Well, being a prose writer who doesn't write for TV or film, I wouldn't be able to eat if I weren't willing to do a certain amount of fact-gathering. If you're going to try to make a living off of being funny in books and magazines and newspapers, you probably need either to do some reporting or be a brand-name cartoonist.

The beauty part of embracing facts is that I can get an assignment and I can get a book deal. Unless you're, say, Steve Martin, you can't get an assignment to write a factless humor piece, and you can't get a book deal to write a novel. But I could go to a publisher and say, "I want to be a Mexican wrestler for a year," or, "I want to interview everyone in Ohio named Barry," and they might cough up some money for that.

How difficult would it be for you to get an assignment to write a factless humor piece?

I still do occasionally write pieces without facts—and like most writers, I labor under the delusion that I'll write a novel one day, just as soon as it drops from the sky onto my head, already written. And, sure, very occasionally someone will assign me a bit o' whimsy. But bookwise, that's a tiny, tiny market, unless you're working on books meant to end up next to the cash register or the toilet.

It's possible that someone would be willing to publish all my *New Yorker* Shouts & Murmurs and the wackier of my op-eds from *The New York Times*, but I'd go into it knowing that it probably wouldn't sell a ton.

There's a fine line between being funny as a journalist and being overbearing—or even mean-spirited. What is that line and how is it best avoided?

I always say, The easiest three ways to make a name for yourself as a journalist are to be a really bitchy reviewer, to write a sex column, or to do Q&As that are heavy on the Qs. So, I've tried to avoid those things, which I usually find overbearing.

With respect to my own work—especially the material where people don't know I'm writing about them—I try never to name or make identifiable anyone that I'm not in a professional relationship with. Like, once I took the National Dog Groomers Association's certification test. I have limited skills in this area, despite my homosexuality. In the throes of the exam, I ended up smearing lipstick on my cocker spaniel's snout and telling the test administrator, "I like a dog with a face." When I wrote the experience up in an article, I made the test administrator identifiable—she and I were in a professional relationship—but not the other test-takers in the room. That distinction seems only fair to me. Likewise, if you're selling me something, or if I've paid you to provide a service, you're fair game. If you're standing in the background, I'm gonna pixilate you.

Also, I self-deprecate a lot. The upside of self-absorption is that you don't pay other people enough heed to hurt their feelings.

Do you ever think you've crossed that line into meanness?

Sure, particularly when I was younger. I did a story in *Spy* magazine once—this is going back twenty-five years—for which I stayed at a bunch of bed-and-breakfasts in Manhattan, tangling with various hosts' unwillingness to tell me whether or not as a paying guest I was allowed to sit in their living room. One host, a distracted woman in her fifties, told me that she was going to be doing some exercises in her living room—"an activity," I wrote, "which I could only imagine involves a lot of crouching and lotion." I reread this line the other day and had two thoughts about it. One, it's sort of mean and ad hominem. Two, I *am* this woman now.

I like to think that my inner compass keeps me from being condescending, but I'm sure there are people who'd be willing to tell you otherwise. Worse comes to worst, a good editor can alert you to condescension. Ignorant: sure, probably have been there, too. No, the more tricky one for me—particularly if people don't know I'm writing about them, or if people who are being interviewed are a little more candid than they should be—is knowing whether or not I can use a juicy, possibly damning comment or revelation. I go through a whole Kübler-Ross, male-menopausal, weather storm-map-ish rinse cycle with those. I'll ask myself, Is it something they would have told me if they knew I was writing a story? Is it worth it to me to ask them if I can use it, only to possibly have them say no? Is the speaker or doer identifiable in the story? I'm inherently a pretty polite, don't-make-a-lot-of-waves, cheery-to-the-point-of-bland, Pepperidge Farms–y WASP, and this orientation doesn't always scream "good reporter."

As a journalist, you enter and write about other worlds: whether it's the hipster community in Williamsburg, Brooklyn, an a capella group at Yale, or a cruise sponsored by the liberal magazine *The Nation*. Since you're an outsider in these situations, I'd imagine you'd want to take extra care not to appear condescending or ignorant.

I'm pretty conscious of the fact that I play on an uneven playing field. Uneven because 1) I'm the writer, so I'm always going to have the last word, and 2) sometimes I know in advance what I'm going to say before I enter the situation. For instance, I knew when I was writing my Brooklyn hipster story for *The New York Times* ["How I Became a Hipster," May 1, 2013] that I would enter a clothing store and ask, "Are your socks local?" When I sang with the Yale Whiffenpoofs [*The New York Times*, "Singing for Their Supper," January 11, 2013], I knew I would tell someone at Yale that Osama bin Laden had been in an a capella group as a teen and that I wished that his group had been called Vocal Jihad. So, I'm semi-armed. Thus, it's particularly important for me to be generous and kind in my coverage, and also to make myself look as much like an ass as possible.

What percentage of jokes, on average, are written beforehand?

Not much. Maybe 10 percent. It's really more of a way to calm my nerves and jittery anticipation before I start reporting. And somehow it helps me focus—maybe it's like an actor reading the whole script before he shoots. Like if you were cast on *Law & Order*, and your only line was "I didn't do nothin', Lenny," but they gave you the whole script, not just your scene to read, you could then really whale on that one line. You could bring seven thousand pounds of subtext to "I didn't do nothin', Lenny."

You mentioned *Spy* magazine earlier, which was infamous for combining journalism with humor. Can you see the direct influence of *Spy* on today's journalists?

I guess I see the influence most directly when I see charticles—something like *New York* magazine's terrific "Approval Matrix" seems like *Spy*'s offspring. I remember reading an interview with Kurt Andersen and Graydon Carter, *Spy*'s founders, who said that they got the idea for funny charts from *Time* magazine, which, after notable plane crashes, would always print illustrations of where everyone was sitting on the plane.

Wit is always pretty timeless, so it's harder to see the specific trickle-down of *Spy*'s particular acerbity. Acerbicity? Acerbitchy? The one aspect of the *Spy* legacy that, in the wrong hands, can sometimes be unfortunate is the insiderness of everything: Yes, I thought it was brilliant that *Spy* devoted a whole column to the Creative Artists Agency, and explained how some Hollywood movies are nothing but "packages," but isn't this the same head that wants to know weekend box-office? Not to go all Kahlil Gibran on you, but who gives a shit about ratings and BO, as I like to call it? *30 Rock* was one of the most brilliant comedies of our time, but it had crappy, crappy ratings. Do you care? I mean, you care if you're Tina Fey or you do props for *30 Rock*, but otherwise, maybe you should consider taking up golf or Chinese brush painting.

What career advice would you give to those who want to combine journalism with humor?

Don't cook up some hilarious essay and then go to the newsstand thinking, Who can I submit this article to? Do it the other way around: Obsessively read and reread a particular section of a magazine—maybe Shouts & Murmurs in *The New Yorker* or maybe the back page of *The New York Times Magazine,* or maybe your local paper's op-ed, or maybe those essays in *Details* where a writer discusses some difficult-to-reach part of his body—and then write something that's tailored very specifically to that section of that publication. This will save you eight hundred thousand man- or woman-hours.

Additionally: Don't do round-ups of unusual but actual state laws ("In Rhode Island, it's illegal to serve crackers to Border collies . . ."), or parodies of year-end holiday newsletters. The world is good on those.

PURE, HARD-CORE ADVICE

....

PATTON OSWALT

....

Comedian, Feelin' Kind of Patton; Voice-Actor; Actor, Big Fan,
Young Adult; Writer, Zombie Spaceship Wasteland,
Silver Screen Fiend

When you're writing something, and it makes you laugh, don't judge that. Even if it doesn't seem to fit. If it made you laugh out loud, it probably belongs on the page. Let someone else see if they can make it work. In the industry, you're always told about this imaginary ethereal audience, like, "People wanna see this, people wanna see that." Actually, let me boil down what I just said even better: Have trust in amusing yourself.

The next step is always the same thing, and it's actually very simple: Just keep going onstage. This is really helpful even if you just want to write, but especially if you want to perform. You're not going to figure out what your next step is unless you do get up onstage. Just keep doing it, and the way will show itself. I know that's frustrating to hear, because it sounds like I'm brushing people off, but it does come down to knowing it when you know it. And the ones that ask,

"But what else?" never make it. It's the ones who just keep going who eventually make it.

The right manager and agent will find you when you're ready.

I know that it doesn't sound like I'm being very helpful, but trust me, I'm being *extremely* helpful right now.

Overlook Hotel
July 4th Ball
1921

DANIEL CLOWES

The sometimes fictional, sometimes autobiographical comic universes of Daniel Clowes's books—he detests the term *graphic novel*—aren't the idealistic utopias conjured up by so many of his comic peers and predecessors. There are no heroes, super or otherwise; no precocious children. His comics, much like Robert Crumb's work, are about not-so-lovable losers who aren't so easy on the eyes. These characters generally live in urban wastelands or mind-numbingly boring suburbs, where nihilism passes for hopefulness, football is understood as "sublimated homosexual rape and Oedipal hostility," and sometimes dogs are born without orifices. He writes about characters with names like Needledick the Bug-Fucker, Hippypants, Peace Bear, Zubrick, Pogeybait, and Dickie: the Disgusting Old Acne Fetishist.

Born in Chicago in 1961, Clowes was by his own estimation a "shy, loner, bookworm kind of kid." He first realized he could draw after attempting (unsuccessfully) to reproduce his favorite *Batman* covers. "I was convinced [the covers] were either done by a machine or they had a special tool that made the lines perfect," he told the *Guardian*. "If I could get that tool, I too could create *Batman* comics."

Clowes majored in illustration at the Pratt Institute in Brooklyn, and graduated in 1984 with few career prospects. But he soon discovered the Hernandez brothers' brilliant and influential *Love and Rockets* comic-book series at a local comics store and decided to submit some of his own drawings to their Seattle-based publisher, Fantagraphics. The editors there recognized his talent and quickly signed Clowes to their stable of artists and writers.

His first series, *Lloyd Llewellyn* (1986–87), a parody of 1950s gumshoe detective noir, lasted only six issues. But his next attempt, called *Eightball*, would evolve into a fifteen-year odyssey. Originally subtitled "An Orgy of Spite, Vengeance, Hopelessness, Despair, and Sexual Perversion," *Eightball* was introduced in October 1989 and featured an array of bizarre story lines and controversial comedic rants, such as "I Hate You Deeply," "Ugly Girls," "Sexual Frustration," and "The Sensual Santa." Clowes became popular with the kind of people who had previously never entered a comics store.

His most famous series, first published in *Eightball No. 11–18* and then reprinted as its own comic in 1997, was *Ghost World*. Set within a suburb with no name and no distinctive characteristics beyond the usual detritus produced by chain stores and fast-food restaurants, it followed the lives of two teenage girls and best friends, Enid Coleslaw (an anagram of "Daniel Clowes") and Rebecca Doppelmeyer, after their graduation from high school as they grapple with the inevitable by-product of the late-teen maturation process: melancholy. Enid feels disconnected from the "obnoxious, extroverted, pseudo-bohemian art-school losers" that surround her, and she ends up befriending a collector of 78-rpm records—a lonely, older male (is there any other type?)—who soon becomes her sole confidant.

When Clowes collaborated with director Terry Zwigoff on the movie adaptation of *Ghost World*, released in 2001, he approached the task with the same all-encompassing devotion he gave to his comics. It took more than five years and nearly two dozen drafts before they finally got it right. In the end, Clowes was Oscar-nominated, but didn't win, for Best Adapted Screenplay.

"Dan has an astute, critical eye," Zwigoff once wrote. "He's been accused of being pornographic, nihilistic, misanthropic, sacrilegious, overly critical, and hopelessly negative. How would I not love the guy?"

In 2010, Clowes published *Wilson*, a book featuring seventy one-page gags about an unlikable middle-aged man. The long-time *Simpsons* writer George Meyer remarked: "Dan is somehow able to dip bucket after shimmering bucket from the roiling depths of his unconscious. Add talent and hard work and courage, and you create blazingly original art like *Wilson*. The book is heartbreaking, wistful, and joltingly funny. I've read it nine times."

Is it true that your first professional published work appeared in *Cracked* magazine?

That's true. I contributed to *Cracked* from around 1984 to 1989, though I think I only published one piece under my own name. For the other pieces I was "Herk Abner" and "Stosh Gillespie"—Stosh was the name my father originally wanted for me.

Any particular reason?

He worked in a steel mill when I was born, and several of his Polish co-workers had the name Stosh. Also, I think he was trying to bum out my mom.

As for Gillespie, it's my middle name.

Were you even a fan of *Cracked*? And, actually, I should probably point out to readers that this was the first incarnation of *Cracked*, not at all similar to the current Internet version. This was for print only, and was, more or less, a direct *Mad* rip-off.

Nobody was ever a fan of *Cracked*. I was buying it at the time because I wanted work in the satire magazine field, but it was just a terrible publication.

Growing up, my friends and I used to think of *Cracked* as a stopgap. We would buy *Mad* every month, but about two weeks later we would get anxious for new material. We would tell ourselves, We are *not* going to buy *Cracked*. Never again! And we'd hold out for a while, but then as the month dragged on it just became, Okay, fuck it. I guess I'll buy *Cracked*.

It was like comedy methadone.

Right. Then you'd bring it home, and immediately you'd remember, Oh, yeah, I hate *Cracked*. I don't understand any of the jokes, and [*Cracked* mascot] Sylvester P. Smythe is the most unappealing character of all time. He wears janitorial overalls and carries a mop.

I don't know if you've ever seen *Sick* magazine—just one of many *Mad* rip-offs over the years—but they actually had an even uglier mascot: Huckleberry Fink. He was just so ineptly drawn that you didn't know what the hell he was. I think he was a freckled hillbilly. And instead of "What, me worry?" [*Mad*'s Alfred E. Neuman's motto], his was something like: "Why try harder?"[1]

Were you given free rein at *Cracked*?

Maybe too much. The very first thing I published was a two-pager called "Aren't You Nervous When . . ." which was a by-the-book *Mad* rip-off. One panel had a gag about noticing a fire engine heading toward your house as you drive home, and the only reference picture I could find was from an old children's book. I remember my roommate looking over my shoulder and saying, "Aren't you nervous when . . . you're being followed by a fire engine from the 1930s."

My friend Mort Todd was the editor in chief for several years,

---

1   Some *Mad* rip-offs since 1959: *Blast* (mascot: Mr. Muggles), *Bughouse*, *Crazy* (mascot: Obnoxio the Clown), *Eh!*, *Flip*, *Frantic*, *Gag!*, *Get Lost*, *Glad*, *Grin*, *Help!*, *Humbug* (mascot: Seymour Mednick), *Madhouse* (mascot: Clyde Diddit), *Not Brand Ecch*, *Nuts!*, *Panic*, *Plop!*, *Ratfink*, *Riot*, *Snafu* (mascot: Irving Forbush), *Thimk* (mascot: Otis Dracenstein), *Trash* (mascot: Norman Nebish), *Trump* (mascot: Jack of Spades), *Whack*, *Wild* (mascot: Orton Leffield), *Zany*.

and we created some truly ridiculous material. We did parodies of TV shows that nobody our age, much less the nine-year-olds reading the magazine, had ever seen—programs like *Ben Casey* [ABC, 1961–66] and *The Millionaire* [CBS, 1955–60]. I don't think we ever bothered with a show from our own era [the eighties], or even the seventies.

Did any *Cracked* readers complain?

Oddly enough, nobody ever wrote in to say, "What in the hell are you doing parodying *Dragnet* and [1950s sitcom] *My Little Margie?*" *Cracked* was a strange place. They had a consistent, revolving audience of nine- and ten-year-old kids who would innocently pick it up at the grocery store for a year or two before moving on. In the front section of each issue there would be photos of children holding up their issues of *Cracked*, or posing in front of giant Sylvester P. Smythe birthday cakes with confused, lukewarm smiles on their faces.

I also remember that one of the publishers had a vanity plate that read "Cracked Man." Sad, but also kind of charming, I suppose.

Cracked did achieve one note of distinction: It managed to somehow convince longtime *Mad* cartoonist Don Martin to leave *Mad* and join *Cracked* in 1988. *Mad* is still upset about this.

I know. There was some below-radar talk about lawsuits, but I don't think they had any real claim. They were furious. Don had been there for more than thirty years.

I remember *Cracked* throwing this big, fancy dinner for Mr. and Mrs. Don Martin in an attempt to woo them over to the other side. Don's wife was really a character. She acted as his agent and was angry about the way *Mad* had treated her husband. She thought *Mad* paid too little. They wouldn't allow Don to own the rights to his own work. Companies would call Don and ask, "Can we make a calendar with your work?" and he'd have to say no.

Both were very happy to jump ship. Don received a little more money per page—I think a hundred dollars more—and he regained the rights to his own work, which was more important.

How happy was Don Martin at *Cracked*?

As far as I could tell, he was happy. I don't think he ever seemed to notice that *Mad* was respected, whereas *Cracked* was loathed.

I left *Cracked* in the early nineties. Once my own comics started to get published by Fantagraphics Books—first with *Lloyd Llewellyn* and then with *Eightball*—I started to receive freelance offers from *The Village Voice* and *Entertainment Weekly* and other magazines.

You became one of the first comic artists to contribute to *Esquire* magazine—or, really, to any major, mainstream magazine. What year was this?

Dave Eggers, who was an editor for *Esquire* then—but who had not yet written his first book [*A Heartbreaking Work of Staggering Genius*, Simon & Schuster, 2000] or published the first issue of his literary journal *McSweeney's*—wanted me to create a comic for *Esquire*'s fiction issue in '98. The story was called "Green Eyeliner," about a slightly unhinged young woman who was arrested for pulling out a gun in a crowded movie theater.

The fact that *Esquire* would even publish a comic for "adults" in their fiction issue was really a big deal, it turned out. No one remembers the actual specifics of that comic, only that it was published.

I wonder why it was such a big deal—your comics had been out for years by that point.

It was one of the many "comics aren't just for kids and fat collector creeps anymore" moments in what has become never-ending fodder for journalists.

Did you ever imagine that you'd one day be producing covers for *The New Yorker* or have a serial comic strip in *The New York Times Magazine*?

Back in the early *Eightball* days? Never in a million years.

Your strip, *Mister Wonderful*, about a shy middle-aged man on a blind date, ran in *The New York Times Magazine* in nineteen installments, beginning September 2007 and ending February 2008. How was it received?

I've received more response to Christmas cards. *The New York Times* didn't have a comments section on their website at the time, but the editors told me that they received some nice letters—although, of course, I never saw any of them.

It's interesting: I'll receive a lot more of a reaction when something appears on a small website than I will when something's published in a major magazine or newspaper. The easier it is for a reader to contact you, the more responses you receive.

Maybe that's a good thing. I have a feeling that a lot of the responses to *Mister Wonderful* would have been negative. It's amazing how sensitive newspaper readers are when it comes to humor. If you look at the syndicated comics, you have to wonder who reads that sort of thing. One would think editors would want to lure readers back to the comics section again, but they're just so terrified of one negative letter.

Were you given free rein by the *Times* to write whatever you wanted with *Mister Wonderful*?

As far as subject matter, they never said a word, but they were very touchy about language—their little "stylebook" is very important to them. Aside from *Jesus*, for instance, I wasn't allowed to use the word *schmuck*. *Mad*'s been using the word for fifty years! It's not as if I were using it in the Yiddish sense: "Wow, that guy has a huge cock!" I even found an old William Safire column from *The New York Times Magazine* about *schmuck*. He wrote something like, "The original meaning of the word has long ago been forgotten, and it's commonly accepted for general use."

I showed this to the editors, but they told me, "No. We can't run the word." I could have acted like an asshole and told them I was going to end the strip halfway through, but this was a really good assignment for cartoonists. I didn't want to be the guy who killed it for everyone else.

I suppose you have to play the game.

Sometimes that can be a good thing. I was restricted—but this restriction ultimately helped the comic. I wasn't allowed to use the words *Jesus* or *God*, but once I was faced with having to replace them, I got more focused on what the character was actually trying to say—or not say—and I realized how much of a crutch the "Jesuses" had become. The central character was a repressed middle-aged guy who was terrible with women, so any time he was further repressed by not being allowed to fully relieve his frustration it only helped.

When I worked on the movie *Ghost World* [in 2000], there were restrictions that you wouldn't believe. For instance, we weren't allowed to show a painting of comedian Don Knotts—unless we had Don Knotts give us permission. It's all about rights, clearances, lawyers. We wanted a character to sing "Happy Birthday to You"—but we couldn't unless we paid something like ten thousand dollars, so we just cut the scene.

In comparison, not being allowed to use certain words in a comic strip became no big deal. You have to work with the situation you're given.

In 2010, you published *Wilson*, a graphic novel that centered on a middle-aged man oblivious to social cues. He may be one of the most obnoxious characters in comic history. One panel ends with him saying out loud, on a playground: "Hey! Can you get that brat to shut up for two fucking seconds!?" And yet I read that you came up with this character as you sat next to your dying father. True?

Yeah. Around that time, I had read a quote from Charles Schulz that was something like, "A real pro cartoonist can sit down at the board for a few minutes and come up with a funny strip." And so I was kind of testing myself to see how fast I could write a bunch of joke comics that were actually funny—at least to me. My dad was in many ways very similar to Schulz, and a big fan of *Peanuts*, and so in retrospect I guess I was trying to gain the old man's approval.

Every story in *Wilson* is only one page. They remind me, in their rhythm, of syndicated comics or even *Mad* pieces. But the material is obviously much darker: death, failed hopes and dreams, inability to connect. It's an interesting combination, similar to hearing canned laughter during a drama.

I'm blind to the darkness. I just genuinely thought the strips in the book were either funny or moving in some way. That format seemed to work for the character, but it's unlikely I'd ever use anything exactly like that for another strip.

What do you think you tapped into while sitting in that hospital? Was it a meditative state?

It was more of a burst of creativity that you can have when trapped in a situation that's both boring and anxiety-inducing. I used to think about enrolling in college courses in subjects I had no interest in so I would be able to achieve that state of restless boredom.

Early in your career, did you find that readers had a difficult time labeling you? The type of work you produced wasn't your typical style of a traditional comic.

They still have a difficult time. I've been called everything from a graphic novelist to a comic-strip novelist to just a cartoonist. I've always preferred cartoonist, because that seems the least obnoxious.

I used to tell people I was a comic-book artist, but they'd look at me as if I'd just stepped in dog shit and walked across their Oriental rug. I never knew what to call myself, but I was always opposed to the whole "graphic novelist" label. To me it just seemed like a scam. I always felt that people would say, "Wait a minute! This is just a comic book!" But now I've given up. Call me whatever you want.

When you started, the graphic novel was such a new form. Growing up, where did you even find inspiration for something like this?

Well, there were a few people doing this as early as the seventies. There was a writer and illustrator named Justin Green who wrote and illustrated a comic book called *Binky Brown Meets the Holy Virgin Mary*, which was published in 1972. It's about a young boy living within the strict confines of his Catholic upbringing as he deals with his sexual awakening and severe OCD symptoms.

Art Spiegelman has claimed that *Binky Brown* influenced his *Maus* books.

The *Binky Brown* comic was out of print for many years, but it's not as difficult to find as it used to be. It is definitely worth buying. I was around sixteen when I discovered it, and, truthfully, I didn't understand it at first. A friend told me that it was the greatest comic ever, but I was not raised Catholic. It was kind of over my head. Then I reread it when I was in my twenties and I really connected with it.

People say that *Binky Brown* is the first autobiographical comic book. I'm not sure if that's exactly true, but, at the very least, it is extremely personal and wonderful.

What were some of your other comic influences when you were growing up?

I have a brother who is ten years older than me, and he gave me his stack of comics from the late fifties and the early sixties—a lot of horror and sci-fi and crappy superhero comics. I never watched TV until I was older. I was obsessed with a lot of early Marvel Comics and DC Comics.

When I was about twenty-one or twenty-two, I bought *The Official Marvel Comics Try-Out Book*, which had a bunch of professionally penciled comic pages printed on good paper. Some of the pages were unfinished to give young artists a chance to ink and color a "pro" drawing. It seemed like it would be fun to test my skills on a few pages of Spider-Man swinging through 1970s New York on his webs. That lasted for about fifteen minutes and then I started giving all the characters afros and exposed tits.

Which did you prefer, Marvel or DC?

I liked DC comics, such as *Superman's Pal Jimmy Olsen* and *Superman's Girl Friend Lois Lane*, because they were about "real" people, with the superhero stuff in the background. I never quite got into superheroes—except on kind of a Pop Art level. I just never got into the fighting. What I found more interesting was the romance and the attempts at conveying some kind of reality in this absurd universe. Like Superboy's dad still working at the general store, even though his son could take over the world—things like that. My friends were the exact opposite. They used to say, "God, who cares about this romance? Get to the punching!"

And, actually, you know what I liked even more? Regular people yearning to become superheroes.

And perhaps failing?

Oh, that I would have found especially fascinating.

Was it always your intention to become a cartoonist?

I had no idea what I was going to do with my life. I really wanted to be a cartoonist, but there was no market for anything I was interested in doing. I just couldn't see myself drawing newspaper strips or working for Marvel Comics. I remember waking up in the middle of the night and being petrified: *What's going to happen to me? What am I going to do?*

I mean, to this day, I have no skills beyond those within the narrow confines of what I do.

So you were laying it all on the line for this?

My parents were like, "Are you sure you want to do this?" It was a ridiculous career choice, which I should have known early on in my life. Thankfully, it took a very long time to hit me just how ridiculous it was.

At what point did you notice that people were beginning to understand what a *graphic novel* actually meant?

For me, there was a sea change by 2001 or 2002, around the time the *Ghost World* movie was released. Average citizens like my parents' neighbors started to say things like, "Oh, you do graphic novels! I love [Art Spiegelman's] *Maus*!" A few years earlier, they would have thought of me as the lowest pornographer.

I assume you never had any interest in creating a syndicated strip for newspapers?

No, that's a whole different genre—an entirely different genus of cartoonist. The ones I've met tend to be these odd, suburban, country-club types. And just because the format worked with audiences in the 1920s doesn't mean it's still the greatest idea today.

It's not very appealing. To create these four-panel increments, day in and day out, week after week, I just don't see how you could accomplish anything of note.

Were there any syndicated cartoonists that had an influence on you?

I guess *Peanuts* would be the obvious one, though I never read it in the paper. *Nancy* was the only strip I read every day throughout my childhood, and it had quite an impact. As the *Mad* cartoonist Wally Wood said about *Nancy*, "By the time you decided not to read it, you already had." I think that's something I always keep in mind with my own comics—always opt for clarity and simplicity.

You grew up pre-Internet. To what degree do you think the Internet has changed comics?

I'm not really sure. There are comics now being created on the Internet, but I'm not interested in reading that sort of thing. I'd just rather wait until it's printed. I don't like the aesthetics of seeing something like that lit up on the screen. That's just my personal take on it—I don't expect anybody else to not read Internet comics for that reason.

One thing I've found about the Internet is that it's very distracting to cartoonists—myself included. Most cartoonists are just looking for any excuse for a distraction. This type of work can be so lonely and tedious and frustrating at various stages of the process.

If I had had a computer in high school, I would no doubt have become obsessed and literally thrown away twenty years of my life. I would not be here talking with you. I would be sitting in front of a TV playing *Grand Theft Auto*. I would have done nothing.

You really wouldn't have become a cartoonist?

I don't think so; I really don't. I would have been way too busy trying to talk to girls in chat rooms. Why would I ever have bothered with comics? I can't imagine.

Do you work alone?

Yes.

You don't have assistants at your disposal, like many syndicated newspaper cartoonists?

No, no. I'd love to hire an assistant, but only to do the lowest shit work. I don't have the right temperament to have an assistant. I'd feel bad criticizing them, and I'd wind up accepting work I wasn't happy with.

I do like the idea of having a whole studio of artists and forcing them to draw in my style and cranking out these huge books every year, but I know I'd never be happy with that. They'd never get it right, and I'd wind up doing everything myself anyway.

Who do you bounce your ideas off of?

I don't. That's part of the fun.

I've tried in the past to gauge people's reactions, and nobody is really honest. I'm not the sort of person who would encourage somebody to be brutally honest; I may really like what I created and not want to hear anything bad. I have to just go with my own instincts. They're not always right, but I'd rather do that than be swayed by somebody who might just be in a bad mood or have these reasons I don't necessarily agree with.

Also, the work becomes more specific if you work alone, more singular.

I'd think that as a comic-book artist you'd have to really commit to an idea. Once you put an idea down onto paper, it would be difficult to tweak it—unless you worked on a computer.

No, I draw everything by hand. But that's right. To change it once you start the process is literally impossible—unless you just start over from the beginning.

What I'll usually do is start with an outline. I try to get the beats of the plot figured out, and from there I just wing it. At a certain point, a cartoonist will have a sense of how long and what rhythm a strip should be. You don't really need to break it down further than that.

Often, when I'm halfway through a story, I realize that if I went in a more promising direction, the strip would have been a lot more interesting. When that happens, rather than starting over, I switch gears. It's exciting to work that way. It's one of the few things about drawing comics that actually *is* exciting.

You never stop once you start?

I've abandoned a few things, but most of the time I try to keep going. That's the thing: You can't go back and redo it over again, because that'll just dissipate your creativity; you lose everything that's interesting and spontaneous. I could spend the rest of my life redrawing everything I've done, but it would just kill everything that's good about it. That would be a total waste of time.

Isn't that a strong creative urge, though? To want to make a work as perfect as possible?

It's similar to when a musician isn't happy with the quality of their early records and wants to record again with a better band. The original work is connected to a specific moment of time; it's never going to become "better." Even when I do a new cover for one of my old books, they always seem sort of condescending to the material.

I can understand the motives, I suppose. I'd love to go back and redo my earlier work. I can see the crudeness of it, as well as the potential, but I just know that it would not be better—it would only be slicker.

Actually, that was the great appeal of writing the scripts to *Ghost World* and [2006's] *Art School Confidential*. The process was very fluid. The ability to just change a character's name is something that no comic-book artist would ever have the luxury of doing. It would be such a pain in the ass to reletter somebody's name or to reorder scenes in comics. I'd just say, "Forget it," and move on.

With the *Ghost World* script, I made a million changes right up until the very last minute. We changed Steve Buscemi's character's name from Sherwin to Seymour the day we handed in the script for the first time, and I'm still not used to it.

How was *Ghost World* green-lit? It was unlike any other Hollywood movie dealing with teenagers I'd seen up to that point—maybe with the exception of *Fast Times at Ridgemont High* and *Heathers*.

Who knows how that film ever happened. It was the most cobbled-together financial arrangement in the history of film. It was held together by spit and Kleenex. It was very low budget. There are a million Sundance films made every year with this kind of money.

The screenplay for *Ghost World* is not your typical Hollywood fare. Even the action descriptions are different from what one would normally find in a script. For instance, this is from the very first page: "A large, hirsute man, wearing only Lycra jogging shorts, watches the Home Shopping Network while eating mashed potatoes with his fingers."

[Laughs] When Terry and I wrote the *Ghost World* screenplay, we would take turns and hand it back and forth to each other. We were just adding detail upon detail to crack each other up. We showed one of our producers the first ten pages, and it was just packed with descriptions: "The high school graduation banner should be sponsored by Dunkin' Donuts."

Never in a million years could we have afforded the rights to Dunkin' Donuts. The producer said to us, "You know, perhaps you should have looked at another screenplay before you started."

It's really a miracle this movie ever got made, quite frankly. A lot of people sort of missed the point of it.[2] Both Terry and I were so green when we were pitching it. We would tell executives we wanted to make another *King of Comedy* [1982] or *Scarlet Street* [1945] or *Crimes and Misdemeanors* [1989]. Big mistake. The executives would look at us as if we were insane. It's like saying, "We'd like to take $6 million of your money and shred it for an art project we're doing." The people who make the decisions in Hollywood are never the oddballs or creative types, so you have to tell them what they want to hear. It didn't take long for us to start saying things like, "We want to make another *There's Something About Mary*." We had no intention of doing that, but you must at least make the effort to be reassuring.

You just mentioned a movie I'm not familiar with: *Scarlet Street*. What is it about?

It's a *noir* movie, but to me, *noir* is more about a state of anxiety and profound loneliness—an awareness of the quotidian grimness of the postwar world. *Scarlet Street* is about a poor, ugly loser [Edward G. Robinson] who gets hoodwinked by a horrible woman and her pimp, almost willingly so, since even this cheap thrill is preferable to his emasculated existence with his harridan wife.

The original version, directed by Jean Renoir, is even better. The [1931] movie is called *La Chienne*, which translates to "the bitch."

---

2   Summary on the Netflix DVD cover of *Ghost World*: "Geeky humor that really snarls pervades this movie riff on the legendary underground comic/graphic novel by Daniel Clowes. . . . But when Enid begins to bond with one of [her] targets, watch out—teen angst might give way to real feeling."

I'm not even sure "the bitch" meant the prostitute, as much as life itself.

What is it about *The King of Comedy* that you like so much?

I think it's Scorsese's best movie—just a perfect little film. I enjoy anything that has an ending that is happy for the characters but is bad for us, the viewers. That ending knocked me to the floor the first time I saw it. I really wasn't expecting it.

I also like any movie that deals with the ugliness of the relationship between star and fan.

And, of course, Jerry Lewis. I think he's very appropriate for the role of the late-night TV host: wired, angry, very close to losing control.

I read an interview with the Asian actor [Kim Chan] who played Jerry's butler in the movie, and he said that the scene when Jerry was yelling at him from outside the house to open the front door was not an act. It was completely real. Jerry was pissed off at the guy for not being able to open the door, and Scorsese luckily had the genius to keep it in the movie.

This next question may very well be the most specific in this entire book, if not in the history of humankind—but here goes anyway. There's a scene in *The King of Comedy* that has always fascinated me. It takes place when Robert De Niro is eating in a dim sum restaurant with a date. There is an extra in the background who stares directly at and mugs for the camera. Have you noticed this?

I have, actually. From what I've heard, this extra was a friend of De Niro's who was just hamming it up. But why would Scorsese have allowed this to happen? It makes no sense. It might be the only time that an average viewer will ever notice an extra. But it somehow adds to the unreality of the film; the scene is very dreamlike.

Were you into teen films growing up?

I never connected with that sort of film. I couldn't relate to the problems of average suburban teens at all.

But I never really considered *Ghost World* to be a teen film. It was more about these two specific characters working through something that felt very personal to me. I wasn't necessarily trying to communicate with teenagers, and I never really imagined they would be as much of our audience as they have.

You say you weren't necessarily trying to appeal to teenagers, but you did manage to capture teen dialogue extremely well.

I wasn't exactly a teenager when I wrote that movie, and I couldn't have told you what an average seventeen- to eighteen-year-old sounded like or what slang they used. It was a total mystery. So I used a modified version of the slang I knew, and I tried not to take it in a too-specific direction. I really wanted the script to be read by somebody of just about any age and not seem dated or corny or overly mannered or overly screenplayish.

All writers want to achieve that with dialogue, but how did you manage to pull it off?

I was really interested in the secret life of girls from the time I was in high school. I've always been fascinated by this alien species. I loved the rhythms of their speech, but I wasn't overly familiar with it. As I got older and actually *had* girlfriends, I'd always ask them to tell me specific stories about what it was like behind closed doors.

It also helped that I had a very special place in my heart for Enid. I have true affection for that character, even though a lot of the audience saw both the movie and the comic as an indictment of Enid. I've always found that strange.

Why do you think that is?

Perhaps they found Enid too judgmental. Also, she's a part of a leisure class and her problems are hardly matters of life and death, but she still complains about every little detail.

Enid tries to create an interesting life out of a potentially dull existence by uncovering—or actually manufacturing—the strangeness beneath this seemingly sterile world. I find that heroic.

If Enid were truly cynical, she would have just gotten a retail job in her town and given up. Enid thinks there's something better out there for herself, and she searches to find it. That has to count for something.

What should also count is Enid's utter disdain for the commercialization aimed at teens her age.

How many teen girls her age are even aware of it? I find it horrible. I find the commercialization and the suburbanization of this country really, really depressing. I'm lucky enough to live in a rarefied part of the country [Oakland, California] where there aren't too many strip malls. But every time I go on a road trip, it's just the same thing over and over again.

What did you learn from your experience as a screenwriter that you later used for writing comics?

I've learned basic rules of dramaturgy that you don't necessarily learn only doing comics. I learned about the nuances of a bigger plot arc, where characters have to travel longer distances emotionally. I learned to rid everything that doesn't work, even though I might have spent a long time on it.

I've always noticed a cinematic flow with your comics.

When I'm doing the comics, I don't think in terms of cinematic flow. Comics have their own rhythm—that's what they're all about. It's the beat to the storytelling that makes them come alive.

Look at *Peanuts*. Charles Schulz had a perfect rhythm in every single strip. They always worked. Robert Crumb also has that talent, as did [the first editor of *Mad*] Harvey Kurtzman.

If you really want to succeed as a cartoonist, you have to do more than merely create cool eyeball kicks.

What does *eyeball kicks* mean?

If you're drawing a really detailed, tricked-out image, and your only concern is how it looks on the page, then that only goes so far in telling a story in comic form. It's just a series of kick-ass images.

How does one learn to create rhythm that's appropriate to comics?

You have to learn it to the point where this rhythm is in your head. You can't overthink it, because if you do, the comic becomes fussy and stupid. It has to arrive with no effort at all.

And that even holds true for the rewriting. You cannot labor over something for too long. If that's the case, just start over and try again.

Really, in the end, each cartoonist has to develop their own rhythm—as well as their own reality.

How have you managed to capture your own reality?

I have to distill all of the elements and then make it into my own. Years ago, cartoonists would have a "morgue file," which contained photos of every imaginable reference: cars, radio sets, boats, buildings. But I don't want anything like that. To me, it's much more valid to *remember* what something looks like.

For instance, if I wanted to draw a Starbucks store, I could take a photo and then trace it. But what I really want is for this Starbucks to be my *internal* impression of what that world is like. Doing that adds value to something like this. It may not be perfect, but it won't be dead on the page, either.

There's a specific paradigm that has frequently shown up in your comics: middle-aged children living with their elderly parents. What is it about this relationship that interests you?

When I was a kid, I spent a lot of time around these old parent figures. I was pretty much raised by my maternal grandparents.

My grandfather, James Cate, was an academic at the University of

Chicago, and he had a lot of interesting friends. His next-door neighbor was Enrico Fermi, who helped create the atomic bomb. Saul Bellow was a friend, as was Norman Maclean, the author of *A River Runs Through It*.

There would be a knock at the door at night, and it would be a professor friend of my grandfather's. They'd sit up until God knows when, two in the morning, and just talk.

Do you think this type of childhood later affected your writing?

It certainly didn't hurt to listen to these brilliant people endlessly converse with each other for hours upon hours. Beyond that, my grandfather was a very, very funny guy—very different. He was born in a tiny little town in Texas and he somehow made himself into this world-class history professor. His whole shtick was that of a back-woods rube, and he used it to disarm people. Every year at the university he used to perform in a series of skits called "The Rebels." He'd write and perform in campus parodies—I loved this as a kid.

On the other hand, my mother was a mechanic. There was a dichotomy in my life. My stepfather, who was a race driver, died in a crash in Elkhart Lake, Indiana, when I was about five. I guarantee you that the crash today would be nothing—he'd walk away from the car just fine. Back then, though, cars were not padded correctly.

I never forgot the details. I suppose it gave me a sense of mortality, in which I knew even at a young age that things could go very badly, very quickly. My earliest memory is of feeling anxiety.

You were obsessed with death?

I was, and, even more specifically, I was obsessed with the Leopold and Loeb murder case. I grew up about five blocks from where they carried out the killing. They went to my high school—obviously, sixty years before I did—but that story just haunted my entire adolescence. It still haunts me.

Why?

They did this horrible thing, and now all they could do was sit there and wait for the authorities to find them. I'll never forget that feeling: Doom is approaching, and there's not a thing you can do about it.

It seems that you remember your childhood with great clarity.

I think most cartoonists remember every little slight, every playground insult. I was telling somebody the other day that I can remember the name of every person in my second-grade class. They were astounded by this, but how could anyone not remember them?

Do you remember your classmates out of anger?

No. I was perfectly happy in second grade. It's not really based on holding a grudge. On the other hand, I can't remember somebody I had dinner with two years ago. It's just the intensity of childhood. It was being with the same group of thirty kids every day for a year and trying to figure out who you are in relation to them.

Everything that's happened to me as an adult seems like a fantasy. For a long time, if someone were to wake me up—this is just hypothetical—and ask me how old I was, I would give an age of about eighteen. I think it's now up to twenty-seven, but that's only recently changed. I still identify with that period between being a kid and being an adult, when you're confused with how exactly you should fit in with the rest of society.

If you woke up and were eighteen again, how long would it take to convince yourself that everything that's happened since has been merely a dream?

Not long at all. Ten minutes.

In November of 2007, you appeared as yourself in a *Simpsons* episode, signing autographs at a comic-book convention. George Meyer, a

writer for *The Simpsons*, said that he once visited you at a convention and that you looked "alert, but dispirited, like a falcon trotted out for third-graders." How do you feel about these conventions?

I've always felt like such an outcast at those events, but in the past it was sort of pleasant. I never used to mind it, and it used to have this weird appeal. Now they're just so horrible; they are like a big media conglomerate. It's like going to Sundance or something—just this hideous group of agents and horrible people trying to promote themselves. No charm at all.

Do you think that today is the heyday of graphic novels and comics?

I think so—certainly in terms of current work, narratively and aesthetically. It would be hard to find an era that was much better. There were certainly people who could draw a lot better in the old days, but it was very rare to find a great writer who could also draw.

What do you see as the future of the graphic novel?

I don't know. When I started out, nobody—none of my peers in art school or anywhere else—would have thought of this as a viable career. They wouldn't have said, "I am going to write and draw a graphic novel." I used to hear classmates from art school say they wanted to work on children's books. Everybody thinks they can write a children's book, and it's something semirespectable to work on.

I receive letters from young writers asking for advice about a "career" in comics. If somebody asks me, I always say not to do it unless you can't *not* do it. If you need encouragement from a stranger, then you shouldn't do it.

Once you are a cartoonist, the best advice I ever received was from Robert Crumb. He told me to just get away from cartooning for awhile. He told me he wished that he had taken up some other form of art, like sculpture; that it was important to do more than just sit at a desk and perform the same repetitive act over and over again. That it was fantastic just to be able to get away from the drawing board, to actually talk to other human beings and to gain some perspective on the many freedoms you take for granted as a cartoonist.

After fifteen years in a room alone, you can start to feel as if you've unwittingly sentenced yourself to solitary confinement. It's no wonder that pretty much every cartoonist over fifty is totally insane.

Do you ever see yourself *not* doing this?

If I get old enough and my eyesight gets really bad or I can't hold a pencil, maybe. Outside of that, I don't see ever stopping.

There's a book that came out more than fifteen years ago—a fiftieth-anniversary index of the members of the National Cartoonists Society. It's a book of photos and short bios of hundreds of old-time American cartoonists, and for some reason a few "younger" nonmembers, such as myself, were included. I was thirty-seven at the time.

There are dozens of photos of these old codgers smiling with these stupid grins on their faces. But you can see the sadness underneath. It's such a grim document. My friend [and fellow cartoonist] Chris Ware told me he had to actually hide his copy of the book, because he can't bear to look at it.

What did you both find grim about it?

All these lives spent behind the drawing board; fifty years on a daily strip that no one remembers.

What's the lesson for you—that you don't want to end up like that?

I sort of *do* want to end up like that—that's the pathetic part about it. I look at that book and I am thrilled to be a part of it. It's sort of like the ending to *The Shining*, when the camera zooms in on that group photo with Jack Torrance at the black-tie party in the 1920s.

There is something so great about becoming that guy.

DANIEL HANDLER, aka "Lemony Snicket"

Writer, *A Series of Unfortunate Events*

Writing Humor for Children

Before you became a best-selling children's author with *A Series of Unfortunate Events*, published under the pen name Lemony Snicket, you wrote books for adults. Why did you make the switch?

My editor read *The Basic Eight* [a 1998 adult novel for St. Martin's Press]. The book is narrated by a teenage girl. My editor didn't think she could publish such a book for young people, but she thought I could write something that she could publish for children. I was sure she was wrong.

Do you think children's books have changed since *A Series of Unfortunate Events* was first published in 1999? Have publishers come to accept the notion that a children's book can be funny without being preachy?

In terms of straight percentages, I don't actually know if that's happening. There seem to be just as many syrupy books for kids as always, but I do think the good books aren't slipping below the radar like they might have in the past. More attention is being paid to children's literature.

Were you a fan of Roald Dahl's? I've always found his work, both for children and adults, to be as dark as the work of any horror writer, and yet incredibly funny.

I was. Even Dahl's lesser works for children have a kind of wondrous quality about them. I always loved *The Magic Finger* [Harper & Row, 1966], which is about a girl with magical powers.

All of Dahl's stories have this chaos and menace where the readers are encouraged to smack their lips over the downfall of nasty people. To me, that has a delicious, yet unsavory, vibe.

Dahl's stories also never seemed to have a real tight arc, which I always appreciated. In *James and the Giant Peach* [Knopf, 1961], a huge peach grows in James's yard. Inside the peach, James finds giant insects. His parents have died, and off he goes with these bugs on adventures. But there's never a sense that James is learning something about himself. It's just a pure, crazy journey.

The older I get, and the fewer tight arcs I've experienced in which I learned something about my life that enabled me to go forward, the more I appreciate these books.

A lot of readers who otherwise would have loved Dahl are put off by his anti-Semitism and reported nastiness. Should that affect whether parents allow their children to read his stories?

I'd think it would affect whether or not you wanted to have him over, not read his work. If you start refusing to read writers who weren't nice people, your shelves are going to be mighty undernourished. Dahl's anti-Semitism is overstated anyway, although his nastiness is understated, so that might balance out.

A favorite childhood book of mine was *Charlie and the Chocolate Factory* [Knopf, 1964]. I reread it recently but had forgotten that the Oompa Loompas were Pygmies from "the very deepest and darkest part of the

African jungle." A far cry from the happy-go-lucky orange cuties who appear in the 1971 film version *Willy Wonka & the Chocolate Factory*.

I do remember that, and it seemed unsettling even when I was a kid. There was a very menacing quality to Dahl's writing. Beyond the Pygmies, there was this bizarre candy in the original book capable of doing all these strange things. They cut this out of the movie, but there's an extended joke in the book about square candy that looks round. The kids look through the window of a lab, and they say the candy is square. Wonka then opens the door and the square candies turn "round" to look at them.

Wonka says, "There's no argument about it. They are square candies that look round."

There's something about Dahl's books that incorporates the fear and the sadness and the chaos that exists in life while also managing to be funny. He doesn't make the world a funny place where only funny things happen. His tragedy is honest, and it doesn't always have redeeming qualities about it.

You don't feel that kids are too young to learn the truth about life?

They already know it. Even if you have an extremely happy childhood, you're going to learn about chaos and heartbreak and all the rest of it on the playground.

Manohla Dargis of *The New York Times* called the whitewashing often found in children's literature the "tyranny of nice."

I think that's a good way of putting it. It's an author using his or her position of power to attempt to force-feed an unrealistic version of the world on those who most likely already know that such a world doesn't exist. That's something I've always tried to avoid, especially when it's come to humor.

You made it very clear at the start of *A Series of Unfortunate Events* that things weren't going to turn out happily for the characters. You

wrote: "If you are interested in stories with happy endings, you would be better off reading some other book. In this book, not only is there no happy ending, there is no happy beginning and very few happy things in the middle."

The books for kids that have stood the test of time—like *Grimm's Fairy Tales* or *Alice's Adventures in Wonderland*—have been strange and chaotic and bizarre. The treacly crap has drifted away. I mean, you can still find Bobbsey Twins books, but they seem to be only for adult collectors and other fetishists. No honest-to-goodness child would ever read that sort of thing.

Was your publisher concerned that some of the scenes in *A Series of Unfortunate Events* were too graphic for kids? In the first volume, *The Bad Beginning*, the fourteen-year-old character, Violet, is nearly married against her will. In *The Vile Village*, the character of Jacques is murdered before being burned at the stake. And, reminiscent of what took place four years previously on 9/11, a large building—in this case a hotel—burns in 2005's *The Penultimate Peril*, the second-to-last volume.

Before I wrote *A Series of Unfortunate Events*, I thought that only kids with happy childhoods would enjoy the books. I thought it would be a safe way for them to explore other, not-so-nice worlds. But I found the opposite to be true. It surprised me, especially considering how tragic certain parts of those books are.

It wasn't so much the publisher who was worried, it was my agent. She was certain that no publisher would ever want to buy books like this, whereas I never saw these books as representing anything that was really all too new.

How did you see them?

I saw them as being part of the long tradition of orphans getting into dire trouble. I also saw it as creating a worldview that was just as much about hilarity as it was about heartbreak. Funny and ghastly at the same time. The tragedy becomes exaggerated, and then the exaggeration becomes funny. The emotions travel on a circular path. The reader feels terrible, terrible, *terrible*, and then suddenly it becomes very funny. That's reality.

Do you enjoy being around children? It seems that many children's authors, including Roald Dahl, weren't too fond of their own audience.

The truth of the matter is that I'm always disturbed by someone who says they like or dislike children. To me, that's like saying you either like or dislike adults. There are so many different types.

Yes, but some adults feel that *all* children are exactly the same.

True. It seems that children are one of the last minorities about whom you can make huge sweeping generalizations and no one will care.

I see this everywhere. I recently read an interview with a woman who was writing about pre-teen culture, and she said that girls love to be pretty and want to grow up to be princesses and want to be rescued by boys, and so on. And I thought, If you were to substitute any other minority for "girls," you'd never work in publishing again.

I suppose kids don't have the representation that other minorities might have.

Also, a lot of adults don't seem to have the thinking skills that are critical to understanding kids. I hate these broad generalizations that adults come up with only because they believe this is how kids *should* think or act. How do *you* know?

Does part of all this have to do with adults forgetting what it was like to be a child?

I think so. It's one thing to forget about your childhood, but don't transfer your incorrect memories onto kids who are now living through that time. Or, at the very least, don't write about it!

When it comes to writing humor for kids, I always think back to when I was a kid myself and teachers would talk to me like I was an idiot. The teachers I really liked were the ones who spoke to me the same way they would to other adults. It was respect.

Do you have any interest in writing humor for adults?

For better or worse, there's just more appreciation of the humor genre within children's literature. Beyond the fact they're very difficult to write, comic novels are also difficult to sell to adults. There are a few authors who get away with it, but, overall, publishers are not excited by humor unless it's a children's book, where there's more room for that type of book in a commercial sense.

Any last words of advice for the aspiring children's writer?

I don't know whether this is true or not, but there's a story about John Coltrane and Miles Davis—they were playing together in the mid-fifties. Coltrane was into playing very, very long sax solos, some lasting for more than an hour. Miles Davis asked him to rein it in a bit.

Coltrane said, "I don't know how."

And Davis said, "Take the horn out of your mouth."

I always think of that story when I'm looking at a beautiful chapter I wrote, and I just can't imagine cutting one word of it. I then think, Actually, yes, you can. It's not that hard.

All of my books are a lot longer in their first drafts than they need to be. I always cut them down drastically. I'm a huge rewriter; it's extremely important. I find this capacity missing with a lot of writers.

I'd also recommend stealing paper from work. And not only paper but printer cartridges. Seriously, I did this for years before I could afford to write full-time. I wrote the beginning of *Snicket* when I worked for a dying man. I was working as an administrative assistant at the City College of San Francisco. My job was to answer my boss's office phone and to inform people, if they asked to speak to him, that he was dying. He managed to live for over a year, so people eventually stopped calling.

I recently met this underground writer—or so she calls herself—who was complaining about the price of self-publishing. I thought, If you don't know how to steal enough paper to print out your own stories for free and to advance and improve yourself as a writer, you're not an underground writer. More than that, you don't *deserve* to be a writer.

That's my advice. Why this isn't taught in the creative-writing programs is a crime.

Finally: I'd avoid reading interviews with writers. None of us know what we're doing. You can learn more from reading a good book than all the floppy advice from the people who make them.

ANTHONY JESELNIK

....

Actor; Comedian; Writer, *Late Night with Jimmy Fallon,*
The Jeselnik Offensive

I wanted to be a writer pretty much my whole life. I wanted to write books. As I got older, I realized what being a novelist meant, and what kind of life that would mean. I decided that that wasn't the life for me. I was in my early twenties, and I didn't want to just lock myself in a room and bang away for the next ten or fifteen years on a novel that might not be any good. So I thought maybe screenplays would be the way to go, but I hated writing screenplays—they're dry and boring, and I found that it was really hard, without connections, to get anyone to read anything you'd written. Even if you wrote a screenplay, to get someone to read that screenplay was a huge pain in the ass. So I abandoned that idea, and I thought, What would be my dream job? Even though I didn't expect to become a comedian, I thought writing jokes seemed like a lot of fun. Being around funny people was the bigger thing. I think a lot of people want a writing job but they don't know what that means. They want to just hang out; they want to be around funny people.

I only had one connection in Los Angeles. My dad had gone to college with a guy named Jimmy Brogan, who was the head writer at the time for *The Tonight Show Starring Johnny Carson*. Jimmy had been a comedian for a lot of years. I went to the Hollywood Improv and watched him do a set—which was the first live set I had ever seen. After, I said to him, "I want to be a joke writer; I want to do what you do." I thought he was going to say, "Okay, show up to the studio on Friday, and bring your ID, and we'll get you in there." But he just said, "If you want to do that, do stand-up." I tell people this all the time, that stand-up, even if you don't want to be a comedian, makes you write, and it forces you to make the material good, because by doing stand-up you're defending your own jokes. You can't just write them down. And I found that that was attractive to me because it made you work.

Stand-up is kind of like getting your bachelor's degree. Or getting a law degree. You can do a lot with it. You don't have to be a lawyer. With a law degree, you can be a teacher. You can have all kinds of different jobs with that degree. If you get into stand-up and you become a producer, or you become an actor, or you become a writer, it's not like you've failed as a comic. It's just that being a comic gives you the skills to move on to the next job. And a lot of times, it might seem to be your dream job, but it might end up being a *job* job. There are a lot of bad comedy writing jobs out there—which I would've taken at the time—but I'm glad I didn't get them. I'm glad I didn't end up on some bad show just churning out crappy stuff. I'm glad I stuck to my guns and just did onstage what I wanted to do.

As my stand-up career kind of heated up, I got hired on *Fallon*. It's hard to get into a place like that, because when shows are hiring writers, they have one spot open, they've been on the air for years, and they usually hire someone's friend. A writer will say, "Okay, I've been here for ten years, you know me, I vouch for this guy, bring him in." And that's how you usually get hired. But when producers have to staff a whole new show like they did with *Fallon*, they have to think outside the box, and this was my opportunity. I kind of talked my way in there and said, "Listen, this is gonna be great. I'll write your monologue jokes," and I was the first monologue writer hired. I recently read something Tina Fey said: "If you hire a writer, it'd

better be someone that you're happy to see in the hallway at 3:00 a.m."
That's a big thing, just to be nice, just to be pleasant to be around.
I had a total blast, and I was fun to be around, so they liked me, and
I thought, Oh, I could do this.

When I was on *Fallon*, they would have these things called "in-
formationals," where young writer wannabes would come into the
office. They'd ask, "I want to be a writer like you. How can I do this?"
And it was me and Jeremy Bronson, another writer at the time, and
we would sit down with this person and they'd be like, "How'd you
guys do it?" And they had their résumé—as if I would ever give a shit
about that—and I would tell them, "Well, I did stand-up for six years
to get to this point, to get this job," and Jeremy would say, "Well, I
worked in news, I worked for *Hardball* for a few years and then submitted for this show," and he had submitted to *SNL* and didn't get it,
but they passed his packet along to *Fallon* and he got the job that way.
People didn't want to hear that. There are all kinds of different paths
to get to places, but you have to work your butt off. You have to work
for a long time to do it. There's no real shortcut. No one cares how
you dress in the interview. It's like a comedian who hands you their
business card. If you're a comedian, be a comedian. I tell a lot of people to start a blog. Start a blog and write monologue jokes every day.
And people don't want to hear that either. To them, it seems like
you're just throwing stuff in the air. But I know Josh Comers got
hired on *Conan* that way. He just had a blog where he'd write monologue jokes every day, and they hired him off of that. So if you have
something to show people, they're gonna be excited by it.

At *Fallon*, we had a fax program for a little while, and people
would send in jokes. And they would send in five jokes a day, but a lot
of times they would be bad. Or the person didn't really work on them;
they would just be sending in jokes for the sake of sending in jokes.
That's a terrible idea. Because when a job finally came up and we were
looking through those packets, we'd be like, "Oh, should we hire
Jenny? Jenny has some terrible jokes." So we'd be like, "No, let's not
hire her." Jenny would've been better off not submitting anything, and
then getting it together. If you're going to submit something, make
sure the jokes are really good. Really work on them. If you've got
twelve hours to do a submission, it might be a better idea not to submit

to that job if you don't have the time to make the packet good. Your name is on top of it, and it's gonna hurt you down the line.

I feel like a lot of people in comedy get frustrated because it's not like school, where you show up and those in charge say, "Here are your classes. Go to this and then you'll take a test at this point." There's no structure to this world. But I just very much wanted to get on the tracks. At the very least, you have to get on the tracks. Think of yourself as the train. And keep throwing coal in there and keep moving down the right path.

Price U.S. 75c   Canada 75c

A 44985
CABIN BOY BLUES
Fox Trot   (SMITH)
Played by
LESTER WIRT AND THE DIXIE RUG BEATERS

THE AEOLIAN COMPANY 1921

ADAM RESNICK

Who's the real Adam Resnick? According to actor Chris Elliott, his long-time friend and writing partner, Resnick is (or was) an enormous Russian who doesn't speak very good English. "The rumor at school was that Adam had grown up in a small town in the Kaluga region of the Soviet Union," Elliott wrote in his 2012 pseudo-memoir, *The Guy Under the Sheets*, "and when the nuclear power plant there had its big meltdown, the radiation gave him gigantism—which was why by age fifteen he stood over seven feet tall, and was by all accounts still growing." According to the book, Resnick and Elliott went on to become comedy co-conspirators—a partnership that, Elliott wrote, soon grew "into a tree of fame, fortune . . . debauchery and a few murders."

Elliott and Resnick have a résumé that'd make any comedy writer worth his or her salt envious; their credits together include working as staff writers on *Late Night with David Letterman* during its golden age (Chris from 1982–90; Adam from 1985–90), the too-hip-for-its-time Fox sitcom *Get a Life* (1990–92), and the initially maligned but now celebrated 1994 feature *Cabin Boy*. Resnick has also written for *Saturday Night Live* and HBO's *The Larry Sanders Show*. But despite the prominence of their work, both men remain somewhat obscure figures, which only enhances their status as cult icons.

"I truly believe my career would have come to a screeching halt a long time ago, as opposed to the slow deceleration I'm currently experiencing, if not for Adam Resnick," Elliott says now. "Anything funny that has ever come out of my mouth, supposedly spontaneously, more than likely came out of Adam's brain first."

Born and raised in Harrisburg, Pennsylvania, Resnick spent a less-than-successful three semesters at New York University's film school before dropping out to intern and then write for *Late Night*, a show still in its infancy. "It was the defining moment of my life—the greatest thing that ever happened to me," Resnick says. "And probably the first time I felt like I belonged somewhere." Meeting Elliott would prove to be a large part of it. As Elliott says now of his burgeoning relationship with Resnick, "We come from different walks of life, and yet from the moment we met we both realized that we shared the same sensibilities, laughed at the same things, and were tortured by the same neuroses. We're two halves of the same coin—like Lily Tomlin and Jane Wagner."

It's not difficult to understand why their various collaborations didn't connect with mainstream audiences. It's remarkable that *Cabin Boy*—a movie about a "fancy lad" named Nathanial Mayweather, a flying cupcake that spits tobacco juice, a boat christened the *Filthy Whore*, and David Letterman selling monkeys to sailors (among many other oddities)—ever got made, much less distributed. It was a failure both critically and financially, but nearly twenty years later *Cabin Boy* enjoys sold-out special screenings at which Resnick and Elliott occasionally do postshow Q&As. Most of the time, they are greeted with standing ovations. They, and their comedy, were ahead of its time.

This argument could be made with almost all of Resnick's projects. More often than not, he was two or three steps ahead of the curve. Much of his work, such as the short-lived 1996 HBO series *The High Life* or the 2002 Danny DeVito–directed feature *Death to Smoochy*, had surreal and darkly subversive worldviews and a giddy lack of morality, not to mention characters who were unapologetically unlikable. Sound familiar? Just look to modern comedy classics such as *It's*

Always Sunny in Philadelphia, *Arrested Development*, and *Eastbound & Down*. While remaining somewhat in the shadows, Resnick was paving the way for some of the best comedy of the twenty-first century.

As Elliott attests, "There are only a few people who think originally in comedy anymore. Adam has never compromised his comedic point of view, so besides loving the guy, I deeply respect him."

In 2014, Blue Rider Press published Resnick's hilarious, horrifying memoir *Will Not Attend: Lively Stories of Detachment and Isolation*.

What comedy did you enjoy growing up?

Growing up, I was always attracted to old movies—W. C. Fields and Laurel and Hardy and things like that. Screwball comedies from the thirties. I always loved the look of that period, from as early as I can remember. And the music—there's something about those Depression-era "cheer-up" songs that always appealed to me. So simple and bouncy, yet dark and wise on some level. And ultimately unrealistic. [Laughs] There's a 1930 song I love by Sam Lanin and His Orchestra called "It's a Great Life (If You Don't Weaken)." Good luck with that!

As I got older, and began to watch a lot of movies, I found I laughed the most at things that tend to feel real, rather than joke driven. Dramas like *The Last Detail*. Jesus, I'm pontificating about comedy already. Everything I was afraid of. And from the *Cabin Boy* guy, no less.

We'll get to *Cabin Boy* soon, don't worry.

Lovely.

You just mentioned the 1973 movie *The Last Detail*. What in particular did you like so much about it?

It's just one of those small movies that says so much about life. The directing, by Hal Ashby, is fantastic. And the performances are so good, especially Jack Nicholson's. Clearly, his character is funny, but he's not playing it for laughs. The dialogue is not about jokes. He's like someone you might meet in real life. I've known a lot of people who are funny characters, but they're not trying to entertain you. My father's a good example. People like that are usually a little tragic on some level. *The Last Detail* is ultimately a tragedy. Same with movies like *One Flew Over the Cuckoo's Nest*, *Goodfellas*, and a lot of Robert Altman's films, including *Nashville* and *Short Cuts*. Those two aren't exactly tragedies, but you know what I'm talking about.

How about contemporary comedies?

[Laughs] Well, it depends on how contemporary. Does a movie like *Election* [from 1999] count? What about [1995's] *To Die For*? As far as studio comedies, I'm not so much into ones that are specifically aimed at a younger audience. Even when I was a teenager, I didn't love movies like *Animal House*. There's a lot of comedy I enjoy; I just hate rattling off titles. Anyway, most comedies today are pretty much for college kids. I'm out of the loop.

Do you think you've changed? Or has the comedy changed?

Well, comedy has just become such a gigantic thing now. There's just so much comedy. Too much comedy. And it all has to be "relatable" or deeply rooted in current pop culture. The audience tends to want to laugh at things they've experienced—weddings, break-ups, hanging out with your buddies, that kind of stuff. For me, the smartest comedy seems to be on TV these days. Shows like *The Office*, *Parks and Rec*, and *Enlightened*—that show blew me away. Not sure I'd call it a comedy, per se.

With movies, a lot of recent comedies are all about this male bonding thing, featuring guys who don't want to grow up. It's all about seeing some version of you and your pals on-screen, hanging out and goofing around: "Hey, remember the time Keith puked all over the waitress at Dave & Busters? It was just like in the movie!" I can't get into that. Hanging out with a bunch of guys and cracking

jokes—that would be my worst nightmare. You realize what I'm criticizing, don't you? Happy, socialized people having a good time. So,
to clarify—maybe the problem is with me, not the movies.

**I, too, have always found that male-bonding obsession kind of strange.
In the real world, do the majority of guys really enjoy hanging around
only with other guys? Especially after the age of twenty-five? But then
again, I say that as someone who never joined a fraternity.**

Right. No, I was never one for male camaraderie. By and large,
guys are assholes. I knew that in kindergarten. I just can't relate to the
bromance thing. And isn't that a lovely term, by the way.

You were never a part of any cliques growing up?

From the first day of school, I couldn't wait to be an adult and get
the fuck out of there—to get away from the teachers, the kids, everyone. So, for me, I don't recognize anything particularly relatable or
truthful in teen comedies. Actually, *Fast Times at Ridgemont High*
did a good job of blending moments of broad comedy with something
that felt recognizable. But in general, I don't recall high school as being all that funny. High school is a deep, dark drama.

I went to a typical, middle-class public high school in Pennsylvania in the seventies. The thing I recall the most was that everyone was
angry—the teachers, the kids, the guidance counselors. *I* was angry.
And if you were a little weird—a "loser" or an "outsider," to use the
great modern comedy trope—you didn't hang around other losers
like you see in the movies. You kept to yourself. Sure, there were stoners and other little factions. But stoners, for example, weren't on the
outside. They were a decent-sized collection of kids who got along
and socialized with each other. This idea that nerds or geeks or losers
stuck together is a fantasy. And the *last* thing they were was funny.
This notion of people like that banding together, even if it's just supposed to be a comedy, kind of drives me nuts. I'm not sure any film or
TV show has accurately captured what school is really like—at least
how I knew it. Maybe *Welcome to the Dollhouse*. Great movie.

How about sillier teen movies? Like *Revenge of the Nerds*?

I remember kind of liking that movie—but just as a flat-out silly comedy. I'm not talking about movies like that. I mean comedies that try to wedge in phony sentiment and moments of so-called "truth." Especially when it comes to relationships. I really remember hating all those Brat Pack movies. Give me a fucking break. I never met kids like that.

Were there any specific comedy writers whose work you grew up admiring?

As far as TV and movies, I liked the writing on *Saturday Night Live*, *SCTV*, Monty Python—those were the big ones for everyone, I guess. Those were the 1970s touchstones that represented a new type of comedy that wasn't for your mom and dad. But, quite frankly, looking back, Paul Henning meant more to me than any of that stuff.

Paul Henning! Now there's a name I don't often hear as a comedic influence.

He was the creator of *The Beverly Hillbillies* and *Green Acres*. I've always had a thing for rural humor, I guess, but I got more enjoyment out of those old reruns than just about anything. And they were really funny and smart. *Green Acres* was surreal at times in a way that was very Pythonesque. I think Henning's humor came out of some sort of a vaudeville sensibility, or a southern Grand Ole Opry tradition. Some might think that the humor is corny, but it's a smart, knowing kind of corny. I wasn't so much a fan of *Petticoat Junction*, which he also created, because that had a bit of sappiness to it, but *Green Acres* and *Beverly Hillbillies*—hilarious. On *Green Acres*, the characters would sometimes comment on the credits as they flashed on the screen. Pretty smart material for the time. I really liked *The Andy Griffith Show*, too. So many great character actors back then. That's the type of thing that's deep in my bones, more than the dope-smoking comedy culture that grew out of the *National Lampoon*.

That's quite a leap from Hal Ashby and his movie *The Last Detail* to Paul Henning and his TV show *The Beverly Hillbillies*.

I guess writers have so many things that influence or inspire them. A lot of the time it's just subconscious. It's probably a mistake to think about it too much. In some crazy way, Henning connects to R. Crumb in my mind—and there's a guy who's really meant a lot to me.

How, specifically?

My five older brothers, who were big potheads, had a lot of underground comics when I was growing up, so I saw *Zap Comix* when I was really young. Probably the first pornographic images I'd ever seen. So there was all this acid-induced imagery of animals and weird characters fucking each other and doing strange things and it reminded me of the old cartoons I loved from the thirties and forties, but with bizarre, graphic sex. As I got older, I just really started connecting with Crumb. Not with his very specific sexual fetishes—God bless him—but for his honesty, what he says about life, work, art, the past, and the decline of American culture. How jazz died after 1932. [Laughs] I've been collecting that same kind of music since I was about thirteen. I've always felt a strong personal connection there that I can't completely articulate. Crumb kind of helped me escape into my own mind.

What were you trying to escape from?

I felt very isolated at home. I grew up in a very dysfunctional family. I always wished that I had had a sister, because I just relate better to women. In general, I think women are superior to men in every way. They're just smarter, more thoughtful, more compassionate. I always thought that if I had a sister, she would've been the one I could've talked to and relied on. It was an insane house. A hell house. Every one of us had padlocks on our doors because no one could be trusted. I can remember hiding the money I saved working for a landscaper, but no matter where I hid it—even in the gap behind the heat register that was literally underneath the floor—it would get stolen. I grew up with such paranoia. If you used the phone, someone would always be listening in. And whatever information was collected would be used against you somehow. Things like that were constant. No sense of privacy. Believe me, I'm not doing this justice. This is the soft overview. [Laughs] I don't have the stomach or the nervous system to go too far down memory lane with all the specifics.

Your situation sounds as if it was a step beyond the typical dysfunctional household.

I'm sure everyone has their stories. Most families are fucked up in one way or another. All I know is, I grew up locked in my room with my books and my old records, and I hardly ever came out. I tried to avoid all interaction with my brothers, and I didn't want too many friends. Sort of a self-imposed isolation based on my circumstances, but I actually enjoyed it. Maybe I would have been like that no matter what. I'm *still* like that.

How did you get the writing job for Letterman in 1985?

Well, Dave's probably the most important person in my life. He gave me my career—which I later set fire to—and basically gave me a reason to live. I was attending NYU film school and came on to *Late Night* a couple of years after the show started. I just cold-called and asked if they had any internships available, and my timing was lucky. I was able to work for Steve O'Donnell, who was the head writer at the time. He's a great guy and was hugely supportive. He bought me a lot of meals in those intern days. It really felt like a family back then. And Chris Elliott, who was already writing and performing on *Late Night*, became my best friend. Chris suggested I start showing my material to Dave. So I began to give monologue jokes to Dave's assistant—those were the days before he was surrounded by the goons with earpieces—and he really liked it.

What was your particular style of joke?

My jokes were barely jokes. I wasn't good at writing topical material, and it really didn't interest me. My material was more about

Dave talking about his white-trash relatives or telling the audience that he spent the weekend sitting on his front porch waving at trucks. A lot of it was just glimpses of things I knew from growing up in rural Pennsylvania, which probably intersected with Dave's Indiana experiences.

Eventually, I was hired as a writer and I dropped out of college. I still look back at *Late Night* as the happiest period of my life, with all due respect to my wife and daughter.

You make your TV days sound so easy, almost like a dream world.

No, it was a lot of work, but so much fun. And the luck of timing! I walked in there at the exact right moment and I happened to be the right guy. I went from an intern to a researcher in the writers' department, which was a paid position, and then I was promoted to writer. But I kept putting those opening remarks on Dave's assistant's desk. And I'll never forget the day Dave called me in and told me how much he liked them. It was a big turning point. Today, it would be hard for an intern to replicate that experience. *Late Night*, and I guess the world in general, was a small shop back then.

Also, *Late Night* was a completely different culture than a place like *SNL*, where you heard a lot of stories about drugs and things like that. Our staff was a direct reflection of Dave, a guy from the Midwest who wasn't impressed with show business and didn't act like a big star. We were all pretty grounded people. The most decadent it got in the office was too many cigars and too much talk about baseball.

What in particular did you find so appealing about Letterman's sensibility?

At the heart of it was his aversion to bullshit, specifically when it came to celebrities and Hollywood. You didn't really see that attitude before Dave. And it was coming from a real place. It wasn't an act or "shtick," to use a beloved Yiddishism. Dave loved doing the show, but anything beyond that was of no interest to him. He never cared about being part of the club or making friends with other celebrities—all the shit that a lot of people relish in the business. They fantasize about that experience. So my thing for Dave, even before I met him, was all about a sense of genuineness. Beyond that, he's still the smartest and funniest guy out there. Since *Late Night* became a big deal in the eighties, so many performers have borrowed the Letterman "aloof, cynical, wiseass" thing, but for most of them, it's not coming from as real a place. It's just a persona. And incidentally, I think Dave's honesty and decency is what cost him *The Tonight Show*. He would never in a million years make a play for Johnny's job as long as Johnny was still doing it. Whereas Jay was sneaking around and going to the affiliates and kissing their asses and all that shit. Dave's a respectful guy. He had too much admiration for Johnny. It's not in him to behave that way. He worked hard all those years and turned 12:30 into a lucrative time slot, and he absolutely deserved *The Tonight Show*. That whole thing was fucked.

How did you come to bond with Chris Elliott, who eventually became your writing partner on the show?

Chris was a writer and performer on *Late Night*, and he was there from day one; he started as a production assistant. He was already performing The Guy Under the Seats sketches when I got there. I was a huge fan, like anyone else who was watching *Late Night* at the time. Before I met him, I assumed he was probably a prick, based on his persona on the show. I could never quite tell if it was a put-on or not. He seemed a little Michael O'Donoghue–esque, the *National Lampoon* writer, who I heard was a real piece of work. Brilliant, but, you know . . . keep your distance. But he wasn't like that at all, and we bonded almost instantly. It was a strangely deep connection. We came from completely different backgrounds, but we had so much in common—how we thought, our sense of humor, the movies we were obsessed with, neither of us could spell. [Laughs] We were the furthest thing from Harvard boys.

You helped Chris create characters for the show. I watched some videos of these characters recently, and I have to say, I still find them just as funny as I did in the eighties—but I also find them just as bizarre and, in some cases, just as frightening.

I don't think Chris or myself—or anyone else who wrote with him—ever consciously tried to make something weird. I think a performer who's got a really original voice, like Chris, doesn't overthink what they're doing. The character he created for the show—and in all his roles he was basically the same character—had been a part of him since he was a kid. He told me that that's how he acted in school with teachers. But what really made it work on the show was Dave sitting there to his left. They were a comedy team in the great vaudeville tradition. Chris was the arrogant idiot who wasn't impressed with Dave, and Dave's reaction to that was just calm amusement. The audience, by nature, was always on Dave's side, so that's a funny dynamic. And quite frankly, it was pretty brave of Chris to always play into that. I think that's where the undercurrent of awkwardness or strangeness came in. You were never quite sure if you were watching a genuine uncomfortable moment or not.

I really think Chris was the first guy to do the modern-day Arrogant Idiot, which is now a staple with a lot of comedic actors. For me, though, no one's done it better or braver than he has. He came at it in such an original way—look at those early characters like The Panicky Guy and The Guy Under the Seats. How often do you see something that's not derivative of a million other things? Chris's work never felt like that.

The studio audiences during Chris's _Late Night_ performances appeared to be almost bewildered. Oftentimes, there was literally no laughter.

That's the risk you take when you're writing something that's more a cockeyed performance piece and less joke driven, although there were plenty of times we thought we had some real jokes in there and they died, too.

But there was never a victory lap for baffling the audience. We _wanted_ people to like the piece. And, most of all, we wanted Dave to be happy with it. Another thing: It wasn't that easy to get a laugh in 6A back then [the Rockefeller Center Studio where _Late Night_ was shot]. I don't know why. You really had to earn it. It was a smallish studio, and I think audiences were different. Whenever I see a late-night talk show now, the audience seems so ramped up. They've been conditioned to behave differently. Or in Leno's case, instructed to run up and shake his hand. Like he was Neil Armstrong or something. First day back from the moon.

Were you involved with the Marlon Brando character that Chris performed on the show?

I was. That came out of Chris and me hanging out and talking about Brando and how nuts he was and how terrible his later movies were, like [1980's] *The Formula*. Chris used to imitate Brando up in the office, but in a way that had hardly anything to do with the actor—it wasn't a classic imitation. It wasn't Brando the actor, it was Brando the mental patient. Brando the cartoon. I don't think we were that far off from what he was really like at the time.

I guess that would explain the dance that the Brando character would perform every time he appeared—a spastic shimmy around a pile of bananas.

The Banana Dance, oddly enough, came from *The Godfather*, but it had nothing to do with Brando. There's a guy in the *Godfather* wedding scene, and you only see him for a second, and he's holding a drink, doing this little dance—he's shaking his hand in a funny way, and both Chris and I remembered the guy doing this little hand movement. The Banana Dance was based on that.

To Chris's credit as a performer, he didn't really seem to care whether he got the laughs or not.

I remember Carrie Fisher was standing backstage once, waiting to go on the show. I doubt she'd ever seen Chris do Brando before, and he walked over to her—in character, in full Brando makeup, holding his little Styrofoam cup of coffee—and said something like, "Miss, if there's anything you need, please don't hesitate to ask. And I wish you the greatest success on your appearance tonight." She looked horrified. Another time there was an astronaut on the show—I forget who—and Chris, as Brando, just drove the guy nuts in the green-room, asking him a million questions and referring to him the whole time as "Mr. President."

Chris was always pretty fearless. But when a piece died on air it wasn't like, "Yeah! We got 'em!" He wasn't like Andy Kaufman that way. The goal was to do something different *and* get a laugh. And when it didn't get a laugh, you just told yourself the audience was too dumb to get it. [Laughs] Classic writer denial.

Chris once came out as himself—which he began to do more and more as the show went on—and he was telling Dave how he was earning extra money by working as a costumed performer on *Sesame Street*. He said, "I landed a new gig as Big Bird's left leg with another guy. There are two other guys who man the right leg, and another five guys up top." And Dave said something like, "Wow, who knew it was that labor intensive?" And Chris said, "Yeah, it gets pretty hot in there . . . so we work without our shirts." To me, that was really funny—the idea of it taking a sweatshop to operate Big Bird. There was also this touch of homoeroticism thrown in to boot—always a cheap, reliable go-to for Chris's character. Anyway, that got nothing from the audience.

Except in the homes of future comedy writers. Did you have any idea, at the time, the mark you were making on pop culture?

Not long after I arrived, we did a show that took place entirely on an airplane going from New York to Miami. When we landed, there was a big crowd of fans waiting for Dave at the airport. I remember then thinking that something was really clicking with people, maybe even more than we realized. But the show was popular almost from the start, before I got there. As far as being an influence on anyone, I don't think you're aware of that when it's happening. It's always looking back, many years later. But, yeah, I think Dave and a lot of the things we did on the show turned out to be hugely influential in the comedy world. I can see Dave's influence in commercials, on You-Tube, on all sorts of things.

The writing staff for Letterman in the mid-eighties was one of the greatest TV-writing rooms of all time.

A lot of really talented people. But the trick was being able to write for Dave, and I think the people who were in that room at the time were just about the only ones who could do it. It's a specific thing—Dave's voice, his sense of humor, his worldview, you had to share some of that to be able to write it. Merrill Markoe was really the one who came up with the template. She and Dave were the creators of *Late Night*, which started back with [1980's] *The Morning Show*. But there were a lot of great writers there in the early days who helped shape it: George Meyer, Jim Downey, Steve O'Donnell, Gerry Mulligan, and some others.

It sounds like you really enjoyed your time there. What made you eventually move on?

I didn't consciously decide it was time to go, but I had been there five years and was starting to feel like I wanted to do more long-form writing. I guess I was thinking about trying to write screenplays. I was definitely not interested in sitcoms. The thing about working for Dave, at least for me, was that it was such a great experience—a somewhat sheltered world—that it made it hard to leave the nest. And I think there was a little fear and a bit of contempt for what was on the other coast.

How did the opportunity to create TV's *Get a Life* occur?

Around 1990, Fox offered Chris a deal to create his own show, so he asked me if I'd write it with him, and because it was Chris, I thought maybe it could be something interesting. But I honestly never thought it would get past the script stage. We'd just write it and that would be that.

We started batting some ideas around, including a show where Marlon Brando moves in with a family and becomes a nanny. That was probably more for our own amusement; I don't think we actually considered it. But it was the launching point of something—the idea of doing something like an old sitcom. Then Chris started talking about a weird version of Dennis the Menace, where Dennis was a thirty-year-old man, and it grew from there—he still lives at home with his parents, he's a paperboy, all that.

We were talking earlier about how you don't necessarily enjoy comedies that feature characters who refuse to grow up. But wouldn't *Get a Life* be an example of just that?

Get a Life was about a guy who was a lunatic. We made Fox *think* it was about a guy who refused to grow up. At the time, in 1990, when we pitched it to the network, they were puzzled by the idea of an adult man still living at home. Wouldn't that just make him pathetic? Or mentally ill? I remember, later, Chris pitching an episode about his character getting his driver's license, and they were instantly all over that: "What thirty-year-old wouldn't have his driver's license?" Chris told them he was actually in the process of getting his. [Laughs] It was true. He was thirty-one, but he'd lived in New York his whole life and never learned to drive. His wife had to take him for the test. She was standing with the other moms.

If you could do it again, would you make Chris's character on *Get a Life* less weird? The character, over the course of thirty-five episodes, manages to set himself on fire in order to join a gang, hears children's voices in his head, and suffers hallucinations involving a roller-skating monkey who wears a gold sequined vest. Not typical prime-time fare.

I guess for the time, it was a little more acid-trippy than other sitcoms. Sometimes Fox would complain and try to shoehorn different elements into the show to make it more normal, like doing more stories about Chris teaching his buttoned-down best friend to "loosen up." But Chris's character was pretty much identical to the one he played on *Late Night*, living in the same strange reality. And we weren't going to change that. As far as some of the surreal bits on the show, maybe it got to be too much at times. I didn't love everything we did. Sometimes going weird is just the lazy way out. But, by and large, I don't think we would have changed too much of that.

In retrospect, would you have changed anything on Get a Life?

Well, I absolutely hated the pilot. That was all about trying to make Fox feel comfortable so they'd pick up the show. It just kept getting further and further away from what Chris and I wanted. Lots of cutesy moments in that first episode. I remember thinking, If that's what the series was going to be, I didn't want to do it. And I always hated the hot laugh track. A lot of people thought that was by design—part of the sitcom parody—but it was just shitty mixing. Way too loud. I don't know why it stayed that way. Generally, as proud as I am of *Get a Life*, I just never felt it was as smart as it could have been. A lot of the episodes are uneven. It never reached a real level of greatness, in my opinion. Maybe we were too distracted by the network beating us up or whatever. It really wasn't a good time in general. Chris and I had a lot of creative differences with certain people and weren't equipped to deal with all the politics that went into it. Again, this goes back to what I was saying about feeling insulated and protected back at *Letterman*. We were rubes and the show got away from us.

What sort of notes did you receive from the Fox executives to "improve" Get a Life?

Essentially, it was always about making it more grounded. I just never understood it. They knew what they were getting into with Chris. They gave him a show based on what he had done on *Letterman*. Why they thought he should be in something more grounded is strange. The whole purpose of the show was to satirize traditional sitcoms, not become another one.

I remember one of the executives being perplexed by the ending of the male model script ["The Prettiest Week of My Life," September 30, 1990], which was fairly silly and straightforward—Chris wins a runway contest. But the executive's reaction was, "I don't get it. What happens? So he becomes a fag?" [Laughs] Yes, that's what happens. He becomes a fag. Sort of like Lon Chaney Jr. turning into the wolfman. So, I mean, how do you even react to something like that?

There were also things like Fox saying Chris can't just be a paperboy, he should be the *head* paperboy. Their thinking being, a thirty-year-old paperboy, well, that's just an imbecile, but if he runs the whole outfit—hey, that guy's going places!

Have you ever, as a TV and movie writer, been saved by executives' notes?

I've had plenty of great notes from executives and producers over the years, and I've also had some bad ones. Like any writer. But with *Get a Life*, there were literally no good notes. There was too much of a creative disconnect.

An entire generation of comedy fans speak about the show in reverential tones, claiming that it was a huge influence. How do you feel about the cult status of *Get a Life*?

It's gratifying. When we were doing the show, there was no sense that anyone was watching. There was no buzz about it. It felt like a failure on every level. Coming from *Late Night*, I knew what it was like to work on a show that people were talking about. That feeling didn't exist with *Get a Life*. So the fact that it's had something of an afterlife is a nice thing. Most of that is due to Chris's fan base, I think. And I don't mean to sound so down on it. We did some good work on the show. We had a lot of good writers. Spent a lot of late nights eating ravioli out of Styrofoam take-out containers. Then I'd drive the forty-five minutes back home, from Sunset Gower Studios in Hollywood to my apartment in Santa Monica, at three in the morning, taking Sunset the whole way because I didn't know the freeways yet. Cherished memories.

***Cabin Boy* is another so-called "cult classic." Can you tell me how that movie, released in 1994, came about?**

Tim Burton was a big fan of Chris's. He knew his work from Letterman and had seen *Get a Life* and wanted to meet with him. So Chris brought me along. It was a fateful moment for both of us. Like when the guys in *Deliverance* pull the canoe over to take a rest. In a nutshell, Tim was about to shoot the first Batman movie, and he decided that for his next movie, he wanted to go back to a simpler time and direct a small comedy like he had done with *Pee-wee's Big Adventure*. So we batted around a few things and somewhere in the process of talks and various meetings Chris and I pitched a movie that would be a cross between [the 1937 movie] *Captains Courageous* and the Ray Harryhausen films, like [1963's] *Jason and the Argonauts*.

We specifically were trying to come up with "Tim Burton–type ideas" and that one stuck. Tim loved it. So Chris and I were very excited; this was a nice little gig after the emotional toll of *Get a Life*—Chris starring in a Tim Burton movie and me writing it. Writing features had been my goal all along, and even though this wasn't something I personally would have written if I were pitching or writing a spec, it was for Tim Burton. After this, I'd be able to write my own ticket! So Chris and I broke the story and I went off to write the script. When I was done, Tim and his producers went crazy for it. I'd never been showered with so many compliments in my life. They sent a gigantic fruit basket with a note that literally said, GREAT JOB! YOU DID IT! I was so emboldened by the prospects of *Cabin Boy*, I immediately sat down and started writing my next script—a 1950s period drama about an incestuous brother and sister that takes place down south on a worm farm. That's not a joke; that was a real project.

Anyway, everything was moving along just fine, and then I got a call one day saying Tim had changed his mind about *Cabin Boy*. He no longer wanted to direct it; he wanted to produce it. He felt it was more of a "Chris and Adam thing." In fact, in an incredible moment of generosity and wrongheadedness, he'd decided that *I* should direct it. Now for the record, as if anyone gives a shit, I was absolutely against that idea. My plan was to sit back and watch my stock rise after writing the smash-hit, Tim Burton–directed *Cabin Boy*, and then collect on that by directing my indie worm farm drama. Anyway, the more I resisted directing it, the more Tim's producers and my agents pushed me to do it: "How often does an opportunity like this come up? You'll regret it for the rest of your life!"

I have to say, that does sound like an opportunity that does not come along often.

Right. And I started to become paranoid that I was sabotaging myself and that I never made the right decisions and that I was a coward and my own worst enemy. And if I didn't do it, everyone would lose faith in me and they'd never want to work with me again. That's basically my brain all day long. So in the spirit of self-improvement, I started to believe what they were saying. Maybe this *was* the right thing for me to do. Maybe Jesus himself was speaking through these Hollywood people, gently leading me down the right path. So Chris and I talked about it—he was always supportive of me directing the movie—and suddenly I was on board.

What was the shoot for *Cabin Boy* like?

Well, an interesting thing happened—it actually occurred during preproduction but continued throughout the process. I realized I didn't like directing. See, I don't really like being around people, and that phenomenon tends to come into play when you're directing a movie. The endless meetings and questions, I just have no stomach for that. And this was a technical movie to a degree, with *special effects*. Shitty effects, but still, I was sitting in three-hour meetings to determine the scale of a stop-motion ice monster. I have zero fascination for stuff like that. I was not one of those kids who took their toys apart to see how they worked. I could not have cared less. Look, the whole thing was doomed from the start. It was done for the wrong reasons—by everybody. And it was a valuable lesson—never do anything just for the opportunity. Always go with your gut—your original instinct. But then again, my gut fails me constantly, so maybe there is no lesson.

Do you think if it had been a script that you specifically wrote for yourself to direct, you would have enjoyed it more?

Probably so. A smaller movie. With a much smaller ice monster.

I was going through some of the newspaper reviews for *Cabin Boy* from that time, and I couldn't quite believe the headlines. Criminals who

murder their families don't receive this level of hatred. "Ugly Cabin Boy Should Be Forced to Walk the Plank," *Fort Lauderdale Sun-Sentinel.* "Cabin Boy Drowns in Nonsense," *The Oregonian.* And my personal favorite: "Who Gave These Morons a Camera?" from *The Fresno Bee.*[1]

[Laughs] Well, who am I to argue with that? Chris and I will never understand why it pissed people off so much. If it were just a simple case of a B movie coming out that bombed and got shitty reviews, fine. I'm pretty sure that happens all the fucking time. But this was something different; this was supernatural. [Tom Green's 2001] *Freddy Got Fingered* will be gone and forgotten one day, but *Cabin Boy* will be infuriating people for generations.

It really put both Chris and me in a dark, awful place for a long time. Our mental states were really off. It was so confusing—why was this silly little movie even on anyone's radar? Why would critics put so much effort and passion into destroying it? It's not like the world was clamoring for this thing and then felt burned.

The day *Cabin Boy* came out, reviews started coming through my fax machine, sent from the Disney publicity department—Disney had produced the movie. It got to the point that whenever I heard the fax machine click on I'd run out of the room. All day long, the reviews would slowly roll out. How many times could I read the headline, "Cabin Boy Sinks"? For days, I was too embarrassed to leave the apartment. And when I did, it felt like my neighbors and everyone on the street averted their eyes when they saw me. I mean, I actually felt I was seeing that happen. I was gone.

And yet, here we are, years later, and *Cabin Boy* has a cult following.

With *Get a Life*, the cult became apparent not too long after it stopped airing. *Cabin Boy* took a lot longer. I think the best thing

---

1 *The Fresno Bee*, March 21, 1994: "Yearn to experience botulism, but just can't bring yourself to open a tin of spoiled meat? Try *Cabin Boy* instead. This movie gives you all the hallucinatory, nonsequential and senseless perceptions that come as a byproduct of a severe bacterial infection, without the chance that you might actually, you know, die. . . ."

that's happened is, Chris and I finally feel okay with it. For a long time we disowned it. If everyone was saying it was that bad, it had to be that bad. But as time went on, more and more people started telling me how much they liked it. Here in New York, Cinema Village and the Ninety-second Street Y did some *Cabin Boy* screenings a while ago, and they invited Chris and me to do a Q&A afterward. And we realized that a lot of the audience had been really young when it came out and had no idea about the bad reviews and all that. So when we talked about that stuff, they didn't really understand what all the drama was about. I'll never forget this nice girl came up to me and looked me in the eyes and said, "Stop being so hard on yourself." [Laughs] It was probably the nicest thing anyone's ever said to me.

Can you see influences from *Cabin Boy* on comedies that came after? Say, the bizarreness on Adult Swim shows? Or with something like 2012's *Tim and Eric's Billion Dollar Movie*, another fan favorite, but one that many critics thought went too far?

I haven't seen that movie, but I doubt anyone was influenced much by *Cabin Boy*. Some people may have liked it, but I can't see it inspiring anyone to go out and create. [Laughs] I don't know. There are a few bands and some hip-hop guys who were into it. The dialogue's been sampled a few times.

How bad was the post–*Cabin Boy* funk for you? Did it prevent you—

Oh . . . can you hang on a sec?

Sure.

[Silence on the other end of the phone line]

Hello?

Did you hear that?

Hear what?

The prostitute screaming.

[Long pause] Are you joking?

No.

Where the hell are you?

My office.

Your office? Where's your office, the red-light district?

On the Upper West Side [in New York City]. It's a tiny studio apartment I rent to get away from home to write. I've never seen her, but I hear her all the time. The walls are so thin. She entertains businessmen during the day. The doorman says it's actually a mother and daughter, and they're both prostitutes. They work separately. They sublet it from some weird guy who's hardly ever there.

I'm, uh . . . this wasn't in your official bio. This actually sounds like a character from Cabin Boy. So . . . does this in any way prevent you from writing? I would think a prostitute screaming would be the opposite of having a white-noise machine.

I liked it at first, but it's just annoying now. And they both have a habit of letting the door slam whenever they leave, and my whole apartment shakes. Prostitutes can be so boorish these days.

The glamour of being a writer.

I guess.

You don't mind being in a room alone all day writing?

No, being alone has always been my MO. There are times, though, if I'm depressed about whatever—and I'm frequently depressed—when I suddenly feel a little lonely and isolated. But then I just go for a walk. I actually think I'd do quite well at Gitmo.

Do you think it hurts your career to be a TV and movie screenwriter in New York rather than in LA?

I guess it doesn't help, but I just can't live out there. And I'm out in LA at different times throughout the year, so it's okay. I love my life in New York and it's where my wife and I wanted our daughter to grow up. So it's a trade-off.

What are you working on now? How do you spend most of your time?

I'm in the middle of writing a screenplay and a memoir [*Will Not Attend*, Blue Rider Press, 2014]. Also, I just finished a pilot for ABC that didn't get picked up.

What was it about?

A nice girl who works in a candy shop in Cape May, New Jersey, gets falsely accused of murder. She's eventually exonerated, but now she's tarnished; a lot of people in town still believe she did it. In retrospect, I think it was a subconscious love letter to Fatty Arbuckle. Maybe I should repitch it that way.

How does pilot season work?

It's a long process that starts around June or July. If you're not writing on spec, you typically find a producer you think would be a good creative match and talk about your idea. If they like it, you take it to a studio. If the studio likes it, you pitch it to the network. If they get onboard, you have to write the script.

But that's no guarantee that the script, even though it was bought, will ultimately be shot and broadcast, right?

No, not at all. In fact, the odds are against it. Studios and networks buy a ton of scripts each pilot season. A fraction of those will get shot, and only a small handful will get episode orders.

Does it work differently with movie scripts?

It's complicated, but in general, the odds are always stacked against getting something produced. And the less commercial the idea, the lower the odds. It's a tough business, but I think it's always been that way. The people putting out money expect to make money. It's a pretty square deal. It's logical. Still, creative people, like myself, will never stop bitching about not selling something or not getting a project produced and crying, "How can they make that other piece of shit when my thing is so much better?" That's normal. You can't think logically when it comes to something you're passionate about. All you can do is keep trying. And write a lot of projects you're *not* passionate about to pay the bills. [Laughs]

Over the years, you've sold two other movie scripts, not including *Cabin Boy*, that were produced: *Lucky Numbers* [2000] and *Death to Smoochy* [2002]. Were you happy with the way either of those films turned out?

No. But this goes to what I was kind of just rambling about. I sold those as pitches. And the end result was extremely painful for me—embarrassing even—but sometimes I have to make myself stand back and look at the business transaction I entered into: I sold an idea, essentially. After I gave them the script, it had nothing to do with me anymore. I got paid; that was the deal. Any further creative involvement was at the discretion of the director—and, of course, the writer doesn't get to choose the director. In the case of those films, I was brought into the process, but it was nothing like a true collaboration, and the directors saw those movies differently than I did. I can bitch all day long about how much better the scripts were, and, believe me,

I did plenty of that, but in the end, you have to accept what the rules were going in. It's not easy, though.

You know what? Maybe it's time for a blow-off question. [Laughs] I can feel my serotonin levels plummeting.

What's the current status of the worm farm script?

I haven't picked it up in awhile, but I'm going to do another pass on it. I've done several, which is always a good sign. Darren Aronofsky [the director of *The Wrestler* and *Black Swan*] read my last draft and really liked it.

And does he want to make it?

Oh, God no.

We never got a chance to discuss your HBO show, *The High Life*.

Let's save that for the new volume. I can't stand to hear the sound of my voice any longer.

Any last words?

I mentioned I wasn't a fan of the Brat Pack movies, right? Look, here's the thing—if you're in this business and you can cover your overhead by writing exactly what you want, you're living the dream. And if you're getting *rich* by writing what you want, you're in an enviable position. But for most writers, it's usually a compromise. The good news is, there's always a chance that everything will click on some project and you'll be happy creatively. And that's what keeps you writing, I guess. For me, every day that I'm not living back in Harrisburg is a victory.

Thanks for doing this, and please give my best to the prostitute.

Oh, I'm going to give her a little something more than that, if you know what I mean. There you go—comedy.

PAUL FEIG

Creator/Writer, *Freaks and Geeks*; Director, *The Office*,
Arrested Development, *Bridesmaids*, *The Heat*; Producer,
Peanuts movie; Author, *Kick Me*, *Superstud*

···
Writing a TV-Series Bible

In 1999, you wrote a series bible for *Freaks and Geeks*. Sometimes called a "character bible" or a "show bible," a series bible is a reference guide that a writer puts together when pitching a new show to networks. It includes details about the show's characters, setting, plot points, and other minutiae. Can you talk about how yours came about?

The bible for *Freaks and Geeks* was for the executives, of course, but I mostly wrote it for me. When you're thinking of something for so long and you have a million thoughts in your head and you keep taking notes—and especially when a show is based on truth, something you actually went through—a series bible is almost this stream of consciousness way to dump all that stuff out and then organize it.

As a writer, all you can really do is to write honest work. You have to really put yourself in the head of your characters, so anything that helps you do that is great. And this really helped me do that.

It was also really a great way to show the writers for the show what I was imagining, what I wanted the show to be. I wanted to let the writers see the continuity of it all. Also, it was for production design, wardrobe, and the sound of the show; I wanted to portray a very specific look and sound. I went through all my old seventies yearbooks and put Post-it notes in them. I still have the yearbooks and they still have all the Post-its.

At the time that I wrote the bible for *Freaks*—this would be the late 1990s—there was a tendency for Hollywood to think, Oh, everything was crazy in the 1970s. It was all leisure suits and disco and all that. And I was like, "No, that's not how it looked. That's not how it sounded to me." So it was really important to me to kill that mentality. By writing this character bible, it was my way of saying, "Here's the guide to the seventies that I knew."

I had never been in charge of a show, and there was a terror for me of pitching to the executives and not having an answer or an opinion when they asked—or of having the wrong opinion. So it also became a way for me to sort it all out.

The details in the series bible are incredible, to the point where you write that the geeks are the ones listening to Electric Light Orchestra and the freaks are the ones listening to Rush.

[Laughs] Right! I mean, it was kind of a fun way to do it. I was surprising myself that all of this was coming out of me, and I was able to go, "Oh, yeah. I remember who liked this. I remember who didn't like that." It was all about defining who were the freaks and who were the geeks. For me, these were the two groups who had never been explored. Even when nerds *were* in movies, they were always the valedictorians; all they cared about was schoolwork. In reality, the geeks I knew liked music; they liked pop culture.

I went into this show so afraid of all that had gone before us, and really wanting to have a defense against the network, or anybody else, who was going to try to force me to do things that had been done before in all those high school shows and movies. And so I really needed to have real-life answers.

Executives will sometimes—but not always—ask to read a series bible when a writer is pitching a TV show. They want to get a sense of who the characters are and what this world will be like. But is it always worthwhile for the writer to create one? It seems like a tremendous amount of work.

Absolutely. It is a ton of work, but it's incredibly helpful to any writer. I'd recommend any writer do it, only to get his or her thoughts in some semblance of order. As a writer, you really need a solid foundation when creating a show—in essence, you're creating an entirely new world, inhabited by characters coming from your imagination. If the foundation isn't solid, everything will collapse. It's a very difficult process. Now, that's not to say that details won't change as the show progresses. But by getting everything down onto paper, and by then organizing this world into a cohesive form, it can only help you if the show is bought and later produced.

When you ultimately got the go-ahead for *Freaks and Geeks* and were hiring writers, what were you looking for? The show is infamous for having one of the best writing staffs for any nineties TV show, and included Mike White, who wrote the 2006 movie *Nacho Libre* and created HBO's series *Enlightened*.

When we were hiring writers for the show, I was not very interested in reading their spec scripts for other shows. I felt that I wouldn't learn anything about a writer if I was reading a *Buffy the Vampire Slayer* script because I'd just be seeing how they could copy somebody else's style. Plus, they would already have these characters at their disposal. I preferred to either read somebody's original pilot or original play or original screenplay in order to see the invention they were able to come up with.

But, keep in mind, that's just me. Most TV shows find writers from spec scripts for their shows. I think it is good to write a spec script, but to always include something original, too. That is really the hardest thing: creating characters from scratch and creating a situation from scratch.

As a writer, what do you prefer to come up with first? Characters or situations?

What happens with a lot of writers when they develop a TV pilot is that they come up with the context first, and then they fill in the characters. That's slightly dicey for a new TV show because the concept is only going to be interesting for so long. What the show really hangs on are the characters and what kind of a life they have. I'd much rather see a writer come up with, "I knew somebody like this." Or, "What would it be like if these three people got mixed together?" At that point, you can then ask, "Okay, what's the best context for them to be in? What situation?"

Are your scripts meant to be performed verbatim, or do you allow for improvisation?

I think the main problem I see with comedy is that a lot of it is overwritten and it's created by people who are very precious about their words. You get that a lot in television, especially with sitcoms where writers are very religious about, "You can't change *this*; you can't change *that*." So, what happens is, there's no life to it.

I do use improv, but sometimes that's just as simple as loosening the wording of a written joke or a sentence to create a kind of naturalness. It also has to do with rehearsal and how you adapt the script to the actors' personalities and how you shoot and how many different ways you have to shoot a scene. Actors are great and they can do scenes over and over again, but, at the same time, there's always going to be a freshness about the first time someone says or does something. You want to get to the point where you're capturing lightning in a bottle. That is the key to comedy as far as I'm concerned: lightning in a bottle. You have to capture that moment when it first happens, because that's when it's funny.

How difficult is it to capture that lightning?

It's hard. Sometimes it's hard just because of the technology involved with making movies and television, like not being able to shoot both actors at the same time. Sometimes it's hard because an actor's not good at doing it. But you also learn from the actors you work with. Some are amazing at being in the moment and others aren't. Some don't know how to handle it correctly, and, if that's the case, you adjust and find a way to make them fresh when it's their turn. Some are better right out of the gate. Others need to warm up. Everyone's different.

When you direct, your head is spinning. That's why shooting comedy is absolutely exhausting. That's why when you come to the end of a full day, you'll have one last scene, and you sometimes feel, My God, I don't know if I can get through it. The temptation is to just shoot it exactly like the script and be done with it. But whatever you do in that one moment is captured forever—you'll always have it—so you have to force yourself to make what is hopefully magic happen.

"Freaks and Geeks: The Series Bible"

(Written by Paul Feig, last revised May 20, 1999. What follows are excerpts.)

General Notes About the Series

This show must be *real*. The teens in this series will talk like real teens. They will never be too clever or grown up sounding. We don't want a bunch of teenage Neil Simons spouting off wittily. These kids generally engage in teenage put-downs, they overextend their language ("Oh, yeah? Well, you're a . . . uh . . . big idiot, that's what you are") and never talk in that writers' "Now that I'm in my thirties, I know what I'd say in that high school situation, so I'll give this kid a snappy comeback" style of writing. These kids have to deal with each other with whatever is in the lexicon of a teenager and nothing more (and despite the fact that most of us think "if I knew then what I know now, I'd really be cool and in control" the sad truth is that if we knew what we know now when we were in high school, we'd probably get beaten up on a regular basis because teenage bullies don't respond well to clever put-downs at their expense).

What They Listen To

Here are some of the bands that the freaks and geeks would be listening to in the Midwest in 1980 (the great thing is that, even though the groups divide pretty cleanly on what they listen to, there's lots of spillover in what they like, partly because of their siblings and parents and partly just because they're kids who are easily persuaded):

The Cars—geeks
Chicago—geeks
Asia—geeks, some freaks
Bee Gees—geeks
Black Sabbath—freaks
Blue Oyster Cult—freaks
Blood, Sweat & Tears—geeks
Eric Clapton—freaks, some geeks
Alice Cooper—freaks and geeks
Cheap Trick—freaks and geeks
Doobie Brothers—freaks and geeks
John Denver—geeks
Eagles—geeks, some freaks
ELO—geeks
Fleetwood Mac—geeks, freak girls
Foghat—freaks
Peter Frampton—freaks and geeks
Foreigner—freaks and geeks
Genesis—freaks
Jimi Hendrix—freaks
Iron Maiden—freaks
Elton John—geeks

Journey—freaks and geeks
Judas Priest—freaks
Kiss—geeks
John Lennon—freaks and geeks
Lynyrd Skynyrd—freaks and farmers
Marshall Tucker Band—freaks and farmers, some geeks
Meat Loaf—geeks
The Steve Miller Band—freaks and geeks
Van Morrison—nobody
Moody Blues—geeks
Tom Petty—geeks, some freaks
Prince (early)—nobody
Rolling Stones—freaks for early stuff, geeks for "Some Girls"
Rush—freaks
Roxy Music—nobody who'd admit it
Santana—freaks and geeks
Carly Simon—teachers
Simon & Garfunkel—teachers
Patti Smith—"Creem"-reading freaks
Bruce Springsteen—not very big in Midwest, some cooler geeks
The Police—freaks, a few geeks
Supertramp—geeks, some freaks
Jethro Tull—freaks
Queen—freaks and geeks
James Taylor—geeks, some freak girls
Jackson Brown—geeks, freaks who smoke lots of pot
Van Halen—freaks
Paul McCartney and Wings—geeks, some freaks
Yes—freaks, some geeks
ZZ Top—freaks, some geeks
Frank Zappa—only the coolest of freaks
Billy Joel—geeks
Bob Seger—geeks, some freaks
J. Geils Band—freaks for early stuff, geeks for "Centerfold" era
Led Zeppelin—freaks
April Wine—freaks, some geeks, lots of Canadians
Jeff Beck—cool freaks

Robin Trower—freaks
Three Dog Night—geeks
B-52s—nobody
Devo—very cool geeks
Elvis Costello—moody geeks, some freaks
Talking Heads—some geeks, some freaks, mostly no one
The Romantics—geeks, a few freaks
Sex Pistols—no one knows about them
The Ramones—them either

What They Wear

Overall note is that all the students will have about four or five outfits they will wear all the time. Pants can stay the same a lot of the time, shirts change daily (except for some poorer kids). Even cool kids and rich kids shouldn't have a lot of different changes. Bottom line, all these kids are blue collar or lower end white collar.

The Geeks

In general, the geeks try to dress well but just don't quite pull it off. Maybe if they were better looking or cooler guys, their clothes would make them attractive. But on them, no matter what they wear, it somehow doesn't work.

Sam

Overall look: Sam looks like a kid who cares about how he looks but only up to a point. He dresses more for comfort and his fashion sense is limited to knowing what other kids are wearing and then trying to approximate their look. He thinks he looks better than he does in his clothes (everything looks fine to him from head-on in the mirror but he doesn't see that what he can't see doesn't really hang well). He's not so much rumpled as the victim of poorly made clothes.

<u>Shirts</u>: Pullover Velour V-neck shirts with collar (a little baggy and ill-fitting), short-sleeved knit pullover with zipper V-neck and collar (white stripe on edge of collar and sleeves), terrycloth pullover with two- or three-button V-neck and collar (shoulder pieces are darker color than rest of shirt, with a stripe on each upper arm), not usually tucked in.

<u>Pants</u>: Brown, green, burgundy jeans, never denim blue jeans (until second season), occasionally polyester slacks.

<u>Shoes</u>: Tan suede earth shoe hybrids with rimpled soles (remember those things? The soles were shaped like two "w's" and the whole shoe looked kinda pumped up like a loaf of bread—see Paul Feig for details), dark suede tennis shoes (occasionally).

<u>Coat</u>: Parka, faux–Members Only jacket (maybe), windbreaker with stripe or father's sporting goods store logo embossed on back (cheap, low-end looking).

<u>Accessories</u>: Always a belt, sometimes with a large copper novelty belt buckle (like a train or Model T car or a tennis racket).

Bill

<u>Overall look</u>: Bill's pretty much a mess. But not a sloppy guy. His family isn't very well off but his mother tries to dress him nice. The result is a lot of clothes from the irregulars bin. He looks like a guy who leaves the house neat but immediately becomes unkempt. Bill is so unaware of his clothes that you get the feeling he doesn't care what he wears.

<u>Shirts</u>: Plaid cowboy shirts, sweater vests (Bill tries to take his fashion cues off of Neal but it's always off a bit), brightly printed button-up shirts, pullover shirts that no one else would buy (different color swatches sewn together, weird patterns patchworked into solid colors, stuff from the irregular bin).

<u>Pants</u>: Off brand jeans, rumpled khakis, occasionally vertically-striped pants.

<u>Shoes</u>: Orthopedic black dress shoes (not jokey looking—just sensible-looking shoes), suede gym shoes (Tom Wolf brand—see Paul Feig for explanation).

<u>Coat</u>: A beat-up, hand-me-down football/baseball jacket with the name of the school on it.

Lindsay

<u>Overall look</u>: Lindsay is trying very hard to look like a freak. She pulls it off very effectively but there's always something a little studied about her look. She dresses down but her clothes are always pretty clean. She tries to be sloppy but can't help primping and neatening herself. A lot of her clothes come from her father's sporting goods store, so they're rather new looking. You'd have to look close to see that she's not truly a freak, but it shows.

<u>Shirts</u>: T-shirts (flower-embroidered, band logo iron-ons), thermal underwear shirts, solid color sweaters (occasionally cowl neck), button-up plaid shirts (tucked in).

<u>Pants</u>: Bell bottom jeans, old painters pants, overalls.

<u>Shoes</u>: Black suede rubber-soled shoes, clogs, old running shoes.

<u>Coat</u>: Old plaid hunting jacket, army field jacket, old worn parka, long wool coat.

<u>Accessories</u>: Worn knapsack for books.

Daniel

<u>Overall look</u>: Daniel has the original grunge look, before it had a corporate name.

<u>Shirts</u>: Plaid flannel shirts with T-shirts underneath (usually black T-shirts).

<u>Pants</u>: Bell bottom jeans.

<u>Shoes</u>: Work boots, old sneakers, snowmobile boots in the winter.

<u>Coat</u>: An old army field jacket, an old sweatshirt under his coat if it's very cold out.

<u>Accessories</u>: Scarf, snowmobile gloves, never wears a hat (it would mess up his afro), a large afro pick is always in his back pocket (although we never see him use it).

Things in the Background

In all the hallway scenes, there will be things happening in the background that typify high school (however, we won't have *too* much stuff going on in the hallway—we don't want it to look like all those period movies that take place in Medieval England where every street in town is filled with people doing activities typical of the era—you know, how every street in *Moll Flanders* and *Shakespeare in Love* looked like a Renaissance Faire was taking place—do we really think that every street in merry olde England had jugglers performing and bear-baiting contests? But I digress). Here's some of the stuff we'll see in the background:

—Two guys having a punching contest (punching each other on the arm seeing who'll get hurt first)
—Band kids selling candy bars
—Drama kids selling suckers
—Drama kids walking around in costume to promote the play they're currently putting up
—Freak couples making out
—Kids harassing the janitors
—Janitors sweeping the halls with red sawdust
—Kids trying to step on other kids' new shoes to get them dirty
—Students carrying wooden planters and cutting boards they made in woodshop
—Students trying to navigate the hallway carrying large sheets of poster board
—Student government kids hanging long painted paper signs advertising dances and school activities
—Freaks tearing the signs down
—Other freaks writing on the signs
—Students making fun of the pictures of former graduating classes hanging on the hallway walls
—Band kids carrying tubas and large cumbersome cases down the hall
—Hearing the school band rehearsing with the door open
—Freaks with large radios (but not boom boxes—just big cassette players or large transistor radios—all low quality)
—Hall monitors (usually women in their fifties who are constantly knitting)
—Science students carrying large science fair exhibitions to and from class

—Kids getting clean-outs from other kids (when you run up behind somebody and knock their books and papers out from under their arm and all over the floor)

—Jocks taking up too much of the hallway and kids trying to get by, not daring to ask them to move

—Guys checking out girls

—Girls checking out guys

—Kids getting wedgies (when you grab the waistband of someone's underwear and pull it up as hard as you can. AKA "snuggies")

—Tough freak girls harassing younger kids

—Girls laughing at anybody and everybody

—Teachers yelling at students in front of their lockers

—Freaks flipping teachers off behind their backs

—Kids tapping their friends on the opposite shoulder behind their backs to get them to turn around the wrong way

—Students in band uniforms

—Farmer kids tripping smaller kids

—Guys high-fiving each other

—A/V guys pushing projector carts down the hall

—Yearbook kids taking pictures of other students (the students pose by doing kick-lines, putting their arms around each other, standing and smiling stiffly, putting up finger horns behind their friends' heads, punching each other, or simply looking like they really don't want their pictures taken)

—Groups of freaks breaking up when a teacher approaches

—Guys delivering love notes to girls for their friends

—Girls coming up to a group of guys and telling one of the guys that some girl likes them

—Students imitating teachers after they've passed by

—Students giving other students "flat tires" (when you walk up behind someone and catch the back of their shoe with your foot, making their heel pop out of their shoe)

—Geeks carrying huge piles of books

—Students rushing to the nurse's office with a cut or a bloody nose

—Students from Commercial Foods class walking around wearing industrial aprons and paper food service hats

—Auto shop students wearing dirty coveralls

—Greasy-haired, dirty "stinky" guys (usually some form of geek—although often a farmer or a freak or just some kid who's a real outsider)

—Scary crazy kids that no one talks to

—Quiet mousy girls with no friends walking quickly down the hallway, clutching their books

—Drafting students carrying blueprint rolls down the hall

—Fights, fights, fights!

—Students on payphones

—Students who are dressed very nice (disco-style clothes)

—Students who are dressed terrible (ratty T-shirts, knit watch caps, old worn parkas, dirty jeans)

—Jocks wearing their school jerseys (usually on game day)

—Girls wearing rabbit skin jackets (short jackets with a patch-work of different colored squares of rabbit pelts)

—Students eating junk food (Hostess fruit pies, Nutty Buddy pre-packaged ice cream cones, Twinkies, cans of soda pop)

—Other students knocking the food out of the other kids' hands

—Kids burning other kids with the "If your hand is bigger than your face, you'll die when you're thirty" gag (the other kid puts his hand up to his face to check and you hit the back of his hand, causing him to get a bloody nose—funny!!!)

[Editor's note: Original version contains nearly twenty-one thousand additional words.]

STEPHEN MERCHANT

....

Stand-Up Comic; Performer; Co-creator, *The Office, Extras,*
Life's Too Short, An Idiot Abroad, Hello Ladies

I was always a comedy nerd. I used to spend a lot of time watching and dismantling comedy to see how it worked, what made it tick. It's about taking pleasure in the process. The fun of it for me is the work. And I don't really like work; I'm naturally lazy. But when I am being lazy, I feel guilty that I'm not being productive. With stand-up and writing, it's about trying to be good at it in the way that my heroes, the people I admire, are good at it. Like Woody Allen, who started as a stand-up and hated stand-up comedy, but his managers told him it was an important process in terms of a gig, getting yourself noticed, building your skills as a writer and as a comedian. It's this philosophy that keeps me doing it. "Oh, I'm just not good enough, I wish I could be better." You never feel like you've cracked it. It's like a tooth that keeps wiggling.

Woody Allen is quoted as saying, "Eighty percent of success is showing up." You can't sit around going, "Man, I would be the heavyweight champion of the world, it's just that I never got in the ring, but I have the physique, people have told me." At some point, you've got to do it.

Sitcom writing is a different skill set than stand-up, because narrative writing has a whole other set of difficulties and complications. There's a different grammar to it. I think sometimes sitcom writers struggle when they try to just simply take their stand-up material and dole it out among different characters. They just regurgitate their observations on airplane food. And if you look at something like *Seinfeld,* where it could've become that, in the end it's so grounded in those characters of George and Jerry and Elaine, allowing what would've been stand-up observations to be played out as real scenarios. The characters are real, not just simply making droll observations about a subject.

Everything's been done. I really think that. All you're doing is variations on a theme. There's an obsession with novelty and freshness, but often that's just repackaging something that people haven't seen for awhile. It's writing something that you think will be funny, that you will enjoy seeing. It *has* to be that to me. What would I want to see? How am I not being catered to? That's the way to do it, rather than something more cynical: "Let me see if I can find a gap in the market." That's just joyless to me.

So much of what we see now is market-tested within an inch of its life. The humor is fine, it makes people laugh, but people sense something missing. It feels mechanical; it feels committee-driven. And the stuff that feels personal and unique—even if the subject matter is very familiar—will become appealing as long as your take on it is specific.

In the end, it comes down to what is satisfying to you. It's hard because we're all seduced by popularity and we're all seduced by money and success, and those things are very alluring, and it's hard to fight that. But you've got to be careful because you might find yourself, five years down the line, working on something you hate—but living in a big house.

I always feel like even with the things I've tried that didn't come off, it was important to go down that alley. Every little avenue is productive, even if you've got to back up again and come back out. I always feel like even with the things I've tried that didn't come off it was important to have done it. Otherwise I'd have this niggling frustration that I didn't try. To me it's useful. Even the missteps are productive, because you're getting something out of your system.

DAN GUTERMAN

Dan Guterman may be the funniest writer you've never heard of.

Over the past decade, Guterman has written for some of the most respected comedy outlets in both print and television, including *The Onion* (1999–2010), *The Colbert Report* (2010–13), and *Community* (2013–). Guterman's also written for *The New Yorker* and coauthored two best-selling books: *Our Dumb World: The Onion's Atlas of the Planet Earth, 73rd Edition* and *America Again: Re-Becoming the Greatness We Never Weren't.*

Guterman clearly cares deeply about his craft: "Dan is one of the most serious funny people I know," says Peter Gwinn, a writer at *The Colbert Report.* "I used to make fun of a scene in the pilot of *Studio 60 on the Sunset Strip* when someone hands Matthew Perry a script. He reads it, and then with a dead-eyed, unsmiling expression, says, 'This is funny.' Because no one is really like that—no matter how jaded a comedian you are, when you read something funny, you at least crack a smile. But Dan comes pretty close. He's constantly thinking about whether something is funny, which to him is too important a pursuit to waste energy on laughing."

Carol Kolb, former editor-in-chief of *The Onion* and the person responsible for hiring Guterman, says, "When Dan started writing for *The Onion*, he was only seventeen years old—a baby! He was just some weirdo kid up in Canada who apparently didn't leave his apartment much, but his ideas were so great and so funny. There was no learning curve with him. He was one of our top writers right out the gate."

Guterman would go on to become the satirical paper's head writer, responsible for some of *The Onion*'s most memorable headlines and articles, including "Black Man Given Nation's Worst Job," following Barack Obama's victory in 2008. From 2004 to 2009, Guterman also penned *The Onion*'s weekly horoscope section. In his words, "They were the perfect vehicle for short-form dark humor." Guterman would spend one day a week crafting these perfect little jewels, an apex of sophisticated comedic thoughts distilled in as few words as possible. Some of Guterman's divination from the heavens:

Aries You'll spend your remaining years hooked up to a machine, which is sad, as it's the kind that checks e-mail and sends out texts.

Cancer Everything will go according to plan, except for the injured hostages, the brief shoot-out with police, and the fact that you were just trying to make toast.

Virgo You've never really thought of yourself as a cat person, but the splicing, trans-binding, and DNA resequencing will soon change all of that.

Gemini Your tryst with a married woman will come to an end this week when she finally asks you for a divorce.

Capricorn The stars fucking give up—if you want another slice of blueberry pie, just go ahead and have another slice of blueberry pie.

In his five years as the writer of the *Onion*'s horoscopes, Guterman penned more than three thousand.

When did you first become interested in comedy?

I was always making people laugh growing up, but I didn't know comedy was an actual *thing* until very late. It never occurred to me that comedy was something that I could do professionally.

I was born in Brazil, and my dad brought our family over to Montreal when I was seven. Growing up in Brazil, the only comedy I was exposed to was pretty broad: large men in diapers banging on pots while large costumed apes ran around in a frenzy. That's all I knew.

Brazilian comedy is lighthearted—it's not the comedy of sarcasm and subversion. So when I first saw *SNL* and *Kids in the Hall*, it freaked me out. It was so loud and aggressive. And it was played straight. It would genuinely frighten me.

Can you give me a specific example?

I remember being really unnerved by some of Jack Handey's work. There was one Fuzzy Memory, about a group of kids pretending to "play pirate," and that meant robbing innocent passersby with these immense machetes.[1] And that scared the crap out of me. I didn't parse it as a joke. I was ten years old and just horrified.

The Chicken Lady sketches [played by Mark McKinney] on *Kids in the Hall* were also terrifying. McKinney played a half-woman, half-chicken creature. It was strange and unsettling, and it imprinted on me in a very visceral way. It makes sense that I ended up writing

---

1   Jack Handey's Fuzzy Memory: "I remember when we were kids, one of our favorite games was to play 'pirate.' We'd dress up like pirates. Then we'd find an adult walking down the street and we'd go up to him and pull out our butcher knives, which we called 'swords,' and say, 'We're pirates! Give us your money!' A lot of adults would pretend to be scared and give us their money. Others would suddenly run away, yelling for help. We played pirate until we were twenty or so."

comedy that draws from darker themes. It had a big effect on me when I was a kid.

Were you a fan of Steve Martin's?

I didn't know who Steve Martin was until I was about twenty. [Laughs] I was totally out of the loop.

The movie *Ghostbusters*? *Animal House*? Any comedy?

No. My parents had nothing like that around the house. No records, no movies, no comedy books. I only found those things much later, on my own. Both of my parents have not-great senses of humor. When I was a kid, I remember my father telling a dirty joke—the kind you'd hear on the playground at school—and I remember him just howling with laughter. I would sit there, dumbfounded, as this fifty-year-old man would be doubled over on the ground. I mean, it's not like it's their fault. It was just a cultural difference.

When you finally did discover comedy, what became your first love?

I was sixteen when I found out about the *National Lampoon*. I discovered "satire" for the first time. And it blew me away.

I had no idea that comedy could be more than just jokes. That the whole thing could be in service of exposing some truth. Now there's nothing wrong with just writing a joke. A great joke is a great joke. But to realize that I could also say something that I believed in, or describe a worldview I shared, or attack a dishonesty that bothered me, through comedy—that changed everything. I was obsessed. I would walk from used bookstore to used bookstore to find old *Lampoon* issues. I'd be in those stores, rummaging through box after box of horrifying secondhand pornography to track them down.

Lampoon pieces like "The Vietnamese Baby Book" [January 1972] by Michael O'Donoghue were amazing. Just so daring and confident, but still measured and nuanced. Targets were introduced and then savagely cut down in a matter of sentences. Jokes like "Baby's First Handprint"—which had three fingers missing due to Agent

Orange—or "Baby's First Word: 'Medic'"—these were more than jokes, they were powerful antiwar statements *phrased* as jokes. To read something like that—something so unexpectedly powerful—was an incredible rush. O'Donoghue was using the rhythms and mechanics of comedy to articulate despair. It was so wonderful.

National Lampoon's 1964 Yearbook Parody [published in 1973 as a book], co-written by Doug Kenney, was also incredible. Youthful idealism bludgeoned by the creeping realization of one's own limitations. Dreams careening headlong into brick walls. It's all very painful and wonderfully funny.

The *1964 Yearbook Parody* proved what could be done with an intricate and sprawling work of parody. This wasn't just a short magazine piece, typeset in the style of what was being parodied—this was an actual one-hundred-and-seventy-five-page physical yearbook, complete with awkward photos, meaningless quotes, and desperate cries for attention. Kenney was creating an entire world, with a giant cast of characters, each with their own intensely average lives.

I think this was also the first time that I realized how effective patience can be. Instead of spilling everything at once, Kenney would slowly leak out details, here and there, until his portrait of fading adolescence came into focus.

Some of the *National Lampoon* material hasn't aged well. A lot of it is shocking and aggressive for the sake of being shocking and aggressive. But the material that was great is still every bit as impressive today.

How about more current comedic influences?

A year or so after finding the *Lampoon*, I stumbled across *The Onion*. I had just gone through a major depressive episode, and reading *The Onion* made me feel so, so good. It was incredible. It was like the *Lampoon*, but, you know, consistent. If you want to read the sharpest satire that's ever been published, track down every issue of *The Onion* between 1999 and 2002. The fact that I got to write for it when I was seventeen is ridiculous. I had no business sitting next to the geniuses who created it.

I remember when I was asked to take over the horoscopes. At the time, the horoscopes were being written by John Krewson, who basically created the model and is probably the most talented writer I've ever worked with. I had admired the horoscopes so much. To me, they represented the pinnacle of comedy writing. So when Krewson said he thought I could handle them, it was overwhelming for me. I just closed the door of my office and started sobbing. [Laughs] In a good way.

What about television comedy? Did anything excite you?

I loved watching *Late Night with Conan O'Brien*. The show would do these high-concept comedy bits on a level I had never seen before. Bizarre sketches that would lead out of the studio and into long pretaped segments. There was a summer episode performed entirely in front of a crowd of six-year-olds. It was silliness on a huge scale and treated with the utmost of seriousness. The perfect blend of highbrow and lowbrow. I couldn't get enough of it.

That was almost twenty years ago. It's crazy. I'm starting to feel like an old man in comedy. Soon I'll be totally out of touch.

Out of touch with what?

With what's popular with the kids. I'm not sure today's generation would go for the absurdist, slyly subversive brand of comedy that *Late Night with Conan O'Brien* did so well. I don't know. Kids today don't seem to want any substance in their comedy.

Would this hold true even for *The Colbert Report* or *Community*, two shows you've written for?

Colbert is a wonderful show. It's filled with great satiric insights on a nightly basis, but I don't know if the kids are watching it. And *Community* is maybe the rarest of shows—a network comedy that's constantly challenging itself both structurally and emotionally. Great, challenging comedy is still out there, but not as part of the mainstream. *Colbert* and *Community* are definitely in the minority.

[Laughs] You're talking like you're ninety. In fact, ninety-year-old comedy writers don't feel this way about "the kids" and their comedy.

Yeah, but I'm not a young sprite, either. I've been writing, without break, for fifteen straight years. *The Onion* snatched me up when I was super young. I'm pretty much done. I've put in my time. I'm very tired.

Tired from having to produce jokes every morning?

Yeah. The stress of constantly having to deliver takes a toll on you. Add deep-seated insecurities on top of that and you end up pushing yourself really hard. I have more than just pride in my work—it's an unhealthy, all-consuming obsession. I want to write a joke so good that it somehow rights the rest of my life. That's the nice thing about having demons. It makes you very productive.

Are you unhappy with your chosen career? If you weren't writing comedy, what else would you be doing?

No. I feel incredibly lucky to get to write comedy for a living. And I'd be miserable doing anything else. But writing comedy isn't carefree and lighthearted work. People think that being a comedy writer is nothing but laughs. And maybe it is for some writers. But for me, it's tied up with all sorts of complicated issues.

The interesting thing about comedy writing is that you're doing this very creative, often very personal thing, but you're expected to produce in this totally noncreative way. My job is to churn out comedy, which is this intangible and temperamental thing, but at the rate and consistency of an assembly-line worker. It's tough. Especially if you're drawing from an emotional place. Synthesizing trauma into entertainment can be great. But having to go to that dark well twelve hours a day is really draining.

What's the hardest part? That you wake up and have a bad morning, you're not feeling funny—maybe you've had a long night or a fight with

your wife—and you then have to head into work and create something funny?

Your job is to be funny whether you feel like it or not—there are people counting on you to deliver. You're there to provide an endless stream of jokes and pitches and ideas. You're there to feed the beast. And the beast doesn't care if you only got four hours of sleep. That said, I don't know if being in a bad mental space makes it harder to create comedy. Oftentimes, you can channel anger or distress into something really good.

There must be tricks you've learned over the years, right? Things that make the relentless demands a little easier to handle?

Sure. When you're exhausted, or feeling uninspired, you can sometimes lean on mechanics and joke construction. Things like manipulating rhythm to deliver a surprising conclusion, or escalating flawed logic, or changing the point of view of a joke halfway through—they all help to bridge the gap between moments of pure inspiration.

But that's getting into a whole other crisis: I wish that my writing was more organic. A lot of it comes from the demands of the job, of course. The crazy deadlines, the pressure one has to produce under—but I still worry that I over-intellectualize the way I write comedy. That I'm not *instinctual* enough. It's a hard thing to explain, but if I were to break it into percentages—and I think it's telling that I'm breaking it into percentages—my writing would be 70 percent inspiration, 30 percent math.

The danger, when you do it for long enough, is that comedy can become a series of variables in a mathematical equation. I know that if I balance the equation correctly, that if I manipulate x and y in just the right way, the end result will be laughter. Maybe some of that has to do with me being a left-brain guy, but the whole thing bums me out. You never want to generate material that feels soulless. It'd be nice to be the kind of writer who drew purely from a place of inspiration. I wish my process was more of a mystery. I wish every joke was a surprise to me as I was writing it.

Yes, but if you were to experience a huge, all-encompassing sense of elation or surprise every time you wrote a joke, you'd go insane.

Maybe. Don't get me wrong—there are still moments of incredible excitement. Especially when I stumble onto something I've never done before. Something that feels completely, totally new. Something where I can't say, "Oh, *this* joke has *this* type of idea from *that* joke, and *that* idea from that *other* joke I wrote." That's when it's really exhilarating.

How did the job at *Colbert* work? What was a typical day like for you?

Every morning there would be a pitch meeting where we'd talk about the latest news and our take on it for Stephen the character. Then Stephen would choose the pitches he liked the most, the writers would be paired off in teams of two, and then everyone would get sent upstairs to write up the chosen pitches into scripts for the day's show. Each team usually had a little over an hour to produce a finished script—which is not a lot of time. Working on the show was a huge adrenaline rush. You'd get back to your office with your partner and the two of you would instantly start pitching jokes for the script while the clock ticked away. It's definitely not a job for the faint of heart.

The show was really good for me. I'm in my head so much of the time. Writing for *Colbert* forced me to be more present. It made me a much better comedy writer.

So you would pitch jokes for the script aloud? How did it go from oral pitches to a written script?

One writer would sit at the keyboard, the other would pace back and forth, and both would start writing the script aloud. Whatever you agreed was funny would get typed up.

And you had only around an hour to do this?

[Laughs] It was crazy.

Was there an advantage to pairing up with another writer?

Writing with a partner was totally new to me. Basically, the show's process borrows a lot from Stephen's improv background. There's this philosophy when you do improv to never say no; to always be open to going down a comedic avenue that's been pitched to you. It's amazing how often we'd stumble onto something that was funny just by seeing where a certain train of thought would lead us.

Also, the nice thing about working aloud, where you're basically talking out every line of a script, is that it kept the show from sounding overly written. When you write alone, and have all the time in the world, you end up rewording sentences, editing and re-editing clauses, playing around with syntax—and your jokes tend to stiffen up as a result. They sound labored over. Your writing is more prone to feeling unnatural. The oral process at *Colbert* was great at preventing that.

At first it was scary. But after I had a couple months to adjust, I calmed down and really loved it. At *The Onion*, I was handed my assignment and then had anywhere from half a day to a day and a half to produce an article. The writers would just go back to their offices and shut everyone and everything off. They wrote slowly; when they were stuck, they left the building and took a walk. It was a process that fed on seclusion and solitude. But at *Colbert*, because we had to produce twenty-two new minutes of comedy every day, there was no time for that kind of luxury. There was no staring at a computer screen for twenty minutes in search of the perfect next sentence; you had to find that perfect next sentence in seconds.

That was the other nice thing about working in pairs. It was this amazingly collaborative and selfless process that allowed for polished material to be created quickly. You'd pitch an idea for a joke, your partner would refine it, you would refine his take on it, and in forty-five seconds you'd suddenly have a great bit.

And the only reason that this sort of back-and-forth works is because Stephen has created an incredibly supportive environment where everyone feels totally comfortable blurting out the first thing that comes to mind. We'd all say things we regretted multiple times a day, but we'd also end up saying something that would crack open a tricky idea or would save a script, and it was all because we weren't overly self-conscious. More so than the brilliance of the writing, it's the communal atmosphere inside those offices that makes that show one of a kind.

When I was interviewed for the job, I remember feeling like they were really happy with my submission packet, and that they had only brought me in to get a sense of what kind of a person I was. They know they've built this comedic Shangri-la, and they don't want to bring in anyone who's going to dismantle it. You get the sense that someone could be an outright genius, but they'd still pass on him or her if they were a fucking asshole.

How involved is Stephen in the daily writing process?

Everything goes through Stephen. Every word goes through Stephen. Depending on the day, he'd rewrite anywhere from a few paragraphs to entire scripts. What that guy is capable of is jaw-dropping. He made us look good all the time. You'd write what you thought was a great joke and then he'd read it and he'd laugh and then he'd instantly pitch a tag for your joke that was twice as funny as the joke itself. To be honest, I've never seen anything like it before. Comedy just poured out of him, and it all came out completely polished and perfect and unexpected and hilarious. And he did it at will.

How much of the interview segments on *Colbert* is written versus improvised by Stephen?

I'd say about 75 percent of his interviews are completely improvised. [Laughs] It's mind-blowing.

Stephen is not just riffing—he's riffing in the voice of a character that is simultaneously a conservative archetype and a comedic deconstruction of that archetype. And he's doing it while arguing with an economics professor, or a presidential biographer, or a botanist specializing in Amazonian plant life. The man is impossible.

What was the difference in writing jokes for *The Colbert Report* versus jokes at *The Onion*?

At *The Onion*, the goal was to never have something sound like a joke. Comedy was delivered as fact. Because of that, I was used to a really dry and understated approach. And you write jokes differently that way. You try to hide the mechanics of them a bit more. Nothing's ever written in set-up/punch line order. You're squeezing jokes into introductory clauses. You're mixing setups and punch lines together. So when I went to *Colbert*, I had to learn how to write a hard joke again.

What does that mean, a *hard joke*?

I just mean a joke that's going to get a big laugh. The advantage of print is that you don't care if your audience laughs or not. You care, but the medium gives you some distance. You're not standing right there when the punch line is delivered. So you're less concerned with whether it's met with a chuckle or a laugh or just a nod of appreciation.

But when you're writing for TV—in front of a live audience—you want laughs. I mean, it's pretty key. At *The Onion*, you can argue, the point was to make them *not* laugh. You were trying to phrase comedy in a way where at first glance someone would mistake it for a genuine newspaper article.

Writing for TV is a different skill set. It forces you to become a performer in a way. The timing is different when something is performed versus when it's read silently on a page. You become more sensitive to some things. Economy of language is really important. You can't weigh a joke down with extra words, or you'll lose that joke on TV.

And how about the difference between writing jokes on *Community* versus *The Colbert Report*?

A lot of what I did at *Colbert* translates to *Community*, but because *Community* is a single-camera show, without a live audience, I can also write the way I used to at *The Onion*. I can sneak in jokes that don't pay off right away or that a viewer might miss the first time. I love comedy that's a slow burn, where it takes a couple of seconds to connect all the different bits of information in a joke before it lands. There's this delayed reaction that is wonderful. Thinking. Thinking. Huge laugh. You can't do that for a show with a live audience—that's death. You can do it every now and then, but you don't want two seconds of complete silence after the end of a joke before you get a laugh. It's awkward. It feels like something has gone wrong.

The great thing about Dan Harmon, and the reason I wanted to work for him, is that he always puts the work first. He's there, day in and day out, trying to write the best possible twenty-two minutes he can. He's not concerned with reviews, or with how the show will do in the ratings, or how hard he has to push himself to achieve the results he wants. The only thing he cares about is quality. And I think that translates on-screen.

Community is also nice because I get to mix emotions. I like comedy that has moments of heart in it, or sadness, or fear. I like comedy that makes people feel different things while they're laughing. *The Onion* and *The Colbert Report* were the same way. It's what I'm naturally drawn to.

You just mentioned the word *fear* and have used it a few times since we began the interview. Are you a fearful person?

[Laughs] I was scared a lot as a kid, especially of animals. I was attacked over and over again by animals.

When I was fourteen months old, living in Brazil, my parents accidentally set me on top of an anthill. I got bit hundreds of times and had to be rushed to the hospital. I have no memory of that, though.

Then when I was around four, a monkey at a zoo threw a hardened piece of feces at my head. Again, no memory of it, but a traumatic event nonetheless.

The one incident I do remember was when I was eleven. My family and I went to the San Diego Zoo, where they had a Birds of Prey exhibit. We sat in this little outdoor amphitheater, and these falcons and eagles flew all around us catching food. At the end of the show, they had a place where you could pose next to the trainer and this bald eagle and get a photograph taken. Everyone lined up for the photo, except for me—I was terrified. So I stood maybe fifteen feet to the side. I remember picking up my head and making eye contact with the bald eagle, and two seconds later that damn thing was on top of me, clawing at my back and pecking at my head. I had to be rushed to the medical tent. I always thought the incident was telling. All that eagle had to do was make momentary eye contact with me, and thousands of years of raw instinct kicked back in—one glance and that eagle identified me as easy prey. That sums me up pretty well as a person. [Laughs] I cast the shadow of a trembling field mouse.

Do you think that comedy writers are more prone to fear and depression? Or is it just that comedy writers tend to talk a lot more about depression than those in other occupations?

It's hard to say if comedy writers are more depressed. It's definitely an image that's been popularized and, to a certain extent, romanticized.

For me, having someone laugh at something I've written is all about getting approval. Sometimes I wonder if I write compulsively because it's the most direct way I have of regulating my brain chemistry. It's all about overcoming a deficiency. Medication helps, but that hit of approval from an awesome joke or script can't be beat.

And it goes way back. When I first started getting noticed for being funny, back in high school, I would keep track in a notebook of exactly how many times per period I would make the class laugh. "Seven times, first period, Monday." And then I would try to beat that number the next day. There was never a honeymoon period with comedy. I took it way too seriously, way too early.

Talent, intelligence, hard work—they all help, but nothing sharpens your writing faster than the desperate desire for validation. Having your self-worth inextricably linked to your work may be unhealthy, but it's also responsible for most of my success.

Well, at least this particular compulsion is productive.

Sure. But, then again, I don't know how productive it is when I'm writing tweets at 3:00 a.m. after fourteen hours at *Community*. Apparently, writing on a critically acclaimed network comedy isn't enough. Apparently, I still need to be told by a complete stranger that I'm funny at 3:00 a.m.[2]

Has this compulsion to write jokes, at all times of the day or night, gotten more extreme over the years?

Actually, it used to be worse. When I met my wife, Mary, I was twenty-two years old, and I was living like an insane person. There was writing all over the walls in my bedroom. They were covered with joke ideas. God bless her heart. I remember when I went down to visit *The Onion* offices in person for the first time in 2000, Mary carefully transcribed every single scribble onto a piece of paper and then painted my walls white. It was the nicest thing anyone had ever done for me.

She's my life. I love her so much, and for a million different reasons. I was a disaster before Mary came along. Still to this day, if she goes away for the weekend, I instantly regress. Three hours after she's out the door, there's suddenly food all over the bedroom floor and I'm naked for some reason. It's terrifying.

Do you ever wonder where comedy will be one hundred years from now? I often wonder if it will be totally indecipherable to us.

I'm not even sure where it's going to be ten years from now. It changes so fast. But in the end—it doesn't really matter. Comedy for me is about expressing something inside myself. And the human condition will always be around.

I'll always keep writing, in some way or another, because it's the healthiest thing I know how to do. Emotionally, I'm a mess. There are a lot of things that I don't like to deal with, personal stuff—the kind of stuff we all face—and comedy lets me confront that stuff as best I can and hopefully get some relief from it.

---

2   A Dan Guterman's Tweet:
    I don't need drugs to have a good time. I need them to focus, avoid depression, endure spring, fall asleep, and maintain an erection.

In the end, do you think you'll ever find anything resembling consistent happiness?

I mean, it's a chemical thing. So I'll never be the kind of person who does cartwheels or stands around parks holding balloons. But that doesn't mean I don't love the life I have. Sometimes I don't remember to enjoy it enough, but I'm extremely happy that I get to do what I'm passionate about.

And I think it's getting better. In recent years, I've worked with comedy writers who are really balanced people, who approach writing in a shockingly healthy way, and they *still* produce funny work. And that's been really good for me to see, because it's proof that you don't have to be this writhing, screaming husk of pain to be a comedy writer. People who aren't tortured can also create satisfying comedy. It's just a myth I was brought up with, even at *The Onion*. This feeling of, "You shouldn't care if your life is a disaster. Go with it because it's only going to produce something worthwhile." I'm now realizing that that's just not true.

At the very least, I don't need to conflate so much of my self-worth with my success as a writer. It's tough. I've spent half my life writing comedy. It's more than an identity—it's all I've accomplished in life. I dropped out of school, there have been disappointing family issues. The one thing, the *only* thing, I've always excelled at has been my writing. But it doesn't have to be that way.

ALAN SPENCER

Working as a Hollywood Script Doctor

You've worked as a script doctor on quite a few major Hollywood scripts over the years. Do you know how much money those films ended up earning, collectively?

They've grossed more than $100 million. One grossed under half a million, but that was mostly from matinee business. Senior discounts knock down your average.

Can you tell me the names of any of these movies?

No.

So, as a script doctor, you're not allowed to talk about the specific movies you've worked on?

No, not in my case, because there are some confidentiality clauses. Many times, before walking into a punch-up session featuring a roundtable of comedy writers and comedians, we've been required to sign a form agreeing not to talk about the project or our contributions. If you don't sign, you're not allowed into the room. It makes you feel like you're in *Mission: Impossible*. There are some movies where people see my name at the end credits, and it will read, "Special thanks to," and they ask, "What's that about?" That's when I've worked on a project as a script doctor. Or maybe just brought a deli platter to the set.

Also, you know what? It's not fair to talk about these things, because it's not my work, ultimately. I didn't incept it. I don't have authorship on that. They're not even stepchildren or adopted—more like I'm babysitting. Unless the idea was generated by me, and unless there was a large amount that I wrote, then no, I don't believe my name should be on the credits as a writer. I tend to only want my name on things that totally reflect my sensibilities. Sometimes the original work from the writer who's been thrown to the lions is really good; it just needs some objectivity to remind everyone why they were drawn to the material in the first place.

My name is on a "Very Special Episode" of *The Facts of Life* [that aired in 1983], and the only things that remained from my original draft were the punctuations. The episode was called "What Price Glory?" and it was a heavy-handed treatise on illiteracy. A football star dating one of the girls [Tootie] was illiterate. Andy Kaufman, who was a friend, watched it and wondered why it wasn't funny. I told him because it was a "Very Special Episode." He asked, "It's very special because it isn't very funny?" I couldn't argue. Anyway, there's just so much inveterate credit grabbing going on most of the time that it should warrant DNA testing.

It seems like the best comedy writers in Hollywood—the most creative, the ones with the most singular voices—oftentimes prefer to work as script doctors rather than going through the difficult process of selling their own screenplays. Why is that?

You know what happens? It's the rejection of this business, of writing scripts you care about, either not having them made or having them not made well, and that starts to affect you. You want to win.

You want your original script to be bought. But if you're emotionally invested in your work at all, then you're in for a really rough time.

Maybe you're invested early on, but not after a lot of failures or unproduced works. And you turn into a short-order cook. You take a little pad and pen and go, "Okay, what do you want?" You start taking orders. And you do it to the best of your ability. If your work is—even to the slightest degree—personal, you'll always take it personally. There's a dearth of personal work out there. It's now a machine with easily replaceable parts. That's why there isn't as much hesitancy about replacing creative figureheads on their own shows. If Rod Serling butted heads with a network today, they'd fire him and call it *John Stamos's Twilight Zone* instead. Actually, I would watch that.

So what happens is that when you rewrite other writers' work, you're now detached. You don't know the baggage and the history and the in-fighting, all the personalities clashing. You just look at the work and say, "Well, here's what you need to do," and you get it going. If you disagree with a note or an idea, you don't resist. This is not *your* car being painted. You make it the best it can be, and they thank you. And you move on. You turn into almost a utility player, and you do the job. You get well compensated for it, but you don't have any emotional baggage attached. And you also don't have the same commitment of time; you're not going to spend years on a project. It's an easier life, and for me it just makes sense.

With the script doctor thing, no matter what you do, it's an improvement. You're brought in to fix something, and there's a sigh of relief. So you're Mighty Mouse: "Here I am to save the day." If it's better, then you know you did your job. And usually, invariably, the script's going to be better or more in line with what they want. And your career and reputation is not necessarily fully at risk, and you move on.

Who are you writing for when you take on a script-doctoring job? The studio executives? The director? The audience? Yourself?

All of them. You bring your own opinions to it. It's similar to the medical profession. You come in, you look at the patient, and you identify what's wrong. Then you describe what you can do to remedy the situation. You're a diagnostician.

In the end, the audience is a major factor. They're the final vote. You have a test score that you need to achieve. You have to bring this number up for the studio to be able to release the product. When you deal with the insecurity and the alchemy of comedy, you need an audience. They're the missing ingredient, so there's always going to be a degree of tension or misunderstanding without an audience to validate you. You ultimately need the vindication. There's a long-standing tradition of nervous executives in a room decreeing what is funny and what isn't—and then an audience enters the equation and casts the deciding vote. It's best to throw yourself on the mercy of that jury rather than argue your case. If people don't laugh, you've been found guilty.

What do you most often notice missing in the scripts that you doctor?

I've noticed that it's very important to have a wonderful third act—a powerhouse ending. Everybody walks out satisfied from that. It can't be a downer these days. It can't be like the ending to *Midnight Cowboy*. I mean, there's a reason you don't see endings in movies anymore like the one that's in *Midnight Cowboy*. Made today, Ratso and Joe Buck would be battling a multitentacled CGI monster attacking their bus.

But if a movie scores a very high rating with an audience, even with a sad ending, would the executives keep it?

Sure. The executives don't care about sad endings if they work. You can't take *Titanic* and reshoot the finale in order for the ship to miss the iceberg or just lightly graze it. But if the audience complains about it—if they're unsatisfied—that's a problem. And executives get greedy, too. A lot of times they'll want the film to score higher—higher, higher, *higher*. There used to be a rule of thumb that if a movie didn't test well it could still find its audience; that they weren't made with a cookie cutter and could still be big hits. Nowadays, if a movie doesn't test well, and even in some instances when it *does* test well, it won't be pushed by the studios.

Who is the typical audience for these screenings?

They tend to be mainly tourists in Hollywood. Everything's formulized, everything is distilled for them. They're told that the movie will be like *Parenthood* meets *Independence Day*. Or *Schindler's List* meets *Jurassic Park*, whatever.

I would love to see the test scores for that last product.

Might just be through the roof—after the dinosaurs were made more likable.

It seems that everyone—screenwriters, executives, studios—prefer landing on the side of safety rather than on the side of risk.

Everyone plays it very, very safe. As a writer, you want your material to be made and to be seen. It's an occupational hazard to confound or to be too outré on the page. For a writer now, security is pre-existing success. It's very important to have something tangible that was well-received to show executives. I've worked on a million shows and movies, and I've created two series, *Sledge Hammer!* [ABC, 1986–88] and more recently *Bullet in the Face* [IFC, 2012]. It's imperative to show something tangible to executives so they'll trust you and feel secure about whatever project you're bringing. Trading roles, we'd require the same. Getting notes from an executive with many hits under his belt feels very different than getting them from Ed Wood.

There was a writer—this would be the first time that this has ever been told, this particular story. There was a writer who sold a pilot to a network. He told them that it was the top sitcom in Ireland and he acquired the rights to it. He had the data and charts showing what a big hit it was and why, and how it made all this money and ran for years. He said, "You know, you can't watch the original show because the accents are so thick, the brogue is heavy. You'll never understand what's being said. But I have the scripts, and we'll retool it for America."

And this writer sold this show to a network in the midst of buying season, around 2005. It ended up not running, but it proved to all be bogus anyway. The show never existed in Ireland. It was a total con job. His presentation was so well-crafted and dazzling, no one checked.

How was the hoax eventually discovered?

It was not discovered.

So how do you know about it?

He told me.

***He* told you? The writer?**

Yes.

You don't have to name names, but is this writer in the industry? Is he well-known?

Uh, he's in the industry. [Laughs] He's got an IMDb page. Then again, so does Charles Manson. I'm not joking; check it out.

What does this hoax tell us about Hollywood?

I don't know. As the old saying goes, nobody ultimately knows anything. Actually, I think marketing people rule the day. They make the decisions. And they like to work with people who have produced something tangible that yields reliable data to analyze. There used to be a time when an executive would call the marketing people in and show them the finished projects. The marketing people would then describe how they would sell the executive's project that he had shepherded and green-lit. Now the marketing people come in and tell the executive what projects to make.

How content are you with your career? Are you creatively satisfied?

Well, I'm content because I've been allowed to do something original over the years. The contentment comes from doing something that's mine and stands out a bit. And I'd think that would be true for anyone: You have to pursue your own projects that no one else could write. Something with your name on it that represents your point of view and your opinions and your vision of the world—or, at the very least, what you'd *like* to see.

It's an interesting world we're in. And it hasn't changed all too much over the years. There's a biography about W. C. Fields that came out in 2003 [*W. C. Fields: A Biography* by James Curtis, Knopf]. There are letters that W. C. Fields had written to the studio about jokes, about his scripts, defending certain cuts, that sound like a comedian today battling an executive. No different. I mean, you could change the date and the language and the things that they're complaining about, but they're exactly the same. The Marx Brothers once battled the studios over a joke. When the executives saw that the joke wasn't cut and was still in the movie, they asked Chico Marx, "Why wasn't that joke cut?" And Chico said, "The god of comedy kept it in."

So it kind of defines what the relationship is always going to be: a comedian versus the executive. A funny person with one expertise and a business person with another. If either one tells the other how to do their job, tensions surface. So, you have to figure out a way to work together or trust things. You have to have a certain pragmatic and diplomatic personality, because if you fight with somebody, you have to remember, first of all, an executive's job is on the line. You also have to remember that it's not your money. If it's your money, you can do whatever you want. But you have to put yourself in the other person's shoes, and nobody wants a writer coming into their office, or into their world, regarding them as an idiot. That's not healthy, and some people starting out have an attitude they're going to war against decades of past battles. There's always a virtue to listening, and there are intelligent people in Hollywood. You have to be a politician and a diplomat. Also, a human being.

It is a struggle. There's always a system to buck. But there's a way to do it. I've been doing it since I was fifteen. You have to have an individual voice, even if you're script doctoring. You have to do it your way and put your stamp on it, so at the end of the day nobody else could have done it the same. The more personal, the better. The more that it's told from your own personal experience, the better.

Also, the moment you start writing things that don't personally make you laugh, you're finished. If you're just being calculating and hedging your bets, if you don't have any kind of belief in how funny it is and are just offering safe and easy laughs and nothing that can ever surprise, then you are done, you know? That's it.

PURE, HARD-CORE ADVICE

MIKE DICENZO

Supervising Writer, *The Tonight Show Starring Jimmy Fallon*;
Senior Writer, *The Onion*

I would say that the best humor comes from things you're passionate about. Write what you're passionate about, and what you know about, and it always translates better. One of my first big bits on *Fallon* was Jimmy impersonating Neil Young singing *The Fresh Prince of Bel-Air* theme song. I'm a huge Neil Young fan, and I'm a huge fan of nineties TV, it's what I grew up with. When you're able to take something you love and put a funny spin on it, it's always going to feel that much more genuine.

I definitely try to watch other late-night shows. I have some friends who work on *Colbert*, which is a great show, and I'll just flip around, or I'll watch clips that I see posted online. But more than anything, I think the important thing is to keep your own sensibility. You should always be excited about what you're writing. Because once you get to the point where you're like, "Ugh, this is a job, and I gotta shit out some jokes," then you're in trouble. It's good to take a step back and remember that you have an awesome job where you write jokes for a living. Of course, every comedy show has a certain quota of jokes that you just have to do. It is a job. But if you can find enough bits that you're in love with, that you're excited about, it keeps you invested and it keeps your sensibility intact. Because when you're excited to write something, you think, This feels right.

I always tell aspiring comedy writers, "Just write as much as you can. That's the only way you're going to get better at it." Do it any way you can—write a bunch of jokes on Twitter, start a web series, start a funny Tumblr—anything. Just produce funny writing and eventually it'll get noticed. All it takes is one person in the comedy business to notice you and find your stuff funny. I've been lucky enough to be in positions where I can help out people I thought were funny, and now a few of them work at *The Onion* and at *Fallon*.

And that's another thing: If you get any success in comedy, help out your friends who are trying to do the same but who might not have a job yet. I was lucky enough to start right out of college at *The Onion*, and I helped a couple of my friends get hired there. Same thing at *Fallon*. You would hope that your friends, if they succeed first, will help you, too. Help each other out, and everybody wins.

MEL BROOKS

In April 1969, Mel Brooks did something that would strike fear into any writer—he walked onstage at the Academy Awards and tried to follow the act of two universally beloved and iconic entertainers: Frank Sinatra and Don Rickles.

Brooks was no comedy novice. He'd cut his teeth on a show with the most legendary writing staff in television history, *Your Show of Shows* (1950–54); co-created (with Buck Henry) the wildly popular TV series *Get Smart* (1965–70); and written and performed on several *2000 Year Old Man* albums with Carl Reiner. But this was different. Brooks was up for Best Original Screenplay for *The Producers*, his feature debut as a filmmaker, and Rickles and Sinatra, the presenters, had the audience in stitches with their impromptu bits about cue cards and fascist Italians.

When Brooks's name was called—his competition included Stanley Kubrick and John Cassavetes—he accepted his award, grumbling to Rickles, "You did twenty minutes. You killed my whole thing already." But he eventually wrestled away the mic, and managed to do the impossible; he upstaged the bigger names. "I'll just say what's in my heart," Brooks said. "Ba-bump, ba-bump, ba-bump."

Born in Brooklyn in 1926, Brooks was raised by his mother, Kate. His father, Max, a process server, died of kidney disease when he was thirty-four and Brooks was just two. He was the youngest of four boys. Although they were poor, "so was everybody else," he says. When he was nine, his uncle took him to see Ethel Merman in *Anything Goes* on Broadway, and he immediately decided that he wanted to go into show business.

At twenty-four, he was hired as a writer for Sid Caesar, first on *Your Show of Shows* and then on *Caesar's Hour* (1954–57), where he worked with future legends such as Neil Simon (*The Odd Couple*), Mel Tolkin (*All in the Family*), and his future collaborator Carl Reiner. Brooks made a big impression on Reiner, who on a 2011 HBO special recalled Brooks's first pitch during a writers' meeting: "This guy I never saw before got up and started talking about his problems as a Jewish pirate."

Brooks went on to write and direct a half-dozen comedy classics, including *The Producers* (1968), *Blazing Saddles* (1974), *Young Frankenstein* (1974), *High Anxiety* (1977), and *History of the World: Part I* (1981). Regrettably, there was never a *History of the World: Part II*. Brooks has also written two hugely successful Broadway musicals based on his own movies, *The Producers* (2001)and *Young Frankenstein* (2007), and probably one more by the time you read this. He's one of only eleven people on the planet who belong to the elite EGOT club—artists who've won at least one award in each of the big four of American creative awards: an Emmy, Grammy, Oscar, and Tony. As Brooks once said in *History of the World*, "It's good to be the king." He was pretending to be Louis XVI (and his head had just been nestled within Marie Antoinette's ample bosom) but he might as well have been talking about his own life and career.

Brooks will never again have a moment like he did at the 1969 Oscars. These days, *he's* the legendary entertainer that nobody wants to follow. But Brooks isn't the kind of comedian to push aside younger performers or hog the spotlight. This was apparent in November 2012, when Brooks appeared as a guest on ABC's *Jimmy Kimmel Live* to promote the DVD boxed set *The Incredible Mel Brooks: An*

Irresistible Collection of Unhinged Comedy. The eighty-seven-year-old comedian didn't just let his considerably younger and less experienced host take the lead; he was also sweetly encouraging when Kimmel's jokes fell flat. "It almost worked," Brooks said after one of Kimmel's gags imploded. "It's a good premise." Dropping a less than casual hint, he added, "I wrote for *Your Show of Shows* for ten years, and I happen to be free now."

You might just be responsible for getting more people into the field of comedy writing than any other person in the history of mankind.

You've left out Charlie Chaplin, Harold Lloyd, and a couple of others.

Yes, but the writers' room at *Your Show of Shows* is seen as the equivalent of the 1927 Yankees—as good as it gets. The image of bantering with writers of such talent, I'm sure, influenced more than a few writers to get into the comedy field.

Maybe, but it wasn't all fun and laughs. It wasn't all like [the 1993 Neil Simon play] *Laughter on the 23rd Floor.* We worked hard. There was a hostility in the air. It was very highly charged. It had to be, you know? The room was filled with this amazing talent, and it was competitive. Sometimes the room was just bathed in laughter. Other times, the competition was fierce. You'd brawl over each line, each joke, each idea.

You're not making it out to be like the writers' room on *The Dick Van Dyke Show.*

When you have that many creative minds fighting over so much creative material, it's bound to get heated. These shows were weekly, live, each of them ninety minutes long.

Looking back, I do think the writing staff was about the best bunch of comedy writers ever assembled under one roof. You had Joe

Stein, who wrote *Fiddler on the Roof* and *Zorba*; Larry Gelbart who created the sitcom *M*A*S*H* and who wrote the screenplay to *Tootsie*. Brilliant. You had Mike Stewart, who was just the typist for the room! He later went on to write *Bye Bye Birdie* and *Hello, Dolly!* This was the typist, not even a writer for the show!

Not as frequently mentioned was Lucille Kallen, who was another tremendous writer. She wrote a lot of the domestic sketches. Very hard worker, she was very talented. And then there was Mel Tolkin, who was our head writer. One of the best comedy writers who ever lived. Just a wonderful comedy writer. He'd sometimes write extraordinarily cheap jokes. You know, "She married a station beneath her. He got off at 116th Street and she got off at 125th Street." Bad, bad, wonderful-bad jokes. He sculpted a lot of the monologues, domestic sketches with Lucille. Also, a lot of parodies of foreign movies.

Your Show of Shows would frequently parody foreign movies, which was rare at the time. How many of the viewers even saw these movies? Did the writers even see these movies?

Well, nobody in America had ever seen a foreign movie, but we, the writers, were from New York. We were New Yorkers. There were a lot of movie houses that showed Japanese movies, French movies, Italian movies, certainly. We were all familiar with the format, the style, the look and feel of these movies. The trick was to make these parodies funny to viewers who hadn't seen the original. But yes, sometimes, we would parody a movie that none of us had even seen. We just assumed that it would look a certain way, and then we'd parody what we imagined.

The writers for Your Show of Shows seem to have been very streetsmart. These weren't writers who studied comedy in college.

Well, you're talking to one of them who never graduated college. I mean, I only had maybe a year of college at the most. I was a street corner comic in Brooklyn. I wasn't the funniest and I wasn't the best. There were many great street corner comics who really would give you the state of the neighborhood, the world, in these one-liners. A lot of what I learned came from those street corners, especially when it came to being funny.

Do you think that affected the comedy, when it was more streetwise? Now, a student can actually major in comedy at college.

I do think the comedy was different. We had real-world experience. A lot had served in World War II. The comedy had to have been affected by that alone.

I don't think there is such a thing as studying comedy writing. There's no way. If anybody could be a teacher of it, I consider it would be me. I've done as much, possibly more, comedy writing than anybody who has ever lived. And yet I can tell you that it's almost impossible to teach. I had a friend who was an actor. His name was Andreas Voutsinas and he was Greek. He played the gay roommate [in the 1968 movie] *The Producers*. He once said to me, "Or you got it or you ain't."

He began the sentence with *or*, which I loved. What he said wasn't grammatically correct, but the point is that you got to have it from the beginning. Either you got it or you don't. You can't teach writing. You can teach some of the basics of writing: act one, two, and three; how to create a premise; how to develop a story; how to sharpen jokes. But you can't ever teach people how to get talent in their guts. You can't teach people how to express this gut-level talent. That's just impossible.

If you learn by anything, you teach yourself. And mostly you learn by your flops. Whenever I lecture at schools, I say, "Don't avoid the flops. The flops teach you what *not* to do in the future." That's just as important, if not *more* important, than teaching you what to do. What *not* do to.

What specifically did you learn from your flops?

Many times, especially when I first left *Caesar's Hour* in 1957, there was a lot of hubris in my writing. There was a lot of arrogance. I would think, The hell with this. If they don't get it, they don't get it. But *I* get it, it amuses *me*. Sometimes I would laugh at very personal, private, obscure jokes, which delighted me. But I realized, How many people is this for? I've got to include some of the audience, or else. I learned from several failures this way.

I wrote a TV pilot in the early sixties for ABC called *Inside Danny Baker*. It was about a little kid with an imagination and a vision. He dreamed of being different things, like all kids do. He was like a young Walter Mitty–type. It's really a good little show; it could have been a nice little series. But it didn't work. It was too personal. I was that kid. I didn't lower myself enough with, you know, sex jokes. You want things to sell; you've got to make them somehow down and dirty and attractive. It was too simple, too pure, and I was pleasing myself. I should have said, "It's just a little too mild to get on television."

What I'm saying is that you just can't be too far in your own head. What I eventually happened upon is a combination of high and low. To give you a specific example, in *High Anxiety*, I had references that people might never have heard of, such as names of psychiatrists, types of analysis, specific references to Hitchcock movies. In *High Anxiety*, an audience would have had to have seen at least three or four Alfred Hitchcock movies to understand what the hell any one scene was about. At the same time, there was action, there was suspense.

That would go for *Blazing Saddles*, too. You had a line like, "The only thing that stands between me and that property is the rightful owners," but there was also a cowboy punching a horse. There were cowboys sitting around a fire, eating beans, farting. You know, just basic thrills that a writer has to give an audience. And I didn't leave those thrills out.

With *Inside Danny Baker*, the show that I mentioned earlier, it was just the story of this kid and his dreams. It was all too personal.

And yet a joke takes place in *Blazing Saddles* that I'd imagine only a very small percentage of audience members would understand. It's in the scene when the Indian chief, played by you, comes across a group of black settlers. The character shouts to the heavens, in Yiddish, "*Shvarzers, loyzem gayne!*" Translated: "Blacks. Just let them go."

Right. Meaning that these blacks were no harm to the Indians. That this was a group even more downtrodden and poorly treated by whites than the Indians. Now that's an example of a joke that I think is high. You have jokes that maybe not many would understand but that serve a higher point. And the point is that there's an underlying sense of right versus wrong. The audience knew where I stood on racism and other issues. You can be silly, but you still have to hew to the underlying truth. If my heart's in the right place, I can go anywhere.

That sense of right versus wrong is consistent throughout your movies.

It is, and I think it helps when writing. I was lucky with *Blazing Saddles* because the black sheriff gave us a *great* little engine that chugged its way through the whole movie. We had lines like, "Kill the nigger! Kill him!" A lot of people, especially movie executives, mistook that for racism. But the point was understood by the audience. There would be no way for me to have written that type of a script if it didn't have that underlying sense of goodness. I wouldn't have written it otherwise. And if I did, none of the jokes would have worked. Audiences never would have liked the characters.

Were there any scenes that you had to cut out of *Blazing Saddles*?

The executives didn't want the farting scene kept in the movie. They wanted that out. I told them I would get rid of it, but I never touched it. Obviously, that scene, as well as others the executives didn't like, were kept.

The scenes that were eventually cut had to do with racial issues. There was an interracial love scene between Cleavon Little [who played Sheriff Bart] and Madeline Kahn [who played Lili von Shtupp] that had to be cut short. What you see in the movie is the lights go out and Madeline says, "Oh, it's true, it's *true*!" The joke we had written was for Cleavon to then say, "Excuse me, ma'am. I hate to disillusion you, but you're sucking on my arm." We had to tone down the racial aspect of that scene. It was too much for its time.

Blazing Saddles is now considered a comedy classic, but at the time it wasn't loved by critics. What do you think they missed when the movie was released in 1974?

I think they missed the irony. They missed the satire. They missed the greater message. As a writer, you can appeal to the critics. It can be done. But you'd lose half the audience.

It was also the subject matter. In *The Producers*, which the critics also despised, the main problem was that we were dealing with a subject—Nazis—that up to that point had never been dealt with. Even now it's hard to deal with. You see a film like *Life Is Beautiful*; it can fail miserably. You've got to know how to do it. It's tricky. You have to have the perfect vehicle, the perfect Trojan horse. For me, that vehicle was the worst musical in the world. And by using that vehicle, I could get across more serious topics. The musical became an orgasm of insanity that allowed everything else.

You've had your issues over the years with those critics who never understood your work. Have your feelings toward critics mellowed?

No. I can learn from my failures when it comes to an audience. I can learn from questions like, "What didn't they like about it? Who didn't like it?" Instead of abandoning it, instead of being angry, instead of getting on my high horse and being arrogant and becoming unapproachable, I can look at why something didn't work.

But I'll never do that with a critic. Critics seem to have some personal axe to grind. They all like to be protagonists, and they all like to be in the ring with you, except they have no right to be in the ring with a creator. You should never take on a critic, ever. They may be dead right, but it's still only one person, one opinion. It is kind of a parallel universe. The critic is in show business, but at the same time, he isn't.

You once described your comedy as midnight blue, not black. What's the difference for you between those two hues?

I've never been hopeless, I've never been despondent, but sometimes I will hit tremendous lows. And I feel that I've got to show that in comedy. I need to show that characters can be despairing but not suicidal. They can be agonizingly despondent, but they will always go on to the next step; they will always get back up the ladder. Midnight blue is that thin brushstroke. It's not pitch black. It's the color just before darkness comes at sunset. Or just after the lightness arrives after sunrise.

What comes first in your creation process? Is it the idea or the characters?

The characters are everything. If you're talented, you'll find a good idea to put these characters in. You'll find a good story. But the characters are what you start with. Everything I've ever done, I've started with characters. I learn what they want, what they need. Where they need to go and how they have to go about achieving that. I listen to them. You can't just have pure action.

Before you began writing the script to *The Producers*, what characters were your inspiration?

For *The Producers*, I started with that little caterpillar who grew into a beautiful butterfly, the little accountant with dreams, dreams, oh, such dreams of glory!, showgirls, and footlights and curtains going up and down, and an orchestra in the pit playing trills! Could little Leo Bloom [played by Gene Wilder] ever really live this life of glory and thrill? That's what I thought of. So I painted this character, this accountant, as loving theater. From there, I knew I needed a producer, a reprehensible producer, a guy screwing little old ladies on a casting couch just to raise enough money so he could have a little extra to stay in show business. Zero Mostel played that character beautifully.

For me, Zero's character, Max Bialystock, is the Id. He's the animal. Gene Wilder, playing Leo Bloom, was soulful. He was the Ego. There's a more poignant aspect to him. In the end, both characters come to realize that they need each other more than they need the money. They needed the joy of working together.

It almost sounds like the combination of high and low we were discussing earlier.

That's exactly what it is, I guess. It's that combination that I've always been fascinated with.

Is it true that you based Zero Mostel's character in *The Producers* on a real-life character that you knew?

I did. I worked for that guy. He was a producer; he put on shows. For one show, I worked everything: I was the stage manager, I was the assistant producer, I was even one of the actors. This was in the early forties. The play was called *Separate Rooms*, and it was about a theatrical event. I played a character named Scoop Davis, and I had one line, the opening line. I ran out on the stage and screamed, "We made it! It's a hit! It's the greatest thing since pay toilets!" That was my opening.

I'd put up advertising cards in barbershops for this producer. I can't tell you his name because he has grandchildren and I don't want them to know he screwed a lot of little old ladies. But that character was based on a real person. There's a line in the movie that comes from real life; it's absolutely true, I heard this guy say it. In the movie, Zero Mostel says to a little old woman, "Make out the check to Cash." And she says, "Cash? That's a funny name for a play." And he says, "Well, so is *The Iceman Cometh*." That comes from real life.

So you were an actor for this production?

Oh, yeah. I had worked as a performer for years as a tummler in the Catskills. A tummler is a performer who does everything. He tells jokes, he sings, he runs around like a crazy person. He'll do anything to get the audience on his side. I started working in the Catskills when I was seventeen. We did a few shows, six nights a week. And when we weren't onstage, we were busy trying to round up the guests to come to another show.

What did all that performing teach you later as a comedy writer?

That every second counts. And that's a very streetwise thing to know. Danny [Simon] and Neil [Simon] were like that. They were street guys. They took advantage of every second and every joke at their disposal. Neil Simon, he never forgot a joke. Neil once said that he never forgot anything that he ever heard that had made somebody laugh, whether he wrote it or not. That's just the type of memory he had. He didn't need to steal jokes; he was so damn talented. But he never forgot, and that's the way you have to be.

Another thing I learned from my time spent at the Catskills is not to be afraid to take chances. To jump off into the unknown, not knowing where you'll land. To take terrifying leaps that can easily leave me bloodied.

Most of all, I knew that I did not want to push a rack of blouses in the garment center all my life. My uncle Jack was a big shot in the railway mail department in Penn Station, and he got me a job to work for a few hours a day around Christmas. I hated it. What I learned from the Catskills was that I had choices. I didn't have to end up in a job in the garment district. It's honest work, but the place reeked of stale coffee. I always hated coffee because of that. I couldn't do it. I had to get out.

You once said that in your writing you had to always get to the "ultimate punch line, the cosmic joke that all the other jokes came out of."

Why do anything else? Why not go as far as you can go, as deep as you can go? Why stop on the surface? It's so difficult to come up with a punch line to a scene or a sketch. It's so hard. The real struggle is to take a premise, the center of it, and blossom it into a punch line. I learned that at *Your Show of Shows*. We managed to do it because it was life or death. We fought like beasts in that room. Our backs were against the wall. And we had great guides and great leaders, like [the show's producer] Max Liebman, to tell us if a joke worked. We were told if an ending to a sketch wasn't great, and we'd have to rewrite it.

But it's almost impossible to create a great ending to a sketch. I would say we pulled it off on *Your Show of Shows* 50 percent of the time.

Your son Max is also a writer. He's the author of two books, *The Zombie Survival Guide* and *World War Z*, but for two years he was a writer on *Saturday Night Live*. From what you've seen and heard, how different was the creative process for a writer on *SNL* versus *Your Show of Shows*?

You know, *Saturday Night Live* is really fun, but Max was one of eighteen writers on the show. That's a lot. He slept under his desk in a sleeping bag. He got very few jokes onto the show, very few. I think he got one or two sketches in the two or three years he was there. For some of them, he'd say to me, "Why did they turn that down?" I'd answer, "I would have used that." He wrote a commercial parody for a medication that had side effects like nausea, headache, abdominal pain. Max added "sudden bouts of anti-Semitism." I think that's great. The things that could happen if you ever took this medicine . . .

Things worked differently on *Your Show of Shows*. We'd never throw anything out that we could piece together or sharpen.

That's a very Depression Era mentality. Never throw anything out.

Absolutely. "Why are you cutting the ends off the sandwiches just to make sandwiches for high tea? What are you doing?! You could live for years on those crusts!" Yeah, the writers grew up with that mentality, and we never threw away a joke that we thought we could eventually use.

In doing research for this interview, I was surprised to find that a major influence on your writing has been Russian literature, particularly the nineteenth-century book *Dead Souls* by Nikolai Gogol. What is it about Gogol's work that speaks to you?

Gogol had two amazing sides to him. One is human, simple, heartfelt. He had tremendous understanding of the human condition. And the other side is absolute fucking madness. Just *madness*. Insanity. He would write about a nose that could speak. Gogol is not bound by the rules of reality, and yet he understands how the heart beats, why it beats. What death is. What love is. He is, of all the Russian writers, my favorite. And that includes a couple of good guys like Tolstoy and Dostoyevsky.

When did you come to Gogol?

It was through the Russian Mel Tolkin, head writer for *Your Show of Shows*. He said to me, "You're an animal from Brooklyn, but I think there is the beginnings of some mind, so I'd like to have you read this book and I know you'll enjoy it." And he gave me a copy of Nikolai Gogol's *Dead Souls*.

And you think that affected your comedy writing?

My whole life. My whole future. I said, "Gee, creativity could be good. Writing could be good!" And Gogol also affected how I could be if I strove—if I never settled for the first joke that came into my head. In fact, Gogol is what drove *Blazing Saddles* to end up like it did.

How so?

For not settling for just writing a parody of Westerns. For digging deeper, for writing about subjects such as racism for blacks, racism for Mexicans, the indignity suffered by Asian railroad workers. Gogol affected my whole life.

What other comedic influences have you had over the years?

An early influence was Buster Keaton. His scenes were so crazy, but he played them with absolute reality. He never winked to an audience. Isn't this grand? Isn't this funny? That was a very important comedic lesson to learn. I've tried to do the same thing in my movies.

Another early influence was Harry Ritz and the Ritz Brothers. They were big in the thirties and forties. Harry had a physical insanity and freedom that no other character ever had. He was eyes-goes, nose-goes, mouth-goes, *all*-goes. He was another Jew originally from Russia. I'm ashamed to say this, but a lot of comedy for the Jews in Russia came from making fun of cripples and unfortunates. Really, they just imitated bad walks, with a hunchback, and they elicited incredible laughs. Harry Ritz was the master of wild walks and facial contortions.

With his brothers, Al and Jimmy, the Ritz Brothers would sing and dance—just perfection. As smooth as silk, every step. They would make movies that were hysterically funny.

Why did the Ritz Brothers never achieve the great fame that the Marx Brothers achieved?

The Marx Brothers were much more intellectual. They had a sense of character and story. The Ritz Brothers had a sense of the *meshugenah*—craziness. They were unfettered by anything normal.

Now that I think about it, I suppose I have a combination of the Marx Brothers and the Ritz Brothers. The *meshugenah* and the intellectual.

How influential was Harry Ritz not only to you, but to other comedians who came of age during his heyday?

You could see it in Danny Kaye, with his voices. You could see it in Milton Berle, with his facial expressions. With Jerry Lewis, you could see it with his crazy walk. But especially Sid Caesar. Sid used a lot of Harry Ritz in my *Silent Movie* [1976]. Sid's in a hospital bed, and he has to swallow a large, white pill. Sid takes a big glass of water. You wait a whole goddamn minute, and Sid swallows and swallows and swallows and then he breaths "Ahhhh," and there's the white pill still stuck on his tongue. That's all Harry Ritz. It's perfectly Harry Ritz.

Speaking of Sid Caesar, for whom you worked for many years, why do you think his career, which started so brightly, didn't sustain itself over the years?

Well . . . [Long pause] My brother Lenny was a waist gunner in a B-17 Flying Fortress in World War II. He told me that unless you fired your .50-caliber machine gun in short bursts, the bullets would go askew. If you shot in long bursts, parts of the rifle would burn out. And you wouldn't be able to get a true aim on an enemy fighter. So short bursts, always short. We knew that Sid would be outrageously funny in short bursts. But too much of a good thing didn't work. You could never have an audience accept Sid in a movie playing a grocery man or candy store owner or a cab driver. There was too much genius. Just too much.

In 1952, I went out to Los Angeles to write screenplays for a thousand dollars a week. Incredible. An incredible amount of money for that period. Nice offices. Secretaries. Palm trees. Real palm trees, not fake and brought in. They were really in the ground! Beautiful. I worked there for two years and then I came back to work for Sid. I said, "Sid, all right. You know, life is temporary, but some aspects of show business don't have to be as temporary as they are. It's like light bulbs—they're designed to be temporary. And in your case, you're going to burn out. Danny Kaye is a big star, but you're better! Bob Hope—funniest guy in the world, but you're better. The smallest movie will last twenty-five or thirty years longer than the best show on television. You make a movie, they put it in a vault, they have Technicolor. It's there forever! It's an amazing way of preserving a performance."

And he said, "You're right. You're absolutely right. I'm not doing it just for money. I'm doing it because I'm good at it and I know it and I love it and I want my art to live." I told him, "Why don't we go out to LA at the end of the season? Give them plenty of warning. I'll direct the movies. I'll write them. We'll make great, memorable movies." Sid warned the executives that he was leaving, and they weren't happy. Then there was a long weekend when I couldn't reach him. He had been sequestered somewhere on Long Island, somebody's mansion. At the end of it, on Monday, he called and said to me, "You know, we'll have to do it some other time. We'll have to wait three years." Then he said, "That's not long. We'll wait another three years and we'll go."

I was heartbroken, of course, but they increased his salary from five thousand dollars a show to twenty-five thousand dollars. Enormous money in 1952. Movies to me were much more lasting. TV happens too quickly, and most is never remembered. I think we could have made good movies.

A lot of your writing seems so improvisational, but I assume a tremendous amount of work goes into your scripts. How important is rewriting to you?

Rewriting is writing. It's everything. The first draft is really full of . . . you know, you can't plant seeds with it. It's full of rocks and pebbles and stones and sand. As you rewrite, you know the characters have a chance of maturing, thriving, and becoming memorable. Rewriting is everything. It's, *Do I really want to get married to this idea?* It's vital.

Can you give a specific example of how long it took to rewrite one of your scripts? Say, *Young Frankenstein*, a script you co-wrote with Gene Wilder?

Gene and I never stopped writing *Young Frankenstein*. I don't know. We wrote, we rewrote, rewrote, rewrote, rewrote, rewrote. We always went back to a scene until we were more or less satisfied. Someone once said that you never finish anything, you just abandon it. We abandoned *Young Frankenstein*.

Were there any particular scenes that you and Gene didn't agree on?

We had a big fight over the scene that showed the monster tap-dancing to "Puttin' on the Ritz." I said, "It's no good. It's tearing the movie apart. It's making it too silly." This was showbizzy stuff. A scene like that only works by just moving an inch or two. With "Puttin' on the Ritz," Gene wanted to move the movie a whole yard. So Gene said, "Do me a favor. Film it and we'll take a look at it. If it doesn't work, we'll throw it right out." And I did. I filmed it, and then I looked up and said, "Gene, not only does it work, but it's the best thing in the movie."

The interesting thing about Gene Wilder's performance in *Young Frankenstein* is that it might very well be the best performance in *any* Frankenstein movie, comedic or not.

Oh, I'm so glad you said that! I think he was Promethean in that role. There was fire in that performance. There was madness in his eyes. Going back to Gogol, you need madness in comedy.

That movie was shot by the great cinematographer Gerald Hirschfeld [*Goodbye, Columbus; Diary of a Mad Housewife; My Favorite Year*]. It looked beautiful. It looked as gorgeous as the early

Frankenstein movies, very authentic. And I directed that movie very seriously. I wasn't trying to be funny in the direction. It was only the situations that were absurd, and that helped with the comedy.

Did you ever have any thoughts over the years of writing a novel? Or short humor fiction for _The New Yorker_, similar to what Woody Allen writes?

Max, my son, has a wonderful narrative skill. His images are beautiful and so perfect, and you always know just where you are and what's happening. And I don't have that. I am a dialogue professional. Nobody can write better Ping-Pong than I can, the back and forth. But you need a great deal of narrative skill, like a Tolstoy, to write a novel. Or you got it or you ain't.

It's odd that even writers considered at the top of their games, such as yourself, notice weaknesses in their work that others might not see.

You'll notice that with anyone, in any profession. You'll see a golfer who looks perfect, but there's something about his skill that won't match his expectations. And, you know, it has to be that way. You should never be totally content with yourself.

Are you still affected after all these years in the business when an audience laughs at something you've written?

Oh, it's the best. The best thing in the world is writing a joke, having an audience get it. I will never grow tired of that. It's magical.

You once said that you were afraid of death, and that humor is your scream and protest against the good-bye. You said this years ago. Do you still believe that?

I kind of do. I kind of do. We're all afraid of dying. When you're laughing, it's hard to think of death. So I think, basically, yeah, that still works.

Do you feel that your work—your writing—is your chance at immortality?

I don't know. I don't think there is any immortality, really. But it's a chance to live a little longer, to be around a little longer, and for your great-great-grandchildren to maybe see something you've done. It's like scratching your name in the bark of a tree. "I was here. I did something. I made my mark. And I will not be completely erased by death."

I think if there's anyone in the business who's earned the right to give advice to a young comedy writer it would be you. What would you tell him or her?

A few things. One, whatever you write has to make you laugh. Not just laugh, but really laugh, from your belly, laugh with your gut. Not just chuckle. If you really laugh, honestly laugh, while you're writing a joke, and if you say to yourself, Oh, they'll like this, then stick with that.

Two, rewrite. Keep rewriting until you get what you want, and then write some more. Rewrite! Rewrite! Rewrite! When you laugh yourself, or when you say, "I can't do better," you can stop. There is no night, there is no day, there is only rewriting comedy until it's glorious.

Last, do not be dissuaded. Don't become brokenhearted. Don't quit. If you believe you can do it, you can do it. It's so easy to be hurt. It's so easy to quit. Don't quit. Do it again. And then again. Do not stop! Learn from the audience and take their advice.

Other than that, I have no more advice.

Anyway, Mike, it was fun. Thank you. I now have to get on with my life.

The End: What Laughter Looks Like
by EDWARD JESSEN

Ex. 11.0 — Frenetic, Pulsing Laughter (Young Girl)

Ex. 20.0 — Rising Cackle

Ex. 04.1 — Short, Disingenuous Male Chortle

Ex. 34.0 — Insipid, Half-Voiced Male Giggle

Ex. 03.3 — Shrill, Teasing Laughter (Female)

Huh — > (A)

Ex. 06.6 — Vigorous Baby Giggles (Oscar, 8 mos)

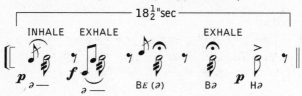

18½"sec

INHALE EXHALE EXHALE

ə — ə Bɛ (ə) Bə Hə

Ex. 09.5 — Dirty Titter

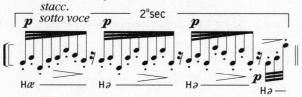

stacc.
sotto voce 2"sec

Hœ — Hə — Hə — Hə —

Ex. 24.2 — Raucous Snigger (Cartoon Animal)

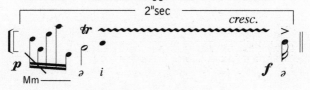

2"sec
cresc.

Mm — ə i ə

Ex. 34.1 — Forced Party Laugh (Male)

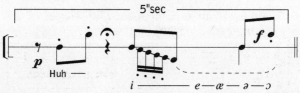

5"sec

Huh —
i — e — œ — ə —
c

ACKNOWLEDGMENTS

A book is never easy to write in the best of circumstances, and it's even more difficult when one doesn't have assistance. Luckily, I had plenty, and I'd like to thank those who contributed and, in the process, made my life easier:

To all who sat for endless interviews

Louise Pomeroy, for her beautiful illustrations

Eric Spitznagel, for researching and co-writing the interview introductions

Lauren Mosko Bailey, for the first copyedit

Lindsey Schwoeri, for the full edit

Douglas Clark, for additional editing

S. P. Nix, for the final edit

Steve Heisler (UCB LA, Splitsider), for greatly assisting me with many of the "Pure, Hard-Core Advice" entries

Bradford Evans, for additional help with the "Pure, Hard-Core Advice" entries

Seth Olenick, for spending an afternoon photographing Jon Hamm in his undershirt (must have been rough)

Jon Hamm, for spending an afternoon with Seth, posing in your undershirt (must have been rough, no sarcasm intended)

Byrd Leavell at Waxman Leavell Literary Agency

To Shimmy, Meir, Alan, Sarah, Brandon, Cindy, Kevin, Bonnie, Howard, Reva, Ken, Jamie, Lauren, Carli, Rafi, Stacey, Bess, Chris, Bob, Marisa, Alex, Christina, Scott, Jen, Stacey

Ellie and John

Ted Travelstead and Julie Wright

Laura Griffin, Scott Jacobson, Todd Levin, Jason Roeder, Will Tracy

Robert Walsh

John Banta

Adam Resnick

Justin, Brendan, Simon, Sue, Michelle, Mary, Alison, David, David, Marnie, Ben, Matt, Michelle, Walter, Louisa, Callie, Jeannie, Bruce, Dana, Jack, Wayne

Gloria and Maria Ayalde, Connell Barrett, Alex Beggs, Melanie Berliet, Steve Bopp, Bill Bradley, Mr. and Mrs. Catfish, Jason Cronic, Brad Engelstein, Adam Frucci, Bruce Handy, Jane Herman, Mike Hogan, Katie I., Todd Jackson, Marco "Meatball" Kaye, Rob Kutner, Austin Merrill, Gina Merrill, John O'Hara, Nathan Rabin, Julian Sancton, Mark Selby, Mark Simonson, Elaine Trigiani, Marie Warsh, Teddy Wayne, Steve Whitesell, Steve Wilson, Claire Zulkey, the library at Montgomery Community College in Rockville, (And Presenting . . . Danny Haynes & Kim Woodman, live in the Gold Room)

Dan Abramson, Lauren Bans, Yoni Brenner, Michelle Brower, Rocco Castoro, Dick Cavett, Michael Colton, Phil Davidson, Gabe Delahaye, Andrés du Bouchet, Janice Forsyth, Michael Gerber, Courtenay Hameister, Jack Handey, A.J. Jacobs, Al Jaffee, Dan Kennedy, Adam Laukhuf, Dan Lazar, Gabe Liedman, Ross Luippold, Merrill Markoe, Sam Means, Daniel Menaker, Richard Metzger, Christopher Monks, Kliph Nesteroff, Don Novello, Dave Nuttycombe, Dan O'Brien, Tony Perez, Alana Quirk, Jason Reich, Eric Reynolds, Simon Rich, David Sedaris, Streeter Seidell, Andrea Silenzi, Becki Smith and Rob Caldwell at WCSH, John Swartzwelder, John Warner, John Waters (and the staff and clientele at the Wigwam), Jim Windolf, Jon Wurster

Andrew Clark and the students and staff of Humber College

Transcribers (a huge thanks): Michal Tamar Addady, Michael Bannett, Caitlin Murphy Brust, Monica Giacomucci, Elizabeth Meley, Maggie Phenicie, Sean Michael Simoneau, Darren Springer

Hair by Keith at Smile

To the upstanding citizens of the planned community of New Granada ("Tomorrow's City . . . Today")

Charlie Cocoa; Fritzy the Bumblebee and The Professor, 143

Contact Information

Steve Heisler, writer: steveheisler.com

Seth Olenick, photographer: www.setholenick.com

Louise Pomeroy, illustrator: www.louisezpomeroy.com

Eric Spitznagel, writer: www.ericspitznagel.com

mikesacks.com

ABOUT THE AUTHOR

A member of the editorial staff at *Vanity Fair* magazine, Mike Sacks is the author of *Your Wildest Dreams, Within Reason*, and *And Here's the Kicker: Conversations with 21 Humor Writers About Their Craft*. His work has appeared in *The New York Times, The Washington Post, The New Yorker, Time, Esquire, Vanity Fair, GQ*, the *Believer, Vice, Salon*, and *McSweeney's*, among others. He is not pictured here.